NUMBER 75

Yale French Studies

The Politics of Tradition: Placing Women in French Literature

Yale French Studies

Joan DeJean and Nancy K. Miller, *Special editors for this issue*
Liliane Greene, *Managing editor*
Editorial board: Peter Brooks (Chairman), Ora Avni,
    Shoshana Felman, Richard Goodkin,
    Christopher Miller, Margaret Miner, Charles Porter,
    Christopher Rivers, Allan Stoekl, Helen Williams
Staff: Lauren Doyle-McCombs
Editorial office: 315 William L. Harkness Hall
Mailing address: 2504A Yale Station, New Haven,
    Connecticut 06520
Sales and subscription office:
    Yale University Press, 92A Yale Station
    New Haven, Connecticut 06520
Published twice annually by Yale University Press

Designed by James J. Johnson and set in Trump Medieval
Roman by The Composing Room of Michigan, Inc. Printed in
the United States of America by The Vail-Ballou Press,
Binghamton, N.Y.
ISSN 0044–0078
ISBN for this issue 0–300–04323–6

JOAN DEJEAN / NANCY K. MILLER

Editors' Preface

1.

If this issue appears as scheduled in the fall of 1988, its publication will mark the fortieth anniversary of this journal's inaugural number. The first issue of *Yale French Studies* was devoted to existentialism, a subject that suggests the new periodical's active engagement in areas of literary controversy. Continuing this commitment, *Yale French Studies* did not wait forty years to tackle the controversial issue to be explored here, the sexual politics of the French tradition: already in 1961, its twenty-seventh issue bore the title *Women Writers*. While Nancy and I were preparing this collection, I thought of no. 27, which I had not yet read, as our precursor. And it is, in a way: the contributors to that issue try to assess the potential impact of noncanonical literary figures who found their initial audience outside contemporary centers of organized literary influence. But the difference that separates our project from the 1961 volume is more revealing than is this surface similarity.

The critics who discussed women's writing in these pages twenty-five years ago by and large do not seem comfortable with their task. The opening essay in *Women Writers*, by Edith Kern, questions the value of women's writing in a canonical economy: "Literature at its best has an androgynous quality" (11). That initial uneasiness situates the volume that follows in a critical no man's land: from reading its essays, it is seldom clear why women writers should be introduced to the audience of *Yale French Studies*. Contributors often seem to exclude from the standards governing their critical discourse the very category to which the volume allegedly will give institutional status. They are quick to point out that the works they are discussing do not meet the criteria according to which they normally judge literature. (Among the criticisms offered: Elsa Triolet isn't as good a writer as she used to be; recent women's novels "leave the reader with the impression of a superficial

1

pastime.") In addition, contributors generally do little to live up to the scope promised by the issue's title. In their discussions, women's writing is limited to the novel; most of the articles are devoted to a single woman writer; with one exception, an article on the comtesse de Ségur, the writers discussed are all twentieth century. Only Henri Peyre suggests that from the long-term French perspective the visibility of women writers from the 1930s on is less noteworthy than the *absence* of a continuous first-rate female presence in nineteenth-century writing, the sole exception in an otherwise brilliant tradition that began in the Middle Ages: "No other history is as rich as that of France in remarkable women" (47).

Upon closer inspection, it turns out that our precursor issue had really prepared the way for us only in this brief section in which Henri Peyre puts the volume's focus into a broader perspective. Still, public recognition of the longevity and the quality of the French female tradition by the long-time chairman of the most powerful French Department in the country in our century is the kind of official acceptance that women's writing has not often won. But how official was that acceptance? Henri Peyre made his remarks public in the pages of a journal openly associated with his Department, yet his enthusiasm for the past did not promote the institutionalization of the female literary presence whose superiority he proclaims. In the Yale Department where I was a student at the end of that decade, reading lists for courses and exams gave little hint that women writers had ever contributed to "literature at its best," the sum total of which was equivalent to the object of our scholarly desire, the canon.

As I looked over the titles of previous issues of *Yale French Studies*, I reflected that such a flagrant discrepancy between recognition, even if ambivalent, of a developing interest among academic readers and subsequent institutional acceptance is not common. The examples of existentialism—or cinema (no. 17), or Sade (no. 35), or even Rousseau at the time when he was the subject of an issue (no. 28, also 1961)—are more typical. In those cases, this journal responded to a growing awareness on the part of academic readers of the value of a subject either not yet institutionalized or the terms of whose institutionalization were about to be rewritten, and in the process predicted, and perhaps helped bring about, canonical revisions. What went wrong with the suggested promotion of women writers from ephemeral status as hot literary property to more lasting presence in the course of study? The interest on the part of academic readers (and I do not pretend that *all* academic readers were, or are, attracted by women's writing, but surely existentialism never won universal acclaim either) has continued to grow, but very little official recognition has been achieved. One need look no farther than the situation in English where, to cite but one example, Gilbert and

Gubar's recent *The Norton Anthology of Literature by Women: The Tradition in English* is the kind of indispensable pedagogical tool that, by eliminating the financial burden for the student and the research burden for the professor, makes it possible to integrate women's writing throughout the curriculum. By comparison, French still has a long way to go.

It was just this sense of the lack of practical gains that originally motivated us to organize this collection. We wanted to focus attention on the gap between wide popularity, even among an intellectual audience, and official disregard within the educational establishment that is a recurrent feature of the history of the reception of women's writing, rather than merely a twentieth-century phenomenon. Thus, a number of the following articles stress the broad readership won at different times through the centuries by works by women writers that did not succeed in gaining admission into the Academy, either as subjects of critical commentary or as pedagogical models for schoolchildren. Other articles examine labels, from realism to surrealism, commonly adopted in critical and/or pedagogical analysis, in order to determine why such generally accepted markers of literary history work against the canonization of women's writing. Finally, other contributions investigate key moments of canon formation, periods during which French literature was shaped into a program in response to a perceived need for a more clearly defined pedagogical tool. These articles attempt to understand both the concrete historical factors and the ideological motivations leading to the exclusion of women writers who had achieved sufficient visibility to merit inclusion in the literary histories and pedagogical manuals whose influence is with us still.

The primary goal of this collection of essays is to explore the possibilities for a new form of *practical criticism* that can actually have an impact on what we as critics do in our other lives as teachers. It is important that women writers gain more than uneasy institutional recognition as a result of renewed critical promotion by an academic audience seeking to offer a challenge to the accepted pedagogical ways. Only when their status as part of the curriculum no longer seems noteworthy enough to merit a number of *Yale French Studies* will we be able to feel that we have made a difference.

—Joan DeJean

2.

> Tradition: fr. L *tradition-, traditio* action of handing over,
> teaching, tradition—more at *TREASON*
> —*Webster's Third New International Dictionary*

What is passed on in the teaching of a national tradition? what betrayed in the handing over of a body of writing from one generation to the next? The essays in this volume point to some of the moves that historically have come to institute a *politics of poetics* across the social text. Of course, on the face of things, at least, these moves may seem merely idiosyncratic, more a "gentlemen's agreement," as Lillian Robinson puts it in "Treason Our Text," than a wholesale project of calculated restrictions and targeted repressions. But as Robinson then goes on to argue: "a gentleman is inescapably—that is, by definition—a member of a privileged class and of the male sex. From this perspective, it is probably quite accurate to think of the canon as an entirely gentlemanly artifact, considering how few works by nonmembers of that class and sex make it into the informal agglomeration of course syllabi, anthologies, and widely commented-upon 'standard authors' that constitutes the canon as it is generally understood" (106).[1]

As a first step in this interrogation of canon making, we have chosen to focus on the exclusionary politics regulating the transmission of French literature; notably, we have wanted to open the question of the exclusion by gender: women writers who are not included in the dominant culture's imaginary, its conscious and unconscious zones of self-representation. To be sure, these are not the only grounds for exclusion from the gentlemen's club. If we think of the canon as a complex social field of intersections and interventions, the cross-hatching lines of class and race, of national "identity" itself—the clusters of differences subsumed under the territorialization of the Hexagon—also need careful siting and remapping. In this sense, while the elimination of women's writing from the cultural record has been our organizing concern here, the question it points to—how can we understand the process by which the cultural record is constructed?—continues to occupy the horizon.

The question of canon formation and especially in the case of women's writing canon *de*-formation—the gestures of selection by which

---

1. "Treason Our Text: Feminist Challenges to the Literary Canon," in *The New Feminist Criticism: Essays on Women, Literature, and Theory,* ed. Elaine Showalter (New York: Pantheon, 1985).

the authorial and reading practices, as well as the social "preferences" of a given cultural moment are erased, forgotten and rewritten as a transcendent literary history—is, as Jane Tompkins has shown for American literature, always a matter of local history. Thus, the essays in the first section of this volume, "Toward a History of Taste," uncover the ways in which the ideologies of gender, art, and national identity collaborate and collide in different moments of French cultural life. They interrogate the categories and vocabulary of literary history itself—period, genre, value, masterpiece, classic, major, minor, etc.—all of which have been at work in the displacement and elimination of women's writing from the scenes of its production. As it turns out, it is indeed from the individual gentlemanly choices of the critics and novelists, Boileau, Abbé Batteux, Sainte-Beuve, Taine, Balzac, Laclos, Etiemble, to name a few ostensibly odd bedfellows, that the collective object called "French literature" emerges.

Despite the typically canonized exceptions—the *named* inclusions of Marie de France, Marguerite de Navarre, Louise Labé, Lafayette, Sévigné, Sand, Staël, and Colette[2]—the tradition remains a story of men's writing. The second group of essays, "Exploring the Underread," reading at an angle to the poetics of the *déjà lu*, looks at genres and modes in which women's participation has been almost completely occulted: the uncanonic lyric, the uncanonic *canso*, theater in the eighteenth century, erotic fiction, and lyric poetry in the nineteenth, avant-garde writing in the twentieth. These essays reopen the questions of margin and center, gender and genre within a familiar tradition's already constituted idea of its history and values, and propose new ways of reading the "invisibilization" of other subjectivities. Whose pleasure, whose text?

In the third section, "Questioning the Canon in the Twentieth Century," the essays point in two directions and signal the etymological intimacies of tradition and treason flagged in the epigraph: on the one hand, the perpetuation in critical discourse and pedagogical enactments of the historical maneuvers of exclusion and repetition as we saw them in the analyses of the earlier periods; on the other, an attention to the dangers lurking in a desire for inclusion unself-conscious of its own repetitions and exclusions. Does the act of replacing women in a periodized history too quickly accept an idea of History we already know to

---

2. Perhaps today, since the astounding success of *The Lover*, Duras would figure as a figure in the national imaginary, as well as Beauvoir, posthumously, for *The Second Sex*, and with a footnote to Marguerite Yourcenar, also posthumously, as the first female "immortal."

It is also important to recognize the serious restrictions that govern which aspects of the *oeuvre* of these writers are in fact retained—Staël's literary criticism, for instance, Sand's *romans champêtres*—and what is actually taught and read.

be blind in its own myths of knowledge to the differences made by gender and that gender makes? Can "French literature" as a concept avoid reproducing hierarchies of fixed identities? Is this enterprise an "American" preoccupation that mistakes the posterity of writing for the petty tyrannies of the syllabus? An academic question?

Dear Friend [Colette replies to Julien Benda's questionnaire on French writers (*Mercure de France*, 1911],
Your letter arrives too late for me to anwer you on the question of Latin: I have no Latin. You ask if Latin helps, as you put it, in the "formation of a French writer" . . . I've no idea. I've never thought about that. It's warm here, I'm enjoying myself, I should be working and I'm not—in a word, everything is for the best.

In the issue of the journal *Critical Inquiry* devoted to the subject of the canon (September 1983), guest editor Robert von Hallberg remarks: "A canon is commonly seen as what other people, once powerful, have made and what should now be opened up, demystified, or eliminated altogether. Rarely does one hear a critic, especially a professor, confess to dreams of potency, perhaps because now that canons are recognized as the expression of social and political power, intellectuals are, by virtue of a consensus as to their adversarial role, almost required to view these aspirations skeptically" (iii).

By virtue of their *particular* adversarial role in intellectual scenes, at an angle or radical asymmetry to the dominant structures of social and political life, feminist critics, I think, may view the requirement of skepticism otherwise. More important for feminist professors than a worry about recuperation (occupying the center of power interests) is, I think, the requirement from *within* feminist practice to place next to the ambitious—potent—fantasy of canon *trans*formation in which women's writing would come to complicate the national topographics, a certain equally productive anxiety about the adequacy of its own maps: the old treasons of new traditions.

—Nancy K. Miller

I. Toward a History of the Formation of Taste: Making Canons in France

ANN R. JONES / NANCY J. VICKERS

Canon, Rule and the Restoration Renaissance

In 1818, as France engaged in the problematic enterprise of recreating monarchy in a form faithful to selected revolutionary principles, the state could scarcely neglect symbolic gestures. Thus in Paris the ceremonial restoration of a sixteenth-century king—the recasting and reinstallation of an equestrian statue of Henri IV—substituted an assertion of monarchic continuity for a painful memory of zealous eradication. Henri's example communicated a message to the weary veterans of the Revolution and the Empire: order could follow civil chaos, and, as a consequence, calm could return to the nation. Then, and only then, literature might disentangle itself long enough from politics to reproduce a noble, classical style, a style possible only within an advanced, peaceful civilization.[1] Thus nineteenth-century "old historicists," not unlike their sixteenth-century predecessors, excavated the past in search of the present. The labels with which they delineated periodicity—"Renaissance," "Restoration"—were figures for repetition.

Like the project of restoring the monarchy to post-Revolutionary France, the project of restoring the Renaissance was fraught with contradictions. Literary historians of the period described the sixteenth century as "catholic and protestant, republican and monarchist"; its riches were deemed "new by being old"; it "progressed" toward truth

---

1. On the restoration of the statue of Henri IV, see Andrew George Lehmann, *Sainte-Beuve, A Portrait of the Critic, 1804–1842* (Oxford: Oxford University Press, 1962), 8–9. On Henri IV as bringing political order to France, see Saint-Marc Girardin, *Tableau de la littérature française au XVIe siècle* (Paris: Didier, 1862), 80–85. On political order as the prerequisite to classical style, see Philarète Chasles, *Etudes sur le seizième siècle en France* (Paris: Amyot, 1848), 33. See also the "Rapport de M. Raynouard, Secrétaire Perpétuel de l'Académie française, sur les concours de poésie et d'éloquence de l'année 1828," in the *Recueil des discours, rapports et pièces diverses lus dans les séances publiques et particulières de l'Académie française, 1820–29* (Paris, Firmin Didot, 1843), 776. References will henceforth appear in the text, as will any references cited more than once.

(Rapport, 773–75). Repeatedly, and often illogically, such writers conflated the language of atemporal verities with that of relentless advances. Consider, for example, the multiple contradictions enacted here through personification: "Such is the 'esprit français'; such the literature and the liberty to whom he gave birth [qu'il a enfantées]. Two immortal sisters, they walk in harmony toward world empire; but they find a fatherland everywhere they go, because they are neither prejudiced nor egotistically nationalistic; they are neither from one century nor one country . . ." ("Rapport," 773; Saint-Marc Girardin, 113–14). French literature and liberty, equally at home at all times and in all places, nonetheless keep walking; they are national, but the term "national" signifies "universal." Literary values are eternal, but literature changes as a result of political, religious, and moral causes.

Returning to the Renaissance, then, constitutes returning to a source that is at once embedded in time and liberated from it. For a long while critics, as if "blinded by the splendor" of the seventeenth and eighteenth centuries, saw "nothing in the more or less obscure times that preceded them"; but now they interrogate origins, look for sources, and, "most of all . . . exhume the monuments of our distant history, to restore them, to study them, to understand them . . ." ("Rapport," 772–74). To the 1820s, the restored Renaissance reveals itself to be a moment of passage and transition in a progress toward maturity, a time "when everything takes shape, but nothing is finished."[2] It is a child prematurely born or an adolescent: "But [the French] genius had scarcely emerged from his infancy and had entered that age which, for nations as for individuals, is made up of those trials and crises upon which the destiny of a whole lifetime depends" ("Rapport," 774–76).

Official exhumations of the monuments of Renaissance culture extended well beyond the restoration of Henri IV to his "rightful" place. Indeed, the French Academy repeatedly proposed Renaissance topics for its annual prize competitions. In 1821 and 1822, for example, a "truly national" and tellingly self-reflexive subject was announced for the poetry prize: "the *restoration* of letters and art under François I" (emphasis ours) (*Recueil des discours*, 687–88, 695–96). In 1828, the eloquence prize shed its own history of generating discourse either in praise of God or of the "numerous and brilliant elite" of great men selected, we are told, not by the Academy but rather by the "nation herself"; this subject matter having been "exhausted," a problem of literary history imposed itself—"the advance and progress of French language and literature from the beginning of the sixteenth century to

---

2. Chasles, 27. On the "unfinished" quality of the Renaissance, as evoked through metaphors of miscarriage in Sainte-Beuve, see François Rigolot, "Sainte-Beuve et le mythe du XVIe siècle," *L'Esprit créateur* 14 (1974):41.

1610" ("Rapport," 773). Thus a complex, varied, and remote body of texts assumed the reified shape of a "history," of a canonical formation invested in the political priorities and assumptions of the moment that created it.

Seven essays were submitted, but two (those by Philarète Chasles and Saint-Marc Girardin) won the judges' approbation. For they stressed a common denominator: the persistence and triumph of the old "esprit français" as it "struggled" against petrarchism and pedantry to achieve the grandeur and majesty of the Classical Age ("Rapport," 780). That "esprit" would, of course, run amuck in the Enlightenment (be led astray by "irreligion and democracy") until, "tired of its error," it would finally settle into the Restoration and determine with "wise boldness" the measure of liberty suited to the 1820s (Chasles, 34; Saint-Marc Girardin, 110–11). The desire to locate a principle of continuity, no matter how chaotic the circumstances, singularly marks the choices of the contest judges. The "re-nascent" France of the Restoration constructs a reassuring, albeit distant, mirror in the gestating nation-state of the Renaissance: if the business of the present remains unfinished, it nonetheless contains the promise of the future.

Charles Augustin Sainte-Beuve's unfinished contribution to that Academy contest, however, never reached the judges' desks. He became so absorbed in his study of sixteenth-century poets that he lost interest in meeting the deadline. But the results of his research, eleven chapters of the *Tableau historique et critique de la poésie française et du théâtre français au XVIe siècle*, were published in *Le Globe*, the liberal journal for which he had begun writing in 1826. Rewritten, the book was published as a whole in 1828 and again, augmented, in 1843 and 1876. Ironically, his version of the Renaissance turned out to be far more influential than those that won the prize: his canon of significant writers and his judgments of their work became the basis for a century of subsequent literary histories, whether they repeated or refuted the *Tableau*.[3]

I. SAINTE-BEUVE'S *TABLEAU HISTORIQUE:* CRITICISM AS THE RULE OF LAW AND ORDER

Sainte-Beuve's enthusiasm for Romantic poetry and for Victor Hugo as its leader shaped his first revision of the *Tableau* (1828). Known for its celebration of Ronsard, whom Sainte-Beuve praised as a great innovator,

---

3. Lehmann discusses the enduring reputation of the *Tableau*, 51. Antoine Compagnon stresses Sainte-Beuve's centrality as model and target for change in his study of curriculum formation, *La Troisième République des lettres de Flaubert à Proust* (Paris: Editions du Seuil, 1983), 174–81. See also Rigolot, 35–43.

his history casts the court poet and the Pléiade as analogues to Hugo and the Cénacle. In his conclusion, Sainte-Beuve reads in the Renaissance an experimental daring that prefigures Romantic renewals of French culture: "The style of our age will be less correct, less savant, freer and more risk-taking [than the sixteenth century] . . . ; it has already recaptured the insouciance and unexpectedness lacking in the monarchical etiquette of the age that followed. . . . In poetry as in politics, we are a young, recently liberated people; who knows where our ascent will take us? . . . The lost lyre has been found; totally unexpected preludes have been heard from it."[4]

But the *Tableau* is far less revolutionary in practice than this critical flight suggests. The monarchical project of the Restoration was more significant to Sainte-Beuve, even as a young man (he was only twenty-four in 1828), than any radical movement in politics or poetry. Indeed, an esthetic of the age of Louis XIV consistently informs Sainte-Beuve's criteria for cultural greatness.[5] Monarchy fascinates him: he begins his *Tableau* with a long love poem by King Charles d'Orléans, whom he praises for his "decent gallantry" (10); every poet ranked as "major" is defined in relation to a royal patron. Marot, he writes, learned his playful delicacy and good taste at the court of François I; Henri II's interest in the arts opened the way for Du Bellay's literary theory; Ronsard's fame as "prince of poets" meant the admiration of rulers including Charles IX, Marguerite de Valois and Mary Stuart (64); Malherbe's power to impose new stylistic norms depended on Henri IV's interest in poetic forms (66).

Whatever historical realism this royalist bias may inscribe, it must be stressed that it excludes individual writers, as well as literary groups, outside the court. And, as a consequence, virtually all women writers are erased. Ladies-in-waiting at court, unlike the rare, exemplarily educated queen, did not write; their role was to attract homage from courtier-poets rather than to compose poetry of their own. But throughout the sixteenth century women poets did perform their work far from court, and in coteries composed mainly of professional men. Humanists and publishers predominated in Lyon, where Louise Labé and Pernette Du Guillet took part in salons; lawyers and judges visiting from Paris joined a later literary circle in Poitiers, in which Madeleine and Catherine des Roches recited the poems they later published as a joint mother-daughter enterprise. Anne Tullone (Mâcon) and Nicole Estienne (Rou-

---

4. Charles Augustin Sainte-Beuve, *Tableau historique et critique de la poésie française et du théâtre français au XVIe siècle* (Paris: Charpentier, 1843), 284. All further references to the *Tableau* appear in parentheses in the text.

5. Roger Fayolle offers an excellent analysis of Sainte-Beuve's political and critical trajectory in *Sainte-Beuve et le XVIIIe siècle ou comment les révolutions arrivent* (Paris: Armand Colin, 1972).

en) also wrote in provincial centers. It was not the court, on which Sainte-Beuve fixated, but rather the city that stimulated the literary production of women.

Sainte-Beuve dismisses such urban groups in passages that reveal the class hierarchy underlying his understanding of "true" Romantic, and thus of "true" Renaissance, poetry as the expression of unmediated emotion. Setting "genius" against "science," in an opposition that would have made no sense in the sixteenth century, he concludes that the scholars and humanists who took part in urban literary and philosophical discussions could not possibly be "true" poets; their concern with the techniques of the professions revealed their inauthenticity: "one did poetry as one did medicine, law, theology, or history; and every literate man could be listed among the poets. . . . But what can we find today in the rhymes of the printer Etienne Dolet, the lawyer Thomas Sebilet. . . ? Wasn't it enough for Pelletier du Mans to be at once a doctor, grammarian and geometer?" (39) Not surprisingly, Sainte-Beuve's notion of lyric as an emanation of feeling rather than of intellect leads him to banish Maurice Scève, the most visible of the Lyonnais, from the elite of poets: "practically unreadable," he wrote poems whose erudition had no appeal for his contemporaries (44).[6] Although women could hardly be accused of professional deformation, they gained no advantage on that account in Saint-Beuve's judgments. He makes no mention whatsoever of Pernette; he criticizes Louise Labé, like Scève, as overlearned. In her *Débat de Folie et d'Amour*, the speeches of the gods are too long and too full of citations; La Fontaine improved on her version by shortening it to a succinct fable (42). Labé's poems, Sainte-Beuve thinks, are few and "insignificant." Taming the striking eroticism of her sonnets, he alludes instead to "the sweetness and purity of her feelings and expression," but even such "sweetness" is qualified by the way in which he identifies and locates her by class and gender. In a single phrase, for example, he marks her social position (through use of her nickname, derived from her husband's artisan status) as well as her problematic literary position (through allusion to her model, Petrarch): "la Belle Cordière soupirait non loin de la patrie de Laure" (42).

The association of Labé with Laura, moreover, not only links her to an *object* of poetry but also to an Italy which Sainte-Beuve imagines as a threat to the naive freshness and evolving good taste that he defines as the virtues of middle sixteenth-century French poetry. In contrast to Marot's tempering of the *vieil esprit gaulois*, the writing, like the behav-

---

6. Scève was raised to canonical status only in the early twentieth century when appreciation for the density of Symbolist poetry disposed critics such as Valéry Larbaud to admire him as a forerunner of Mallarmé. See Verdun Saulnier, *Maurice Scève* (Paris: Klincksieck, 1948), 1, chap. 21.

ior, of groups far from the court supposedly coarsened what was already "primitive" in medieval culture: "outside the court, in the depth of the provinces, especially in those foreign to the center because of their close links to Italy, such as Anjou and Poitou, the wildest merriment [la jovialité la plus effrénée] sustained its traditions and maintained its greedy feasts" (42). This dismissal of unruly regions, such as Rabelais's Poitiers and Labé's Lyon, characteristically implicates Italy as the grotesque Other.[7] Sainte-Beuve retrospectively defines Renaissance genius as consisting of purity of language and delicacy of sentiment. Both must be protected from corruption by foreign influences from which he presumes the sixteenth-century French court was in essence free. But what Renaissance court could Sainte-Beuve have in mind? François I surrounded himself with Italian artists; Catherine de' Medici was the wife of Henri II, the mother of Charles IX and Henri III. The culturally heterogeneous courts of early modern France seem wishfully reconstructed to conform to a tidier paradigm—the triumphantly centralized national court of the Sun King.

In 1850, in a note for an article on criticism under the Empire, Sainte-Beuve wrote, "Criticism is what puts order into Letters. The rule [règne] of criticism is the rule of proper order in literature. After political crises, after revolutions which have overturned everything, criticism has inherited a tutelary power; [thus it] accomplishes its task and the restoration of proper morality."[8] As the police of literary law and order the critic's task is embedded in a timeless tradition of corrective and stabilizing assessments of literary merit: playing Malherbe to the Restoration, Boileau to the Second Empire, Sainte-Beuve lays claim to a sacred responsibility to preserve the values of the elite, even (or especially) in the aftermath of political rebellion. This view of the critic's role governs an essay written the same year, "What Is a Classic?" Sainte-Beuve opens with a passage from the late Roman grammarian Aulus Gellius, who uses the word "classicus" to denote a citizen belonging to the highest rank of taxpayers; in Sainte-Beuve's paraphrase the term means "a writer of worth and note . . . who counts, who has solid possessions, and who is not to be confused with the crowd of proletarians."[9] Rather than

7. On Italy as a feminized and feminizing threat to the "esprit francais," see "Rapport," 776; Saint-Marc Girardin, 89; and Chasles, 1–5 and 27. For an analysis of strategies through which the grotesque is used to banish oppositions and to consolidate cultural identity, see Peter Stallybrass and Allon White, *The Politics and Poetics of Transgression* (Ithaca: Cornell University Press, 1986).

8. Cited by Fayolle, p. 57.

9. "Qu'est-ce qu'un classique?" in *Causeries du lundi,* 3rd. ed. (Paris: Garnier, n.d.), 3, 39. All further references to this essay appear in parentheses in the text. Ernst Robert Curtius cites Gellius as follows: "but it was not until very late, and then only in a single instance, that the name *classicus* appears: in Aulus Gellius (*Noctes Atticae,* XIX, 8,

questioning this conflation of economic and literary value, Sainte-Beuve takes it as proof of Roman discernment: "such an expression implies an epoch advanced enough to have already carried out a census and classification of literature" (39). Despite the fact that he is narrating metamorphoses of taste, his images endow writers whose fortunes have in fact been unsteady with enduring autonomy. Restoring the measure and taste the Middle Ages lacked, he writes, the fifteenth and sixteenth centuries enabled the great authors of antiquity to "stand out luminously" from the mass and to "group themselves harmoniously" on the two peaks of Parnassus (39). And paradoxically, this emergence of "true" judgement of founding texts is attributed not just to the revival of classical perspectives but to the emergence of the nation-state. It was, Sainte-Beuve suggests, the attainment of political order that made possible the "true" judgment of a literary order—a judgment secured not through any process of argument but through its transparent self-evidence. The French had only to look back upon the triumphant state culture of Louis XIV's reign to recognize "immediately what a classic was without having to reason about it" (41).

Although Sainte-Beuve takes issue with the literary-historical strictness of the Academy's 1835 definition of a classic ("a writer who has become a model in a particular language"), in his own definition he systematically evacuates history of any kind from canonical works. He calls, contradictorily again, for eternal verities and moral progress. In practice, as his example proves, both these qualities are inevitably to be judged from a particular standpoint in the present; but Sainte-Beuve suppresses the changing situations of readers and critics through a fantasy of the great writer's consistently direct relationship to an evolving communal mind: "A true classic . . . is a writer who has enriched the human spirit, who has genuinely increased its treasure, who has made it take a step ahead, who has discovered an unequivocal moral truth" (42). The accumulated antitheses in his description of classic style do not resolve the contradiction between his defense of new forms and his demand that thematic content be communicated in a way transparent to all readers in all times: classic style must speak "to everyone in a

15). . . . The thing to do [writes Gellius] is to follow the usage of a model author: 'some one of the old orators or poets, that is, a first class tax paying author, not a proletarian'. . . . The *proletarius,* whom Gellius mentions by way of comparison, belongs to *no* tax class." In *European Literature and the Latin Middle Ages,* trans. Willard Trask (Princeton: Princeton University Press, 1948, rpt. 1973), 249–50. Stallybrass and White comment on the passage as follows: "From the first it seems that the ranking of types of authors was modelled upon social rank according to property classifications and this interrelation was still being actively invoked in the nineteenth century. In recent times we have been inclined to forget this ancient and enduring link between social rank and the organizing of authors and works," 1–2.

style of his own" yet be innovative—"new and ancient, easily contemporary to all epochs" (42).

Finally Sainte-Beuve, revealing the local interests that his positing of a transhistorical canon denies, explicitly links the requirement of lasting readability to political moderation. In order to be received into the canon, the classic writer must ultimately support the status quo; even if he goes to "extremes," it is only to achieve equilibrium: "a classic author may have been revolutionary at a certain moment, or have seemed so, but he no longer is; he pillaged everything around him at first, turned his constraints upside down only in order to reestablish balance, very quickly, for the benefit of order and beauty" [au *profit* de l'ordre et du beau] (42, emphasis ours). Novelty, then, is acceptable in classic authors and in classic ages only if carefully circumscribed; measure and order, the reassertion of unchanging values, are all: "the Temple of taste," says Sainte-Beuve, needs expansion, but in the form of restoration (50). The basic ground plan must be preserved.

The architects and owners of "the Temple" are, of course, gendered: the writers Sainte-Beuve praises as "classics," and the readers with whom he identifies, are men. If, like Molière and La Fontaine, they were indifferent to the rules and models of their day, he celebrates them as *virile* free spirits: "as far as classics go, the most unexpected are still the best and the greatest; seek . . . those male geniuses truly born immortal and perpetually flourishing" (50). His ideal reader, too, is a man, a gentleman of leisure who has read widely and returns to well-known books at the end of his life. A class and even a religious decorum is implied in his closing advice to the would-be appreciator of the classics. At some point he must stop sampling new texts: "for one must choose, and the precondition of good taste, after having comprehended everything, is to stop traveling, to sit down and take a position. Nothing dulls and dims taste more than endless voyages; the spirit of poetry is not the Wandering Jew" (53). The discerning reader, then, is a settled bourgeois, ready for the refined enjoyment of the familiar that comes with age: "it is then that the word *classic* takes on its true meaning and is defined for every man of taste by an irresistible predilection and choice" (54). And the rewards that the canon guarantees to this man of taste include "a conversation at any moment, a friendship that does not deceive or leave us, and that habitual impression of serenity and affability that reconciles us, as we often need to be, with other men and with ourselves" (55).

Underlying Sainte-Beuve's definition of a canonical purpose—being "reconciled" with "other men and with ourselves"—are assumptions that both include and exclude. On one hand, the complacency implicit in his notion of "reconciliation" serves to marginalize all literary radicals and explorers, adventurous readers as well as writers who would question and provoke rather than soothe. On the other, the man who reflects upon other men and himself has predictably little to say about women or the texts they produced. Although he logically entertains a cross-cultural perspective on, for example, epic poetry (other men), he erases genres in which women traditionally became visible, such as letter writing and the short novel. When Sainte-Beuve introduces women writers into his history of "taste," he does so to survey and correct, to enforce modest silence on too often erotic matter, to muffle sex(ts) rather than analyze texts.[10] Consider, as examples, his readings of Marguerite de Navarre and Louise Labé, the two most visible women in traditional histories of sixteenth-century French literature. For here Sainte-Beuve tellingly invokes evaluative criteria that inform the ongoing canonization of Marguerite and the alternating decanonizations and recanonizations of Louise.

II. RULY AND UNRULY WOMEN: MARGUERITE DE NAVARRE AND LOUISE LABÉ

Sainte-Beuve's focus on royalty as the center and source of culture leads him to privilege the sister of the king, the princess poet, Marguerite de Navarre. But his approval depends largely on her patronage of Clément Marot; his remarks for the most part are restricted to an enumeration of her relationships to significant men. In the *Tableau historique* his first sentence about her consists of praise for her devotion to Marot: she was "la protectrice de sa vie" (33). Sainte-Beuve dispenses with discussion of Marguerite's short stories and plays in order to conjecture about the sources for her poems, which include "several easy songs that suggest that she knew how to profit from the model and the services of her valet de chambre" (34). His implication goes beyond the claim that she was indebted to Marot as mentor or even as ghost writer; at the same time that her status as a member of the royal elite would include her in Sainte-Beuve's history, her status as a woman would exclude her.

Marot's patroness may well have been a queen, but, like any woman, she was subject to sexual conquest. In an aggressively leveling footnote, Sainte-Beuve sums up with titillating ambivalence the debate over whether Marguerite and Marot were lovers: "there is no doubt about Marguerite's elevated morals, but there are certain moments in anyone's youth" (34). From this apparently gender-neutral axiom, he moves to a second innuendo that arises from a complex of assumptions about

10. Here we paraphrase Hélène Cixous, though in a contrasting context: "let the priests tremble, we're going to show them our sextes." In "Le Rire de la Méduse," *L'Arc* 61 (1975), 47; translation by Keith Cohen and Paula Cohen in *New French Feminisms*, ed. Elaine Marks and Isabelle de Courtivron (Amherst: University of Massachusetts Press, 1980), 255.

feminine self-exposure and masculine dominance. Any woman who goes public as a writer must have questionable motives and sources: "whenever a woman writes, one is tempted to ask, smiling, who is behind her" (34). Sainte-Beuve's generalization says a great deal about the conditions under which he will admit a woman into the canon. She must serve men in one or more ways: as a patron, as a literary imitator, as a sexual partner, and so on. And her work in turn serves as a pretext for criticism that links literary and sexual relations in ways rarely invoked in analyses of male writing.

This uneasy tension between royalist admiration and sexual suspicion persists in Sainte-Beuve's longer essay on Marguerite in a "Causerie du lundi" (1853). By this time his political views had hardened. After his break with Hugo, his disenchantment with the Saint-Simonians and his revulsion at the Revolution of 1848, he increasingly saw the functions of the critic as the purification of taste and the protection of standards against the commercialization of contemporary literature (Fayolle, 60–77). His 1853 assessment of Marguerite arises almost entirely from his conviction that criticism should act as the watchdog of moral order. This version of Marguerite is a portrait of the ideally virtuous woman of the 1850s, combining sweet domesticity (he cites at length her letters to François I, including one in which she tenderly describes his children) and appreciation of her male contemporaries.

In her own time, Erasmus praised Marguerite for intellectual and spiritual qualities admired by the Renaissance in men as well as women: prudence "worthy even of a philosopher,"[11] moderation and piety, an invincible strength of spirit, indifference to worldly things. Sainte-Beuve, however, concentrates on her protection of protestant thinkers, an activity that implied specific intellectual and political positions in Marguerite's time that he then recasts in terms of his own. First, her alliance with Calvinists was a sign of liberal tolerance, never of radical sympathies: "she behaved like a person who, around [17]89, would have supported liberty wholeheartedly, without desiring or predicting the Revolution" (442). Second, he sees no intellectual coherence in her position; although she defended protestants in letters in which she even uses the "jargon of Calvinism," her writing generally shows engagingly "feminine" inconsistency on religious matters: "one must not expect much rigor either in her ideas or in her expression of them" (443). He discusses her *Heptaméron* (which, in a new edition, is the ostensible topic of his essay) only briefly, praising the subtlety of dialogue in the frame tale but dismissing the collection as a whole as written "without art, composition, or the sense of an ending" (449).

11. Sainte-Beuve cites Erasmus's letter to Marguerite in "Marguerite, Reine de Navarre," *Causeries*, 7, 441. All further references to this essay appear in parentheses in the text.

Then, in a move typical of the critical policing carried out by the canonical mentality as it deals with women writers, he shifts to a denunciation of the coarseness of the tales, their "licence et grossièreté" (450). The real issue for Sainte-Beuve, the quality he requires of a woman writer, is not skillful narration but verbal propriety. He takes Marguerite's anthology as proof that elegant and proper conversation evolved only in the seventeenth century; "professors" of "bon ton," such as Mlle de Scudéry, would have to spend years "preaching decorum" before the elegant discretion of middle seventeenth-century "entretiens" was attained (450). Women, according to Sainte-Beuve's moral system, are responsible for maintaining decency: "in all times, respectable women have had to listen to more things than they themselves say; but the decisive moment, the one to be noted, is the moment at which they ceased saying these unsuitable things themselves, and saying them to such an extent that they preserved them in writing without imagining that they thereby fell short of virtue" (431). Sainte-Beuve anachronistically imposes his version of the double standard by assigning a natural and transhistorical "pudeur" to women without recognizing that sexual differentiation in the Renaissance, whatever its marked hierarchies, allowed the hybridization of popular and courtly discourses even in "virtuous" women's texts.

The "license" Sainte-Beuve noticed in the *Heptaméron* has tended, until very recently, to be effaced in criticism of Marguerite's writing. Her piety and generosity as a patron—that is, her religious and "maternal" service to the men in her milieu—are foregrounded. The woman who ruled won attention as a queen, but she also had to be rewritten to represent the ruly woman: chaste, pious, a "protectrice" to the heroes of Renaissance culture. Castex and Surer, for example, in their manual designed for students preparing for their baccalaureat, stress the "pure and moving impulses of her soul" and "the moral and religious scruples" she applied in transforming Boccaccio's material. Their brief literary commentary, moreover, is framed by her careful positioning in relation to notable men: they begin, "Marguerite of Angoulême, sister of François I, initially married the Duke of Alençon, and later the King of Navarre, Henri D'Albret, her second husband"; they conclude with a celebration of the protectress of Bonaventure des Périers and Marot; and only two intervening paragraphs discuss texts surprisingly thought to be composed by Marguerite "*herself*" (emphasis theirs).[12] Lagarde and Michard limit their evaluation to one sentence: "In his role as ['Father of Letters', François] was seconded by his sister, Marguerite of An-

---

12. P.-G. Castex, P. Surer, and G. Becker, *Manuel des études littéraires françaises, XVIe siècle* (Paris: Hachette, 1966), 6. The defense of the *Heptaméron* as a purification of Boccaccio began as early as Brunetière in an essay on Marguerite in his *Histoire de la littérature française classique* (Paris: Delagrave, 1904), 175–80.

goulême, duchess of Alençon, then queen of Navarre, protectrice of Marot and author *herself* of the *Heptaméron*" (emphasis ours).[13]

Although in some senses subject to similar descriptive strategies, Louise Labé—"the 'belle cordière' (her husband was a ropemaker)" (Lagarde/Michard, 31)—constituted a more problematic site for judgments conflating poetics and anxiety about female sexual behavior. Hers has been a story of the unruly woman, whose writing was read— negatively and positively—as a transgression of cultural norms. Class and political interests interacted with gender ideologies in the first responses to the woman and the writer; they still do. The fixation on feminine sexual propriety helps to explain Sainte-Beuve's extremely idiosyncratic reading of Louise Labé, both in the *Tableau historique* and in a later essay written in 1862. He accepts the early myths about the poet: she fought in the battle of Perpignan, loved the aristocratic Olivier de Magny more than her rope-maker husband ("so unappetizing in his greasy apron,")[14] and died young, still grieving over unrequited love. In an about-face from the *Tableau*, he praises the "ingenious elegance" of Labé's *Débat de Folie et d'Amour*; he takes it as an example of the superiority of prose to poetry at this stage of French writing and emphasizes its conformity to his notion of feminine charm (306). His first comment on Labé's sonnets, however, is rather deprecatory: they are hard, rough, obviously constrained by rhythm and rhyme. But he then employs an axiom of Romantic aesthetics in order to save the poet: the sincerity of her feelings justifies the imperfection of her style.

What feelings, however? The striking thing about the 1862 commentary is that Sainte-Beuve selects three of Labé's most sublimated poems, repressing those in which she demands "chaleureux" kisses from her beloved, for example, or deploys her fame as a writer in a seductive appeal for his love. Clearly, the critic would make Labé into a Romantic heroine. Sainte-Beuve concedes that Labé suffers from a dubious reputation; he sums up the debate over her promiscuity by acknowledging that too much is said about her to believe that she "kept her ardors only for her poems" (101). But he reforms her by rewriting her as a pure spirit, a poet of "burning" force (311), a precursor of Romantic intensities and melancholies. His anachronism here, as in the *Tableau*, is interwoven with his androcentrism; Sainte-Beuve absorbs Labé into a masculine literary scheme that privileges *men's* Romanticism, which remains his constant point of reference. In his conclusion, he shifts his focus from Labé to a "woman poet of our days," Mlle Ackermann, the dedicator of

13. André Lagarde and Laurent Michard, *XVIe siècle: Les Grands auteurs du programme* (Paris: Bordas, 1965), 9.
14. "Oeuvres de Louise Labé, la belle cordière," in *Nouveaux lundis*, 4, 305. All further references to this essay appear in parentheses in the text.

"Stances" to Alfred de Musset. The essay ends with a line from Acker-mann's poem, which Sainte-Beuve offers as an epigram worthy of the male poet's tomb: "Hélas! chanter ainsi, c'était vouloir mourir" (341). This relay of meritorious suffering from a Renaissance woman to a nineteenth-century male writer accounts for Sainte-Beuve's continuing interest in Labé: she is the pretext for praise of a youthful *hero* of Romanticism. Whatever differences exist between Musset and Labé—her manipulation of sixteenth-century rhetoric, her critique of Petrarchan conventions, her demand to be recognized as a woman poet by her contemporaries—are effaced. Her *Euvres* are rewritten as an episode in literary history that satisfies a nineteenth-century fascination with suffering "femininity" and advances the construction of literary history as the history of men writing about and for men.

Of the various threads in Sainte-Beuve's assessment of Labé, his reference to her damaged reputation had many historical precedents. There is no real proof that Labé led a life of sexual excess: her inheritance of wealth from a rich merchant father and her marriage to another wealthy ropemaker assign her to a socioeconomic class much above the fallen gentility or poverty from which successful courtesans fought their way to prosperity. Twentieth-century critics are fairly well agreed that attacks on Labé arose from her fellow citizens' disapproval of her participation in bourgeois literary coteries that challenged the cultural hegemony of the aristocracy. An example is an early charge against her by Philibert de Vienne, a Lyonnais nobleman who wrote, in his *Philosophe de cour* (1547), that Labé was at least less avaricious toward her "serviteurs" than a courtesan such as Lais of Corinth had been.[15] But he was never a member of Labé's circle, which was open to men of letters whether or not they were aristocrats; it may well have been his exclusion that motivated his charge about behavior of which he had no direct knowledge.

In fact, most accusations that Labé was a courtesan and an adulteress have been revealed as strategies through which men attempted to settle scores with other men. In 1552, one M. Ivard, a former neighbor of Labé, was seeking a divorce in Geneva; he accused his wife of trying to poison him as a result of the dissolute life to which she had been led by "her cousin, la 'Belle Cordière'."[16] In order to rid himself of one woman, Ivard defamed another who no longer had a powerful clansman to keep him in order (Labé's father had died in the same year). Tension between two men also produced one of the most serious attacks on Labé: Calvin

---

15. Cited by Ferdinand Zamaron, *Louise Labé, dame de la franchise* (Paris: Nizet, 1968), 67. See also Karine Berriot, *Louise Labé: la belle rebelle et le françois nouveau* (Paris: Editions du Seuil, 1985), 187.

16. For exonerating discussions of this case see Zamaron, 67–68; and Berriot, 187.

described her as a "common whore" in a Latin pamphlet he wrote from Geneva in 1561 (Zamaron, 68; Barriot, 188–89). But this pamphlet was directed at Gabriel de Saconay, a liberal churchman of Lyon, where several young Genevan protestants had been burned in 1551. In order to denounce Saconay, Calvin descended to sexual insult, accusing him of frequenting brothels and employing the services of Labé, "a famous whore, that is, la 'Belle Cordière'."[17] Caught in the crossfire of the Reformation, Labé was used again as ammunition for men's enmity and ambition. Aristocratic envy, a man's divorce suit, churchmen's polemics: such were the determinants of Labé's sexual reputation.

And critical opinion has continued to judge the writer according to myths about the woman. Léon Feugère, a contemporary of Sainte-Beuve (whom he cites admiringly in an 1860 study), typifies the conflation of sexual rumor and critical evaluation: "Louise Labé expresses the transports of passion in a language too indiscreet to be easily accepted by the modern reader."[18] Like Sainte-Beuve, Feugère censors the sonnets, leaving out the openly erotic ones in favor of those "that breathe out a tender melancholy." Even in the twentieth century, investigations into the poet's private life continue.[19] The obvious reason for this critical anxiety is a persistent critical commitment to purity in women's bodies and words. In 1955, for example, Léopold Senghor defended the poet and her texts together: "it would be impossible to find in our entire literature more chaste love poems. Truly, Louise Labé has no sense of sin, she is innocent at heart and in the flesh, she remains the greatest poetess to be born in France."[20] Robert Sabatier reverses the terms of earlier judges by praising the intensity of physical "frémissement" in the poems; indeed, he reads Labé as a magnificent masochist, citing Marie Bonaparte on essential feminine painseeking.[21] Even in 1976 the erotic in a woman's text remains a problem; whether it is repressed or celebrated, it still needs to be contained by selective censorship or interpretive sublimation.

Labé's reputation has been constructed through other biases as well, particularly the kind of assumption Sainte-Beuve made about Marguerite de Navarre: if a woman writes, a man must be behind her. "Cherchez l'homme": this obsession appears everywhere in commentary on Labé's *Euvres*. In 1584, about twenty years after Labé's death,

17. The Latin text is cited by Dorothy O'Connor in *Louise Labé, sa vie et son oeuvre* (Paris: Les Presses Françaises, 1926), 184.

18. Léon Feugère, *Les Femmes poètes au XVIe siècle* (Paris: Didier, 1860), 19.

19. For example, in her appendix to *Louise Labé* O'Connor includes a list of witnesses in order to prove that Labé was a courtesan, 185–89. Zamaron invokes his experience as a police inspector to draw the opposite conclusion from the same evidence, 100.

20. *Anthologie des poètes du XVIe siècle* (Paris: Bibliothèque Mondiale, 1955), 13.

21. *La Poésie du seizième siècle* (Paris: Albin Michel, 1975), 115–16.

Pierre de Saint-Julien asserted that her *Débat* was too witty and learned to have been composed by a "mere courtesan" and that it must therefore have been the work of Maurice Scève (Berriot, 196). Other lovers who influenced Labé as a poet have been suggested: Henri II, Marot, Olivier de Magny.[22] The arguments and counterarguments about these presumed mentors reveal very little about actual influence but a great deal about the critical desire to subordinate women's writing to men's. A recent case in point is Paul Ardouin's glossily illustrated celebration of the Ecole lyonnaise, which turns Scève into Labé's teacher.[23] Here the gender biases of influence studies contribute to the decanonization of the woman poet by denying her literary autonomy. Gender bias individualizes women's literary relationships to such an extent that they are represented as writing in thrall to a single romantic and literary model rather than responding to the conventions and vocabularies shared by male poets in their time.

Androcentric logic produces an opposite conclusion in the view that Labé was nonpareil, a unique poet untouched by the intricacies of sixteenth-century lyric theory. Sainte-Beuve's positive judgment of her arises from exactly this idea. She had nothing in common with the Pléiade, he writes: "her verses do not derive from it or show its influence, they know no other star but the Star of Venus! She belongs to no compartment or school, to no classification" (311). But the attribution of originary creativity brings problematic assumptions in its wake when a woman writer is at issue: Labé's "sincerity" has come to connote spontaneous artlessness. Max Jasinski, for example, conjectured that her poems isolated her because the Pléiade "doubtless found her work too naked, too untaught, too far beneath the high art to which they had proudly raised themselves."[24] Like Jasinski, other influential literary historians emphasize the genuineness of her feeling without quoting any of her texts. The one-line summary of her sonnets in Lagarde and Michard's literary manual demonstrates that this critical response has solidifed into a cliché: "another poetess from the Lyon group must be mentioned, Louise Labé, . . . whose sonnets are remarkable for the *sincerity* of their sentiments" (31). The representation of artlessness as the gift of a woman poet apparently dispenses readers from actually examining her work.

If, on the contrary, a critic decides to take Labé seriously, to focus on her technique and form, the gesture is likely to efface her womanhood.

22. Luc Van Brabant argued for Henri II and Marot in *Louïse Labé et ses aventures amoureuses avec Clément Marot et le Dauphin Henry* (Coxyde-sur-mer: Les Édifiants de la Belle sans sy, 1966).

23. *Maurice Scève, Pernette du Guillet, Louise Labé: l'Amour à Lyon au temps de la Renaissance* (Paris: Nizet, 1981), 41–42.

24. *Histoire du sonnet en France* (Paris: Brugère, 1903), 66.

Lawrence Harvey's respectful formalist study of Labé's sonnets opposed the obsessive dwelling on her private life endemic to earlier criticism, but his desire to rehabilitate Labé, to make her conform to the laws of the canon, blinded him to the thematic and rhetorical gendering of the poems. He downplays Labé's addresses to women and her self-representation as a woman by treating such performances as "fictions," explorations of what love might be rather than autobiographical confessions.[25] Thus he can defend Labé as a universal poet—understood as masculine. This assumption is transparent in the phrasing of his final paragraph where he argues that Labé's achievement lies elsewhere than in the history of confessional literature: "it is surely clear that its true value lies elsewhere: in the poet's *mastery* of a form that is both fixed and flexible, in the expressive effect this form attains as it recreates a coherent vision of the *human* condition, and finally in this vision itself— of the Renaissance, yet *universal*—that calls up the powerful, poignant drama of *man's* yearning and striving toward an ideal that forever lures *him* on and remains, eternally, inaccessible" (emphasis ours) (84).

We also, in contrast, now have a Labé defined entirely in terms of gender, as Woman. A canon of the quintessential female, being constructed in France and elsewhere, draws new political and theoretical concerns into the assessment of women writers. In a recent book, Evelyne Sullerot uses Labé as an instance of the eternal feminine: "It behooves us to listen to woman sing of the mystery of the seductive spell [man] casts over her . . . —a mystery which proves as powerful as that of the woman for the man, that eternal refrain that we have heard so often through the ages."[26] This rhapsody to heterosexual nature is expanded in Sullerot's presentation of Labé as typical of all women in all times: "Louise Labé is the perfect expression of the vision of life, the emotions, the suffering, the feminine experience, of the woman in love" (75). The romantic valorization of spontaneity reappears here; so does the Sainte-Beuvian fusion of the poet's erotic life and her written texts. Labé's eroticism is celebrated rather than muffled, but is there any change in the presumed eternal verities—that women love only men, that love entails suffering, that sexual attraction is a perpetually unknowable mystery—smuggled in under Sullerot's praise for Labé?

One of the tasks feminism has assigned itself since the 1970s is that of challenging assumptions like these. And indeed, the lessons of that labor would seem to demonstrate that the inequalities imposed by the politics of canon formation can be righted neither by arguing that writ-

25. *The Aesthetics of the Renaissance Love Sonnet: An Essay on the Art of the Sonnet in the Poetry of Louise Labé* (Geneva: Droz, 1962), 14 and 51.

26. *Women on Love: Eight Centuries of Feminine Writing*, trans. Helen Lane (London: Jill Norman, 1979), 75.

ing transcends gender to achieve "universality" nor that it marks an essential, a-historical "difference." It is not difficult to show how early historians of Renaissance literature reproduced their own moral and political biases by translating them into judgments of taste, presumably objective and therefore above analysis; it is harder to recognize the contemporary ideologies informing the construction of new canons. Perhaps the canon-building project itself should be abandoned; its history has certainly had little to offer women as writers or readers. This would, of course, require suspending the traditional categories of "value" in favor of other categories and questions. How invested are women writers in the articulations of difference—be it difference from men or difference from other women? How are they positioned at specific historical moments? How have they negotiated the constraints of race, class, and gender in relation to inherited discursive models? For new answers, new questions. Sainte-Beuve's instinctive sense of the "classic" need neither be re-membered nor regendered. Rather its motivating suppositions and strategies require a suspicious rereading so that the corrective measures of the present not duplicate the corrective measures of the past: "our criticisms judge us more than they judge others," noted Sainte-Beuve.[27]

Louise Labé was celebrated as a heroine of the Revolution in Lyon. In 1790 a division of the National Guard displayed her portrait on their banner, accompanied by the following motto: "you foresaw our designs, Charly, Belle Cordière; to break our chains, you were the first to fly. Belle Cordière, your hope was not in vain."[28] Clearly this radical canonization of Labé rewrites her as much from the perspective of the present as do her conservative decanonizations. And an analysis of the interests motivating such inclusion and exclusion constitutes a genuinely productive position for feminist critics. For such a strategy both escapes the cataloguing of eternal women worthies and exposes the historicity of literary value. Perhaps we need not only to imagine "flying beyond" canonical chains but also to interrogate the processes that forge them.

27. In a letter to Hortense Allart (6 November 1845) in the *Correspondance générale*, ed. J. Bonnerot (Paris: Stock, 1949), 6, 272; cited by Rigolot, 43.
28. Cited by Zamaron, 78. The French text reads: "Tu prédis nos desseins, Charly, Belle Cordière / Car pour briser nos fers tu volas la première."

JOAN DEJEAN

Classical Reeducation: Decanonizing the Feminine

Each age has its canon, its own peculiarly idiosyncratic vision of the literature of preceding centuries. One way of approaching the study of canons is palimpsest-style, by peeling back superimposed layers of critical judgment in search of the hierarchies and the process of inclusion-exclusion that commentators of a given period developed to package contemporary literary production and that of earlier ages for pedagogical dissemination and consumption. In the case of seventeenth-century literature, the stripping away of canonical layers would take us back to the period from the end of the seventeenth century to the middle of the eighteenth century during which two related developments transformed the meaning of "classic" in French. In the first place, modern (French) authors were placed on an equal footing with their ancient precursors as models for pedagogical instruction, thus becoming "classic" according to the most standard usage, the primary sense of the term attested in seventeenth-century dictionaries ("author who is taught in classes, in the schools"). In the second place, selected authors of the second half of the seventeenth century (the period that baptized itself France's Golden Age) gradually became accepted as "classic" in another sense of the word, this time one particular to the French language and one included only in modern dictionaries: "that which pertains to the great authors of the seventeenth century and their period, considered as expressing an ideal" (Robert dictionary).[1]

In the course of this semantic drift, these two meanings of classic are often considered synonymous; in many periods it is almost universally

1. There is considerable confusion about the origin of this usage. To date, I have not been able to reach a satisfactory conclusion. However, I do not accept the attribution of this sense of "classic" to Voltaire. The Robert dictionary states that this usage was only introduced at the turn of the nineteenth century by Staël. If this is true, we have still another indication of Staël's sensitivity to semantic innovation. (Time and again, I have traced the origin of terms crucial for the history of women's writing to her works.)

understood that "the great authors of the seventeenth century" are alone worthy to be taught in the schools. At the same time and as part of the same evolution of linguistic usage and pedagogical practice, the most influential women writers of the Golden Age are pronounced unworthy of membership in the class of "great authors of the seventeenth century" because the "ideal" their works express is deemed unfit to be proposed to schoolchildren as a model. However, these women writers are still proposed as models as long as the original canon of French literature, a canon, as we will see, for adult readers rather than schoolchildren, still survives (roughly until the beginning of the nineteenth century). In search of an explanation for the exclusion of women writers from classic status, I will contrast the two types of pedagogical programs available in France from the late seventeenth century until shortly after the Revolution, what I have just referred to as the canon for adults and the first canon for schoolchildren to include modern authors.

In the closing decades of the seventeenth century, French writers begin to draw up lists of their precursors and then to edit anthologies of their representative works. The best known of these is the *Recueil des plus belles pièces des poètes français,* published anonymously in 1692 and considered the work of either Fontenelle, a man of letters sympathetic to women writers, or a noted woman writer of the day, Marie-Catherine d'Aulnoy.[2] This compilation is in many ways a model for the most central early tradition of anthologizing. It is devoted exclusively to French authors and almost exclusively to seventeenth-century writers. Its editor makes no claim to be a literary arbiter: all authors are included who have acquired a certain "reputation," whether or not they can be considered "great" authors. The editor makes no attempt to dictate literary taste but tries simply to give a sense of the field.

Today's readers familiar with the French pedagogical tradition probably think of anthologies exclusively as works intended to introduce literature into the classroom in order to mold the taste of schoolchildren. However, in France for over a century until just after the Revolution, almost all these volumes were compiled for adults who wished to keep abreast of the literary scene. The principle of inclusion on which the Fontenelle/d'Aulnoy anthology is based makes it clear that this anthology, like the dozens that imitated it throughout the eighteenth century, was destined for a precise public, the adults who

2. *Recueil des plus belles pièces des poètes français depuis Villon jusqu'à M. de Benserade,* 5 vols. (Paris: Barbin, 1692). Initially, the anthology was generally accepted as d'Aulnoy's. Only later is Fontenelle's name attached to it and, even though no convincing reason for the change in attribution has ever been offered, it has gained wide acceptance. (G. Reed, *Claude Barbin* [Geneva: Droz, 1974], 40, n. 1). Today, the compilation is most often referred to as the Recueil Barbin, after the publisher who signs its dedicatory preface. (He was the publisher of many early women writers.)

frequented milieux like the salons, in which literature was a major topic of discussion and who wished to have a sense of the range of modern literature, a subject not yet part of the curriculum at the time of their official education. These early anthologies are therefore pedagogical in a sense of the term perhaps closest to the recent usage "continuing education." In the vision of literary production they propose, the canon is made up of works read by an adult public active in the world rather than a public isolated in an educational establishment, a pedagogical role for literature promoted actively at least until the early nineteenth century. Indeed, prior to the mid-eighteenth century, the only canonical status to which *French* authors could aspire was inclusion in worldly anthologies compiled for adults, a canonical status that was never officially legitimated. Only under the most exceptional circumstances did a new work become canonical in the original French sense of the term, that which is introduced into the classroom as a model for students. Prior to the mid-eighteenth century, the classics, the works taught in the *collèges*, were all Greek and Latin, whereas modern works could become influential only by appealing to the worldly adult public.

The view of the literary scene found in the continuing education anthologies of the late seventeenth and early eighteenth centuries is remarkably different from the vision of that era presented in today's manuals. Perhaps the most striking difference concerns the presence of women writers. In anthologies devoted to writers in general, women writers are admitted in numbers far more important than at any time since. In addition, between the late seventeenth and the late eighteenth century, at least a dozen literary anthologies devoted exclusively to women writers were published. Before presenting the canonical revision that was the end result of the new literary pedagogy of the Enlightenment, I will consider very briefly two of these continuing education anthologies, one near the beginning of the tradition and one at its end, in order at least to suggest the magnitude of the options eventually sacrificed to the remodeled classical ideology.

Marguerite Buffet's *Nouvelles observations sur la langue française, avec l'éloge des illustres savantes tant anciennes que modernes* (1668), one of the first such anthologies, is a fascinating critical hybrid. Buffet's volume is the clearest demonstration of the genre's goal of contributing to the continuing education of an adult public: its first half is a French grammar and a treatise on correct usage and orthography destined for a general audience and in particular female readers who had been denied formal linguistic training. These grammatical considerations are joined to a portrait gallery of literary women in which Buffet, alone among the representatives of this worldly tradition, broadens the definition of the literary to include demonstrations of the linguistic excellence she defines in her grammatical treatise, oral as well as written. She is thereby able to record accomplishments, such as conversational brilliance, otherwise excluded from the domain of literary criticism, and to privilege the particular artistic manifestations then being developed in the salons. Volumes like Buffet's—as well as those of her contemporaries Jean de La Forge, Jacquette Guillaume, and Claude de Vertron—provide information on numbers of influential seventeenth-century literary women who have been virtually lost to readers since the demise of the worldly canon after the Revolution.[3]

Early anthologies like Buffet's have none of the pedagogical qualities of the eighteenth-century compilations whose techniques we will analyze. They are often closer to collections of eulogies than to literary manuals from which a potential student of any age could obtain information on what an individual author actually wrote, much less on what that literary production was like. By the end of the worldly anthology tradition, however, editors had made great progress in the pedagogical presentation of material, clearly having learned from their predecessors (almost every such compilation contains references to precursor volumes) as much as from the rival tradition of manuals for classroom instruction. Both the most eloquent and the most pedagogical of the worldly anthologies is one of the final examples of the tradition, an enterprise that would clearly have realized the genre's potential, had it not become still another victim of the events of 1789.

The fourteen existing volumes of Louise Keralio Robert's *Collection des meilleurs ouvrages français composés par des femmes* (1786–1789) stand as a monument to the tradition's potential for growth. Furthermore, as she makes clear in the preface to volume one, Keralio had initially planned a venture far more vast, "about 36 volumes" that would have presented a panorama of French literary history from the Middle Ages through the end of the eighteenth century, with the lion's share devoted to the "classical age" of French women's writing, the seventeenth century.[4] Had Keralio completed her anthology, she would have provided an alternative history of French literature until the Revolution, a narrative demonstrating the deficiency of any French literary history that omits the contributions of women to every period, a history challenging the adequacy of the notions of periodization then commonly accepted—many of which are still accepted today—to account for the production of women writers. But Keralio did not come close to

3. Buffet, *Nouvelles observations sur la langue française, avec l'éloge des illustres savantes tant anciennes que modernes* (Paris: Jean Cusson, 1668); La Forge, *Le Cercle des femmes savantes* (Paris: Loyson, 1663); Guillaume, *Les Dames illustres* (Paris: Thomas Jolly, 1665); Claude Charles Guionet, seigneur de Vertron, *La Nouvelle Pandore ou les Femmes illustres du siècle de Louis le Grand*, 2 vols. (Paris: Veuve Mazuel, 1698).

4. Louise Félicité Guinemet de Keralio Robert, *Collection des meilleurs ouvrages français composés par des femmes*, 14 vols. (Paris: Lagrange, 1786–89), 1: i–ii.

finishing her history. After the initial five volumes devoted to the Middle Ages and the Renaissance (Christine de Pisan alone is allotted two volumes), she jumps ahead to Scudéry. She then skips over volumes 7 and 8, which she leaves blank, as she explains, in the hope of returning some day to fill in the gaps, and proceeds directly to Sévigné. It is easy to offer a historical explanation for Keralio's failure to complete the ambitious contract she initially offered her readers: the last volumes of her collection appeared in 1789, surely an inauspicious date, as Germaine de Staël would soon observe, both for feminist writing in general and for the until then largely aristocratic tradition of French women's literature in particular. No one would ever fill in the gaps in Keralio's history, although the tradition she represents was killed off by a movement that began long before 1789, and one that was hardly revolutionary in its politics.

The volumes Keralio did manage to complete are astonishingly well-researched and put together and could easily be used today as the basis for a curriculum in French women's writing. Her format is highly pedagogical: biography followed by selections from major works, with an important innovation found in no other early anthology. Keralio understands that the best literary history presents an overview, a framework in which individual pieces can be situated. Thus she alternates her treatment of women authors from a given period with a history of French literature, presented in segments, from its origins (defined as the time of the Gauls), always integrating the women writers she is about to discuss in the general literary context of their day. And Keralio's volumes are the logical summation of the movement that begins with Buffet and her contemporaries. An examination of early French literary histories shows that, until the dawn of the nineteenth century, women writers were just about as likely as their male counterparts to be included in canonical compilations. However, at the same time as the editors of worldly anthologies were learning to make their case more forcefully, the countertradition was developing that would in the long run become so influential that it would succeed in establishing its program of French literary classics as the only vision possible of the early history of French literature.

No sooner had the first anthologists established the existence of a French tradition (by the early eighteenth century) than the power of the pedagogical canon began to be recognized. Historians have traced the movement whereby, from the sixteenth to the eighteenth century, the family gradually turned over to the *collège* the boy's preparation for professional life. Yet, despite the fact that the student was supposed to enter a profession directly upon leaving the *collège*, schools continued throughout the eighteenth century to rely almost exclusively on literary texts to teach all subjects. In the course of the eighteenth century, theorists began increasingly to call for a "national" education, a "uniform" education that would replace "provincial prejudices" with "homogeneous ideas of civic and religious virtue."[5] Contemporaneous with the development of the desire to standardize the teaching of Frenchness is the movement to give French authors at least equal importance in the curriculum that was to perform this new pedagogical mission. In a standarized, national educational program whose primary goal was to use the teaching of literature to form model Frenchmen, educators realized that the newly recognized French literary tradition should play a major role. Under these circumstances, pedagogical authorities initiated the process of teaching teachers how the works of literary moderns could be held up as models of Frenchness.

This project for the ideological packaging of literature took shape over the first half of the eighteenth century. Scholars gradually developed the anthology into a full-scale literary program: in 1740, for example, Goujet produced an eighteen-volume *Histoire de la littérature française* still directed at a post*collège* public, no longer governed by the principle of the worldly anthologies—that is, an author should be included if he or she is being talked about. On the contrary, Goujet's aim was strictly judgmental: "I want to lead my readers by the hand through our literary riches, to teach them what we have in each literary domain, to show them what they should choose and reject".[6] Goujet transforms the worldly anthology into the arm by which critics could police the reading habits of the "honnête homme" and could thereby shape both his taste and his national prejudices. Such a project would in effect be a form of reeducation, an undoing of the vision of the contemporary literary scene spread by the worldly anthologies. He concludes his "preliminary discourse" with a call for a similar effort on the part of pedagogues, who should be adapting the texts of literary moderns the better to accomplish their task of making their young charges into "good Christians" "useful to civil society" (xli).

Pedagogues quickly heeded his call to arms. The ancestor of the modern system of national exams, the *concours général des collèges parisiens*, at its inception in 1747 had a double prize, *amplification française* side by side with *amplification latine*. From this point on, Parisian professors of rhetoric "categorically" demanded that French poets and orators be introduced into the curriculum and that students begin to write *in* French about French authors (Chartier et al., 199). At

5. Roger Chartier, M.-M. Compère, and D. Julia, *L'Education en France au XVIIe et XVIIIe siècles* (Paris: PUF, 1964), 209. Subsequent references to this work will be included in parentheses in the text, a practice I follow with all works I cite more than once. All translations from the French are my own.

6. *Bibliothèque française; ou Histoire de la littérature française*, 18 vols. (Paris: Mariette, 1740–56), ii.

the very same time that the system of *concours* was being founded, the pedagogical philosophy and even the pedagogical tools that are still used today to prepare students for the national exams were given their original formulation. L'abbé Batteux's companion volumes *Les Beaux arts réduits à un seul principe* of 1746 and his *Cours de belles-lettres* of 1747 were designed to provide teachers with both what we know from Lagarde and Michard as a *"program* of *great* French authors" and the techniques for using these authors to teach Frenchness, most notably the reduction of works deemed masterpieces to *morceaux choisis* made pedagogical through an *explication de texte.* The canon that can be assembled on the basis of the worldly anthologies is quite different from the program for the study of seventeenth-century French literature generally proposed today. The ancestor of the manuals in which those of us currently teaching received our first ideas of the period is Batteux: the "reduced" canon he proposes is remarkably close to what, for better or for worse, we think of as the classic French canon. Batteux throws his considerable authority as holder of the Chair of Greek and Latin philosophy at the Collège de France behind a program for the study of the French tradition that aims to eliminate all literature deemed dangerous to civic virtue, especially the women writers who figure so prominently in the nonpedagogical anthology tradition. Before taking up the question of women writers and the case Batteux builds against them, however, I will first discuss the strategy on which Batteux's pedagogy is founded.

For his reform, Batteux calls on pedagogues to follow the new scientific model, "to collect data as the basis for a system that reduces their findings to common principles."[7] In *Les Beaux arts réduits*, Batteux defines the nature and the origin of the unique artistic principle he claims to have unearthed, and he also demonstrates the ideological goal of this method of literary and critical reduction. Let me outline the reasoning on which Batteux's model pedagogical system is founded. Good taste is unique: "there is only one good taste, that of nature" (1: 127). There is, however, progress in the spread of good taste because the public "allows itself, without noticing it, to be taken in (*se laisser prendre*) by the examples [it encounters in literature]. . . . One shapes oneself unconsciously on that which one has seen." Since moderns have the advantage of access to a greater number of authors, it is logical that good taste has become more widespread and that modern taste provides the definitive guide to classical status. On the basis of these two rules, Batteux constructs the following scenario: there is only one "natural" taste. The great artists are those who have "exposed" the natural design in their works. An educated public is able immediately to appreciate

7. I cite Batteux in the four-volume 1774 reedition of his works, *Principes de la littérature* (Paris: Saillant), 1: 126.

and to "approve" this greatness and then, instinctively and without even realizing it, to form itself according to the standards proposed by the classic literary texts. Then, as a matter of course, the model esthete becomes a model citizen: "One wishes to seem good, simple, direct; in other words, the complete citizen will be revealed" (1: 145). The ideal citizen, furthermore, is also a perfect Christian, and the artistic manifestations of good taste inspire both civic virtue and Christian ideals (1: 146).

Batteux's logic, which he calls "simple, straightforward," is based on a premise never clearly exposed in his initial treatise: good taste may be unique and innate, but it must also be taught, for only an educated public immediately understands great literature. The implied conclusion of Batteux's theory of universal taste and esthetic progress is that the French educational system should use its power to create the ideals and the standards of Frenchness. This service Batteux himself provides in the companion volume to his reductionist theory, in which he selects the precise examples that should be imposed upon the minds of those to be made into model Christian citizens, to mold them, without their knowledge, into the recognition of socially correct greatness. In his *Cours de belles-lettres*, he provides the outline for the teaching of literature designed to produce educated French male Christians. He gives examples from Greek, Latin, and French literature, although "of course French letters will occupy the first rank" (2: 9). Both his volume's organization and his description of it are resolutely direct:

We will cover all the genres in succession, beginning with the simplest. We will give a summary presentation of the nature, the parts, and the rules of each of them; we will briefly trace its history; after which we will apply the rules to the most famous works in each genre, which will be analyzed both in terms of their content and in terms of their form. [2: 9–10]

In the three volumes of his curriculum, Batteux proceeds genre by genre, giving first general history and principles, followed by a short biography of each author, and finally, selected passages from each author's work, passages which—and this is his work's major long-term innovation— he then analyzes. In the *Cours de belles-lettres*, anthologizing is always accompanied by a demonstration for teachers of how to use literature in the classroom. The *Cours de belles-lettres* is the first example in France of the pedagogical genre we now call a literary manual.

When Batteux begins the course itself, it quickly becomes apparent that "our" taste simply singles out again and again those works that conform to "our" preconceived notions of what a work on a specific subject should say. When he sets up his presentation of La Fontaine, Batteux lays out the foundation for his method for reading literary texts, a method with a prodigious future in the French pedagogical tradition. His technique—"which presupposes real genius"—"consists in the comparison of a work with nature itself or, *that which amounts to the same thing, with the ideas that we have about what one can, and what one must say about the chosen subject"* (2: 61, my emphasis). He illustrates his method with a reading of La Fontaine's "Le Chêne et le Roseau" that is a classical model for the critical/pedagogical genre today known as *explication de texte.*

Before examining the text, however, Batteux shows why it deserves to be singled out as an exemplary work: "Before reading it, let us try to see for ourselves what ideas nature would present us on this subject" (2: 61). He then shows how the major elements in La Fontaine's fable correspond to "our" preestablished ideas of what they should be. In his *explication de texte,* furthermore, Batteux goes on to demonstrate that "our" expectations, when properly fulfilled, produce a work that is the perfect embodiment of all the stylistic and formal qualities previously characterized as the highest literary values. The great work, the classic, is the work that contains no surprises for the educated critic/reader and the work that conforms perfectly to the French male Christian critic's ideas of (human) nature. All "we" have to do to explicate literature properly is to articulate "our" prejudices and proclaim as classics those works that best exemplify "our" vision of what the world should be.

Thus Batteux's program reveals that the teaching of literature in France has been founded from its origin on the phenomenon that Anne-Marie Thiesse and Hélène Mathieu, in an indispensable recent study of the evolution of the canon of French literature in the nineteenth century that has been expanded and translated for this volume, refer to as "l'histoire littéraire par les textes" [literary history through texts]. Just as in the nineteenth-century process whose unfolding Thiesse and Mathieu retrace, in Batteux's formulation of "l'histoire littéraire per les textes" works are initially singled out allegedly only because of their value as examples, that is, for the extent to which they lend themselves to the techniques of the *explication de texte.* Yet the overall implication of his work, and of the nineteenth-century programs that follow his example, is that literary history can be written solely on the basis of the works thus isolated.

Batteux's program is also a monument to the official exclusion of the novel from the pages of literary history, and therefore of the women writers who were until then its most illustrious practitioners. The self-styled Boileau of his age (his collected works appear in 1774 to coincide with the centenary of the publication of the *Art poétique*), Batteux continues his precursor's battle against prose fiction. Boileau, however, had at least discussed the novel, if only to dismiss it, in the *Art poétique* and in more detail in the *Dialogue des héros de roman.*[8] But even the

---

8. Lack of space prevents me from repeating any part of an argument I have already developed elsewhere: for Boileau, the novel is dangerous first and foremost because it is marked by the values of the women writers who dominated the genre's production in his

scornful condemnations of the premier critic of the Golden Age had not succeeded in diminishing the genre's popularity in Batteux's day: seventeenth-century novels continued to be reedited throughout the eighteenth century and were given enormous coverage in the worldly anthologies, proof that they remained an essential part of the canon for adult readers that, at least until the Revolution, offered a challenge to the classic canon being developed by Goujet, Batteux, and their colleagues. Batteux's resolute avoidance of the novel could well have been a new tactic for eliminating the genre that for decades had proved stubbornly resistant to the decree denying it classic status. Since Batteux does not allude to the genre's existence, even in the volume he devotes to prose forms, it might be possible to explain his omission on the grounds that the novel was perhaps the mode least malleable to the demands of the *explication de texte.* However, this explanation is invalidated by the terms on which Batteux judges the only two women writers he chooses to include.

In the volume Batteux devotes to prose genres, he concludes with a discussion of the letter, for which his representative modern author is Sévigné. However, the goal of the *explications de texte* he performs on her epistles is to point out their defects, to prove that she is not a suitable pedagogical model. Her letters are so full of "dead time" (*longueurs*) that they frequently "languish" (355–56). Her arguments are "without body" (356). Her style, in short, is an appropriate model only for "overly tender mothers" (354), and it is unworthy of exemplary status because it is too "risky (*hasardé*) for anyone but her, and especially for a man of letters" (354–55, my emphasis).

This reasoning becomes even clearer in Batteux's treatment of Deshoulières, the only other woman writer he includes. (She was, in 1671, the winner of the first prize for poetry awarded by the Académie Française, and she is the ideal example of the woman writer always part of the worldly adult canon, but since eliminated, following the judgment of Batteux's followers, from their canon for children.) Her pastoral poetry is judged "the most delicate," "the *softest* possible," but

unfortunately, the doctrine —the "esprit de mollesse," the "essence of flabbiness or pliancy"—that her poetry fosters is conducive to a weakening of moral fiber, and turns it into a sort of epicurianism entirely opposed, not only to Christian morality, but also to that vigor of the soul, to that *male force,* that is the foundation and the support of true integrity. [2: 188, my emphasis]

Thus Deshoulières, like Sévigné, seems to have been included in the first pedagogical canon of French literature the better to justify the exclusion of women's writing in general. These token women achieve

---

day. See my "Sappho's Leap: Domesticating the Woman Writer," *L'Esprit créateur* 25, no. 2 (1985): 14–21.

exemplary status above all as illustrations of the threat to "vigorous" male Christian standards represented by the "softening" and "languishing" tendencies of female literary models. Women writers, Batteux warns, had to be eliminated from the curriculum because they were a direct threat to church and state.

Classicists have long been sensitive to the central role in the preservation of Greek literary texts played by the anthologies edited for schoolboys in antiquity. For example, of the forty to forty-four comedies of Aristophanes known to the ancients, we know only the eleven edited by a grammarian as "selected theater" for classes. Similarly, all that has come down to us of the vast production of Eschylus and Sophocles are the seven plays selected for the curriculum.[9] In the case of French literature, one cannot, of course, speak of a phenomenon as dramatic as the permanent destruction of works. Nevertheless, for nearly two centuries it has been as if the works of most of the French women writers included in the early canon for adults no longer existed. Once modern writers had entered the pedagogical curriculum, within decades the anthologies for a cultivated adult public ceased to be compiled, and the other canon they had kept alive began to be forgotten. Increasingly, the modern writers who continued to be read were only those who could be promoted as French classics, that is, as part of a national, and a nationalistic, literary program. The educators entrusted with the creation of a literary model for the exclusively male public of the *collèges* followed Batteux's lead and excluded the "dangerous," the "inimitable" as Lafayette would have it, examples of virtue provided by women writers.[10]

The terms in which Batteux eliminated women writers were frequently repeated as the original French pedagogical canon was set in place. I will cite one example from another pedagogue-critic of the day because I believe that the importance of repetition in canon formation must never be underestimated. Critics-pedagogues most often just reiterate the judgments of others. "[Villedieu's] works are little read today, and I dare say that they are still read too much, considering the danger that young men above all cannot fail to run from their reading" (Goujet, 18: 138). When women writers are evoked by any of the eighteenth century's literary pedagogues, it is almost always simply to explain in

9. Henri Marrou, *Histoire de l'éducation dans l'antiquité* (Paris: Seuil, 1948), 225.

10. There were occasional attempts to found a pedagogical canon for schoolgirls, the most celebrated of which was drawn up at Saint-Cyr for and by the Marquise de Maintenon. These curricula always make frequent use of women's writing—witness the impressive role played by Scudéry at Saint-Cyr. However, given the tiny percentage of girls among the schoolchildren of the day, it is obvious that these alternative pedagogical curricula are largely merely utopian artifacts.

summary fashion why their works should no longer be read. Often, Batteux's argument about their threat to the nation's male fiber is restated. Just as often, the pedagogue turns to the argument Boileau used, quite prematurely, about Scudéry (in his *Dialogue des héros de roman*): "she is no longer read." Their pronouncements are just as premature as their master's—Villedieu, for example, continued to be reedited throughout the eighteenth century; but that is not the point. Women writers were so threatening to the ideology of the developing pedagogical canon that their elimination had to be reimposed until the new curriculum was firmly established.

Thus, in the sixteen-volume compilation that may best represent the view of the canon that the nineteenth century inherited from the eighteenth, *Lycée ou cours de littérature ancienne et moderne* (1797–1803), the Voltaire disciple and longtime journalist La Harpe uses this argument, virtually without exception, whenever he evokes a woman writer. He mentions eleven seventeenth-century women, not an unimpressive list, but for all but Lafayette and Sévigné, the entry is limited to: "her boring novels, plays, etc., have been forgotten," or "her works are no longer read." La Harpe devotes fully half of the *Lycée's* volumes to the literature of his own, not quite finished, century. In these eight volumes, however, he includes only four women writers: Tencin, de Beaumont, Riccoboni, Graffigny. La Harpe's compilation demonstrates that the flowering of the pedagogical tradition brought about the termination of the worldly tradition. Contrary to what you probably imagine, his *Lycée* is intended not for the formation of schoolchildren but as "a supplement to [the studies they've already done] for people of the world who don't have the time to begin new studies."[11] (The *Lycée* is, in fact, the record of La Harpe's lectures at what has been described as a worldly Sorbonne with an elegant public.) This is the first work of adult education to be a work of *reeducation*: La Harpe is trying to destroy the influence of the tradition of worldly anthologies, to make over the vision of the canon proposed for adult readers in the image of the pedagogical canon drawn up for schoolchildren. In the worldly anthology thus brought into the nationalistic line, women writers were virtual nonentities. This new pedagogical nationalism arrived just in time for its message to be heard by those who were involved in the canonical revision of the 1820s, whose influence on the image of sixteenth-century French literature still projected by today's manuals is demonstrated by Ann Jones and Nancy Vickers in this issue.[12]

Such consideration of canonical genealogies seems naturally to call

11. *Lycée ou cours de littérature ancienne et moderne*, 16 vols. (Paris: Lefèvre, 1816), vi.

12. La Harpe's compilation is reprinted four times between 1813 and 1816 alone.

for reflection on the process of canon formation taking place today. The critics who seem most inclined to consider the type of question—if not pronouncing on the value of a literary text, at least championing a text for inclusion in a curriculum—that was the exclusive concern of their classical precursors are for the most part those, whether feminists of the so-called American persuasion or supporters of other minority traditions, who ask that the canon be revised in order to include voices that have traditionally been excluded. The most visible contemporary canonical gestures have taken the form either of the critique of existing curricula and other pedagogical tools, or the promotion of parallel canons to which students are to be exposed at the same time as more traditional programs. Not since the turn of the eighteenth century have pedagogues been faced with the choice between two opposing plans for the programmatic packaging of French literature, one of which would systematically grant a place to women writers. It is hard to predict the ideological grounds on which a decision will be made this time.

It is, of course, possible that there is now room for more than one canon of French literature. Certainly the dissemination of French culture is no longer the relatively manageable phenomenon that it was the last time this canonical option was available: various centers, more or less distant from the source of French nationalism and with more or less regular transfusions of native blood (presumably, those trained at the source are more likely to share received ideas of Frenchness) now promote visions of the canon that may well become gradually more irreconcilable with that formulated by and for the French national educational system. Finally, it is even possible that new technologies might inadvertently generate a challenge to received ideas of the canonical.[13]

Consider the example of the ARTFL (*CNRS*/University of Chicago *Trésor de la langue française*) data base. Many American universities now subscribe to this program that allows users, for an hourly fee, to have access on their computers to a long list of works of French literature from the Middle Ages to the twentieth century. (A new list is due soon; the one I consulted includes some seventy texts from the seventeenth century alone.) The data base was constituted by the Institut National de la Langue Française rather than one of the branches of the CNRS more directly entrusted with a pedagogical mission. Texts were selected for the ARTFL data base solely on the basis of their linguistic richness (the project's long-range goal is a new dictionary of the French language).[14] In the meantime, anyone at a subscribing institution has

13. In an interview for this volume, Julia Kristeva expresses the belief that there will no longer be canons because of the influence of the media. I think rather that mass communication will revise traditional methods of canon transmission.

14. I would like to thank Bernard Quemada and Evelyne Martin for this information.

access to what looks for all intents and purposes like a computerized canon of French literature with nothing to indicate its lexicographic mission. For some time, I derived great satisfaction from the list, which I imagined to be some sort of subversive canon of French literature, generated in the bosom of the CNRS: the data base includes, among other texts that are since the Revolution no longer part of literary programs, a good selection of the poetry of Deshoulières (the very verse Batteux castigates as a danger to "Christian morality" and "male force"), as well as no fewer than seven works, both fairy tales and travel literature, by d'Aulnoy, the possible editor of the original worldly anthology. My satisfaction continues even now that I know that the French intend to propose these women writers as models only of linguistic variety. After all, no one will be around to instruct the evergrowing ranks of American students who, far from the Hexagon, rely increasingly on computers rather than any printed source of information, that the works so readily available on their screen (when they may have been out-of-print for decades, if not centuries) are valuable solely for their word-count. Without a critical apparatus to direct their judgment, students might even take Deshoulières for the classic author she was for generations of adult French readers. The first canon of classic French literature just may be due for a revival.

NANCY K. MILLER

Men's Reading, Women's Writing: Gender and the Rise of the Novel*

> The latest enemy of the vitality of classic texts is feminism.
> —Allan Bloom, *The Closing of the American Mind*

I will begin academically with the matter of a footnote.

About six hundred pages into Frances [Fanny] Burney's nine-hundred page novel, *Camilla*, the heroine receives the visit of the ebullient Mrs. Mittin. Mrs. Mittin eagerly tells Camilla the story of her getting to know Mrs. Berlinton.[1]

> I happened to be in the book shop[1] when she came in, and asked for a book; the Peruvan Letters[2] she called it; and it was not at home, and she looked quite vexed, for she said she had looked the catalogue up and down, and saw nothing she'd a mind to; so I thought it would be a good opportunity to oblige her, and be a way to make a prodigious genteel acquaintance besides; so I took down the name, and I found out the lady that had got the book, and I made her a visit, and I told her it was particular wanted by a lady that had a reason; so she let me have it, and I took it to my pretty lady, who was so pleased, she did not know how to thank me. [606]

Burney's 1796 novel was republished by Oxford University Press in 1983 in an edition established by Edward A. Bloom and Lillian D. Bloom. Their footnotes are abundant, authoritative in tone, and, on the face of it, carefully documented. Thus on this passage, for "book shop" they offer: "obviously a circulating library. In *The Southampton Guide* (6th ed., ca., 1801, pp.74–75) [the story takes place in Southampton] there is a description of such a library: 'T. Baker's Library, in the High Street, contains a well chosen selection of nearly seven thousand volumes, forming a more general collection of useful and polite literature than is usually found in circulating libraries. The books are lent to read,

---

*Earlier versions of this essay appeared under the title "Authorized Versions" in *French Review* 9(3) (February 1988): 61 and in *Novel* (Winter and Spring 1988): 21.

1. I am grateful to Rachel Brownstein for bringing this note to my attention.

at 15s. the year, 4s. 6d. the quarter, and 5s. for the season.'" As someone who rarely does this kind of research herself, I love having access to information provided with such detail. The precision of it—4s.6d. the quarter—feeds the fantasy (which I think it must remain) that one might be able to reconstruct the material contexts of a past of reading.

Despite the seductions of its information, however, this is not the footnote I'm after; rather its pretext. The note in question comes (next in sequence) to explain the title of the volume requested, the "Peruvan Letters." The Blooms opine: "Mrs. Mittin meant either Charles de Secondat Montesquieu's *Persian Letters* (trans., 1722) or George Lyttleton's *Letters from a Persian in England to his Friend in Ispahan* (1735). In her ignorance she failed to distinguish between Persia and Peru" (949–50). The failure to distinguish between Persia and Peru, however, is neither securely nor uniquely a matter of Mrs. Mittin's ignorance. The editors themselves, of course, in their own geo-graphics, in their map of misreading, miss Graffigny on a border with Montesquieu. Françoise d'Issembourg d'Happoncourt Graffigny's *Lettres d'une Péruvienne* were translated in England as the *Peruvian Letters* in 1771, 1774 and 1782. At least.[2]

What shall we make of this scholarly lapse? Omissions like these, born less of prejudice, presumably, than oversight—after all, why Burney and not Graffigny?—come nevertheless to figure the set of references that through the either/or of its logic, Montesquieu or Lyttleton (!), constitutes the canon of a national literature. Taking off from this instance of exclusion, I want to focus more closely here on some of the ways in which the reading and writing practices of a given period are recorded, reconstituted, and re-formed in the image of a certain pleasure of the text that by the terms of its own discourse displaces the works of women writers. I will take as my particular piece of the territory (mapped in part by Peter Brooks in his 1972 *The Novel of Worldliness*), those eighteenth-century novels that articulate and explore what I will call, borrowing Joan Kelly's well-known formulation, "the social relations of the sexes" (822–23).[3] More acutely, though I will only touch upon it here, I am interested in the particular figure of the human subject who emerges from this literature and the ways in which this subject is produced and kept alive at the expense of others. In order to understand this construction of a privileged positioning, it

<hr/>

2. An account of the translation history is provided by Gianni Nicoletti in his critical edition of the novel, (Bari: Adriatica Editrice, 1967). English Showalter, who is an expert on Graffignygraphia, tells me that Nicoletti missed some of the translations of the novel.

3. Joan Kelly-Gadol, "The Social Relations of the Sexes: Methodological Implications of Women's History," *Signs* 4 (Summer 1974): 809–24.

is necessary to look at the specific repertory of values animating the choices of a certain literary history.

In his wonderfully erudite and still timely study on the eighteenth-century novel, Georges May makes the observation that the "history of the French novel remains to be written." "The volume devoted to the eighteenth-century novel," he adds, "is especially lacking,"[4] and he wonders about this missing piece of literary history. Twenty-five years after the publication of *Le Dilemme du roman au dix-huitième siècle,* despite several excellent books on the novels of this period, the task, I think, still lies before us, if, by a history of the French novel, one has in mind a history that includes women's foundational role in its development. As a feminist critic concerned with imagining the volume devoted to the eighteenth-century novel still to be written, I find myself twenty-five years later returning to May's introduction (and the long chapter "feminism and the novel") for a place from which to begin again, for, among other things, a *gendered* account of authorship: men *and* women writers. Thus, in a rollcall of novelists publishing between 1715 and 1761, he names (in this order): Prévost, Marivaux, Crébillon, Duclos, Tencin, Graffigny, and Riccoboni and characterizes them as the "least forgotten" writers of this period (3). The inclusion of women's names as a matter of course (even among the least forgotten) may not be taken for granted in 1963 or today.

In "Classical Reeducation: Decanonizing the Feminine" Joan De-Jean shows how anthologies in seventeenth- (and eighteenth-) century France served as a kind of "continuing education" for adults "who wished to keep abreast of the literary scene"; anthologies were organized pedagogically not only to supply literary material, but to shape a generation's taste by supplementing its ideology. Let us turn now to what I see as a modern version of this mode, René Etiemble's collection of eighteenth-century prose fiction in the 1966 two-volume Pléiade, *Romanciers du XVIIIe siècle.*[5] I have chosen this volume precisely because, as Etiemble himself argues, the Pléiade edition constitutes a form of recognition meant to assure a posterity of reading. The Pléiade edition "of itself" confers legitimacy and provides authorizing versions of the included texts.

Of May's list Etiemble includes only the male writers to which he adds others. Now, Etiemble has read Georges May, and concurs with his position that one needs a history of the eighteenth-century novel; that it

---

4. *Le Dilemme du roman au XVIIIe siècle: Etude sur les rapports du roman et de la critique (1715–1761)* (New Haven: Yale University Press, 1963), 1.

5. René Etiemble, *Romanciers du XVIIIe siècle* (Paris: Gallimard, 1966).

is wrong to justify the ignorance of the general reading public who see in the novel only Balzac and Stendhal instead of Rétif, or Duclos, or Crébillon and miss the eighteenth century completely. But nowhere, in a preface and introduction both of which demonstrate a high degree of self-consciousness about the grounds for inclusion and exclusion at work in the anthology, and a sympathy for what he calls the "human reference" (2,xx), does it seem to cross the critic's mind that women writers were central to the production and formation of the very fictional forms he is so eager to present to a sophisticated reading public ("aux gens cultivés," 8).

Etiemble explains that a reader who wants a more complete picture of the evolution of the genre ought to "reread" *other* works not included in his volumes, (*not* included, because unlike his selection, these have received their own individual Pléiade "consecration"). Readers, he specifies, are to *return* to the novels of Montesquieu, Marivaux, Diderot, and Rousseau interweaving them in chronological order along with his choices if they are to have a complete picture, more than "a glance of what the French novel becomes in the eighteenth century" (7). Thus, despite Etiemble's awareness of the importance of women writers of this deconsidered form in the seventeenth century—he names Scudéry and Lafayette (1, 7)—and his admiration for Georges May's mapping of the terrain, neither Graffigny, Tencin, nor Riccoboni, for example, figures in this "tableau" of the French novel. Why was Etiemble, who is not beyond a major saving operation in this anthology, not moved to make a case for women writers? Why Sénac de Meilhan, or Cazotte, and not Riccoboni or Tencin? (I have, of course, no idea whether Etiemble ever read any of the women's novels I'm thinking of; read them and rejected them. What interests me are the effects produced by the posture of his selection: a stance that in passing over women writers in silence authorizes a form of ignorance.)

To be sure, one could argue that the category of the "woman writer" was not a vivid one in 1966. Or rather that the category of "la romancière" very precisely left the question of the specificity of women's writing either moot or intact.[6] One could also, and perhaps more interestingly, suggest that what attracts Etiemble to his corpus is the lure

---

6. Thus in his massive *La Destinée féminine dans le roman européen du dix-huitième siècle* (Paris: Armand Colin, 1972), in the chapter called, "La romancière," Pierre Fauchery states categorically: "In the eighteenth century, the myths of feminine destiny, of masculine creation, are for the most part accepted whole cloth by the women novelists. The latter, moreover, far from claiming their autonomy, take shelter behind the authority of the great writers of the other sex" (93).

of identification, a form of "reading as male bonding" that Susan Winnett, in a shrewdly theorized paper on "narrative and the principle (s) of
pleasure," identifies as a "homoaesthetic subtext," a set of assumptions
that follow from a "legalized, entirely male circuit of desire."[7] Etiemble, for his part, seems drawn to the form of male memoir epitomized in
Louvet's *Les Amours du Chevalier de Faublas.* From the list of "si
j'aime le *Faublas* c'est . . ." let us retain this formulation: "It's in particular because of the slightly disreputable women who work at satisfying
Faublas for the amusement of the well-endowed reader" [C'est à cause
en particulier des femmes un peu moins honnêtes qui s'emploient à
combler Faublas, pour l'amusement du lecteur bien constitué (2, xxv)].
Although to be fair this invocation of the well-endowed (redblooded
might be a better translation) reader is not Etiemble's *only* explanation
for his textual preference, it is difficult to resist the impression that his
evaluation of Crébillon, Duclos, Denon and company is finally inseparable from a highly masculinist mode of critical pleasure (very specifically, reading as a French, relentlessly heterosexual, terminally misogynistic though always elegant and gallant male [2, xxvi]): in a word,
reading *like* a man.

I want to suggest further that if Graffigny, Tencin, and Riccoboni do
not appear on Etiemble's screen it may also be because in addition to
their status as women writers (hence their general invisibility), they
specifically produce what I will call *feminist writing* on the same subjects. These fictions of dissent call into question the fulfillment of the
virile subjectivities that typically structure libertine texts, by which I
mean here the recollections of a man's life as organized by and narrated
through his sexual experience—whether a list of encounters or the
obsession of a single passion, like *Manon Lescaut.* I am prepared to
argue that this particular plot of heterosexual engagement provides the
basic psychosocial design of the memoir novel, one of the two dominant
novelistic forms in the eighteenth century. Feminist fictions take another, harsher, and less jubilant view of the sexual and social stage of
human relations; and in these novels female subjectivity is the figure,
not merely the ground of representation against which the tropes of
masculine performance display themselves.

In *Subject to Change* I make the claim that it is important to locate
any poetics of feminist writing in relation to a historicized national and
cultural production; indeed that a "poetics of location" is the only way
to work against the universalizing tendencies of a monolith of "wom-
en's writing."[8] Although the individual works that I treat there range in

7. Susan Winnett, "Coming Unstrung: Women, Men, and Principle (s) of Pleasure."
Unpublished MS.

8. *Subject to Change: Reading Feminist Writing* (New York: Columbia University
Press, 1988).

time from *La Princesse de Clèves* (1678) to *La Vagabonde* (1910), I draw implicitly on the powerful body of eighteenth-century women's texts for my general understanding of this writing. The novels of women writers in eighteenth-century France may be characterized by what Rachel DuPlessis has called a "poetics of critique";[9] more specifically I focus on the *figuration* of dissent from the plots of the dominant tradition that marks these fictions. In these eighteenth-century novels— most dramatically, perhaps, Riccoboni's *Lettres de Mistress Fanni Butlerd* and *Histoire du Marquis de Cressy*, and Tencin's *Mémoires du Comte de Comminge*—the conventional sex/gender arrangements that underwrite masculinist stories (the complacent fantasies of the "ro-man-liste," for instance) are vividly undermined.[10]

In this sense, then, in order to understand the patterns of inclusion and exclusion that shape the history of the novel in France, it is not sufficient to speak simply of men's or women's writing. Retained for posterity among the eighteenth-century novels devoted to the social relations of the sexes, is, we might more usefully say, libertine and not feminist writing. Put another way, at an angle to the notion of a literature of "worldliness," we want to emphasize the differentiation of the viewpoint from which the world (and its discursive domains) is perceived, entered, and experienced.

To understand the history of the French novel, especially as it played itself out in the eighteenth century which in so many ways made the nineteenth-century realist novel possible, it is crucial to perform two gestures: first to restore feminist writing to the body of fiction that becomes the Novel; the second, to reread the texts retained by literary history through this supplemented and redoubled vision.

9. Rachel DuPlessis, *Writing beyond the Ending: Narrative Strategies of Twentieth-Century Women Writers* (Bloomington: Indiana University Press, 1985).

10. *Lettres de Mistress Fanni Butlerd* offers perhaps the clearest instance of a feminist critique of masculine advantage: when Alfred (Mylord Charles Alfred, Comte d'Erford) abandons the woman in love with him to move on to the next and make a fashionable marriage, the woman goes public with their story; her letters, like the narrative of *Histoire du Marquis de Cressy*, reveal the psychic and social cost to women of a socially unregulated male sexual "freedom." Both Riccoboni's *Cressy* and Tencin's *Mémoires du Comte de Comminge* rewrite the masculine suffering embodied by Des Grieux as a form of blindness and narcissism. Thus, in the end, both Comminge and Cressy are forced to witness the spectacular death of the superior woman they have failed: unlike Manon, however, Adélaïde and the Marquise de Cressy are neither mythical nor enigmatic; it is instead their human complexity *as women* that the men in love with them prove unable to comprehend.

> Flaubert was writing the new novel of 1860, Proust the
> new novel of 1910. A writer must bear his date, knowing
> there are no masterpieces in eternity, only works in
> history; and that they survive only to the extent that they
> have left the past behind them and announced the future.
> —Alain Robbe-Grillet. *Pour un nouveau roman*

Let us consider a recent example of the old literary history; unlike the Etiemble volumes, this is not an anthology, but another legitimating instance of eighteenth-century letters, a mainstream exercise in cultural diffusion: the volumes published in 1984 by Arthaud, specifically the volumes of *Littérature Française, 5, De Fénelon à Voltaire* and 6, *De L'Encyclopédie aux Méditations.* (The former is edited by René Pomeau and Jean Ehrard, the latter by Michel Delon, Robert Mauzi, and Sylvain Menant.)

The problem of inclusion and exclusion in these manuals, by which I will mean for the purposes of this essay the difference in treatment of men's and women's writing, is related to a problem of category and definition: the men appear in the table of contents with their names under the large headings: "Great Works, Great Authors." Except for Staël (and she is part of an ensemble along with "Benjamin Constant et le groupe de Coppet") no women's names appear in the table of contents, or in the bibliographical sketches at the back of the book. But the hidden bodies are there, of course, slotted into the subset of a literary historical category: the sentimental novel, under "Forms and Genres." Under the more promising heading, "Toward a New Novel," Tencin and Graffigny are located within the subheading, "le roman des coeurs sensibles," the novel of sensitive hearts (for sensitive souls). We also find: Riccoboni—less talented than Richardson and Diderot in her ability to create the illusion of reality (Riccoboni "ignore le pittoresque," 216); and at the end of the century, we find in a short list Krudener, Charrière, Cottin, Staël ("Staël elle-même"[!])—as servile imitators, "who borrow from Rousseau their characters, situations, settings and the means of moving their female readers, for these women are addressing a female audience" (Delon, 221).

Although in their analyses of the production, distribution and consumption of books, the authors of the manual rarely distinguish by gender, they note the role played by education in the formation of a reading public and the fact that women are excluded from the scenes of knowledge: with a few exceptions, they observe, women are not seen as fit for studying serious subjects: "women are granted the novel, the frivolous genre, without anyone suspecting that it is to them that the novel will owe its surprising development" (45). Unfortunately, this acknowledgment of the material conditions of literature and its paradoxical relation to women's social inferiority stops there and congeals into a commonplace. It does not take the next step to reflect upon its own categories of analysis, categories that by their language—Great Works, Great Authors—return women to invisibility, to the clichés of the *lectrice:* of a female reading public on the one hand, and of women writers as inferior imitators of a perfected male-authored model and novel of the feminine to boot—Richardson and Rousseau.

In their unexamined adherence to the masterpiece codes of the dominant tradition according to which they (re)construct a male genealogy, the Arthaud editors fail to see women writers on the one hand, as the continuers of a powerful tradition of seventeenth-century women writers, and on the other as the producers of new forms and new reading practices. I cannot stress too heavily the degree of canon-*de*formation this failure of vision represents.[11]

What we need in order to write a history of the eighteenth-century novel are some new ways of thinking about what goes on in a "republic of letters," restoring its heterogenity and reopening the question for criticism of the relations between social values and literary forms. Although in my own research I have been specifically concerned with the "cultural work" performed by women's writing[12] and with the social values defining woman's place that subtend a national literature at a given historical moment, the implications of such an emphasis in fact require a reimagination of the whole picture: the mix of writing that has been sorted out to become the narrow and fixed literary tradition we study, write about, teach and pass on.

> There's no cause for alarm. I'm not going to talk either about the play *Cénie,* or even about the *Lettres péruviennes,* works that were somewhat appealing in their time and that are completely passé today. I'm going to talk mainly about Voltaire; Mme de Graffigny brings us into his home and helps us to discover him in a rather new or at least very natural light. (Monday, 17 June 1850)
> —Sainte-Beuve, *Lettres de Madame de Grafigny, ou Voltaire à Cirey.*

11. The masterpiece model, which assumes that a work both exemplifies and transcends its historical moment, seems particularly inappropriate to the eighteenth-century novel, since its "most important" instance, Rousseau's *Nouvelle Héloïse* remains both largely unreadable and unread. I should also add here, in an autobiographical moment, that I wish I had read more women's writing earlier in my own work on the eighteenth-century novel, and taken the measure of the difference women's writing makes in its history. To the extent that seen from the perspective of women's writing, the dominant literature is *only* men's writing, I would have had to radically restructure my own contribution to this discussion in *The Heroine's Text.*

12. Jane Tompkins, *Sensational Designs: The Cultural Work of American Fiction: 1790–1860* (New York: Oxford University Press, 1985), xv.

Let us reconsider now the case of Mrs. Mittin's mistake. Graffigny's *Lettres d'une Péruvienne* is a novel that like most women's writing in France enjoyed tremendous popularity when it was published, and in this case even a certain posterity: thirty editions, including ten in English and Italian, until 1777, and then continuous publication until 1835. Despite its contemporary critical recognition (the "*Lettres d'une Péruvienne* were among the most widely read books in the eighteenth century," Delon, 210), the novel rarely appears in the standard accounts of eighteenth-century fiction, nor until recently has it been collected in standard editions. Unlike many female-authored novels, however, the *Lettres d'une Péruvienne*, had a reprieve of sorts. In 1967 an Italian scholar, Gianni Nicoletti, brought out a critical edition of the novel which had not been republished since the early nineteenth century.[13] And in 1983, more important, perhaps, a paperback edition, based on Nicoletti's work, was published by Garnier Flammarion, in a collection of epistolary novels. This volume has made it possible for the first time to teach the novel as a matter of course. Will this be the case?

Despite the work's material availability, without a rethinking of the value paradigms that have overdetermined our reading habits, without a critical reflection about the act of women's writing as a type of cultural intervention, it is not at all clear that the *Lettres d'une Péruvienne* will emerge from the margins to be read alongside, for example, the Persian ones. (The Professors Bloom are only a case in point.) The very fact of classifying the novel for publication as a love-letter novel ("romans d'amour par lettres") maintains the hierarchy of classifications that as we saw in the discourse of the Arthaud manual trivializes female authorship.

The reconstructive project of reading women's writing, then, necessarily involves textual strategies that acknowledge the peculiar status of this literature in the library: there, but in opposition to the "already read," the *déjà lu* of the canon—"underread"—"*sous lu*," cut off from the kind of historical and metacritical life that characterizes the works of dominant French literature. Learning to read women's writing entails not only a particular attentiveness to the marks of signature that I have called "overreading"; it also involves "reading in pairs" (or, in Naomi

---

13. Sainte-Beuve, we might say, finished Graffigny off for several generations of readers. In his caustic portrait of her in *Lettres de Madame de Grafigny ou Voltaire à Cirey* (written in 1850 and published in *Causeries du lundi* (Paris: Garnier, 1858), v. 2, the critic, in another instance of literary criticism as male bonding, reviews Turgot's reservations about the novel's ending. Having commented enthusiastically and at length on the novel's ideas, ideas that inspired writings of his own he concludes: "All these pages of Turgot are excellent, and I recommend reading them, as much as I can't recommend rereading [rouvrir] the *Lettres péruviennes*" (224).

Schor's coinage, "intersextually").[14] By this I mean looking at the literature of men's and women's writing side by side to perceive at their points of intersection the differentiated lines of a "bi-cultural" production of the novel—Persian *and* Peruvian—more complicated than the familiar, national history of its tropes.

I want to offer now an example of the stakes of this revision and the difficulty of sorting out the values at work in such a project. In a long review essay on Fanny Burney's *Cecilia* (1784) Laclos elaborates a comparative (French and English) and gendered poetics in which he makes the claim that women are particularly well suited to novel writing because the genre requires the three requisite skills of "observing, feeling, and depicting."[15] "[Women's] education," Laclos writes, "their existence in society, all their praiseworthy qualities, and if one must tell all, even some of their flaws, promise them successes in this career that they would, in our view, seek vainly in every other." Laclos explains that he doesn't have the time to develop his theory (readers can supply their own examples) but moves instead to situate Burney in his survey of the field: "Among the women whom one could cite as having placed themselves beside [*à côté de*] our best novelists [*meilleurs romanciers*], there would be few more distinguished and more surprising than the Author of the Work we are going to review" (501). What I want in my own hurried way to suggest here is that writing literary criticism toward the end of eighteenth century Laclos reads women's writing through a set of clichés of femininity that leave the category of novelist masculine and originary: for Laclos the class of novelists is male. Thus, despite the high praise he has bestowed upon *Cecilia*, despite the relation of contiguity—*à côté de*—that grounds his rhetoric, in the end, Laclos replaces Burney's novel with a clearly ranked and conventionally gendered hierarchy of difference: "Finally, we think that this novel must be counted among the best works in this genre, with nevertheless the exception of *Clarissa*, the novel in which one finds the most genius, *Tom Jones*, the best constructed novel, and *La Nouvelle Héloïse*, the most beautiful work ever produced under the title of the novel" (521).

In this move from metonymy (the aleatory contacts between writers) to metaphor (the fixed relations between the sexes) we have, I want to argue here, the principle of selection that guides the anthologies of literary history. Laclos had already elaborated the logic of this poetics of

14. On "overreading," see "Arachnologies: The Woman, The Text, and the Critic," in *Poetics of Gender*, ed. Nancy K. Miller (New York: Columbia University Press, 1986); on the intersextual, "La Pérodie: Superposition dans *Lorenzaccio*," *Michigan Romance Studies* 1 (1982): 73–86.

15. Choderlos de Laclos, "Le Roman: Cecilia," in *Oeuvres complètes* (Paris: Gallimard, 1959).

gender in his exchange of letters with Riccoboni. In the correspondence
between Riccoboni and Laclos that followed the 1782 publication of the
Liaisons dangereuses, to Riccoboni's critique of Laclos's representation
of women—notably of the portrait of Madame de Merteuil in which, in
her words, he would have "decorated vice with attractive features"—
Laclos replied by inviting readers to turn to the "charming tableaux" of
Riccoboni's own novels for more "gentle feelings." In his self-justifica-
tion and explanation for the difference between his fictional universe
and hers, Laclos, in what by now is a commonplace in eighteenth-
century critical commentary, returns to the eternal nature of women
and men for supporting evidence:[16] "women alone possess this precious
sensibility, this easy and cheerful imagination that embellishes everything it touches, and creates objects as they should be: but . . . men,
who are condemned to a harsher labor, have always acquitted themselves well when they have rendered nature exactly and faithfully!"
(688). (In "Idealism and the Novel," Naomi Schor, citing the Ric-
coboni/Laclos exchange, makes the important argument that the mapping of idealism onto femininity, and the identification of masculinity
and realism, play a crucial role in canon formation in the history of the
nineteenth-century novel.)

In "Idée sur les romans" (1800) Sade writes literary criticism according to the same principles, indeed proclaiming in a parenthesis women's
generic superiority to men: "as if this sex, naturally more delicate, more
suited to writing novels, could not in this genre lay claim to many more
laurels than we" (27–28). Praising the works of Gomez, Lussan, Tencin,
Graffigny, Beaumont, and Riccoboni for "honoring their sex," he names
"Graffigny's *Lettres péruviennes*," which he goes on to assert, "will
always be a model of tenderness and feeling, like [the letters] of Mylady
Catesby, by Riccoboni; they will eternally serve those who only aspire
to grace and lightness of style. But let us return to the century where we
left it, pressed by the desire to praise the lovely women who in this genre
taught men such good lessons" (28).[17] I want to emphasize two points
here: the way in which the category of the writer remains the male-
universal against which the woman as writer is judged, and the self-
appointed role of the male writer *as critic*. As a result, both the categories of the discussion and the positioning of the voice of critical discourse reproduce the content of the judgments.

Almost two centuries after Laclos and Sade's closural moves of putting the woman in her place, Delon et al., we have seen, make the same

16. See May's discussion of the coexistence of this discourse on women's special
aptitude for novel writing with an undisguised misogyny, 218 ff.
17. Sade, Donatien-Alphonse-François, "Idée sur les romans," (Paris: Palimugre,
1946).

gesture. In each instance the protocol that regulates the social relations between the sexes takes the place of—at the very least displaces—literary criteria. What grounds the reproduction of this discourse?

In "[Why] Are There No Great Women Critics? And What Difference Does It Make?," Susan Lanser and Evelyn Beck raise the question of the *"woman critic"* and ask what difference to the history of critical discourse her voice might make.[18] Lanser and Beck do not conclude about the judgments of women theorists, but they plausibly imagine that their poetics would constitute "a challenge to traditional generic classifications" (87). In the current absence of a history of women's critical writing (not to say a self-consciously feminist poetics), for now we can begin by turning to the prefatory moves of a woman writer who situates her work in relation to an already gendered literary history.

In the original preface to *Evelina,* Burney begins with a paragraph almost identical in its language to the beginning of Laclos's review article (499). Writing as a man, Burney, like Laclos, observes that "in the republic of letters, there is no member of such inferior rank, or who is so much disdained by his brethren of the quill, as the humble Novelist."

But in the detail of her editorial remarks she places her authorship in this fraternity somewhat differently. Despite the powerful models of Johnson's "knowledge," Rousseau's "eloquence," Richardson's "pathetic power," Fielding's "wit," and Smollett's "humour," Burney will not pursue, she explains, "the same ground which they have tracked." Unlike the other Arts, where "a fine statue, or a beautiful picture, of some great master, may deservedly employ the imitative talents of young and inferior artists, "in books," she argues, "imitation cannot be shunned too sedulously; for the very perfection of a model which is frequently seen, serves but more forcibly to mark the inferiority of a copy." In her conclusion, however, she backs away from any implications of self-promotion in these poetics: "I have, therefore, only to intreat, that my own words may not pronounce my condemnation; and that what I have here ventured to say in regard to imitation, may be understood as it is meant, in a general sense, and not be imputed to an opinion of my own originality, which I have not the vanity, the folly, or the blindness to entertain" (n.p.).[19]

---

18. It is here that the much cited formulation of women's "double-voiced discourse" is first articulated. "The writings of women who are struggling to define themselves but have not yet given up a patriarchal frame of reference may betray a tension so strong as to produce a virtually 'double-voiced' discourse" (86). The essay was originally presented as a paper in 1977 and published in *The Prism of Sex: Essays in the Sociology of Knowledge,* ed. Julia A. Sherman and Evelyn Torton Beck (Madison: University of Wisconsin Press, 1979).

19. *Evelina, Or The History of A Young Lady's Entrance Into the World* (New York: Norton, 1965). Burney's novel is framed by an "Original Dedication: To the Authors of the Monthly and Critical Reviews," in which the authorial persona is that of a young writer

In the preface to her letter-novel, Graffigny, in the familiar ironic style of eighteenth-century philosophical discourse, like Burney, also raises the problem of imitation. In what I see as a similar defense of new ground, and that beyond the canonical tropes of authorial modesty I "overread" as a claim for the originality of a woman writer, she invites the public of novel readers to decipher another story. Writing as an editor/publisher of letters translated from the original, Graffigny regrets the power of prejudice that leads "us" (the French) to scorn other nations, notably the Indians, "except to the extent that their customs imitate ours, that their language resembles our idiom" (249). As feminist critics "we" might today reinterpret this utterance—"we recognize what mirrors and mimes us"—as a historical gloss on the status of women's writing in the dominant culture: the canon retains what it knows how to read, when it recognizes its own idiom.

By locating her subject of difference in writing and language in France (as opposed to the precursor's "Oriental" scene of the seraglio) and by placing her at the end of her fiction retired from the world in solitary study in the library, Graffigny stages another reading of Enlightenment categories. In the construction of her Peruvian other, Graffigny produces not so much minor fiction for "coeurs sensibles" as a minority literature of protest which of necessity demands to be read in majority context, against what we have learned to see as the monuments of the dominant culture. "The work of a woman," Myra Jehlen has argued, "—whose proposal to be a writer in itself reveals that female identity is not naturally what it has been assumed to be—may be used comparatively as an external ground for seeing the dominant literature whole" (585).[20] The effect of reading from this point of view that "in itself" challenges the complacency of the "normative universal" is a displacement of positionings of identity that keep the canon alive.

As a provisional answer to the question of canon formation as it might be posed in eighteenth-century French studies, then, I want to summarize the three local points I have been arguing for in this essay. First, that in the range of works that make up the packaging of "the eighteenth-century novel," the very categories that traditionally have

---

without a name—the gender is implicitly one constructed on a continuity with the Gentlemen of the press, and a preface.

In Riccoboni's second letter to Laclos she rejects the title of *"un auteur"* and denies any self-importance: "I am so barely an author that in reading a new book I would find myself quite unjust and foolish if I compared it to the trifles that issue from my pen and thought my ideas qualified to guide those of others." She writes instead as a woman, a French woman (Laclos, *Oeuvres complètes*, 689). This also figures in a poetics of gender.

20. Myra Jehlen, "Archimedes and the Paradox of Feminist Criticism."*Signs* 6 (Summer 1981): 575–601.

defined this corpus serve as effectively to suppress a wide range of women's writing by narrowing its project; when, for instance, women's novels are placed in the category of the sentimental (for "coeurs sensibles") and not read, as men's writing conventionally is, as realistic fictions of social life, what results is a radical impoverishment of the complexity that characterizes literary exchanges in the eighteenth century.[21] My second point is that the exclusion of these voices of critique from a highly dialogic sociality is naturalized through a critical discourse of male bonding; flattered by the mirrors of his own representation, the masculinist critic sees himself, say, in Faublas. This narcissistic identification both emerges from and reinscribes a general ignorance of (and resistance to) female and feminist traditions of writing and rewriting that did not wait for Rousseau or Richardson to take shape. Finally, in order to register the heterogeneity of the cultural record of writing that becomes the history of the novel, we need to take another look within the period at the sites where the intersecting discourses on femininity (as the inflected term of the masculine/feminine couple) and fiction become—like the recklessly heterosexual couples of the social text they also articulate—permanently and dangerously entangled.

> I am convinced that the practice, as against the theory, of feminist criticism has in many cases weakened the critical enterprise.
> —Richard Poirier, "Where Is Emerson Now That We
> Need Him? Or, Why Literature Can't Save Us"

In "Woman in France: Madame de Sablé," George Eliot, filled with admiration for French women writers—especially "those delightful women of France, who, from the beginning of the seventeenth to the close of the eighteenth century, formed some of the brightest threads in the web of political and literary history"—celebrates, among others, Germaine de Staël: "Madame de Staël's name still rises to the lips when we are asked to mention a woman of great intellectual power" (55).[22] On our way to a conclusion about the place of women writers in the liter-

21. Melinda Sansone, currently a graduate student in the English doctoral program at Columbia University, has begun research on the ways in which the sentimental tradition in England has been relegated to a preparation for "Romanticism." She argues that by virtue of its emancipatory powers for women writers, sentimentalism was seen as threatening to dominant arrangements and historically repressed in favor of a male mode of expression; she calls it interestingly a "lost poetics."

22. "Woman in France: Madame de Sablé," *The Essays of George Eliot,* ed. Thomas Pinney (London: Routledge and Kegan Paul, 1963).

ature of the eighteenth century, and a revisionary strategy for teaching their works, I will just point to the case of Staël, who both represents the culmination of a great tradition of women writers in France, and a challenge—never met—to the novel of the nineteenth century.[23] What, for instance, of *Corinne*, the great feminist novel that punctures the illusions of masculine subjectivities and images the vision of a dramatically new voice and place for women writers?

Etiemble, defending Sénac de Meilhan from obscurity, manages to work in a swipe at Staël (the only woman mentioned in the second volume). He uses the literary historian Albert Thibaudet to set her up. Thibaudet goes on about the merits of *L'Emigré* as "a figure of the cosmopolitan novel less decorative, but more lively, more moving and more true than *Corinne.*" Etiemble comments: "That's a fair judgment of *Corinne;* still, despite Thibaudet, despite his *Histoire de la littérature française* where I cull these few lines, it's *Corinne* that is edited, glossed, taught, admired and pitied. Poor students! [Pauvres potaches]!" (2, xxvi–xxvii). Anyone who tried to find an edition of Staël's novel in a library or bookstore before its recent republication by des femmes in 1979, and the Gallimard Folio in 1985, or looked at a reading list, in this country at least, for exams or syllabi on the eighteenth- or nineteenth-century novel will be amazed by these claims. Staël's name, however, does of course have a place in the landscape of French studies: as a writer of literary theory who imaged and imagined comparative literature.[24]

Courses on women writers, either in the form of a historical survey, or by genre and period, offer a simple, if conventional way to address the exclusions of the canon. The very gesture of reconstructing the histories of women's writing provides a standpoint from which to dismember the universal subjectivity enshrined in dominant literatures. It also establishes a ground from which to address the question of the work performed by women's writing and the value one wishes to ascribe to that work. But at the same time the establishment of such a parallel history (or curriculum) runs the risk of generating, and perhaps guarantees an even greater indifference to the question of women's writing itself on the part of those authorizers and disseminators of cultural value, who, as we have seen, are happy enough to have a women's chapter which

23. On the relation of *Corinne* to women and the history of the French novel, see Joan DeJean's "Staël's *Corinne:* The Novel's Other Dilemma." *Stanford Literature Review* (Spring 1987), 10 (1): 77–88.

24. Another odd footnote about women's names and their function in the cultural record. In the Norton edition, "An Authoritative Text," established by Richard D. Bamberg (New York: Norton, 1975) of *A Portrait of a Lady* a footnote explains the allusion to Corinne, "the American Corinne, as Mrs. Osmond liked to be called" by a reference to the sixth-century poet, Corinna, that completely occults the text of Staël's heroine. Perhaps this blind spot would be impossible today after Moers's work on Corinne's legacy.

leaves their story intact. It may be that the pleasure of this new text requires another pedagogical politics.[25] It may be that to produce a literary history that articulates the complexities of the cultural record, it is as important to conceive a pedagogy that leaves less already in place. This would mean among other things a commitment to the practice of gendered poetics that also rereads men's texts in the weave of women's.

The question, then, of "placing" women writers in French literature must be understood finally as a double operation. If the first move inevitably takes the form of a replacement that appears to leave the field intact, or rather, subject only to minor *dis*placements (one in the stead of the other) that respect the original body, this must not be seen as its aim. Rather, seeing the first as immediately doubled by an interrogation of the body itself, it becomes possible to start another project altogether.

25. Margaret Switten and Elissa Gelfand have already conceived and taught such a course at Mount Holyoke called "Gender and the Rise of the Novel" (which I have appropriated for the title of this essay) in which the notion I describe earlier as "reading in pairs" is imaginatively enacted. I am grateful to them for sharing their materials with me.

Following several introductory sessions on the beginning of the *roman* in the Middle Ages, the *querelle des femmes*, early poetics and contemporary feminist criticism, the students of "Gender and the Rise of the Novel" read Tencin's *Comminge*, Prévost's *Manon Lescaut*, Graffigny's *Lettres d'une Péruvienne*, Rousseau's *Nouvelle Héloïse*, Diderot's *Jacques le fataliste*, Charrière's *Caliste*, Riccoboni's *Fanni Butlerd*, Laclos's *Liaisons dangereuses* and the correspondence between Laclos and Riccoboni.

In the same spirit, one could also imagine reading Montesquieu's *Lettres persanes* or Prévost's *Histoire d'une Grecque moderne* "with" *Lettres d'une Péruvienne*; the *Lettres portuguaises* with the Graffigny; Duclos's *Les Confessions du comte de**** with Riccoboni's *Histoire du Marquis de Cressy* or *Lettres de Milady Juliette Catesby*. Finally, to circle back to the question of *Corinne*, and as a move into questions of the nineteenth-century novel, one could reread the canonical tropes of the "psychological" novel *Adolphe* in the light of a male subjectivity brilliantly supplied by *Caliste* and *Corinne*. Their own account of the course appears in the *French Review* vol. 61 no. 3 (February 1988) under the title: "Gender and the Rise of the Novel."

NAOMI SCHOR

Idealism in the Novel: Recanonizing Sand*

> L'amour où le prendrons-nous? Telle femme l'irait cher-
> cher dans Balzac. Mieux vaudrait madame Sand. Il y a là
> du moins toujours un élan vers l'idéal.
> —Michelet, *La Femme*

> Cette querelle des réalistes et des idéalistes est fatigante
> et sans fin. Il y a de grands esprits et petits esprits, il y a
> des esprits masculins et des esprits féminins.
> —Champfleury, *Souvenirs et portraits de jeunesse*

Let me begin with an anecdote: in June 1986 I participated in a conference at Georgetown University on "The Representation of the Other." My paper dealt with the representation of men in women's writing and my examples were drawn from the fictions of several major French women writers, among them George Sand, whose novel *Indiana* I discussed in some detail. When I sat down after having delivered my talk a fellow panelist, a respected male professor at a major ivy-league institution, leaned over and whispered confidentially in my ear: "that was very nice Naomi, but you still haven't convinced me to read *Indiana*." I begin with this comical but unfunny episode because it has everything to do with the reasons that I have undertaken to write a critical study of George Sand. Boldly stated: in 1986, sixteen years after Kate Millett's *Sexual Politics*, thirty-seven years after Simone de Beauvoir's *The Second Sex*, fifty-seven years after Virginia Woolf's *A Room of One's Own*, to cite some of the landmarks of feminist criticism and theory, many if not most of my colleagues still believed that it was incumbent upon *us*—and when I say "us," I refer in general to we feminist critics, in particular to we Sand scholars—to convince *them* that Sand (but also many other major women writers) are worth reading. Ours is of necessity a rhetoric of persuasion.

We may respond to this challenge in a number of ways: disbelief, derision, dismissal, deconstruction, but the question of the canon re-

*This essay is to be the first chapter of a critical study of Sand. It was written with the generous support of the ACLS, which is hereby gratefully acknowledged. My thanks also to Sima Godfrey for bringing the second epigraph to my attention.

56

mains and it will not go away, for as Leslie Fiedler has observed: "we all know in our hearts that literature is effectively what we teach in departments of English; or conversely, what we teach in departments of English is literature."[1] If we assume for the moment that we can simply substitute French for English—no small assumption—then the situation becomes quite clear: as long as works by Sand are not included routinely in surveys of nineteenth-century French literature, on reading lists for prelims and orals, on the program for the Agrégation, etc., however many colloquia we may hold on Sand, however many studies we may devote to her oeuvre, however many texts of hers we may reedit, she will remain beyond the pale of literature, in its strong institutional sense. Two possibly controversial assumptions ground that statement. First, that the task, rather one of the tasks of feminist criticism is to infiltrate and remodel the existing canon. My quarrel here is with the position provocatively argued by Lillian S. Robinson in her anthologized article, "Treason our Text: Feminist Challenges to the Literary Canon." Robinson's claim is that upgrading women writers already marginally in the canon from second to first rank is a misguided feminist enterprise, as it leaves the criteria for canonization in place: "the case here consists in showing that an already recognized woman has been denied her rightful place, presumably because of the general devaluation of female efforts and subjects. . . . Obviously, no challenge is presented to the particular notions of literary quality, timelessness, universality, and other qualities that constitute the rationale for canonicity."[2] My effort here is to show that on the contrary a reflection on the particular circumstances of a *de*canonization can produce results that exceed the case of an "already recognized woman" and do call into question the value system grounding the canon.

Second, that Sand deserves a place in the new, revised French canon of nineteenth-century literature. More precisely, Sand deserves to recover the eminent place she occupied in the old, unrevised French canon established by the Sorbonne between 1871 and 1914, during a period of intense national reaffirmation following the humiliating defeat of 1871. As Elaine Showalter has remarked: "it is a curious fact of literary history that canon formation has been particularly aggressive following wars, when nationalist feeling runs high and there is a strong wish to define a tradition."[3] The ideological constraints that presided over the formation of the French canon at the turn of the century are clearly at

1. Leslie Fiedler as quoted by Elizabeth A. Meese, "Sexual Politics and Critical Judgment," in Gregory S. Jay and David L. Miller, ed., *After Strange Texts: The Role of Theory in the Study of Literature* (University of Alabama Press, 1985), 86.

2. In Elaine Showalter, ed., *The New Feminist Criticism: Essays on Women, Literature, Theory* (New York: Pantheon Books, 1985), 109.

3. Showalter, "Introduction," *The New Feminist Criticism*, 11.

work in the promotion of Sand's so-called rustic fiction that went hand in hand with her canonization. It is after all as a novelist of the *terroir*, or countryside, the author of such classics of French children's literature as *Fanchon the Cricket, The Country Waif*, and the adult's favorite, *The Bag-Pipers*, that Sand was initially inscribed into the canon.[4] Somewhere around 1890 a consensus was reached regarding the canonicity of Sand's pastoral mode. Already in 1887, Emile Faguet had written: "hers was the genius of the idyll." According to him it is the works written in what he terms Sand's "third manner," the peasant idylls sited in her home region, the Berry, that are destined for immortality: "she found there her superior works, the ones that will endure, *Fadette, Le Champi, Jeanne*, and above all, *La Mare au Diable* and *les Maîtres sonneurs*."[5] And, in an important and thoughtful assessment of Sand's literary achievement, Georges Pellissier asserts in 1890: "What will remain of George Sand are her pastorals, a few simple and touching love stories set in a natural framework. . . . She is par excellence a painter of the fields. . ."[6] To recanonize Sand, then, cannot be merely to reinstate her earlier position and positioning, it must entail a reexamination of the premises of her earlier canonization, as well as a recognition of new ideological pressures. For if Sand is reinscribed into the canon at the turn of the twentieth-century it will almost certainly be as the exemplary feminist author of such novels as, *Indiana, Valentine*, and *Lélia*.

But, above all, to recanonize Sand must involve a better understanding than we now have of the conditions of Sand's decanonization. For Sand's fall from aesthetic grace has been spectacular. Writing in 1949, Van Tieghem declares: "Sand's fictional oeuvre has singularly declined. It is difficult to imagine the glory and the esteem that surrounded her."[7] Indeed, a writer of international stature in her lifetime, Sand was widely read, admired, and imitated by such far-flung readers as Margaret Fuller,

4. And it is as an author of rustic fiction that she survives in those ultimate repositories of the French canon, the "manuels" (e.g., the Lagarde et Michard) destined for high-school students preparing for the Baccalauréat examination. In a recent survey of women as they are represented in textbooks, the author of the section on literature notes: "her oeuvre is generally reduced to her rustic novels, whereas her production is very diversified," in Brigitte Crabbé et al., *Les Femmes dans les livres scolaires* (Brussels: Pierre Mardaga, 1985), 57. All translations are mine except where otherwise noted. According to the same author (Evelyne Wilwerth) women writers are subject to two strategies of exclusion: "occultatiot. and reduction caracterize the treatment of women's writing" (57). As one of the two "monuments" of nineteenth-century French literature—the other being, of course, Mme de Staël—, Sand's contribution cannot be elided, hence the "reduction" of her immense oeuvre to her country fiction.

5. Emile Faguet, *Dix-Neuvième Siècle: Etudes Littéraires* (Paris: Boivin & Cie, 1887), 395 and 398.

6. Georges Pellissier, *Le Mouvement littéraire au xixe siècle* (Paris: Hachette, 1890), 243–44.

7. Philippe Van Tieghem, *Histoire de la littérature française* (Paris: Fayard, 1949), 468.

the Brontë sisters, and Fyodor Dostoevsky, as well as by the greatest of her French contemporaries. Allowing for the season in purgatory all French writers endure in the immediate aftermath of their deaths, after 1876 (the date of Sand's death), Sand's place in the pantheon of great nineteenth-century French authors, as noted above, appeared secure. In the introduction to selected passages from her writings published in 1924 in a series called *Pages Choisies des Grands Ecrivains,* the editor writes: "the century which witnessed the birth and death of George Sand is scarcely over, and already she takes her place among our classics."[8] And yet, already in 1890, Pellisier concludes his exceptionally intelligent and sympathetic assessment of her achievement, by saying: "George Sand is hardly read any longer."[9] And, by 1938, Virginia Woolf speaks of Sand, as a "half-forgotten author."[10] Unread in 1890, half-forgotten in 1938, what happened to George Sand?

I

The steady decline of Sand's artistic stock in the course of the twentieth century is inextricably bound up with a major remapping of the topography of the nineteenth-century French novel. For, in the critical tradition instituted and widely disseminated by the Sorbonne, Sand's works are classified under a rubric which has since disappeared, seemingly without leaving a trace: the idealist novel.

In the nineteenth-century, following Kant's formulations in *The Critique of Judgment,* realism was yoked to idealism. Initially, realism appeared as idealism's binary opposite, as in G. H. Lewes's characteristic formulation: "of late years there has been a reaction against conventionalism which called itself Idealism, in favour of *detailism* which calls itself Realism."[11] Realism in the nineteenth century signified *only* in relation to idealism, so much so that to consider one term

8. George Sand, *Pages Choisies des Grands Ecrivains* (Paris: Armand Colin, 1924), np.

9. Pellissier, 243.

10. Virginia Woolf, *Three Guineas* (New York: Harvest, HBJ Books, 1966), 188, n.49.

11. G. H. Lewes, *The Principles of Literary Success in Literature* (Boston: Allyn and Bacon, 1891), 83. Lewes is in many ways a crucial figure in this realm of aesthetics: a significant interpreter and disseminator of Hegel's idealist philosophy, an insightful supporter of women novelists (Brontë, Sand, and of course, Eliot), Lewes emerges as one of the prime theoreticians of realism/idealism in Victorian criticism. In fact, for Lewes who espoused what one commentator has called a "modified Realism", idealism and realism were not incompatible, not true opposites; for him, writes Alice Kaminsky, "idealism is simply a special kind of realism." Thus Lewes writes: "realism is . . . the basis of all Art, and its antithesis is not idealism but Falsism." Alice R. Kaminsky, *George Henry Lewes as Literary Critic* (Syracuse: Syracuse University Press, 1968), 45. For Lewes on Sand, see "Balzac and George Sand," *Foreign Language Quarterly* 33 (1844): 265–98, and "George Sand's Recent Novels," *Foreign Language Quarterly* 37 (1846): 21–36.

in isolation from the other is to deplete, even distort its significance. Because the opposition between idealism and realism is viewed as an immanent mental structure, it is a commonplace of nineteenth-century literary criticism. Pellisier's account of the evolution of the novel is in this respect typical. After passing through a lyrical, then a historicist stage, the novel, he writes:

Leaving behind history for contemporary society . . . in the end divided itself, without exceeding this very framework, into two very distinct genres corresponding to two irreducible tendencies of the human spirit: some, viewing real life through their imaginations enamored of beauty, truth, happiness, produced a portrait always idealised in its very truth; the others, fortified with a wise and penetrating analysis, directed their energies at seeing reality as it is and at representing it as they had seen it. [233][12]

And yet so massive, so crushing has been the triumph of realism that at least in the field of literature—in painting where the opposition first arose, the story is quite different—idealism has all but vanished from our critical consciousness, taking with it the literary reputation of its most eminent French representative, George Sand.[13]

There is, then, a general recognition among Sand's posthumous promoters that her declining literary fortunes are linked to the triumph of Balzacian realism over the idealism associated with Sand's name:

For the last twelve or fifteen years her success diminished, though her talent had not flagged; it is just that fashion had shifted elsewhere. The positivist and scientific spirit has taken over literature; today a more exact imitation of things,

12. Cf., Christopher Robinson, *French Literature in the Nineteenth Century* (Newton Abbot: David & Charles, 1978), whose survey of nineteenth-century French literature is informed by the opposition between "idealists" and "pragmatists," an eternal opposition given renewed impetus in the nineteenth century, "not only because of the crisis of values caused by the social cataclysm of the end of the previous century, but also because continued progress in the sciences undermined belief in accepted notions of reality itself" (8). Curiously, Robinson's generalization of the category of idealism to include most major developments in nineteenth-century French literature does not correspond to a reevaluation of Sand's fiction. Of the writer who was arguably the preeminent idealist of her time, he writes: "even a thinker so congenitally feeble as poor George Sand could see this [that during the July monarchy "problems of social inequality were substantially moral too"]. It is the very core of her revolt against society in those novels compounded from a jumble of absurd utopian and spiritualist theories, e.g., *Consuelo*; it underlies such ludicrous idealizations of the peasantry as *Petite Fadette* or *François le Champi*. Even in her early novels, with their grotesquely melodramatic stylizations of adultery at its most clichéd, *Indiana* or *Jacques* (. . .), the moral corrosion effected by the social structure is constantly felt as a primary cause of individual inadequacy" (105–06).

13. More accurately, Sand and idealism are forever linked in the half-life of the literary manuals, where the pace of change is inscribed in the longest of "durées"; like a fossil preserved in amber, the Sandian idealist novel remains embalmed in the unscientific sample of manuals and introductions to French literature I have consulted.

characters more like those one encounters daily, absolutely precise descriptions recorded on the spot, in short a detailed, literal and micrographic copy of reality are what is wanted. The novel is in the hands of Balzac's successors.[14]

Consequently, all hopes for and predictions of Sand's return to favor are tied to a return to or of idealism, a turning away from a spent realism. In his 1910 *Cours de littérature*, Félix Hémon announces that that double return is imminent:

. . . since Balzac, we have for so long savoured the humiliating pleasure of contemplating our portraits as we are, that we are seized by a violent desire to be flattered, idealized, fooled if need be about our poor human nature. And that is why favor is returning to this mixed oeuvre, within which one nevertheless asks to pick and chose. [43][15]

My thesis then, is this, Sand's spectacular aesthetic devaluation cannot be ascribed in any simple terms to her gender; it is not because Sand was a woman, rather because (like so many other woman authors) she is associated with a discredited and discarded representational mode that she is no longer ranked among the canonic authors.

The question then becomes: what is the relationship if any between femininity and idealism? A brief comparison of the literary fates of "the two Georges" (Sand and Eliot) should serve to dispel at the outset any notion of the essential femininity of idealism as a literary practice. Speculating on the reasons for George Eliot's easy superiority over the other George, whom she read so admiringly and to whom she owed so much, Patricia Thomson writes: "in the long run, George Eliot has easily outdistanced the other George to whom she was indebted for so

14. Hippolyte Taine, *Derniers Essais de critique et d'Histoire* (Paris: Hachette, 1894), 130–31. Cf., Henry James who, in his essay on George Sand, included in *French Poets and Novelists* (New York: Grosset and Dunlap, 1964), explicitly indebted to Taine's, also links Sand's falling out of fashion with the dissemination of realism: "During the last half of her career, her books went out of fashion among the new literary generation. 'Realism' had been invented, or rather propagated; and in the light of '*Madame Bovary*' her own facile fictions began to be regarded as the work of a sort of superior Mrs. Radcliffe" (168).

15. Cf., Rocheblave who explicitly links Sand's literary fortunes to a long deferred return to the ideal: "while waiting that the public, at last done with a sad realism, come back fully to idealist literature" (np). James, in his aforementioned piece, is far less sanguine about the prospects for a return to Sandian idealism, imagining instead that in a future "world . . . given over to a 'realism' that we have not as yet begun faintly to foreshadow, George Sand's novels will have, for the children of the twenty-first century, something of the same charm which Spenser's 'Fairy Queen' [sic] has for those of the nineteenth" (180–81). Though it may be argued, as does Katherine Hume in *Fantasy and Mimesis* (New York: Methuen, 1984), that Realism was a short-lived movement and that postmodernism marks a return of the fantasy repressed by realism. The return of fantasy is not the same as the return of idealism, though there is a definite connection between the two. The Sand that has returned to favor, at least in the United States, is the feminist Sand. Sand's idealism has not been revalorized by contemporary feminist readings.

many insights and such a great enlargement of her horizons. It is not simply that the idealist, optimist and romantic has less of value to communicate than the writer with a deep and realistic sense of the irony and tragedy of life—although for modern readers this is surely a vital distinction."[16]

The difference in the literary fates of "the two Georges," while not reducible to the opposition idealism-realism, does overlap with it in interesting ways. For Eliot's poetics was, it will be recalled, explicitly antiidealist, classically realist. In chapter seventeen of *Adam Bede*, entitled, "In which the story pauses a little," Eliot stops to explain why, deliberately frustrating her implied readers' desire, she chooses not, "to represent things as they never have been and never will be," not to "touch" up the world with a "tasteful pencil", not "make things better than they were."[17] She prefers instead to offend her "idealistic friend" (233) by the representation of the vulgar details that inhere in the representation of the commonplace and the homely. As Eliot writes in "The Natural History of German Life," "the unreality" of the representation of the common people is a "grave evil," for it directly prevents "the extension of our sympathies" that is art's "greatest benefit": "appeals founded on generalizations and statistics require a sympathy ready-made, a moral sentiment already in activity; but a piece of human life such as a great artist can give, surprises even the trivial and the selfish into that attention to what is apart from themselves, which may be called the raw material of moral sentiment."[18] For Eliot the superiority of realism over idealism is then moral; only a deidealized portrayal of the people can enable the sympathy for the Other that great art can uniquely inspire.

There are few prophets in the world; few sublimely beautiful women; few heroes. I can't afford to give all my love and reverence to such rarities: I want a great deal of those feelings for my everyday fellowmen, especially for the few in the foregound of the great multitude, whose faces I know, whose hands I touch, for whom I have to make way with kindly courtesy. . . . It is more needful that I should have a fibre of sympathy with that vulgar citizen who weighs out my sugar in a vilely assorted cravat and waistcoat, than with the handsome rascal in red scarf and green feathers. . . . [224–25]

The opposition between Eliot's realism and Sand's idealism is, however, neither simple nor neat: as many commentators have noted, Eliot is in

16. Patricia Thomson, *George Sand and the Victorians* (New York: Columbia University Press, 1975), 183, emphasis added.

17. George Eliot, *Adam Bede* (Harmondsworth: Penguin Books, 1980), 221, 222, and 223. All subsequent references to this novel are incorporated in the text.

18. George Eliot, *Essays of George Eliot*, ed. Thomas Pinney (New York: Columbia University Press, 1963), 270.

her own way an idealist, thus the very figure of the common working man, Adam Bede—who has been compared to Sand's Meunier d'Angibault—is itself heavily idealized, and Sand's idealism is in turn informed by some of the same moral and social imperatives that animate Eliot's realism.[19] But finally, the question of the differences between Eliot and Sand is mooted by the realization that the triumph of realism over idealism owes less to moral than to aesthetic considerations. Or rather, that the triumph of realism over idealism makes visible the interpenetration of the ethical and the aesthetic. If realism has triumphed over idealism, and Eliot and Balzac over Sand, it is in large measure because the aesthetic legacy linking referential illusion and political efficacy with the detailed representation of a blemished reality has remained with us in the age of the simulacrum. Even in those works, structuralist and poststructuralist, which have in recent years subjected the "order of mimesis" (Prendergast) to a radical critique, some of the underlying assumptions of classical realist aesthetics remain undisturbed. As Barthes observes in *S/Z:* "beauty . . . cannot be induced through catachresis other than from some great cultural model (written or pictorial): it is stated, not described. Contrariwise, ugliness can be abundantly described: it alone is 'realistic', confronting the referent without an immediate code (whence the notion that realism, in art, is concerned solely with ugliness)."[20] To recanonize Sand must of necessity entail a critical rethinking of both the aesthetic and ethical valorization of the ugly and the consensual equation of the real with the unsightly, for as we shall see, it is on these linked assumptions that her decanonization rests.

II

So far we have relied on a vague and commonsense understanding of idealism to ground our discussion. If we are to advance and to avoid the pitfalls that result from an indiscriminate use of the term idealism, at this point some understanding of how it was used in nineteenth-century aesthetic discourse becomes necessary. It is in a section of the French philosopher Hippolyte Taine's immensely popular and influential lectures on aesthetics, *Philosophie de l'Art,* entitled *De l'Idéal dans l'Art,* that we find the elements of a specifically late nineteenth-century theo-

19. At the conclusion of his reading of chapter 17 of *Adam Bede*—which I read after having drafted this essay—J. Hillis Miller makes the point that the very difference Eliot seeks to promote between the arts of "irrealism" and "realism" tends finally to collapse. See J. Hillis Miller, *The Ethics of Reading* (New York: Columbia University Press, 1987), especially 66–70 and 78–80.

20. Roland Barthes, *S/Z,* trans. Richard Miller (New York: Hill and Wang, 1974), 59.

ry of the ideal in art, and an indigenous French one to boot. Now, admittedly there is something circular about bringing the aesthetics of one of her most ardent admirers to bear on Sand's literary practice. Indeed it is difficult to separate Taine's theory from Sand's practice: for no one was more keenly aware of the necessity to devise a poetics of idealism specially adapted to the idealist text to allow readers with a realist horizon of expectations to read Sand with pleasure: "to take pleasure in them [Sand's fictions]," writes Taine, "we have to adopt their point of view, take an interest in the depiction of a more beautiful and better humanity."[21] Taine develops his notion of the ideal in two key chapters of his aesthetics: "the degree of importance of the character" ["Le degré d'importance du caractère"] and "The degree of goodness of the character" ["Le degré de bienfaisance du caractère"]. What then does Taine mean by "character"? Character, as he explains in the inaugural section of his aesthetics, is an essential, salient feature of an object:

This character is what the philosophers call *the essence* of things; and, because of that, they say that the purpose of art is to make manifest the essence of things. We will leave aside this word *essence* which is technical, and we shall simply say that the purpose of art is to make manifest the central character, some salient and notable quality, an important point of view, a principal manner of being of the object.[22]

Despite his positivist trappings—Taine grounds his hierarchy of distinctive features in the realm of art on the notion of variability in the life sciences—in "Le degré d'importance du caractère" Taine does little but reinscribe the main tenets of neoclassical aesthetics: The notable character that is the marker of the ideal is essential, unchanging, universal. The supreme work of art is installed in what modern historians call *la longue durée*; it is built on the bedrock upon which the superficial and transitory products of the moment merely glide. As an example of such a perennial masterpiece, Taine cites l'abbé Prévost's *Manon Lescaut*; so "durable" is the "type" created by Prévost that *Manon* has been repeatedly rewritten and adapted in response to the changing times. It is here that Sand makes her first appearance in *De l'idéal dans l'art*, for in her novel *Leone Leoni* she rewrites *Manon* reversing the roles.

Based on this section of Taine's work it would appear difficult to make the case for Sand as an idealist author, for it cannot be claimed that Sand ever created in her own right the sort of universal type Taine has in mind. It is only when we turn to the second major section in Taine's text, "Le degré de bienfaisance du caractère", that we can begin to grasp the sense in which Sand could be described as an idealist novel-

21. Taine, *Derniers Essais de Critique et d'Histoire*, 132.
22. Hippolyte Taine, *Philosophie de l'art*, I–II (Paris: Ressources, 1980), 33.

ist. In these pages Taine establishes a new hierarchy, one ordained not by scientific principles of durability, but rather by moral principles of goodness. Following this second classificatory system, the highest ranked works of art are not those featuring universal types, but rather those representing heroes and heroines: "all things being equal, the work which expresses a benevolent character is superior to the work which expresses a malevolent character" (2, 289). It is according to this ethical scale of values that Sand is promoted as an artist of the ideal for, writes Taine, along with Corneille and Richardson she undertakes deliberately ["de parti pris"] to represent "noble feelings and superior souls." Taine singles out for particular praise several of Sand's fictions, including *Mauprat* and *A Country Waif* for their depictions of "native generosity" (2, 295).

What Taine's lectures make apparent in a way distinct from that of a long line of theoreticians of the ideal in art stretching all the way back to Plato, is the necessary slippage between the heightening of the essential and the promotion of the higher good that constitutes idealism in the realm of aesthetics. Only in the light of Taine's *double definition of aesthetic idealism* does Balzac's celebrated statement to Sand regarding their differences become fully intelligible. Writing of her poetics of idealization in her autobiography, *Story of My Life*, Sand attributes the following remarks to Balzac:

> You seek man as he should be; I take him as he is. Believe me, we are both right. Our paths meet in the end. I love exceptional people too; I *am* one. Besides, I need them—to set off my vulgar people—and I never sacrifice them needlessly. But these vulgar people interest me more than they do you. I magnify and idealize them in reverse, in their ugliness or folly. I give their deformities frightening or grotesque proportions. That you could never do, and you do well not to gaze too closely on the beings who give you nightmares. Idealize only toward the lovely and the beautiful: that is woman's work.[23]

Initially Balzac casts his formulation of the difference between himself and Sand in terms all too familiar to generations of French *lycéens:* Balzac is to Sand as Racine is to Corneille. Theirs is but a replay of the paradigmatic French confrontation between realist and idealist writer. Almost immediately, however, Balzac undercuts this neat antithesis, arguing instead for an underlying commonality of purpose and method. In keeping with Taine's first definition of the term, both Sand and Balzac are idealist novelists; idealization is here taken to be synonymous with hyperbolization, a form of excess in writing that strains at the limits of verisimilitude. Enunciating her theory of writing earlier in

23. George Sand, *My Life*, trans. Dan Hofstadter (New York: Harper, 1980), 218. Cf., the recasting of this dialogue in the "Notice" of *Le Compagnon du Tour de France, 1* (Paris: Michel Lévy, 1869), 1–2.

the same section of her autobiography, Sand explicitly links idealization and implausibility:

> Áccording to it [this theory], the novel is a work of poetry as much as analy-
> sis. Authentic, even real, characters and situations are required, ranged about a
> figure who must exemplify the chief feeling or idea of the book. This figure
> usually represents passionate love. . . . This love must be idealized . . . the au-
> thor should not fear to give it exceptional importance, unusual power, and
> charms and sufferings beyond the common run of human things, and even
> beyond the bounds of probability. [218]

The difference between Sand and Balzac's idealizations is in the end
one of quality not quantity, it is of a thematic rather than a rhetorical
order. The conflation in Sand's writing practice of hyperbolizing and
meliorative idealization are what, in Taine's eyes, make her the paradigmatic idealist novelist, whereas Balzac, for all his larger than life character types, remains mired in the lower ethical spheres of realism. Seen
in this unfamiliar perspective, realism appears as a lesser, even a failed
idealism; it is idealism, not realism that is the more inclusive term. The
perceptible drift in this passage toward a stunning hierarchical reversal
is, however, checked when in the last sentence Balzac suddenly aligns
idealization with gender. Earlier we asked what was the relationship, if
any, between idealism and femininity. Balzac's statement offers the
elements of an answer. Idealism in the novel is a priori sex-blind; the
feminization of the idealist mode of representation is bought about by
aligning sexual difference with a *difference within idealism*. This align-
ment produces a splitting: associated with masculinity, negative idealization becomes the positively valorized term, henceforth known as
realism, while positive idealization, linked up with femininity, becomes the negatively valorized term, a diminished and trivialized
idealism.

The gendering of poetics inevitably results in their degeneration into
stereotype. Thus, responding to a letter from the novelist Mme Riccoboni, critical of his seductive portrayal of the evil Mme de Merteuil in
Les Liaisons dangereuses, Laclos writes:

> . . . to women alone belongs this precious sensitivity, this easy and cheerful
> imagination which embellishes everything it touches, and creates objects as
> they should be, but . . . men, who are condemned to a harsher labor, have al-
> ways acquitted themselves well when they have rendered nature exactly and
> faithfully.[24]

---

24. Chloderlos de Laclos, *Oeuvres complètes,* ed. Maurice Allem (Paris: Gallimard,
Pléiade, 1951), 688.

The division of literary labor along gender lines rests on a series of highly questionable assumptions: mimesis is man's work; the faithful representation of "nature," a sort of Adamic curse visited on male writers, condemns them to a literary life of referential servitude. Women writers, congenitally unable to view the world without the benefit of rose-colored glasses, are essentially idealists. Hierarchy insinuates itself into this paradigm less through its blatant naturalization of women's weakness, than through its more insidious and far-reaching assumption that aesthetic value resides in the (virile) depiction of the horrors of unembellished nature. What is at stake here is, finally, woman's relationship to truth. Thus Zola, a preeminent representative of the school of Balzac, attributes Sand's failure in her peasant novels to, "her idealist temperament which prevented her from seeing *true truth* and above all from reproducing it."[25] The woman writer in rose colored glasses stands as the necessary antithesis to that figure of the philosopher's imaginary, woman-as-truth. For the logic of misogyny is a no-win logic where whatever is connoted as feminine—e.g., an excessive proximity to or distance from truth—is devalorized. Thus, the stereotypical association of woman artists and the ideal is the obverse of an equally long and powerful tradition that condemns woman to the servile imitation of the nature with which she is so closely identified, that views her as congenitally incapable of transcending immanence to attain the ideal.[26] For James, whose generally sympathetic account of Sand in *French Poets and Novelists* is a tissue of sexual stereotypes, Sand's disregard for truth is doubly determined by her sex and her nationality; like the heroine in the song, the French woman writer is one who sees "la vie en rose":

Women, we are told, do not value truth for its own sake, but only for some personal use they make of it. My present criticism involves an assent to this somewhat cynical dogma. Add to this that woman, if she happens to be French, has an extraordinary taste for investing objects with a graceful drapery of her own contrivance, and it will be found that George Sand's cast of mind includes both the generic and the specific idiosyncrasy. (155)

25. Emile Zola, *Oeuvres complètes*, (Paris: Cercle du Livre Précieux, 1968), vol. 11, 772.

26. For more on the detail-woman association, see my *Reading in Detail: Aesthetics and the Feminine* (New York: Methuen, 1987). Interestingly, in Eliot, according to Miller, the gendering of the realism/idealism paradigm is reversed: "The impulse toward falsehood is given an implicit male gender, the gender of the narrator himself [in an idiosyncratic strategic gesture Miller insists on referring to Eliot throughout as "he"] whereas the faithful representing of commonplace things is therefore implicitly female" (68). If Miller is right, then we can perhaps identify Eliot's writing as inaugurating the transvaluation of the traditionally negative association of femininity and detailism pursued by modern feminist writers and critics who have often (re)claimed the realistic representation of (female) experience as the hallmark of women's writing.

The essay concludes with an enlisting of a by now familiar color code, although in this instance the rosiness has been transferred from the lens of vision to reality itself:

George Sand's optimism, her idealism, are very beautiful, and the source of that impression of largeness, luminosity and liberality which she makes upon us. But we suspect that something even better in a novelist is the tender appreciation of actuality which makes even the application of a single coat of rose-colour seem an act of violence. [185]

Though we may today smugly mock the innocent sexism of a Laclos, a Balzac, or a James, the valorization of realism—the masculine mode— remains largely unexamined in contemporary theories of representation and the canonic hierarchies they serve to secure, for the theory of realism from Lukács to Barthes is essentially a theory of a single fictional practice, Balzac's. In other words, the ongoing critique of representation stops well short of questioning the realist paradigm (and Balzac's status as the paradigmatic realist) and its underlying sexism. Even those critics who have most acutely exposed the complicity of realism with bourgeois ideology, countering realism's claims to a specular objectivity by demonstrating the active part mimesis plays in legitimizing the apparatus of the Law, the network of disciplinary mechanisms that repress all exceptions to the norm, the sexual fix, even these critics have continued to be fascinated by the canonic figures, especially Balzac.[27] To begin to grasp the not so subtle ways in which idealism has been feminized and hence devalorized is to begin to ask what it might mean

27. I am thinking here of the work of what might be thought of as the English or Cambridge school of critics (Tanner, Heath, McCabe, Prendergast) who, working in the wake of Barthes, are engaged in rethinking realism. Significantly, however scathing their critique of realism, it has remained completely divorced from a critique of the canon. The work of Prendergast is in this respect symptomatic: while recognizing fleetingly that the laws of verisimilitude repress "feminine desire" with a particular vengeance, Prendergast's corpus is resolutely male. The surprising annexation of Nerval's *Sylvie* to the standard works in the library of realism only serves to point up the critic's blind spot; indeed, one almost suspects that *Sylvie* is appropriated in lieu of a text by a woman. The references here are to: Tony Tanner, *Adultery in the Novel* (Baltimore: The Johns Hopkins University Press, 1978); Christopher Prendergast, *The Order of Mimesis* (Cambridge: Cambridge University Press, 1986); Colin McCabe, *Theoretical Essays: Film, Linguistics, Literature* (Manchester, UK: Manchester University Press, 1985); Stephen Heath, "Realism, modernism, and 'language-consciousness'," in ed., Boyle, Nicholas and Martin Swales, *Realism in European Literature* (Cambridge: Cambridge University Press, 1986), 103– 22. This is perhaps (also) the place to make explicit what is implicit throughout this essay: to say that Balzac is the paradigmatic realist (or Sand, the paradigmatic idealist) is not to endorse the reductionism of the canon. Balzac's representational versatility, his own practice of (Sandian) idealism are not the issue here. What is at issue here is that the same criteria of canonicity (derived from and confirmed by Balzac's realist fiction) that serve to decanonize Sand serve to decanonize Balzac's (and other writers) nonrealist fiction.

to read "otherwise," to ask specifically what poetics would have to be elaborated to take into account the Sandian text, to bring it into the pale of the readable, and more important the rereadable, for as James devastatingly remarks: "all the world can read George Sand once and not find it in the least hard. But it is not easy to return to her. . . . George Sand invites reperusal less than any other mind of equal eminence" (181). Once again Taine points the way when in his late essay on Sand he characterizes idealist prose in ways that interestingly renew earlier normative idealist aesthetics: "It is," he writes,

an ideal world and to maintain the illusion, the writer erases, attenuates and often sketches a general outline, instead of depicting an individual figure. He does not emphasize the detail, he scarcely indicates it in passing, he avoids going into it; he follows the great poetic line of the passion he pleads or the situation he describes, without stopping over the irregularities which would break the harmony. This summary way of painting is the property of all idealist art. [132]

In this postrealist definition of idealism, idealism appears as a signifying practice of lack. Whereas prerealist idealism, by which I mean the idealism promoted and practiced before the emergence of the specifically nineteenth-century literary movement known as Realism, prescribed idealization as selection—the construction of the ideal through the combination of ideal parts abstracted from imperfect wholes—Sandian idealism is an art of deliberate erasure. For Sand was keenly aware of the link between details and realism, defining realism as a "science of details."[28] To be erased, passed over lightly, the detail must then be there to be erased; it is a case of emphasis subtracted. The idealist effect is produced by the evacuation of those very superfluous details that create the illusion of the real (Barthes). To read idealist fiction necessarily entails a painful renunciation of the pleasure of the detail and the illusion of referential plenitude it provides. Other renunciations, similarly painful (at least in my own experience), follow: for just as the idealist text eschews the redundant descriptive detail, it refuses the booby-trapped hermeneutic code that propels the classical realist text forward, even as it undoes conventions of characterization.[29]

The difficulties posed by the modern idealist novel are not, of course, unique to Sand—except insofar as her sex exacerbates them. They are notably intrinsic to the field of nineteenth-century German fiction. The great tradition of realist fiction so grandly embodied elsewhere in Eu-

28. George Sand, "L'Education sentimentale par Gustave Flaubert," in *Questions d'art et de littérature* (Paris: Calmann Lévy, 1878), 421.

29. On the breakdown in Sand's fiction of the difference between characters that grounds psychological realism, see my "Female Fetishism: The Case of George Sand," *The Female Body in Western Culture: Contemporary Approaches*, ed. Susan Suleiman (Cambridge: Harvard University Press, 1986), 363–72.

rope is, as is well known, strikingly absent in the history of German prose fiction. In his chapter devoted to German literature, "Miller the Musician," Auerbach speculates at some length on the reasons why a "contemporary realism" (as opposed to the realism bound up with Historicism) failed to develop in Germany despite what he calls a "favorable aesthetic situation":

> Contemporary conditions in Germany did not easily lend themselves to broad realistic treatment. The social picture was heterogeneous; the general life was conducted in the confused setting of a host of "historical territories," units which had come into existence through dynastic and political contingencies. In each of them the oppressive and at times choking atmosphere was counterbalanced by a certain pious submission and the sense of historical solidity, all of which was more conducive to speculation, introspection, contemplation, and the development of local idiosyncrasies than to coming to grips with the practical and the real in a spirit of determination and with an awareness of greater contexts and more extensive territories.[30]

Whether or not one accepts Auerbach's definition of realism and his explanation for "the problem of nineteenth-century German realism" the connection he makes between representational modes and sociopolitical circumstances is one with interesting implications for our study of Sand. We will want to ask how Sand's politics inflected her idealism: is there, for example, any connection between Sand's regionalism and her idealism? Is there a politics of idealism? Is idealism the representational mode of choice of an aristocrat with populist blood and leanings?

III

If in Balzac's formulation realism is but a subcategory of idealism, albeit the most prestigious, Sand's idealism must nonetheless be understood as a response to what was to become known as Balzacian realism. For, if idealism is not (any more than its opposite, detailism) an essentially female representational mode, the practice of an aesthetics of idealism was unquestionably for Sand a strategy for bodying forth her difference, and that difference is in part sexual. Feminist critics have traditionally emphasized transhistorical specificities of women's writing, but I

---

30. Erich Auerbach, *Mimesis: The Representation of Reality in Western Literature*, trans. Willard R. Trask (Princeton: Princeton University Press, 1968), 445. See also Martin Swales, "The Problem of Nineteenth-Century Realism," in *Realism in European Literature*, 68–84. Sand's well-known debt to Goethe—*Jacques*, for example rewrites the *Elective Affinities*—appears here in a new light, because for Auerbach, Goethe's aesthetic choices, his aristocratic rejection of realism decisively inflected the history of German literature. It is because Goethe is the central canonic figure of German literature and because Goethe eschewed bourgeois realism that realism failed to take hold in Germany.

would argue that female specificity in writing is (also) contextual, local, a microspecificity that shifts opportunistically in response to changing historical and literary historical circumstances. Writing in her auto-biography of her literary beginnings, Sand makes it quite clear that to begin writing is to take one's place on a scene of competing representa-tional modes (and all represented by men):

... in those days writers wrote the oddest things. The eccentricities of the young Victor Hugo had excited the younger generation, who were bored with the threadbare ideas of the Restoration. Chateaubriand was no longer suffi-ciently romantic, and even the new master, Hugo, was barely romantic enough for the fierce appetites he had whetted. The brats of his own school . . . wanted to "sink" him by outdoing him. [216]

Sand's choice of idealism was surely overdetermined—her moti-vations were political as well as psychological (the idealization of her dead father)—but what is significant is that it was a choice, albeit a difficult one. Traces of the difficult emergence of Sandian idealism from the matrix of Balzacian realism can be clearly made out in *Indiana*, the very novel Sand was working on at the moment of her conversations with Balzac. The celebrated double response of Sand's mentor Latouche to his star pupil's first solo novelistic venture accurately reflects the text's straddling of representational modes. After quickly scanning the opening pages of *Indiana*, Latouche is said to have exclaimed: "come now, this is a pastiche, School of Balzac! Pastiche! what do you mean by it?" However, having spent the night reading the entire novel, the very next morning Latouche saluted Sand's achievement in the following terms: "your book is a masterpiece. I stayed up all night to read it. No woman alive can sustain the insolence of a comparison with you . . . Balzac and Mérimée lie dead under *Indiana*."[31]

The emergence of Sand's distinctive writing mode from that of her genial friend takes two forms to which I can only allude here in passing: first, the movement from the conventionally realistic inaugural section to the controversial epilogue which so spectacularly exceeds the bounds of bourgeois realism. Second, the elimination in the 1833 edition of the interventions designed to persuade the reader of the original 1832 edi-tion of the narrator's allegiance to the main tenets of the realist credo and his rejection of competing novelistic trends, notably idealism:

The current fashion is to depict a fictional hero so ideal, so superior to the common run that he only yawns where others enjoy themselves. . . . These

31. George Sand, *Histoire de ma Vie* in *Oeuvres autobiographiques*, (Paris: Gal-limard, Pléiade, 1971), vol. 2, 173 and 1342–43, n.1. The translation is by Nancy K. Miller as it appears in "Arachnologies: The Woman, The Text, and the Critic," in Nancy K. Miller, ed. *The Poetics of Gender* (New York: Columbia University Press, 1986), 281.

heroes bore you, I'm sure, because they are not like you, and that in the long run lifting your head up to watch them float above you makes you dizzy. I place mine firmly on the ground and living the same life as you do.[32]

And yet, the double-edged irony of this passage suggests that even within these digressions designed to guarantee the author's realist credentials and hence his legitimacy, another aesthetic is being promoted.

In what sense, then, can we speak of *Indiana* as an idealist novel? Indeed is it one at all? No less a Sand scholar than Pierre Salomon, author of a general introduction to Sand's life and works and editor of several of her novels, states categorically that *Indiana* is not an idealist novel, basing himself on the deidealized representations of the male figures, notably Raymon, the vile seductor allegedly modeled on Sand's lover, Aurélien de Sèze: "if sometimes George Sand appears to be an idealist writer, it is certainly not here. The analysis is cruel, and one may well wonder at so much harshness directed against a man once beloved."[33] If, however, we recall Sand's own definition of idealism in the novel, it becomes immediately apparent that the ideal in this novel resides in the figure of its heroine and not its hero, for it is Indiana whose passionate love story exhibits the implausible extremes Sand identifies as constitutive of the fictional ideal. And yet, as useful as is Sand's explicitation of her idealizing techniques, it does not fully account for the idealism in *Indiana*. To do so we must bring into play Taine's theory of the biaxiality of the ideal in art, for what sets Indiana apart from other sadomasochistic female protagonists in nineteenth-century French fiction, notably Emma Bovary, her most illustrious descendant, is that in her story the quest for the love ideal is inseparable from an aspiration towards an ideal world. For all her reading of silly women's novels, when Indiana fantasizes, it is not as Emma later will of the beautiful people and Paris, rather of freedom for herself and for all her fellow slaves:

A day will come when everything in my life will be changed, when I shall do good to others, when someone will love me, when I shall give my whole heart to the man who gives me his; meanwhile, I will suffer in silence and keep my love as a reward for him who shall set me free.[34]

In keeping with Taine's theory, idealism in Sand's inaugural fiction consists, then, in a distinctive concatenation of the erotic and the moral, not to say the political. Moreover, and this returns us to the question

---

32. George Sand, "Notes et Variantes" in Béatrice Didier, ed. *Indiana* (Paris: Folio, 1984), 380, n.13.

33. Pierre Salomon, *George Sand* (Paris: Hatier-Borcier, 1953), 29.

34. George Sand, *Indiana*, trans. George Burnham Ives (New York: Academy Press Limited, 1978), 46.

of the gender specificities of idealism, Sand's idealism bespeaks a yearning to be delivered both from the base desire for carnal possession characteristic of male sexuality and the injustices of a man-made system of laws that enables the enslavement of both women and blacks. Balzac's feminizing of positive idealization, though wrong-headed, is finally not entirely wrong: idealism, as appropriated by Sand, signifies her refusal to reproduce mimetically and hence legitimate a social order inimical to the disenfranchized, among them women. Idealism for Sand is finally the only alternative representational mode available to those who do not enjoy the privileges of subjecthood in the real. To recanonize Sand will then require nothing less than a reconsideration of realism as it constructs and supports the phallo- and ethnocentric social order we so often confuse with reality. Finally, to recanonize Sand will call for the elaboration of a poetics of the ethical.

II. Exploring the Underread

STEPHEN G. NICHOLS

Medieval Women Writers: *Aisthesis* and the Powers of Marginality

> "You did not respond to most of my arguments about preferring love to wedlock, and freedom to chains."
> —Heloise to Abelard

MODERN CANON FORMATION AND OLD-FRENCH LANGUAGE

As readers and writers, medieval women played a paradoxical role. Their autonomy and power were marginalized, strictly speaking, yet they managed to effect changes in cultural perspective by their peculiar double relationship to literary production: active—as readers and writers—and passive—as patrons and poetic theme. No woman embodied this double identity more paradoxically than Heloise, mistress and wife, nun and lover. In her first letter to Abelard, she summed up the contradiction of the feminine with her vigorous blend of affirmation and self-reflection:

Wholly guilty though I am, I am also, as you know, wholly innocent. It is not the deed but the intention of the doer which makes the crime, and justice should weigh not what was done but the spirit in which it was done.[1]

To take the measure of their contribution, therefore, we must heed Heloise's injunction and examine the "intention of the doers" by looking closely at the nature of the literary language twelfth-century women developed and its social consequences. Modern scholars have tended to view the contribution of women from the perspective of inclusion or exclusion from canon formation, with the attendant assumption that literary disenfranchisement is homologous with political disestablishment.[2] But, as John Guillory recently observed: "histories of canon

---

1. *The Letters of Abelard and Heloise,* Translated with an Introduction by Betty Radice (Harmondsworth, England: Penguin, 1974), 115.
2. "Yet this sense of representation, the representation of groups by texts, lies at a curious tangent to the concept of political representation, with which it seems to have been confused. . ." John Guillory, "Canonical, and Non-Canonical: A Critique of the Current Debate," *ELH* 54 (1987), 483–527: 484. Further references to this article will henceforth appear in the text.

77

formation in themselves explain nothing" (504). It is in the social context of text production, particularly at the linguistic level—the relationship between the language of literature and sociolects—that the question of the noncanonical becomes theoretically meaningful.

The most conspicuous aspect of the current legitimation crisis is surely the fact that the non-canonical is not that which does not appear within the field of criticism, but that which, in a given context of reading, *signifies exclusion*. The non-canonical is a newly constituted category of text production and reception. [484]

The issue here is not canon formation, then, but the nature of women's relation to literacy, and the meaning of that link. Women did write in the twelfth century and their texts were noncanonical. But, since all vernacular writing in the twelfth century was noncanonical, the interesting questions lie in the direction of women writers' relation to literary language, their success in crossing over from the discourse of the everyday world to that other language, the discourse of writing. As Guillory says, "the question of reading and writing belongs to the whole problematic of social reproduction, because what one learns to read is always another language" (501).

Twelfth-century women explored this alterity of language in a double sense. First, they created or adapted new kinds of texts in which they incorporated a range of linguistic codes suggestive of the heterogeneity of spoken language.[3] This awareness of the heteroglossia of everyday experience in urban centers was not scientific, but rather linked to the second aspect of alterity, a manifest fascination with the dimensions of human psychology concealed by language: "beneath the thin ice of language lies the ocean of the psyche" (Guillory, 505).

With as much candor as originality, women explicitly confronted the hidden dimensions of desire. By translating images of fantasy into sensual perception, or *aisthesis*, writers of the period used the noncanonical situation of vernacular literacy to give cultural expression to a subject that had been explicitly proscribed, and consistently denounced, by canonical authority.[4]

In the early twelfth century, vernacular literacy had a clear role of social reproduction to play. French was itself noncanonical, a discourse unconstrained by grammar, spoken by the *laicus*, or laity (a Latin term signifying exclusion from the clergy, the body responsible for can-

3. See my article: "Working Late: Marie de France and the Value of Poetry," in *French Women Writers*, ed. Michel Guggenheim (Stanford: Stanford French Studies), forthcoming.

4. On the canonical attitudes towards sensual expression, see my article, "Rewriting Marriage in the Middle Ages," in *The Legitimacy of the Middle Ages*, a special issue of *Romanic Review*, forthcoming, Winter, 1988.

onicity). Unlike Latin, Old French was institutionally unconstrained, an instrument defined by its users, rather than by formal schools. In the midtwelfth century, Peter Helias, professor of rhetoric and grammar in Paris from 1135–1160, cited as a hypothetical case the possibility of establishing a French grammar.[5] The reference shows that French was recognized as an autonomous language. More importantly, it reminds us that French had yet to be subjected to the constraints of grammar as a formal discipline of the schools and grammar as a key instrument of canon formation.[6] In other words, French had yet to be coopted by the agents of power.

Such an inchoate sphere of creativity whose language was still inventing itself, may be exploited by anyone of passable poetic talent. Literacy was the principal requirement for entrée into this sphere, and, as we shall see, a significant number of women, and not only of the upper classes, were literate.[7] It is less the medieval scene that suppressed the role of women in Old French, than modern canon formation which has devalued their importance in creating a literature of dialectical dissonances within medieval culture.[8]

Since the eighteenth century, the medieval canon has been defined hierarchically in terms of the major narrative genres: epic, chronicle, and romance. Lyric poetry has been selectively admitted according to a principle of association with male figures whose poetic talent was per-

5. "Et possunt huius artis species crescere, hoc est plures esse, ut si grammatica tractaretur in gallica lingua, quod possit fieri facile" [And the number of these species of grammar may grow still more, as for example if one were to make a grammar of the French language, which would be easy enough.] Petrus Helias, *Summa super Priscianum*, Appendix 1. Quoted by Serge Lusignan, *Parler Vulgairement: Les Intellectuels et la langue française aux XIIe et XIV siècles* (Montréal: Les Presses de l'Université, 2nd. edition, 1987), 21.

6. Lusignan, 21. Guillory explicitly links formal grammar as a school discipline to canon formation, 494–504.

7. "From the texts assembled thanks to the diligence and erudition of Léon Gautier and Édmond Faral, it's clear that female *jongleurs* were numerous. These texts show them exercising various occupations: dancers, acrobats, singers, musicians (that's how they're portrayed in miniatures . . . of Spanish manuscripts), but they do not say that they were given to poetic composition." Alfred Jeanroy, *La poésie lyrique des troubadours* (Toulouse: Privat, 1934), vol. 1, 314.

8. "The *trobairitz* whose names have come down to us were more or less high born "ladies" occupying an honorable social position and who wrote poetry because they had a taste for it and to make a name for themselves as clever. Most of them only wrote in the lower genres which required minimal poetic effort (debate poems, verses, dialogues). Only five raised themselves to the heights required of the *canso*; and of these, three left a very small number of songs, as insignificant for their form as for their content. For only two of them, the Countess of Dia and Castellosa, is the poetic legacy sufficiently extensive to enable us to appreciate their talent, which seems to me, I admit, to give evidence rather of an elegant facility than of originality and forcefulness." Jeanroy: 1, 315. [See also the next note.]

ceived as extraordinary because joined with high political status (the poet-princes), or because attuned to modern views of romantic or symbolic expressiveness (troubadour love poets), or virulent social critiques (e.g., Marcabru, Bertran de Born, Rutebeuf, Villon).

Consequently, modern readers learned to view medieval vernacular literature as a male phenomenon with the occasional woman writer emulating the dominant literary culture.[9] How does this view affect what Mary Jacobus calls "the nature of women's access to culture and their entry into literary discourse," one of the problems "central to feminist literary criticism"?[10] In one sense, it should help us to understand *better* the nature of women's access to medieval culture and literary discourse.

For one of the fascinating aspects of medieval women writers in France was their innovative nature. Marie de France and Christine de Pizan come immediately to mind but in almost all instances, we find women writing in a new key, or a significantly modified one. But even when we cannot positively identify a work as being by a woman, as in the case of the anonymous lyrics of the "chansons de toile," or spinning songs, we find the feminine inscribed as a controlling presence, a force associated with social factors in which they exercised far greater determinacy than we have been led to believe.

By way of illustration, let us look at three different areas of the Old-French literary tradition: the anonymous *chanson de toile* or spinning song (traditionally viewed as a women's genre), the erotic religious ode, a song by a woman troubadour, and a letter by Heloise. In each instance, we find less a sense of oppression than of self-assertion, an assumption of the right to interrogate and to act.

A DIALECTICS OF THE UNCONSCIOUS: THE UNCANONIC LYRIC

1. The Chanson de Toile

A well-known Old French *chanson de toile* begins:

1. Bele Doette as fenestres se siet,
   Lit en un livre mais au cuer ne l'en tient;

---

9. "I imagine that our *trobairitz*, slaves of tradition, incapable of any analytical power, contented themselves with exploiting known themes, with employing current formulas, by simply reversing roles. We can speak only, in their work, of literary exercises, not, it is true, entirely devoid of merit. Hypothesis for hypothesis, it seems more natural to grant to these "noble and educated" women, a certain languor of mind, an obvious lack of taste, rather than any shocking lapse from modesty and decency." Jeanroy: 1, 316–17.

10. "The Difference of View," in *Reading Woman: Essays in Feminist Criticism* (New York: Columbia University Press, 1986), 28.

De son ami Doon li resovient
Q'en autres terres est alez tornoier.
    E or en ai dol!

[1–5]

Fair Doette sits at the windows
She reads in a book without taking it in;
She's thinking about her lover Doon
Who has gone to the tournaments in other lands.
    And how it grieves me![11]

The song goes on to recount dramatically the return of Doon's
squire, overcome by grief at having to report to his lady the death of her
husband in a tourney. She responds to the blow by determining to found
an abbey in which she will become a nun. But the abbey will not simply
be a monument to her love for the dead Doon; more insistently it will
exclude unfaithful lovers, and shelter those who have been harmed or
abused in love. Already of great size, it will continue to expand to
accommodate love's victims:

VIII. Bele Doette prist s'abaiie a faire,
    Qui mout est grande et adés serai maire;
    Toz cels et celes vodra dedanz atraire
    Qui por amor sevent peine et mal traire.
        E or en ai dol!
Por uostre amor deuenrai nonne a l'eglise Saint Paul.

[36–40]

Belle Doette began to build her abbey
Which is already big and soon will be bigger;
All those men and women she would attract inside
Who have known suffering and abuse for love.
    And how it grieves me!
For your love I will become a nun at Saint Paul's Church.

A good deal of sentimental nonsense has been written about this
song by those who have concentrated solely on the apparently pathetic
narrative of the grief-striken wife whose noble acts of self-abnegation
and commemoration appeared just the reverse of the shrewish com-
plaints of the "mal mariée."[12] Such naïve readings fail to take account
of the diegetic and linguistic anomalies that abound in the text.

---

11. *Chanter M'Estuet: Songs of the Trouvères.* Ed., Samuel N. Rosenberg and Hans
Tischler (Bloomington: Indiana University Press, 1981), 18. All translations mine unless
otherwise indicated.

12. Gaston Paris was offended by the *Chanson de mal mariée* which presented marriage, "'as a servitude from which the wife had the right to escape, and the jealous husband
as an enemy against whom everything may be permitted,' even though the only charge
against him was precisely that of being the husband." *Mélanges de littérature française,*
601 [Quoted by Jeanroy: 2, 302].

First, the song turns upon a juxtaposition of sensuality and religion:

"Ou est mes sires cui je doi tant amer?"

[22]

Where is my lord whom I must love so much?"

"Por vostre amor vestirai je la haire
Ne sor mon cors n'avra pelice vaire."

[28–29]

"For your love I will wear a hairshirt
Nevermore on my body to wear gleaming furs."

"Por vos ferai une abbaïe tele"

[31]

"For you I will make such an abbey"

"Si nus i vient qui ait s'amor fauseie,"

[33]

"If anyone comes there who has been false in love"

"*Por uostre amor deuenrai nonne a l'eglise Saint Paul*"

[31, 36, 41]

For your love I will become a nun at Saint Paul's Church

Then we must account for the multiple perspectives—some contra-dictory—the text uses to represent Belle Doette. Most evident are the omniscient and personal narrative viewpoints (third person and first person) unusual as a lyric combination. Doette is both third-person subject (principal actor) of the discourse *and* first-person speaking subject. The narrative ambivalence extends to her different social and do-mestic roles: she is secular noblewoman and, by the end of the song, a nun; she is wife, mistress, and widow. She is represented as both reader and poet (of refrain and lament); she is founder and builder of the abbey, abbess, and gatekeeper.

Finally, the song enacts two comprehensive movements: an initial rigorous separation of the masculine and feminine worlds according to the logic of historical reality, followed by a reversal of that division according to a scenario in which genders merge in an imaginative space projected from the feminine unconscious. From the first line (*Bele Doette as fenestres se siet*) the woman physically constitutes the line of demarcation between masculine and feminine, as well as controlling the narrative point of view. She motivates the inner space of the cha-teau—the sphere of the feminine—in contradistinction to the shadowy male world beyond the windows.

At the same time, from the first stanza, we find Doette endowed with an imaginative power that transforms the inner, domestic space to include a masculine presence—a presence created according to her own erotic economy. She rejects the heroes of the book she reads, to evoke an image of her own lover, Doon. The difference between her perception and imagination and that of the male figures appears in the confrontation between Doette and the squire who returns from the "far away lands" to report his master's death.

The squire represents fact, the sequential narrative of material presence or absence. Doette, on the other hand, demonstrates a more complex and different kind of perception. *Aisthesis*, sensual perception, motivates her intention of the world. This is a form of cognition in which the sensate, inner being—the *cuer* of line two—joins with the mind to project images of the world which are not necessarily material images.

According to the philosophical anthropology of John Scotus Eriugena (late ninth century), espoused by the Chartrians in the eleventh and twelfth centuries, gender should be considered rather as an accidental than an essential category of human existence. In the original divine model, Eriugena postulated, humans were not spatial but spiritual, and thus whole rather than divided into two sexes. Eriugena held that humans had external cognate faculties, *nous* (intellect) and *aisthesis* (sensual perception). On the basis of grammatical gender, *nous* was seen as "a kind of male in the soul" and *aisthesis*, a kind of female. All humans possess this dual configuration of faculties and thus contain within themselves, as part of their essential makeup, the "masculine" and "feminine" qualities of sense and intellect. Significantly, it is the so-called feminine quality of sensual perception, *aisthesis*, that integrates the outer being to the inner as a kind of messenger shuttling back and forth between them.[13]

Aisthesis provides a dialectical matrix for cognition in a manner that incorporates diverse and contradictory impulses. It encourages a layered, multilevel narrative whose logic incorporates the emotional unconscious. It is the opposite of the straightforward matrix of *historia*, i.e., narration according to an ideology of history so characteristic of the canonic medieval genres. In short, *aisthesis* authorizes a poetic expression grounded in desire, a narrative of mind and body. Women authors did not discover the principle, but their literature consistently exploits it beyond the potential males found in it.

In our *chanson de toile*, the first stanza establishes the inner space of

13. [*De Divisione Naturae*, ed. I. P. Sheldon-Williams (Dublin, 1972), 98; Migne, *Patrologia Latina* 122, 569C–D]. For a further development of this concept, see my article "Rewriting Marriage in the Middle Ages," *Romanic Review* (forthcoming, Winter, 1988). For a discussion of *aisthesis* related to medieval theories of imagination and judgment see Kathy Eden, *Poetic and Legal Fiction in the Aristotelian Tradition* (Princeton: Princeton University Press, 1986), 75–90.

Doette's being as one where sensual perception and rationality fuse. Doette's mind and body collaborate to project a fantasy of her real lover, Doon, perceived as preferable to the subject of the book which her inner being rejects: "*Lit en un livre mais au cuer ne l'en tient*" (2). In short, the imaginative space of the song is entirely given over to the mediation of the external world by Doette's inner faculty of *aisthesis*.

The male figure in this song is neither dominant nor powerful except as a focus of the woman's feelings. Indeed, despite traditional readings, one may argue that the dynamics of the poem turn on a progressive substitution of the feminine expressive space for masculine values. Traditional readings have failed to identify the ambivalent valence of Doette as signifier. In his edition of the poem, Constans gave the traditional explanation of Doette's name:

Doette. Diminutive of *Do*, nominative form of *Doon*. The wife bears the feminized form (here with the addition of a diminutive suffix) of the husband's name in accordance with old custom (and modern, outside of the large cities).[14]

This reading is philologically and culturally correct. In terms of the textual unconscious, however, we may see another system at work. In accord with the dual-perspective structure of the poem, "Doette" may equally be seen as a diminutive of Old French *doe* signifying "dowery," and its extension *doee*, "wife." Note how this reading reverses, at least analogically, the connotation of the husband's name. "Doon" is disyllabic, but a homophonic neighbor to the OFr. pair *don* (masc.), *done* (fem.) "gift." Liberality on the part of the courtly seigneur, as Chrétien de Troyes and others made clear, was a desideratum. To the extent that the dowery (*doe*) of the wife (*doee*) contributed significantly to the ability of the noble husband to distribute largesse (*don*), one may posit a reciprocal homology to the *Doon* >> *Doette* formula: Doon: Doette::Doette:Doon. The homology conveys both the dual perspective and the reversal of dominance from masculine to feminine in the song's dynamics.

Furthermore, *doement*, the action of bringing a dowery, or the dowery itself, has, as an extension, the connotation of an endowment to establish a religious foundation (church or abbey). In short, rather than a specific, historical individual, Doette signifies a universal condition of woman as a prime financial factor within the economy of a patriarchal culture. Her name may signify the feminine diminutive of her husband's, *Doon* >> *Doette*, but at this second level, it also figures the paradox of her condition: the dowery that constrains her to marriage in the first place, but which enables her gesture of autonomy once widowed.

14. L. Constans, *Chrestomathie de l'ancien français (IXe–XVe siècles)*. 1918 Reprint (New York: Stechert), 99, n.1.

The paradox of the woman's presence—as name and situation—destabilizes even the genre or tone of the song. A lament for the loss of a lover, it also celebrates a gain: the realization of her own name on her own terms. The lyrics assert Doette's power to protect her autonomy of action, an autonomy she is not about to surrender by considering remarriage.

We see this generic destabilizing at work in the linking of religion and sexuality. The pairing creates a burlesque undertone to the oxymoronic conjunction of elegy and celebration. For if the song stresses the register of grief (*dol, duel*) it also enacts the gesture of *doer* "donation," "endowment" of the abbey ostensibly as a material correlative of that grief. But *doer*, the verbal form of the seme *do-* in her name, also means "to gratify" as in the fulfillment of desire.[15] Doette implements both senses of *doer* in her "lament" in stanzas six and seven where she states and reiterates her intention of founding an abbey.

The term *"abbaïe"* itself becomes equivocal in this context. While we have no firm evidence for an equivocal meaning attached to the concept from this early date, attestations from the thirteenth century onward, including a passage in Jean de Meun's *Roman de la rose* and an octet from Villon's *Testament* (ll. 1551–58), link abbey with places of sexual indulgence. We read, for example, in a thirteenth-century song quoted by Godefroy:

> Mal et vilanie et pechié
> Fist tel pucelette
> Rendre en abiete
> Honnis soit de Dieu
> Qui me fist nonette.
> [13th c. French Song, *Somme le Roy*, ms. Troyes, f. 7a]

Evil, baseness, and shame made such a young virgin enter the abbey; may God curse the one who made me a nun.

Jean de Meun's jealous husband in Ami's discourse denounces abbeys and cloisters, and the women who inhabit them as notorious enemies of chastity, *Roman de la Rose*, 8983–991 (Lecoy edition): Chastity . . . certainly does not lack opponents: everywhere in cloisters and abbeys, the nuns are all her sworn enemies (8988–91).

Villon's passage occurs in the octets leading up to the "Ballade de Grosse Margot" with its famous refrain: *En ce bordeau ou tenons nostre estat!* [In this whorehouse where we keep our state]. In the octets immediately preceding this ballad, Villon associates religious foundations and prostitutes. Lines 1557–58 are clearly ironic: Si ira maint bon cres-

15. Godefroy's entry for *doer* gives the following example: "Veuillez que vostre mere m'ame de s'amour *doe*" (*Berte*, 864, Scheler).

tien/Voir l'abbaye ou il n'entre homme [There enters many a good Christian (masc.)/To visit the abbey where no male ever enters]. In the *Dictionnaire . . . érotique,* Pierre Guiraud comments: "abbaye des s'offre à tous, abbaye de clunis, 'whorehouse'. These expressions are slang words formed by analogy with such expressions as "Monte-à-regret abbey," "the gallows," "Saint-Lasche abbey," "goldbrickers union," where the abbey stands for the "common house," "the head-quarters" of the "guild" or "union." To the erotic variations we're dealing with in these cases, is added a religious implication: love is a "cult," the whorehouse a "convent" in which the prostitutes are the "priestesses," the "nuns," the "novices," and the Madame is the "ab-bess." As for the Abbey of Clunis, it is a pun on the Latin *clunis,* "but-tocks" (by extension, "ass") and the famous Abbey of Cluny (120).

2. Eros in the Cloister

While the specifically erotic connotations of Doette's lament may be speculative, the linking of religion and sexuality, as an assertion of equal access to sensual enjoyment constitutes an important element of feminine self-expression in the early Middle Ages. A nun named Cons-tance in the convent of Le Ronceray (Angers) equates the written page with the body, and reading with intercourse in a late eleventh-century letter, written in Latin to an older monk, Baudri of Bourgeuil:

> Night hateful to my study, envious of her who reads. . . .
> I put the letter under my left breast—
>   they say that's nearest to the heart. . . .
> At last, weary, I tried to get to sleep,
>   but love that has been wakened knows no night. . . .
> I lay asleep—no, sleepless—because the page you wrote,
>   though lying on my breast, had set my womb on fire.[16]

Constance joins such eroticism to equally fervid affirmations of chastity: "I am chaste, I am chaste in manner, I wish to live chaste, O if only I might live as the bride of God!" "Custom and law guard our love,/ A chaste life justifies our games."[17] Like *Belle Doette,* her rhetoric thus deploys two languages in tense balance: the erotic and the spiritual. Constance's verse letter or *carmen,* responds to one previously written to her by Baudri. Yet she imparts to her letter a vivid eroticism wholly

16. Quoted in Peter Dronke, *Women Writers of the Middle Ages: A Critical Study of Texts from Perpetua to Marguerite Porete* (Cambridge: Cambridge University Press, 1984), 88.

17. Lines 114–15, 122–23 of *Perlegi vestram . . .* Letter of Constance to Baudri, 239, 346–47, of *Les Oeuvres poétiques de Baudri de Bourgueil (1046–1130),* ed. Phyllis Abra-hams (Paris: Champion, 1926).

original, as Dronke points out. That eroticism, however, exists without contradition as a kind of eroticism of virginity. In Constance's letter, the same themes found in Baudri become charged by her explicit use of her own body as the expressive space on which she maps the contending impulses of sexuality and chastity. Whereas Baudri treats the erotic wordplay as a literary game of outdoing Ovid—the *Heroides* are the principal subtext—Constance transforms the stakes by figuring a psychological drama in which sexuality and spirituality constitute not so much contradictions as complementary desires on a single complex continuum.

She exploits the potential of *aisthesis,* affective perception, for evoking images that transform the act of writing and reading into sensual terms without the material basis of the sexual act. This enables Constance to articulate her sexual desire while avoiding the material fulfillment that would destroy the equally desired countervailing pole of chastity.[18]

Constance's focus on the erotic tension of their exchange, rather than on its spiritual resolution gives dramatic impact to her verse, but more importantly dialogizes the issues which Baudri raised to begin with. His song seems pale when set against Constance's. Nevertheless, Constance continually keeps the image of Baudri's letter before her. If she illustrates the graphic equivalence of the female body as an expressive space of erotic tension, she also includes Baudri.

Beginning with her first line:

> Perlegi vestram studiosa indagine cartam
> Et tetigi nuda carmina vestra manu
>
> I read your letter with embracing zeal
> with my hand I have touched your naked songs

she interweaves his language and thought consistently into the fabric of her response. The first word, *Perlegi* "I read," announces her compliance with the repeated imperative at the beginning of his letter: "*Perlege . . . Perlege . . . Perlege.*" Her first two lines distill a series of word games from his letter into a tight response that both echoes and transforms the original. She does not imitate Baudri, but rather makes her rhetoric perform the zealous enfolding of his letter (*studiosa inda-*

---

18. Constance's technique offers a practical application of Aristotle's theory of the psychological image worked out in the third book of *De Anima.* "To describe the workings of the imagination's power to receive, retain, and retrieve images, Aristotle depends largely on his treatment of perception (*aisthesis*). Imagination or *phantasia* is a kind of movement activated by perception, and its images (*phantasmata*) resemble percepts (*aisthemata*), except that they lack matter. These images, moreover, enable the mind to think." (My emphasis). Kathy Eden, *Poetic and Legal Fiction in the Aristotelian Tradition* (Princeton: Princeton University Press, 1986), 75.

gine cartam—she recharges the equivocal word *indagine*[19] picked up
from him) announced in line one. Her rhetoric does so by conjoining
their bodies and minds in the one *carmen*. Her body, like her ode, has
become a representative space for both of them as she provides him with
a lesson in erotico-spiritual creative writing:

> Hoc jacet in gremio dilecti schedula nostri,
> Ecce locata meis subjacet uberibus

[68–69]

> Here lies on my breast the record of our desire
> There placed lying under my breasts.

3. The Uncanonic Canso

In a secular setting where women enjoyed greater political freedom
as in the Langue d'oc region, we find examples of women turning the
lyric canon of the *canso*, or love song, into a subtle dialectical instrument for suggesting the difference in the equation *canso* (song), *cors*
(body) when the poetic voice is that of a woman.

One is tempted to call the Comtessa de Dia, the earliest of the
trobairitz or female troubadours, the René Magritte of that most canonic of all poetic forms of twelfth-century aristocratic culture, the *canso*. Like Magritte's 1928 painting, *The Treason of Images* ["Ceci n'est
pas une pipe"], the Comtessa's *cansos* expose the rule-governed forms of
the genre, forcing us to reflect upon its (male) narcissism. At the same
time, she deploys a rhetoric of sensual perception that reclaims the
genre for the feminine other—reified as the love object or *domna* in the
canonic examples.

Bernart de Ventadorn, the most representative troubadour of the first
period, provided an *ars poetica* of the genre in a song whose first stanza
reads:

> Chantars no pot gaire valer
> si d'ins dal cor no mou lo chans,
> ni chans no pot dal cor mover
> si no i es fin'amors coraus.
> Per so es mos chantars cabaus
> qu'en joi d'amor ai et enten
> la boch' e·ls olhs e·l cor e·l sen

[1–7][20]

---

19. *Indago* possesses the connotations of the hunt, war, and philosophical introspec-
tion associated with the metaphoric language of love. *Indago* connotes encircling, closing
when hunters encircle game with nets; the surrounding of enemies in a war; and searching
or examining or investigating as in philosophical reflection.

20. *The Songs of Bernart de Ventadorn*, ed. Stephen G. Nichols et al. (Chapel Hill:
University of North Carolina Press, 1962), 81.

There is no use in singing if the song does not spring from the heart; and the song cannot spring from the heart if there is no true love there. And so my singing is superior because I have joy in love and devote my lips and eyes and heart and mind to it.

Bernart here codifies the convention whereby poetry and love become synonymous. The song is a rhetorical mirror showing how poetic language arises from the same source, the seat of the inner being, as the sentiment of *fin'amors*. The poet's body, fragmented into the sense organs in the last line of the stanza, exists primarily to create a poetry— *chantars, lo chans, chans, chantars*—whose chiasmatic symmetry will reflect its source: the poet's body.

The aggressively masculine rhyme scheme of the *coblas unisonans*—monorhymed stanzas—underlines the exclusion of the feminine, the ostensible coefficient of *fin'amors*. When he does mention the woman later, she functions, like the song, as a mirror, confirming, and prolonging, the poet's existence:

> C'aicel jorns me semble nadaus
> c'ab sos bels olhs espiritaus
> m'esgarda, mas so fai tan len
> c'us sols dias me dura cen.

[46–49]

The day when she looks at me with her beautiful, spiritual eyes seems like Christmas to me; and she does it so lingeringly that one single day lasts me a hundred.

The Comtessa, too, makes the *canso* a kind of rhetorical mirror. Rather than the Narcissuslike mirror of solitary reflection of Bernart de Ventadorn, though, she makes a gendered mirror that focuses on sexual division as a function of amorous misperception. In terms of the troubadour canon, her *cansos* must ultimately be seen as uncourtly because they expose masculine self-reflexivity—the exclusion of the feminine viewpoint (in distinction to the views of the feminine which abound in the canonic *canso*)—as a major impediment to love.

One of her best-known *cansos* self-consciously incorporates rhyme schemes based on grammatical gender to represent the philosophical differences between male and female in the love situation defined by the genre. By playing on its gender presuppositions—principally the expectation that the poet-speaker will be male—the Comtessa throws these expectations into bold relief. In her song, love and poetry are only incidentally synonymous, and so undermine the formalist assumptions of the *ars poetica* codified by Bernart de Ventadorn. For the Comtessa, the *canso* becomes an instrument of shared analysis and communication.

In *Ab ioi et ab ioven m'apais*, she uses grammatical rhymes to assign key words from the courtly vocabulary reciprocally to herself (the poetic I) and her lover. Poetry provides the matrix for her lesson, but a poetry that analyzes the love situation in terms of both partners rather than playing the role of a substitution for love by one of them.

> Ab ioi et ab ioven m'apais
> e iois e iovens m'apaia,
> car mos amics es lo plus gais
> per qu'ieu sui coindet' e gaia;
> e pois eu li sui veraia,
> be taing q'el me sia verais,
> c'anc de lui amar no m'estrais
> ni ai cor que m'en estraia.
>
> [1–8]²¹

I feed myself on pleasure and youth/ and pleasure and youth feed me,/ because my lover is the most gay,/ that's why I am beautiful and gay;/ and since I am so faithful to him,/ I want him to be faithful to me,/ for I can never stop loving him/ nor do I have the heart to stop.

The key words occur in the grammatical rhyme, a device by which the same word can be given a masculine and feminine form. The first and last two lines of the stanza end in grammatical rhymes based on two verbs: *apaisar* "nourish" (1–2), and *estraire* "take away" (7–8). The middle four lines rhyme variants of adjectives having to do with physical and ethical states: *gai* (3–4), *verais* (5–6). The verb forms refer to the female speaker/poet, the active partner in the love; the adjectives ascribe the same states of reciprocity in love to both partners.

The uncanonic basis for the song derives from the identification of the speaker, the active agent in declaring love, with the feminine love-object of the traditional *canso*. The Comtessa does not simply reverse the masculine-feminine roles as Jeanroy suggested (notes 8 and 9 above); she speaks from the marginalized position of the *domna*, or love object itself. The effect is akin to that of a speaking statue; the created object addressing its creator(s).

Line four—*per q'ieu sui coindet'e gaia*—provides the pivotal substitution of this song. *Coindet(a)* is the feminine diminutive of *coind*, *conhda*. As used here, the adjectives *coindet'e gaia* symbolize the dual status of the Comtessa. *Coinde* derived from Latin, *cognitus*, "known" which originally connoted one "who knows something."²² The first troubadours gave it the sense of "attractive, gracious, agreeable." In the poetry of Guilhem IX and Jaufré Rudel, the term may be one of self-reference or describe the psychological effect of love on a male.²³ The

21. Gabrielle Kussler-Ratyé, "Les Chansons de la comtesse Béatrix de Dia," *Archivum Romanicum* 1 (1917), 161–82.

22. Glynnis M. Cropp, *Le Vocabulaire courtois des troubadours de l'époque classique* (Geneva: Droz, 1975), 108–09. Further references in the text.

23. Guilhem IX: "Mout ai estat *cuendes e gais*" [I was very pleasant and gay] ["Pos de chantar m'es pres talenz," l. 29[. Jaufré Rudel: "Et quant hom ve son jauzimen/ Es ben

implication in such cases within the context of courtly society, Glynnis Cropp argues, was the necessity, for a lover and poet, "to know (*connaître*) the best way of conducting oneself agreeably, to know how (*savoir*) to please" (Glynnis Cropp, 109). Later, with poets of Bernart de Ventadorn's generation, the two epithets, *conhd'e gai*, are used to designate qualities of the *domna*. Thereafter, the term *coinde* tends not to be used to describe the woman.

Only the Comtessa de Dia uses these marked terms simultaneously to describe the poet as lover and the woman as love object. By conflating the two roles in one, she does not simply mark her song as extra-ordinary. She also recasts the courtly lexical register of her song, marking it with ethical, psychological and erotic descriptors that assert a feminine activism in a normally masculine code.

The noncanonical expression, *coindet'e gaia*, sets ethical parameters for the kind of courtly knowledge *coindeta* denotes: reciprocal fidelity (*Veraia/verais*). By setting a standard of fidelity herself, she urges a standard of ethical reciprocity in love. The Comtessa does not command reciprocal behavior—although as the *midons* or *domna*, seigneurial honorifics designating the lady as lord in troubadour poetry, she presumably might have done. Instead, the Comtessa's speaker uses logic: "Since I am faithful (*veraia*) to him/I certainly hold that he ought to be (subjunctive) faithful (*verais*) to me." The root (ver-) shows the similarity of principle, while the grammatical rhyme figures the difference in practice: *verais* may not be *veraia*.

Coindeta also casts the erotic register in a light of feminine insight. By her explicit affirmation of desire, the Comtessa takes the *canso* back to its prefigured form in the *vers* of Guilhem IX, the first troubadour. Lines 1–2, 7–8, identify key terms of *fin'amors* as applicable to both subject and object, male and female, the speaker and her lover.

She focuses in the first two lines on the equivocal terms *joi e joven* which she links to the verb *apaisar* "to nourish." The terms link inversely with the speaking voice: in line one, they are predicates of the speaker, "I feed myself with *joi e joven;*" in line two, they are the subjects of the verb, the speaker, its object: "*jois e jovens* feed me." The meaning of the two words ranges from unambiguously sensual complements of *amor* for Guilhem IX ("Et er totz mesclatz d'amor et de joy e de joven"), to moral qualities of human love in Guilhem's immediate successors. In the second half of the twelfth century, the terms were applied to the courtly spirit of the *domna* (Glynnis Cropp, 419).

In the circularity of her first two lines, the Comtessa creates a usage of *joi e joven* without precedent in their doubly gendered referen-

---

razos e d'avinen/ Qu'om sia plus *coyndes e guays.*" [And when a man sees his delight/ it is right and fitting/ that he be more agreeable and gay] ["Belhs m'es l'estius e·L temps floritz," ll. 5–7].

tiality—figuring both the motivation of the speaker as poet and the poet as *domna*—and in the evocation of their full range of meanings, sensual as well as moral. The circular rhetoric cleverly evokes the different meanings as one repeats the lines: *apaisar* has the dual meaning of to nourish and to slake; the moral connotations of *joi e joven* suggest the former meaning of *apaisar*, while the sensual connotations call up the notion of satiety. Although the moral and sexual connotations may be associated, they are not the same. Once again, the Comtessa uses the grammatical nuance of gender differentiation to suggest profound philosophical differences in the attitudes and consequences of love. She has betrayed the *canso* into expressing images of sensual interrogation never intended by the troubadours.

4. Conclusion: Heloise and the Alterity of Aisthesis

The difference of viewpoint expressed by the Comtessa's songs is not dissimilar to those we have already seen, and could find in many other examples of women's writing of the period. Such examples remind us that there was a powerful culture of women reading and writing in the Middle Ages, marginal in terms of political power, but located squarely in the mainstream of society. In an extreme form, their outlook may be summed up by Heloise's statement to Abelard—quoted with such amazement by Jean de Meun's jealous husband:

> "Se li empereres de Rome,
> souz cui doivent estre tuit home,
> me daignet valair prendre a fame
> et fere moi du monde dame,
> si vodroie je mieux, fet ele,
> et dieu a tesmoign en apele,
> estre ta putain apelee,
> que emperiz coronee".
> [Lecoy: 8777–8794]

"If the emperor of Rome, to whom all men should be subject, deigned to wish to take me as his wife and make me mistress of the world, I would prefer," she said, "and I call God as my witness, to be called your whore, than to be crowned empress."

Of the women we have looked at, Heloise has the broadest scope, the most deeply philosophical outlook. She does not simply express an attitude toward marriage in her letters to Abelard. Even more than her contemporary women writers, she has strongly articulated feelings about the relation of the personal to the institutional. Whether it be marriage, the religious life, or an amorous relationship, Heloise and the others question cultural assumptions, articulated in canonic texts, which do not recognize their difference of view.

Heloise will voluntarily associate herself to Abelard on condition that their bond be one of mind and body joined. That is her definition of love (*amor*) and the social bond (*amicitia*) predicated upon it. "My spirit (*animus*) was not with me, but with you; now especially if it is not with you, it is nowhere: truly it has no purpose without you."[24] Heloise here articulates the same principle of reciprocity we saw in the Comtessa; like Constance and the Comtessa, she encircles and then incorporates the male viewpoint into a more inclusive perspective. Reciprocity, the ideal of mind and body joined by *voluptas*, the principle of *aisthesis*, motivates her letter. Her suffering and fidelity have proved that the "carnal pleasures I delighted in with you" [tecum carnali fruerer voluptate][25] were in fact amor rather than simple male libido.

Writing, for Heloise, will be to their present state of physical separation what the caress was earlier, an act of contact: "Since I am robbed of your presence, at least by offerings of your words—in ready supply with you—present me the delight of your image" (Monfrin, 116). Heloise's letters are carefully constructed rhetorical propositions adumbrating a plan for a renewal of their intercourse adapted to their changed circumstances. With great dialectical force and perceptive analysis, Heloise lays out the conditions for a union no longer based simply on physical love, although far from devoid of physical desire, as her second letter makes abundantly clear. That union must be predicated on willingness—particularly on Abelard's part—to see her as she is in body and spirit, a spirit continually dialogized by the body: "more than ever you should fear for me, now that my incontinence can no longer find in you a remedy" (Letter 4).

Heloise's frank analyses, like those of the other women writers, uncover a fundamental truth about love and its relationship to the feminine. They show the power of the noncanonical to express the essential contradiction of humans poised between "the thin ice of language and the ocean of the psyche." For me, the greatest testimony to the prescience of these women occurs in rediscovering their insights echoed in the words of a twentieth-century philosopher, Emmanuel Levinas:

The difference of the sexes does not lie in . . . the duality of two complementary terms. For two complementary terms presuppose a pre-existing whole. To say that sexual duality presupposes a whole, is to presuppose love as fusion. But the pathos of love lies in the insurmountable duality of beings. It is a relationship

24. From Heloise's first letter to Abelard. Peter Abelard, *Historia Calamitatum*, ed. Jacques Monfrin (Paris: Vrin, 1978), 116.
25. Monfrin, *Historia Calamitatum*, 117.

with the fugitive. A relationship does not in itself neutralize alterity, but preserves it. The pathos of desire lies in the fact of being two.[26]

Medieval women writers of the twelfth century understood Levinas' concept of "le pathétique de l'amour" only too well, as we have seen. The duality of love was not in itself uncanonical; their attempt to express the second viewpoint, the view from beyond the divide, was.

26. Emmanuel Levinas, *Le Temps et l'autre* (Paris: Quadrige/Presses Universitaires de France, 2nd Edition, 1985), 78.

ENGLISH SHOWALTER, JR.

Writing off the Stage: Women Authors and Eighteenth-Century Theater

The great playwrights of the Century of Louis XIV endowed their nation with a corpus of dramatic literature which, for a century and a half, defined literary greatness for the French. The preeminence of the Comédie Française depended on more than taste and tradition, however; royal institutions ensured that the theater, the easiest genre to regulate, would also be the most secure and lucrative for writers. For simple practical reasons—the number of people involved, the need for a fixed site, the public nature of the spectacle—a clandestine stage was almost inconceivable. The theaters of the fairs and street entertainers occasionally flouted the law with a parody or political satire, but these impromptu performances could not last long. Unlike the broader publishing industry, in short, the theaters were successfully controlled by the state, and authors who wrote for the Comédie Française were rewarded with performance royalties, publication privileges similar to a copyright, and memberships in the academies. Although the authors' freedom of expression was severely restricted, their other rights were better protected than in any other mode of publication.

Very few women enjoyed the economic benefits of writing for the stage, however. Barbara Mittman remarks that "the eighteenth century could claim a dozen or more women whose works were performed on the public stages of Paris—a considerable increase over the three or four that the seventeenth century had produced."[1] Mittman's figures are low for both centuries, especially the eighteenth; but simply counting authors gives a misleading impression. Most of the eighteenth-century women playwrights were in some way marginal. At least seven women wrote a play for the Italians, two for the Théâtre des Variétés, and one for Nicolet's theater; by the standards of the time, these were automatical-

---

1. "Women and the Theatre Arts," in *French Women and the Age of Enlightenment*, ed. Samia I. Spencer (Bloomington: Indiana U P, 1984), 163.

ly less prestigious works, regardless of their intrinsic merit. All but one of those plays, as well as works by four other women, were of one, two, or three acts, and were therefore considered minor. Finally, the majority of these authors wrote only one play that was performed in public. This small output inevitably reduces their significance as playwrights, and the regularity with which women abandoned the theater after one play points to a powerful deterrent force at work.

Although the number of women playwrights in Old Regime France was low, there were some illustrious names, and contrary to Mittman's conclusion a tradition seems to have begun with some vigor and then died out. In the seventeenth century, Marie-Catherine de Villedieu wrote for the Comédie Française in the 1660s before turning exclusively to the novel; before the end of the century she was followed by Catherine Bernard and Antoinette Deshoulières. Between 1700 and 1717, Marie-Anne Barbier had four full-length verse tragedies staged, and Madeleine de Gomez three. But it appears that constraints tightened in the eighteenth century. Barbier and Gomez openly expressed an interest in fame, and they inserted themselves with pride into a tradition of women writers, including Madeleine de Scudéry, Henriette de La Suze, and Antoinette Deshoulières *fille*, as well as her mother and the other dramatists. But from 1717 to 1749, no new plays by women were produced. In 1749 Marie-Anne Du Boccage tried to revive the sense of tradition with *Les Amazones*, but the play failed; and Françoise de Graffigny, whose *Cénie* in 1750 and *La Fille d'Aristide* in 1758 were the last full-length plays at the Comédie Française by a woman until the Revolution, sounded a note of modesty and self-deprecation, both in her prefaces and in her private correspondence, and did not want to be regarded as an author or as a bluestocking.

The relative exclusion of women from this field had a far-reaching impact, even though the eighteenth-century French theater has not retained its place in the canon as the seventeenth century's has. Leading tragic dramatists like Crébillon and Voltaire would be stunned to discover that even the best of their numerous tragedies go unread and unstaged today, while "frivolous" novels and tales are studied and respected, and Marivaux is regarded as the century's great dramatist. The continuing revision of the canon has, in recent years, led to the rediscovery of several women novelists—Tencin, Riccoboni, Charrière, for example—who, like their male colleagues, took advantage of the freedom of a minor or forbidden genre to produce an original literature that is still gaining in stature. Given the scant attention now paid to the mainstream theater of numerous prolific male authors like Baculard d'Arnaud, Destouches, Gresset, Houdar de La Motte, La Chaussée, and Marmontel, it would be remarkable if, by modern standards, any of the rare women playwrights had coped more successfully with the limitations of the stage. While one or two of their plays might well claim as much right to inclusion in the recent Pléiade anthology as most of the ones chosen, the rediscovery of lost works is not the only reason for studying them. It is equally important to realize that the institutional privilege of the theater disenfranchised women in fact if not in principle, and in denying them the possibility of writing for the stage effectively disbarred them from writing for a living.

The careers of the four women—Barbier, Gomez, Du Boccage, and Graffigny—who managed at least to have a full-length play staged reveal many of the factors that enabled them to succeed where other women failed, and also many of the obstacles, enacted in regulations or simply established in custom, that only hindered them but discouraged other women entirely. All four began with close connections to the literary world, often to the theater itself. They needed the strong support of male friends, lending plausibility to the inevitable rumor that a man was the real author. Even when her first play succeeded brilliantly, none of the women made a real career of writer for the stage, although many men of little talent managed it; Barbier's four tragedies and one comedy constitute the greatest number of plays by one woman staged at the Comédie Française until George Sand's sixth was produced in 1888. But they did not lose interest in writing; they turned to another genre, or wrote plays without trying to have them produced.

For those who were writing for the income, abandoning the theater entailed a real sacrifice. In rough terms, the author of a five-act play was entitled to one-ninth of the box office receipts, as long as they did not fall below 500 *livres* for two consecutive performances. To illustrate what this might mean, Graffigny's popular play *Cénie* ran for 25 performances in 1750 with an average box office of 2153 *livres*. Actual figures on her royalties are not available, but must have been close to 4000 *livres*. The first edition of her *Lettres d'une Péruvienne*, in 1747, one of the most popular novels of the century, brought her a mere 300 *livres*. Even after the success of *Cénie*, when Malesherbes helped Graffigny reclaim her rights to the novel from the original publisher, so that she could bring out a revised edition with a privilege, she received only 900 *livres*.[2] The conclusion is inescapable that social and institutional barriers to staging a play proved a fatal deterrent to women. As a result, most of the century's best known women writers—Tencin, Riccoboni, Charrière, Du Châtelet, Madame Roland—depended for their live-

2. See my articles "*Les Lettres d'une Péruvienne: composition, publication, suites*" (*Archives et Bibliothèques de Belgique*, 54 [1983]: 14–28) and "The Beginnings of Madame de Graffigny's Literary Career" in *Essays on the Age of Enlightenment in Honor of Ira O. Wade*, ed. Jean Macary (Genève, Paris: Droz, 1977), 293–304. Claude Alasseur has detailed the economics of the Comédie Française of the eighteenth century in *La Comédie Française au 18e siècle, étude économique* (Paris, La Haye: Mouton, 1967).

lihood on some other source of income, often a husband or inherited wealth. For women, writing was sometimes an avocation, sometimes a form of self-expression, sometimes an obsession; but it was not a livelihood, as it was for a host of male hacks.

The present low regard for eighteenth-century theater is ironic, for it was a theatrical age. Sociability, one of the era's most highly prized qualities, was primarily an art of self-presentation. The literature of the time revels both in describing the art and in exposing the artifice. Men and women played unequal roles, however, and the theater reflects this situation both in the plays and in the fate of women playwrights. As Laclos's Marquise de Merteuil explained with acid precision, Valmont's bad reputation simply becomes part of his role, even with the virtuous Présidente. He chooses his own stage and invents his own characters. For women the choices are restricted; they must play a role scripted for them by society, and they must never break out of it. They must behave so that they may be taken by surprise at any time and still appear to be in character. The least involuntary gesture, a tear, a sigh, even a private action like the Princesse de Clèves knotting ribbons alone in her pavilion, can betray the true self and lead to ruin.

This inequality would be handicap enough, but women's roles demand that they be reserved, if not silent. They must not assert even their virtue too ostentatiously; the *prudes*, who dramatize their strict morality, and the *dévotes*, who dramatize their piety, drew the satirists' scorn as surely as the aging coquettes and the bluestockings. Much eighteenth-century literature is built around the pretext that justifies the heroine's display of her virtue. In Graffigny's last play, Aristide's daughter sells herself into bondage, a shocking gesture, but simply the logical extension of all the dutiful daughters who settle their fathers' debts in the bonds of marriage. Outside literature, however, most never have the chance to confront the world with the magnitude of their sacrifice; it is taken for granted, or worse yet, assumed to fulfill the woman's own desire. Graffigny's farfetched plot, in other words, legitimates the woman's speaking out and even acting. What she says and does, however, represents a far more routine and ordinary human reality.

Obviously, the heroine's brief empowering as a victim pushed to the limit may also symbolize a woman's coming to writing. Writing, especially for the stage, threatened a woman's reputation. Graffigny's other stage heroine, Cénie, wishes to have her confession torn from her, just as Graffigny herself wished to have her manuscript torn from her. Only in this way could she present herself to the public without seeming proud and bold. Even so, she felt constrained to write in prose rather than poetry, lest she seem too ambitious. The dilemma, or double bind, extends even to the dedication of *La Fille d'Aristide:* Graffigny must simultaneously praise her patroness, the Empress Maria Theresa, and obey an express order not to; she must present the play as a tribute while denying its worth and the Empress's need for it.

These women's plays, produced under adverse circumstances, thus merit some special attention; if read attentively they tell something of their authors' struggles. This is not to claim a distinctive mode for women's drama; Voltaire's Zaïre is surely as much a martyr to silence and a patriarchal order as any heroine of the century. It is to suggest rather that the conventional plots, stock characters, and formulaic speeches conveyed a truth to which we are no longer fully sensitive. Both male and female authors were drawn toward pathetic heroines, silenced by their own sense of honor, paralyzed by their own loyalties, victimized by their own virtue; and as the century progressed, the heroes also tended to become pathetic. In many cases, a providential ending appears to undermine even the implicit criticism of the existing political order; but it is our distance from the situation that allows us to prefer a realistically hopeless outcome or a character who revolts by cynically exploiting the social fictions. The relief of a staged happy ending did not prevent contemporary spectators from knowing how most real conflicts were resolved; and an up-beat finale did not wipe out the spectacle of suffering in the first four acts. A general rereading of eighteenth-century French theater is no doubt overdue; if women authors are privileged here, it is because their lives make it easier to sense the authentic human voice masked by a conventional discourse.

Of all the women playwrights of the century, Marie-Anne Barbier was the most outspokenly feminist. Her life is little known; born in Orléans around 1670, she frequented a literary society that included Boursault, Pellegrin, and Bignon. By her own account, in the preface to her first play, *Arrie et Petus*, she was urged to write for the stage by Boursault, who had read some of her elegies and who knew her taste for the theater. As happened to virtually all women writers, her works were attributed to a man, Pellegrin, although the abbé de La Porte reasoned that she was neither rich nor beautiful enough to have motivated Pellegrin to sacrifice his writings to her glory, and that therefore she probably wrote them herself under his guidance. Writing just two decades later, La Porte gave the date of her death incorrectly—it was 1742—and he failed to mention that she was married and had a daughter.[3]

Barbier's first three plays are dedicated to women patrons, her prefaces take up feminist issues, and her plays always have strong female

3. Abbé Joseph de La Porte, *Histoire littéraire des femmes françoises* (Paris: Lacombe, 1769), vol. 4, 84–93.

characters. In the preface to *Arrie et Petus*, she discusses the reactions to it:[4]

> For the rest people found it good, maybe better than I ought to have hoped, since some took the occasion to say that a woman was incapable of doing so well. Truly I would never have imagined that what pleased about my work would count against me, or that anyone would refuse people of our sex the merit of producing good things. I realize that one could praise my play no higher than by finding it better than a woman could do, and that my vanity should be flattered. But I confess I was not insensitive to that injustice, and I could not help feeling annoyed that people wished to rob me of the most precious fruit of my labor. [xiv]

To buttress her case for women's ability to write, she cites her recent predecessors Scudéry, La Suze, the Deshoulières, and Bernard (xv).

The plot of *Arrie et Petus* sets the pattern for the other three plays; Petus and Arrie love each other, and their love is politically forbidden. Petus conspires against Claudius, is discovered, and plans to escape; but Arrie refuses, preferring an honorable suicide, to which she summons Petus in dying. In the preface to her next play, *Cornelie, mère des Gracques*, she stated some of her principles of dramatic composition:

> Cornelie, daughter of Scipio Africanus, and mother of the Gracchi, was one of the most illustrious ladies of Ancient Rome. Her love of the people, her courage amid dangers, and her constance in adversity shone forth so brightly during the Tribunates of her two sons that I thought I could put nothing on the stage more glorious for our sex [83] . . . . Nothing is more capable of producing interesting situations than love between two people whose parents are irreconcilable enemies. The conflict of love and duty produces the sort of feelings that are the soul of Tragedy. [84]

Like the first play, *Cornelie* ends with a suicide, and the third play, *Tomyris*, concludes with a murder, a death in combat, and two more suicides. The intransigeance of all the passions, especially love, which is supremely irrational, combined with an absolute inflexibility of principles, means that no solution is ever possible, except death. The characters stall for time, but even when an accident provides a way out, honor usually prevents them from taking it. The plays, more Racinian than Corneillean, show people waiting in forlorn anguish for the inevitable to occur.

4. The works of the women playwrights are cited from the following source editions; the translations are my own: Graffigny: *Œuvres complètes*, New edition (Paris: Briand, 1821); Barbier: *Théâtre de Mademoiselle Barbier* (Paris: Briasson, 1745); Gomez: *Habis*, tragédie (A Paris, chez Pierre Ribou, 1714; *Marsidie, reine des Combres*, 1716, in *Le Nouveau Théâtre François* (Utrecht: Etienne Neaulme, 1735), v. 7.; *Cléarque, tyran d'Heraclée*, 1717, dans *Le Nouveau Théâtre François* (Utrecht: Étienne Neaulme, 1733), v. 4; *Semiramis*, 1716, in *Le Nouveau Théâtre François* (Utrecht: Étienne Neaulme, 1737), v. 9; Du Boccage: *Recueil des Œuvres* (Lyon: Frères Perisse, 1762 [1792]), 2 vols.

The regular repetition of Racinian despair in the early eighteenth century suggests that French audiences continued to find it a persuasive image of their condition. Some of Cornelie's lines invite contemporary application: "Force the people to be happy, what a new kind of slavery!/ Already you speak the language of the Senate" (II, 5); "You know the Gauls, they are an unconquered people,/ Who count freedom as the supreme good" (III, 4). One might describe Barbier's heroines as theorists of passive resistance. Even in the Optimistic midcentury when the tragic mode gave way to the pathetic, the passivity remained; the characters waited just as forlornly, but waiting was more often rewarded by Providence. And even as French minds were turning away from the divine order and toward the political, the plight of powerless women still served to represent man's fate, in Montesquieu's harem and Diderot's nunnery. It is perhaps no accident that Racine's greatest figures were women; in his Jansenist universe where humans struggle in a contest they are fated to lose, it is as if the tragic heroines reenact women's usual social roles writ heroically large, while the heroes, confronting an unaccustomed sense of powerlessness, appear weak, unnatural, diminished—in a word, feminized.

Barbier's final play, La Mort de César, exposes the exhaustion of the classical formula, all the more because Shakespeare's version of the events is so well known. In Barbier, the characters have no flaws and the political question is ignored; the story is built around love conflicts and propelled by the doubts and hesitations of the leading men. Or rather, the political conflict is transposed into the domestic and sentimental sphere; the sign of Caesar's authoritarian ambitions and the proof of their danger lie in his arbitrary treatment of the women. Antoine and Octavie, Caesar's niece, are in love, as are Brutus and Porcie, Caton's daughter; Caesar decides to marry Porcie to Antoine, Octavie to Brutus. As usual, Barbier's women hold more rigidly to their principles than the men: Octavie warns her uncle that if she marries Brutus she will no longer be free to denounce the conspiracy. One might see in this attitude a tactic of the powerless, forcing the patriarchy to self-destruct by a "work-to-rule" adherence to their subordinate status.

The most generous reading, however, cannot completely dissipate the problems in making Octavie's engagement the central issue in Caesar's assassination. The play was poorly received, and Barbier was severely criticized for taking liberties with historical facts. After its failure, Barbier wrote no more; but with five plays staged and her outspoken defense of a female tradition, she clearly could have served as a model for later women playwrights. Instead, she seems to be the last representative of the seventeenth-century "femme savante," about to succumb to social ridicule and institutional obstacles. None of her plays were revived.

Madeleine de Gomez was born Madeleine Poisson in 1684, into a theatrical family: her grandparents, parents, and brother were all actors, and her grandfather had written for the stage. The biographical dictionaries say that she married a Spanish nobleman, believing him to be rich, only to discover that he was deep in debt, and that she was thereby forced to write to earn a living. Her first plax, *Habis,* was produced in 1714 and enjoyed considerable success. It was revived in 1732, an honor reserved for only 56 of the 719 new plays staged by the Comédie Française between 1701 and 1774. Lancaster says that only four other plays of the period 1700–1715 had greater success and that *Habis* is the most successful tragedy written by a woman in France.[5]

Needless to say, Gomez was accused of having had a man write her plays for her, and she replied bluntly in the preface to *Habis:*

I am too jealous of my glory to suffer patiently that anyone take it from me or share it; and I would blush with shame to accept praise that belonged to another. If it seems surprising that a woman of my age undertook a work of this importance, people should get over their surprise by looking at the women who have immortalized their name. I can even say on behalf of my sex that the works of its mind are no longer regarded as prodigies. One cannot then, without offending the sex, deny me the merit of having made this play, alone, and without any help; and I cannot imagine that there are people bold enough to say or imply that they had a hand in the versification or the story.

The plot centers on an aging tyrant, Melgoris, king of the Cinettes, who long ago killed his grandson, Habis, because of an oracle predicting that the grandson would take his supreme power from him. Since then, he has held his own daughter prisoner. But Habis is of course alive, and in fact the leader of Melgoris's own triumphant armies. As the play begins, Melgoris is about to marry Erixène, whose father promised her in return for Melgoris's military aid; predictably, she and Habis are in love. Rumors of Habis's return circulate. Melgoris's old fear and cruelty rise up again; his daughter, his prime minister, his bride-to-be try in turn to persuade him to forgive Habis. Finally, Habis himself, still disguised as the general Hesperus, pleads his case, and succeeds. Everything ends happily; the tyrant not only welcomes his grandson, but gives him the throne and Erixène.

Gomez does not develop the tragic potential of an obsessed character like Melgoris. Instead, she envisions him as an embodiment of authority, King and Father, and as such he is in a sense exempt from attack if not from criticism. The other characters demonstrate their virtue by their blind acquiescence in his follies and submission to his injustice. From the first scene, when Habis's mother hears rumors of his return, she

5. H. Carrington Lancaster, *Sunset: A History of Parisian Drama in the Last Years of Louis XIV, 1701–1715* (Baltimore: The Johns Hopkins University Press 1945), 79.

expresses concern that he respect the tyrant who has kept her in jail for twenty years, caused the suicide of her husband, and attempted the murder of Habis himself: "And if to avenge himself my Son took up arms,/ Whom should he strike? A King? A Father?/ Whom my heart still reveres despite his mad furies . . ." (I, 1). The identity of Habis is revealed to everyone except Melgoris early on; the scene where he finally recognizes and forgives Habis is inevitable. There, too, Habis succeeds by reaffirming his absolute trust in legitimate authority; having made his case, he places his life in Melgoris's hands, stating that he prefers a virtuous death to a revolt against his king and father.

This servility pervades eighteenth-century literature, especially the French theater. The temporary errors of authority figures seldom prod the heroes to revolt or the narrators to question the political structure. Female characters were held to an even more groveling acquiescence to the unreasonable demands of their masters. Rebellion of any sort was unseemly, fit only for villains. Contemporary readers and audiences enjoyed instead the heartrending spectacle of suffering virtue, knowing that patient endurance would be rewarded in a climactic scene of recognition, forgiveness, and reconciliation. To twentieth-century readers, such texts seem to preach a foolish faith in an already moribund political order, advising the oppressed to accept their lot without challenge, imagining wisdom and benevolence in the oppressors. We prefer works that resist and thematize the excesses; self-conscious villains and calculating role-players, like Versac and Valmont, Marivaux's coquettes and Diderot's parasite, impress us as revolutionary figures whose every word questions the bases of the established order. It is not certain that we read the eighteenth century well, however, and if "revolutionary" is anything more than a critical hyperbole, the sensibility was formed by their canon, not ours. The complacent suffering of these characters, finding pride in their refusal to resist, can be as insidiously subversive as the lessons of libertine novelists or materialist philosophers. The eighteenth-century spectator did not mistake the providential ending for realism; at most it was an exhortation to those with power in the real world, but in any case it stood in ironic contrast to the situation as it had stood until the final act. The happy ending provides a release to painful tensions; without it audiences might have found the play unbearable. But they did not forget the pain they had seen, nor were they unaware of the other possible outcomes and the arbitrary thin line separating poetic justice from disaster.

Gomez's second play, *Marsidie, reine des Cimbres*, was published but not staged. The central figure is a strong heroine, who overcomes political treachery and male vacillation, but does not anticipate the magnanimity of her Roman adversary and conqueror, Marius, who sacrifices his own love for her in favor of the vanquished Gotharsis. Marsidie, however, expecting a choice between death and dishonor, has already taken poison. The unhappy conclusion is pathetic rather than tragic, an accident of timing rather than the inexorable consequence of fate and passion. It is no accident, however, that suicide is the woman's choice, or that the misfortune falls to one who resisted Rome, the archetypal symbol of virile order.

After *Marsidie* Gomez returned to happy endings, but with little success. *Semiramis*, staged in 1716, ends with the death of the traitor Menon, whose exposure makes possible the marriage of the heroine with Ninus, the man she loves, the fulfillment of the treaty between Syria and Arabia, the reunion of Simma with his long-lost children, and the happy disposition of Ninus's rival Aretas, who is actually Semiramis's brother. *Cléarque, tyran d'Heraclée*, staged the next year, is based on a familiar hostage plot: Cléarque holds both Aristophile and her father Entigesne prisoner, threatening the old man's life as a way of forcing the daughter to accept his hand. Entigesne instructs Aristophile that she may honorably murder Cléarque before she marries him, but not afterwards; if she finds herself in his power, she should commit suicide. Luckily, Leonidas shows up to assassinate the tyrant, so that this play also ends happily for everyone except the villain.

After *Cléarque* Gomez ceased writing for the stage, but continued to turn out fiction in large quantities, her best known work being the thirty-six-part collection *Cent Nouvelles Nouvelles*, published between 1732 and 1739. Unlike Barbier, Gomez expressed no explicit feminist consciousness in her plays and gives no clue what her motives for writing were or why she abandoned the genre. Her enormous productivity would have enabled her to earn a substantial income as a novelist; like Prévost, Marivaux, and Crébillon fils, she produced multi-volume works, thereby capitalizing on her popularity. According to the biographical dictionaries, she lived until 1770, but appears to have given up writing altogether after the last volume of the *Cent Nouvelles Nouvelles*.

For over thirty years after *Cléarque*, from 1717 to 1749, there were no new works by women at the Comédie Française.[6] All the more understandable then, that the flamboyant Marie-Anne Du Boccage set Parisian tongues wagging with the announcement of her tragedy *Les Amazones* in 1749. Born Marie-Anne Le Page, in 1710, a native of Rouen, Du Boccage frequented a literary society, as had Barbier; Fontenelle, Collé, Trublet, and Voltaire's correspondent Cideville were

6. Unless one counts *Thélamire*, which had a brief run in 1739. It has been attributed to a Denise Lebrun, but the attribution is dubious; it has also been attributed to a marquis de Thibouville, and had the author really been a woman, the event was unusual enough that her identity would probably have been revealed. Nothing is known of either person, in any case.

among her friends. She was said to be rich, and her husband supported her in her literary ambitions. She traveled to England in 1750 and to Italy in 1758; after 1758 she opened her salon to a group of distinguished men of letters, and continued to receive them after her widowhood in 1767, and even through the Revolutionary years, when she was impoverished. She died in 1802, in her nineties.

The title of her play proclaims a feminist awareness, and the published text includes a preface addressed "Aux Femmes." To a 1980s reader, however, the material seems disappointing. Du Boccage does not take up the defense of a female literary tradition or even of the individual woman writer's right to equal treatment. The choice of Amazons as heroines must signify an interest in female power and in radical solutions to the problems of gender relations, but the play develops conventionally, The situation might be described as a reversal of the usual hostage plot: two Amazons, Orithie, the queen, and Antiope, a princess, hold Thésée prisoner, and have fallen in love with him, in violation of Amazon law. Of course, Du Boccage was not the first to have given such power to a woman. In this instance, the debate over whether to kill Thésée or not is rendered moot by his escape. Thésée loves Antiope, and a nice loophole allows Amazons to marry in order to save the state. Thésée generously restores Orithie to her throne and freedom, but she commits suicide out of shame and passes the crown to Ménelippe, who swears eternal enmity to Thésée.

This denial of what appears to be a happy ending is the most subversive aspect of the play. Without saying so, perhaps even without knowing it, Du Boccage follows in the course traced by Barbier and Gomez: suicide is the only possible solution for the female protagonist. Thésée's power, both as warrior and as seducer, is a mortal threat to the Amazons, however magnanimous he may appear. Du Boccage uses a double plot. The most obvious is a typical tragic passion, love conflicting with dual duties, those of friendship between two rivals in love, and those of obedience to the law. This plot reaches a conventional happy outcome: one love is rewarded, the other consoled, and a political solution is found. But the second plot, which emerges only when the first is resolved, casts the first into doubt: Orithie cannot be consoled, and no political solution can be devised in the conflict between irreconcilable opposites, Amazons and men. Orithie's destiny cannot be subsumed in a patriarchal happy ending. Her love for Thésée destroys her identity as an Amazon, but not her fidelity to the Amazon ideal. In death she assures the preservation of the ideal, and from the Amazons' perspective the marriage of Antiope to Thésée must be viewed, not as a happy ending but as a sacrifice, a virgin offered to propitiate the monster.

Les Amazones met with little success. It lacks dramatic movement and Du Boccage's verse does not compensate for the static plot. If the critics recognized its subversive feminist qualities, they kept silent about them; the play did not succumb to controversy but to a lack of audience response. As happened to Graffigny after *La Fille d'Aristide,* once the failure was certain Du Boccage's public friends gave free rein to their malice in private; Collé notes that audiences snickered, sniffled, and yawned, while Cideville wrote that "fair-minded people think she did a lot for a woman, and sensible people think that, even so, she would have done better not to release the play."

Du Boccage herself wrote to Cideville: "I do not know if I will set out again, the work is too painful. Besides the pain of the work, the trouble of putting it on stage is excessive. Monsieur Du Boccage did most of it, but at every rehearsal I made changes which exhausted me" (1 August 1749).[7] Indeed, she did not return to the theater, although she continued actively to pursue fame as an author, with her epic poem *La Colombiade* and translations from the English. She could afford to ignore the financial aspects of her career; she was working only for glory and personal satisfaction. Her motives for giving up the genre will be echoed and amplified in Graffigny's account of getting *Cénie* staged a year later. Besides the work of writing, a great deal of labor was required to bring the play to the stage. Someone had to negotiate with the actors and supervise the rehearsals; a woman could not undertake those responsibilities. The factors that served to protect the proprieties at the Comédie Française functioned not only to enforce political and religious orthodoxy, but gender roles as well.

Graffigny observed Du Boccage's activities with scornful interest, and refused to receive her socially, considering her too brash and brazen. Graffigny was already famous for *Lettres d'une Péruvienne,* and publishing the novel had been a delicate balancing of proper feminine modesty with the need for public exposure. When Du Boccage's tragedy was staged, Graffigny had already been working for several years on her own play, *Cénie.*[8] Much of what Graffigny says about the composition of *Cénie* could probably be said of any play: the days spent writing, listening to criticism, revising, having copies made; the moments of enthusiasm and of weariness; impatience with the actors and anxiety as the premiere approached. Some of her concerns, however, arose from her position as a woman. After Du Boccage's play was presented in the

7. Cideville and Collé are quoted in Grace Gill-Mark, *Une Femme de lettres au XVIIIe siècle: Anne-Marie Du Boccage* (Paris: Champion, 1927), 153, 154.

8. Graffigny's correspondence is almost all in the Beinecke Rare Book and Manuscript Library of Yale University and is quoted with permission. A team headed by J. A. Dainard is editing the *Correspondance complète.* Volume 1 (letters from 1695 to June 1739) was published in 1985 (Oxford: the Voltaire Foundation); the introduction contains the best information about locating specific letters within the collection.

summer of 1749, the rumor circulated that Voltaire's niece, Marie Louise Denis, had also written a play for the coming season. In April 1750, Denis actually read her play to Graffigny, but lamented that Voltaire had refused to let her present it. Graffigny thought it very mediocre, and agreed with Voltaire's judgment, and perhaps they were right to condemn it; but without this censorship there might have been one more woman playwright. At the same time, Denis's play might have prevented Graffigny's from appearing; Graffigny wrote to her correspondent Devaux that she did not want to be seen as part of a trio. This is a classic dilemma for writers from a minority: if they are alone, they are treated as freaks or tokens; but if they are not alone, they are bracketed with others they dislike and do not want to resemble.

In the spring of 1749, Graffigny had written a version of *Cénie* in three acts; over the summer she expanded it to five and made other changes. Devaux asked whether she was going to versify it; she replied that prose was more decent from the pen of a woman, a belief confirmed by her friend, the former actress Jeanne Françoise Quinault. According to Graffigny, verse bespoke the pretentions of a bluestocking, whereas prose suggested only a "femme d'esprit." Nothing suggests that we should regret Graffigny's failure to versify *Cénie*; indeed, the obligation to write classical verse stultified most of the century's playwrights, and the best turned to prose. For the woman writer, prose could have been a positive sign of difference, the adoption of a more natural idiom, like the familiar letter; the history of women's writing reveals a frequent transformation of imposed genres into powerful means of self-expression. As Graffigny presents it, however, the prose form seems rather a lowering of ambition, the acceptance of a secondary achievement as the only appropriate one for a woman. Although women were arguably better off outside the mainstream because they had greater artistic freedom, it meant that they had less hope for becoming professional authors earning their own living. The costs of losing that freedom cannot be calculated.

Du Boccage confessed that her husband had had to do much of the work to bring the play to the stage. Graffigny had no husband, and so her first task was to win the patronage of a man in a position to get her play accepted. It was the prince comte de Clermont who took up the cause; he had his own private theater at Berny, where he later staged a one-act "féerie" by Graffigny. His rank as a prince of royal blood endowed him with considerable authority over the actors of the Comédie Française, and his knowledge of the theater augmented his influence. First, however, Graffigny had to make additional changes to meet his criticisms. Eventually, in February 1750, Clermont got the play read and it was soon accepted, as Graffigny heard from the author and academician

Duclos in mid-March. Graffigny herself could not have dealt with the troupe as men like Clermont and Duclos could. She could, and did, arrange to meet the actors socially, or ask one to come to her loge at the theater. She tried in this way, with small success, to get plays produced for numerous friends, including Devaux, Saint-Lambert, and Palissot, although after the triumph of *Cénie* she got better results. But she could not go to the actors' and actresses' dressing rooms, or hang around the theater, or besiege a key member of the troupe, or flirt with the male stars.

Du Boccage cited the fatigue of seeing a play through to production as a reason never to try again. In late May, Graffigny still thought that she would escape with no more trouble than a few social calls: "I'll go to that rehearsal at la Gaussin's and that's all. I'll have Sarrasin to dinner with Dromgold and Duclos so they can both try to get him not to treat his part so nonchalantly. I think that will be my whole job" (29 May 1750). A few days later, however, she wrote, "Ah, truly, my friend, you were right. It is no small affair to get a play acted" (1 June 1750). The tale of problems goes on for three pages, and setbacks kept occurring throughout rehearsals, virtually to the eve of the premiere. Male authors suffered the same treatment, but they were free to act on their own behalf. For Graffigny, the problems came as last-minute surprises and the solutions depended on waiting for a suitable assistant to happen by.

Du Boccage's fatigue supplied the pretext for the rumor that sitting through all the rehearsals had developed a boil on her bottom which opened and left a hole large enough to put a finger into. The sexual innuendo in this salacious story hardly needs pointing out. The age was never kind to the author, male or female, of an unsuccessful work; with women the satire regularly took the form of reduction to the sexual body, the object of male penetration and domination. The alleged locus of Du Boccage's failure thus becomes the site of a resexualization, whose painfulness and unnaturalness serve to emphasize its punitive and stigmatizing function.

A woman author's reputation was especially vulnerable to such attacks, because women were supposed to be modest and self-effacing. Graffigny's choice of prose was an effort to minimize any semblance of self-display. She explained to Devaux in February, as Clermont was presenting the play to the actors, that she did not plan to stay anonymous, but that she hoped to give the impression that Clermont had taken the manuscript against her will. Hence she was not displeased that early rumors attributed her work to Duclos. She was extremely grateful to the actor Roseli, who caught a potentially laughable line at the last rehearsal. Despite the overwhelming popularity of the play, which drew packed houses even in the off-season, and which was so wildly applauded people choked on the dust raised by stomping feet, when the satirist Charles Roi wrote an epigram about her,[9] she wished she could withdraw the play:

I had just been devastated by learning that Roi, the vile Roi, has written a horrible epigram, not against the play but against me. They say no one wants a copy, but slanders always get around. Mlle Quinault and Duclos came and said all the reasonable things one can say about it. They calmed me for the moment but when I'm alone all I see is the horror of being the object of a horror like that one. Ah, I'll never write again, that's for sure. The good is not worth the bad. If I could do it without seeming crazy, I'd withdraw the play this minute and never show it again. I won't be at ease as long as it's playing. I'll await the end of its run like the end of a great affliction.

The vehemence of this reaction passed; not only did *Cénie* remain on the boards to the end of its summer run, it returned in the winter season and was revived four years later. Moreover, Graffigny wrote a second play, *La Fille d'Aristide*; it was a dismal failure when it was staged in 1758, but Graffigny took the bad reviews more philosophically than Roi's satiric doggerel.

The plot of *Cénie* is complicated and implausible, although not un- usual for the period. Cénie has been raised as the daughter of Dorimond and Mélisse; but she is really the daughter of her governess Orphise and an unjustly exiled nobleman. Two brothers, Méricourt and Clerval, love her; Méricourt learns the secret from Mélisse on her deathbed, and tries to use it to get Cénie (and Dorimond's fortune). Cénie of course refuses, and tells Dorimond everything; Dorimond belatedly realizes that he has been deceived by Mélisse and Méricourt, tries to repair the situation by adopting Cénie or marrying Orphise, but they are too noble to accept such charity and are on their way to a convent when the nobleman reappears, having been pardoned by a minister *ex machina.*

The heart of *Cénie* is the dilemma of women expected to remain silent yet forced to speak. The heroine's part is full of lines like: "Don't force me to blush in front of you. . . . That's what I feared the most. This fatal confession puts the final touch on your woes. Clerval, remember that you tore it from me" (III, 4); "My disastrous adventure would become the latest gossip and I would be the object of public curiosity" (IV, 1); "Courage and silence are the nobility of the unfortunate" (V, 3); "Permit me to spare you confidences which should be told only to people with hardened hearts" (V, 5). The men in *Cénie* have mis- governed, but by mistake. The women suffer unjustly, but can remain in the right only by passive submission. Eventually, truth will out, and the

---

9. Roi's epigram is quoted in Georges Noël, *Une Primitive oubliée de l'école des coeurs sensibles: Madame de Graffigny* (Paris: Plon, 1913), 240. It implies that "bel esprit" is equivalent to prostitution for women no longer young and beautiful enough to earn a living from the latter.

real natural order replaces the apparent one; then the virtuous characters are rewarded and the wicked punished.

Far from disbelieving the plot, Graffigny's contemporaries circulated rumors that "Cénie" was an anagram of "nièce," and that the
story was based on the life of Graffigny's ward, Minette de Ligniville.
Graffigny denied it to Devaux, and certainly nothing in Minette's noble
background resembled Cénie's story of uncertain origins and belated
recognition. The play nonetheless reflects the situation of the two
women in important ways, Orphise being the surrogate mother to Cénie
as Graffigny was to Minette. More importantly, however, the response
to the play must arise from a powerful sense on the audience's part that
the emotion was genuine. The mute resignation of Cénie and Orphise
translates a situation familiar to the spectators of 1750. Even as it ostensibly celebrates and rewards the virtue of silence, *Cénie* allows the
women characters to speak, and itself constitutes an act of speaking out.
The enthusiastic reception of the play suggests that audiences responded to that boldness far more than to the bland reassertion of conventional moral ideas.

The first thoughts of the play that became *La Fille d'Aristide* appear
in Graffigny's letters while *Cénie* was just getting underway. This work,
completed shortly before the author's death, erases the last distinctions
between the pathetic tragedy and the tearjerking drama of the mideigh-
teenth century: like the drama, it combines a serious tone with a happy
ending, and is in prose; but like the tragedies, it is set in ancient Greece,
with such exotic trappings as the Athenian Senate and slaves. The public responded unfavorably and Graffigny withdrew it after four performances. As in *Cénie*, the central figure is a virtuous woman at the
mercy of false impressions. Her legitimate lover goes away for a year and
sends no word; he returns to find her persecuted in various ways by two
old men and one young one, and of course leaps to false conclusions
about her feelings. The point of the awkward and unconvincing plot is
to permit the heroine, Théonise, to be suspected of indecent behavior,
when in fact she has performed the supreme self-sacrifice of selling
herself into slavery to pay her benefactor's fine. Needless to say, the
lover rescues her and the benefactor, and everyone else repents and
apologizes. In *Cénie* the women silently prepare to enter a convent; here
Théonise secretly sells her freedom. The deeds finally dramatize what
propriety forbids speaking: neither desire nor virtue, but the utter hope-
lessness of the woman's situation. Self-sacrifice if not suicide is the only
issue.

After Graffigny's death, no more women wrote full length plays for
the Comédie Française. Some of the women novelists of the last half of
the century might well have been major playwrights under different
conditions. Marie Jeanne Riccoboni had been an actress at the Théâtre

Italien and had written for that stage; her translations of English plays and her correspondence with Diderot about the craft of playwriting prove her continuing interest and her intelligence on the subject. Isabelle de Charrière left a large number of unpublished plays; they contain some of the liveliest dialogue and freshest scenes in the entire century. But the novel afforded a better avenue for these women's creativity, in part no doubt because of its freedom from formal rules, but also in part because the theater demanded a degree of self-promotion and managerial activity that women could not easily provide.

In one area, however, it seemed appropriate for women to hold authority and to write their own script: the education of children. Félicité de Genlis is generally credited with the invention of the genre of children's theater, and she certainly popularized it through the publication of her *Théâtre de l'éducation* (1779) and the expanded seven-volume version, *Théâtre à l'usage des jeunes personnes* (1785). In fact, Graffigny had already written a number of plays with a similar purpose, which were used in educating the Imperial children in Vienna; the titles include *Ziman et Zenise* (1749), *Les Saturnales* (1752), *Le Temple de la vertu* (1750s), and perhaps others. In the domestic sphere, a woman could assume the role of moral guide, teacher, or governess; in certain cases she could also cast the play and direct the actors. In retrospect, a children's theater seems a natural and almost inevitable response to the frustrations women encountered in the mainstream theater and the larger society it represented.

LUCIENNE FRAPPIER-MAZUR

Marginal Canons: Rewriting the Erotic

The "interest model," which construes canons "as the expression of the interests of one social group or class against those of another,"[1] goes a long way to explain the marginalization or total exclusion of works by women and minorities. But this antagonistic model neglects less obvious instances of exclusion and inclusion. For example, through their engagement with generic constraints and prescriptions, writers are active agents of canon variation. Since authors of canonic works may also be readers of noncanonic works, even noncanonic writers may indirectly play a role in canon formation and ultimately become institutionalized. Sade's covert presence in nineteenth-century canonic texts (such as Balzac's *La Peau de chagrin* or Flaubert's *La Tentation de Saint Antoine* and *Salammbô*) and his still growing visibility today provide a magnified example of this phenomenon. The role of noncanonic writers may account for the changing status of erotic and pornographic fiction (erotic *poetry* has always had a higher status), which now inspires critical and scholarly anthologies, bibliographies, books, essays, and articles, and even dictionaries.[2] While primarily the result of cultural and ideological factors, this evolution of the status of pornography helps problematize the general notion of canon formation: can one speak of a "marginal canon" of works often widely read by major writers but not

1. Robert von Hallberg, "Editor's Introduction," in *Critical Inquiry* 10 (September 1983): iii.

2. I have reviewed all the texts listed in Louis Perceau, *Bibliographie du roman érotique au 19e siècle* (Paris, 1930), and a selection of those listed in *Dictionnaire des oeuvres érotiques* (Paris, 1971), ed. Pascal Pia, *Anthologie historique des lectures érotiques*, ed. J.-J. Pauvert (Paris: Simoën, Ramsay, Garnier, 1979, 1980, 1982), and Claudine Brécourt-Villars's excellent anthology, *Ecrire d'amour. Anthologie de textes érotiques féminins (1799–1984)* (Paris: Ramsay, 1985). For male low pornography *circa.* 1889–1890, see Marc Angenot, "Pornographie fin de siècle," *Littérature populaire: recherches québécoises*, in *Cahiers pour la littérature populaire* 7, (Fall–Winter 1986): 38–54. The genre as such begins to appear in the sixteenth century and slowly follows the evolution of the novel.

belonging to the academic institution? Since pornography is a highly codified genre, and since the canon is modified by the introduction of new works or subgenres and by changes in generic models, what is the relation of code to canon? What is the relation of low to high literature, which partially overlaps that of pornographic to erotic?

When pornographic works are written by women, a parallel series of questions arises. Do their character and status differ and, if so, how? Are they addressed to the same audience as those written by men? What can we learn from their traditional position as twice-removed from the official system of literary value—belonging to a marginal corpus and written by a marginal group? My purpose is to examine this double relation within its historical framework, taking into account questions of periodization, themes, and narrative forms. This will require defining a model, which will necessarily be masculine (even while ostensibly addressing female narratees as in *Margot la Ravaudeuse* [1760] or in the author's footnotes to Sade's *Histoire de Juliette* [1797], erotica have traditionally been designed for men); identifying turning points at which women have written erotic literature; examining exemplary texts by women; and considering whether these texts have been instrumental, either directly or indirectly, in the evolution of the literary canon.

Trying to deal consistently with a common but fluctuating terminology, I will use the collective term *erotica* and the qualifier *erotic* to refer to all the texts I shall present, by which I mean that, while retaining the basic motifs of commercial *pornography* and illustrating its formulaic model, they also go beyond its limits. The sole goal of pornography is to be sexually stimulating and, whatever its form, its primary generic identity is as pornography.[3] *Eroticism*, on the other hand, denotes a quality, and erotic texts may belong to a variety of generic categories. Eroticism and pornography often blend in the same texts. This is the case for all those erotic stories whose female authorship is documented. They all refer to a literary intertext and rely on textual work as well as pornographic motifs. And since women's erotic stories constitute the focus of my study, I shall not analyze any "raw" pornography. I call erotic those stories which represent a succession of sexual acts connected by a narrative thread, and which are perceived at some point in time as transgressive because they violate both the norms of discourse and of sexual behavior.[4]

---

3. *Obscene* recurs in most of its dictionary definitions, and although the sense of obscenity may vary, pornography uses language crudely enough to render frivolous any concern for matters of contextualization.

4. I am indebted to Susan Suleiman for this distinction, which she elaborates in her essay on "Pornography, Transgression, and the Avant-Garde: Bataille's *Story of the Eye*," *The Poetics of Gender*, ed. Nancy K. Miller (New York: Columbia University Press, 1986), 117–36.

Discursive transgression may be lexical and/or textual. The texts I am studying all rely on semantic associations as much as on a lexical register for their erotic impact. Some of them are quite literary. As for transgressive *acts*, they must break common or fundamental interdictions in order to hold full transgressive potential. But transgression may assume different forms—metaphysical, somber and violent, or lighthearted and without guilt. Many variations and some overlappings can occur between those two veins, whose eighteenth-century prototypes are respectively Sade and Andrea de Nerciat. Finally, the explicit reference to the law, when it occurs, entails a large amount of doctrinal, frequently anticlerical discourse in favor of freedom.[5]

The requirement for transgression accounts for the indispensable motifs of erotica—defloration, rape, masturbation, bisexuality, sodomy, group sex—whose varying frequency may well reflect the (male) reader's preference for certain forms of substitute gratification, but whose main interest for us lies elsewhere. Barthes's description of Sadean orgiastic motifs, which he compares to the "rhetorical figures of written discourse . . . the *metaphor,* which indifferently substitutes one subject for another, . . . the *asyndeton,* an abrupt succession of debaucheries . . ."[6] emphasizes their codified character, but it also reduces this accumulation to a textual exercise. These motifs constitute multiple variations on power relations; as such, they bear an ideological significance which contradicts the discourse of transgression, its plea for freedom and apparent subversion. The erotic scene represents a fantasized version of sexual dominance and can stand as a (more or less) playful outlet, or a metaphor, for other forms of control. Cultural anthropology has shown that our perception of the body is mediated and socialized, that the human body is a universal metaphor for the social body: the erotic scene often manifests the sociocultural determinants of erotic modes,[7] and, most frequently, it has assigned the dominant position to men and the submissive one to women.[8] In order to achieve its sharply contrasted hierarchy, it has mostly relied on implicit stereotypes about "man's nature"—strong, rational, and all-knowing—and

5. A few examples in the anticlerical vein: *Thérèse philosophe* (1748), *L'Education de Laure* (1783) and of course Sade's novels, then weak examples like *Le Tartuffe libertin* (1830), *La Tourelle de Saint-Etienne* (1831), or *Amours secrètes de M. Maveux* (1832).

6. Roland Barthes, *Sade, Fourier, Loyola* (Paris: Seuil, "Points," 1971), 137.

7. Nerciat provides an interesting variation: he represents sexual equality among aristocrats, while the sexual obedience of servants, hairdressers, etc., of either sex reflects the social hierarchy.

8. For the intricate interaction of the cultural and the intersubjective in this distribution of gender roles, see Jessica Benjamin, "Master and Slave: The Fantasy of Erotic Domination," in *Powers of Desire,* ed. Ann Snitow, Christine Stansell, and Sharon Thompson (New York: Monthly Review Press, 1983), which includes a subtle analysis of *Histoire d'O.* The branch of pornography that caters to male masochism is outside the scope of my study.

explicit ones about "woman's true, hidden nature"— sexually un-
bridled, or generally feebleminded, or with a vocation for suffering—
whose effect, after the eighteenth century and until recently, was increasingly the silencing of the woman: at best "spoken" but not speaking, at worst physically eliminated. The whole Barthesian pornogram-
mar is not immune from this original motivation.

The body of the silenced woman becomes the main narrative object
and locus of meaning, opposite the phallic synecdoche which refers to
the male subject and his active inscription of woman's body. Extreme
violence is not necessary; the will to power often expresses itself in the
minor mode. Historically, the two most recurrent motifs have probably
been defloration and lesbianism, two euphemized forms of domination
in male erotica: if not brutal, defloration has to be markedly painful for
the woman, and lesbianism is a pretext for scenes of voyeurism, in
which secret observation asserts the observer's superiority.[9] Furthermore, a number of characteristic relations and situations reinforce the
alliance between the political and the sexual. They are incest, especially
father-daughter incest, the epitome of male sexual dominance in the
pornographic imagination; prostitution, which directly conflates sexual relations and class subjection; elitism and social inequality, either
represented between the sexual partners or implied by the protagonists'
wealth and leisure. A crossing over of the boundaries of consciousness,
often with a metaphysical dimension, may lead to the linking of sex and
death.[10] Most of these relations manifest the will to suppress the self, or
the other.[11]

Women authors respect the canon of motifs even when they treat it
differently: Defloration appears with comparable frequency, but it is
much less painful, and the pleasure that follows is more moderate.
Masculine impotence is a prevalent situation which easily assumes
castrating connotations when treated by a woman writer. I have found
very few allusions to incest in works by women:[12] this may be related to

9. Some women writers have emphasized this significance of voyeurism and translated it into scenes of overt scopic aggression. In *Histoire d'O*, Sir Stephen watches O and
her lesbian lover with O's complicity, and eventually persuades her to masturbate in his
presence. Such scenes are frequent in *F.B.* and *La Punition*, by Xavière (Paris: Christian
Bourgois, 1970, 1971). In one of them, a patron simply sits in front of the prostitute, and
terrifies her by silently watching her naked on the bed.

10. Even in *L'Enfant du bordel* (Paris: 1800), a popular, tongue-in-cheek novel by
Pigault-Lebrun, the narrator and the servant make love next to the mistress's corpse, as a
way of remembering and mourning her.

11. See especially Anne-Marie Dardigna, *Les Châteaux d'Eros* (Paris: Maspero, 1980),
25, 30–32, and the whole of ch. 1 for her historical survey of the term *érotisme* and her
keen comments on the political implications of eroticism in literature and film.

12. See, however, the gleeful, humorous treatment of a father-daughter incest narrated by the daughter in Belen [Nelly Kaplan], *Mémoires d'une liseuse de draps* (Paris:
Pauvert, 1973), quoted in Claudine Brécourt-Villars, op. cit., 326–27.

its special significance in men's writings. Sodomy, group sex, voyeurism, female masturbation, and lesbianism are omnipresent motifs, but the last three acquire a very different significance according to the sex of the writer, as we shall see. The prostitution of women, equally frequent, is viewed as good in male erotica and often glorified as a high mode of exchange, communication, and bonding among men: *Emmanuelle* celebrates it with pretentious enthusiasm, *Histoire d'O* subtly suggests its homosexual component, but most works by women condemn it even when they use it as an erotic motif. Recent stories by women prostitutes offer its most complex representation. Men often use a cruder vocabulary than women writers, who tend to prefer the clinical term to the vulgar one. Both male and female authors, even today, rely a great deal on euphemisms, stylistic clichés and metaphors to describe sexual acts—this is an enduring tradition in France. The differences just outlined seem almost self-explanatory. As to the power relations which found the erotic scene, nineteenth-century and a few twentieth-century women writers have systematically reversed them. After the Second World War, women writers have returned to a representation of male dominance, with a shift in narrative viewpoint.

In the eighteenth century, when it was still entirely male-authored as far as can be ascertained, erotic fiction evolved from a juxtaposition of episodes, as in the dialogues of *L'Académie des Dames* (1660), to a loose initiatory structure describing a progressive stripping of all sexual constraints, a narrative model which still survives. This progress is lived by the usually female protagonist either as joyful liberation or gradual debasement. Sometimes it leads to conjugal bliss and fidelity: the heroine recognizes the superiority of heterosexual, monogamous love and will confine the practice of her erotic science to the conjugal bed. With this general framework, it is the link between voyeurism and lesbianism—extending to female masturbation—which provides the basic narrative situation and highlights the primacy of the female body as narrative object in relation to the reader.[13] The voyeuristic character actualizes the reader's own position as voyeur and this specular relation enhances the staging of the female body and its erotic effect on the omnipotent reader. In male erotica, in general it is men who hide to observe lesbian couples, an occupation often leading to a threesome during which the male observer secures active control of the situation. Conversely, if women hide, it is most frequently to observe *heterosexual* couples, for instance in *Thérèse philosophe* (1748) or *Félicia* (1775), by Nerciat. This difference is related to the hierarchy between male-

13. See A. de Nerciat, *Félicia*, 1775 (Paris: Nouvelles Editions Françaises, 1929), 3, ch. 15, 186–88, for a euphemized example of male dominance. Men spy over lesbian couples in *Les Dames de maison et les filles d'amour* (n.d., circa 1830) and *Le Tartufe libertin, ou le triomphe du vice* (n.d. circa 1830).

female and lesbian loves: in most works by men, lesbian pleasures, like others, first appear as prodigious and may be glorified as antinatural, but only to be finally revealed as inferior to those a man can dispense. *Gamiani*, almost totally a pastiche, epitomizes the state of the art around 1833: "I have divorced nature," says Gamiani, the lesbian protagonist, and her pleasure is described as "horrible . . . incomplete."[14] Lesbianism, as we shall see, constitutes a central reference for a comparative study.[15] It figures prominently in works by women, in which it undergoes a very different treatment.

I will limit my examination to works whose female authorship is known, either directly or indirectly, and first compare their signatures to those of other nineteenth-century women writers.[16] The latter often used a pseudonym and, for obvious reasons, women erotic writers all did, but they distinguished themselves by favoring *female* pseudonyms (with the exception of Marc de Montifaud, born Marie-Amélie Chartroule de Montifaud, who favored traditional anticlericalism and erotic double entendre in her stories). Female signatures have erotic value— indeed, many male pornographers, unlike other male writers, resort to female pseudonyms. The Countess de Choiseul-Meuse, like other eighteenth- and early nineteenth-century women, signed "Mme de ***," and in 1883 *Le Roman de Violette* was published anonymously. Otherwise, the signatures of women's erotic novels fall into four groups: 1. typical of the first half of the nineteenth century, the aristocratic signature, which usually concealed a commoner—women erotic writers used it longer than other writers (for example Jane de la Vaudère, 1898), but not as long as male erotic writers, as testified by the example of "Jean de Berg" (Alain Robbe-Grillet, *L'Image*, 1956);[17] 2. the first name,

14. *Gamiani*, fac-simile of original edition, Paris, 1833 (Geneva: Slatkine, 1980), 4 and 1. Most scholars now agree on Musset's authorship, although the possibility of a joint endeavor, perhaps with Gautier, should not be discarded. This hierarchy between homo- and heterosexual love also appears in many novels by women, e.g., *Histoire d'O* (1954) or *L'Espace d'un livre*, by Suzanne Allen (Paris: Gallimard, 1971), 232.

15. With the notable exception of Sade, one finds relatively few representations of male homosexuality in eighteenth- and nineteenth-century erotic writings. Courtilz de Sandras describes a homosexual brotherhood of young noblemen and their pranks, which culminate in a sadistic attack against a prostitute's genitalia, in *Les Intrigues amoureuses de la Cour de France* (1685), 21.

16. This comparison is based on the findings in Roger Bellet's "Masculin et féminin dans les pseudonymes des femmes de lettres au XIXe siècle," in *Autour de Louise Colet, femmes de lettres au 19e siècle* (Lyon: Presses Universitaires de Lyon, ed. R. Bellet, 1982), 249–81. His starting-point, like Brécourt-Villars's in *Ecrire d'amour*, op. cit., is J. M. Quérard, *Les Supercheries littéraires dévoilées* (1869).

17. Anagram of "Je bande ARG." See Brécourt-Villars, 31–32. An exception: "Jeanne de Berg," pseudonym of a woman married to a known novelist, who published *Cérémonies de femmes* (Paris: Grasset et Fasquelle, 1985), noteworthy for its first-person female narrator and the theatrical staging of her sadistic performances on consenting (mostly male) victims.

after the example of Rachilde in the Decadent years, a practice which is still current; 3. the ordinary pseudonym—a female first name and a surname (for example Claire Senart, pseudonym of Mme Louis Figuier, 1860), which became more frequent in French literature in the second half of the nineteenth century when women writers began to feel more secure, and which Renée Dunan, a libertarian anarchist, may have been the first erotic writer to use in 1928 when she signed *Les Caprices du sexe* "Louise Dormienne"; 4. the real name, perhaps also first used by Renée Dunan, whose example has only recently begun to be followed. Today, the most frequent signatures are either a first name, now limited to the erotic genre, or the female ordinary pseudonym, but some women also use their real names. Unlike many men's publications in the eighteenth and nineteenth centuries, whose title page bore made-up, often obscene publishers' names, women's erotic fiction was published by specialized, but not clandestine, houses. Today, like men's, it is often published by major publishers.

Starting with Scudéry, women's novels, when first published, were often attributed to male authorship or collaboration: Sand's, Rachilde's and Colette's early novels, Liane de Pougy's *Idylle saphique*, were first published under a man's name or with a cosignature. Men's works, which may also benefit from discussion and collaboration, do not usually encounter this form of reception. *Histoire d'O* is of interest to us in this respect. When it first appeared, "Pauline Réage" was said to be a man, or several men—Jean Paulhan had written the preface and he was most often quoted as the main author or collaborator. Today, conflicting rumors are still going on, and make it virtually impossible to assess the respective share of each collaborator. Whether factually accurate or not, "Pauline Réage" 's assertions in *O m'a dit* and *Une fille amoureuse* constitute a public acknowledgment, or rather a claim, of female authorship.[18] She insists that the first sixty pages of *Histoire d'O*, which correspond exactly to the first chapter, were "given" to her, as if dictated from within. Despite her repeated statements, one can speculate that her novel elaborates other fantasies than her own,[19] but the question of whose fantasies *Histoire d'O* inscribes is irrelevant to its authorship. On the other hand, the special twist of the narration deviates from the model of male fiction.

18. Pauline Réage, *Une fille amoureuse*, in *Retour à Roissy* (Paris: Pauvert, 1969) and Régine Deforges, *O m'a dit* (Paris: Pauvert, 1975).

19. As suggested by A. Robbe-Grillet in "What interests me about eroticism," a comment he qualifies by adding that people's actual fantasies are often those theoretically ascribed to the opposite gender (*Homosexualities and French Literature: Cultural Contexts/ Critical Texts*, ed. George Stambolian and Elaine Marks [Ithaca & London: Cornell University Press, 1979], 91). See also Brécourt-Villars, 47: "Si Pauline Réage continue à défendre à bon droit son incognito, elle est bien en réalité une femme."

The first French erotic novel to be signed by a woman, *Illyrine, ou l'Ecueil de l'inexpérience,* by G . . . de Morency (Suzanne Giroux), appeared towards the end of the revolutionary period, in 1799–1800, and the next few between 1802 and 1909 by the Countess Félicité de Choiseul-Meuse, whose best-known novels in that category are *Amélie de Saint-Far ou la fatale erreur* (1802) and especially *Julie ou j'ai sauvé ma rose* (1807). They did not have any followers until the 1880s, when the "vicomtesse de Coeur-Brûlant" published the facile, sentimental and socially conformist *Les Cousines de la Colonelle* (1880),[20] and Rachilde published *Monsieur Vénus* (1884), a Decadent novel she wrote at the age of twenty-four and which launched her into a long and successful literary career. After the Decadent period, women's erotica became infrequent until the years following the First World War, and again from the late 1930s to the late 1960s.[21]

A few sociohistorical considerations can account for the dates of the two nineteenth-century turning points, and the void that separates them. When one remembers the extreme misogyny and puritanism of the Convention and its legislation regarding women,[22] one hesitates to ascribe the appearance of *Illyrine,* whose female authorship was no secret, to any encouragement given by the French Revolution to literary expression, erotic or otherwise, on the part of women. It is more likely that the general licentiousness of the eighteenth century, and the amiable *libertinage* of contemporary erotica, which recognized female desire as a matter of course among men and women of the best society, created a favorable climate for this kind of writing. But perhaps the social turmoil brought by the Revolution was still needed for self-censorship to be overcome: at first, the Revolution did raise women's expectations of social equality, before disappointing and even condemning them. The return of the monarchy saw a general decline in the production of pornographic literature. Perceau's bibliography lists many more reissues than first publications, and among the latter none by women until the Decadent years. The adoption of the Napoleonic code and the rise of bourgeois values sealed what has been called the "confinement" of nineteenth-century middle-class women within the family structure and the suppression of civic rights for all but single women. Divorce, which had been instituted in 1792, was abolished in 1816 and reinstituted only

20. She was the marquise de Mannoury d'Ectot, born Le Blanc.

21. Brécourt-Villars's introduction examines in detail those fluctuations and their relation to censorship laws.

22. See for example Simone de Beauvoir, *Le Deuxième sexe* (Paris: 1949), ch. 5; Evelyne Sullerot, *Histoire de la presse féminine en France, des origines à 1848* (Paris: 1966), ch. 4; Harriet B. Applewhite and Darline Gay Levy, "Women, Democracy, and Revolution in Paris, 1789–1794," in *French Women and the Age of Enlightenment,* ed. Samia I. Spencer (Bloomington: 1984), 64–79.

in 1884. Nodier's response to the feminist explosion of 1831–32 alludes to women's "prolonged, delightful childhood and legal minority" and gives a fair idea of the general reception of feminism at the time: "What, for a few miserable social rights which you have been deprived of by the universal [*sic*] institution, you would run the risk, Mesdames, of losing our protection and love?"[23] In written discourse, the traditional split between the virgin/mother and the courtesan received new emphasis.

One can hardly speak of turning points again in relation to women's erotic writings until the late 1960s and early 1970s. In France, the link with the 1968 "events" seems unmistakable. 1968 launched the women's movement which, despite many feminists' hostility to erotica, has inspired more women to "write themselves" in their own words, hence an unprecedented upsurge of erotic novels whose tone is altogether new. And the prostitutes' movement, itself an offshoot of the women's movement, also linked to the protests and political demands of 1968, has given rise to some autobiographical fictions of an erotic character.

Limiting myself to the most significant differences between erotic stories by men and women, I will first contrast their respective treatments of lesbianism. I will then consider the use of first- and third-person narration.

In women's fiction, the female body remains central, and this adds to the overdetermination of lesbian motifs which, as in men's fiction, are invariably associated with female narcissism. The light satire of lesbian love and narcissism contained in *Gamiani* (1833) provides a typical contrast with the complacency that characterizes their treatment in women's writings. But the essential difference between the two groups is that, in nineteenth-century women's fiction, lesbianism signifies a refusal of male dominance.

As early as 1807, *Julie ou j'ai sauvé ma rose* ends on a lesbian episode and combines distinct narcissism with a remarkable will to power. Julie has two goals in life: domination of men and sensual pleasure. This is presented as a dilemma, since men *always* forsake the women who surrender to them. Her solution is *never* to lose her virginity, while coming as close as possible to granting "the last favor" in order not to discourage her lovers. Thus, she will maintain a position of strength. A female Don Juan, she never swerves from this line of conduct. One of her lovers, angered by her resistance, turns to another woman, but she seduces the woman and separates the pair. The man comes back to Julie who, having regained absolute control on both fronts, conducts the two affairs simultaneously. A few details—Julie's excitement the first time she sees the ballet dancers at the Opera and her passionate female

23. *L'Europe littéraire* (March 1833). Cf., Sullerot, ch. 11.

friendships—suggest a covert proclivity towards lesbianism. To this day, most erotic novels by women, even when respecting the hierarchy between homo- and heterosexual love, attach great value to female friendship and make little distinction between female bonding and erotic love.[24] This is all the more noteworthy in the face of generic models that tend to represent an impoverished affectivity and concentrate on performance.

With the relaxation of generic prescriptions in the nineteenth century, the narcissistic relation of female characters to their own bodies began to differ more and more according to the gender of the authors. Descriptive codes had become less conventional, and when erotic writings surfaced again during the 1880s, they bore the mark of Decadent aesthetics, which allowed more play for imagination and subjectivity. This trend has asserted itself ever since. In *Idylle saphique* (1901), by Liane de Pougy, the two lesbian partners relate their unrestrained narcissism and their love of the same to their love of Beauty and artifice and to the praise of perversion and sterility. They celebrate "the chastity of the supreme embrace during which nothing penetrates and Dream hardly dares touch you," a counterpart to the fear and dislike of "devouring femininity" expressed by male Decadents.[25] Clothes and fashion play a great role in their self-celebration, including, not surprisingly, cross-dressing, since hints of mental and physical bisexuality almost unfailingly accompany the representation of lesbianism. And bisexuality, although first an erotic ingredient, leads directly to the question of power relations and the reversal of the male model.

In *Le Roman de Violette* (*circa*, 1883), the lesbian pairs enact an active/passive, masculine/feminine polarity, which is represented first by the costume, next by the erotic practice, and finally by a physical characteristic—a magnificent fleece [*toison*] which covers the chest and stomach of the actress Florence,[26] a virile virgin whose dislike of men arises from her fear of domination and her own wish to dominate, which she carries to an extreme: armed with Diane de Poitiers's ancient ivory dildo, she performs her own defloration in front of a mirror, out of a wish

24. In this respect, women's erotic novels simply actualize the unconscious or unavowed sexual component of romantic female friendships. A common occurrence in the lives of women through the beginning of the twentieth century, these friendships were considered asexual and usually did not arouse any blame or suspicion. See Lillian Faderman, *Surpassing the Love of Men. Romantic Friendship and Love Between Women from the Renaissance to the Present* (New York: William Morrow and Co., Inc., 1981).

25. Liane de Pougy, *Idylle saphique* (Paris: Editions J.-Cl. Lattès, 1979), 145. See Jean de Palacio's article "La féminité dévorante. Sur quelques images de la manducation dans la littérature décadente," *Revue des Sciences humaines* 168 (1977): 601–18.

26. *Le Roman de Violette* (Lisbonne: 1870), 138, 153–54. It actually appeared in 1883 according to Perceau, who attributes it to Mme de Mannoury, the author of *Les Cousines de la Colonelle*.

to experience vaginal orgasms with her lesbian lover. The recourse to defloration and voyeurism, those traditional manifestations of power over the female other, turns this act into an assertion of self-mastery whose treatment is not, however, totally devoid of burlesque. The novel privileges phallic eroticism[27] and, with the addition of a few sentimental touches, is written in the salacious, lighthearted eighteenth-century vein. It at once inverts and respects the traditional model, and its intent is not entirely clear.

In 1884, *Monsieur Vénus*, by Rachilde, developed motifs and themes of cross-dressing and female dominance around a "bisexual" couple. With its clever subversion of Decadent motifs, it can be read as an attempt to leave behind ordinary notions of bisexuality and as an experiment in the radical scrambling of definitions.[28] Rachilde seems to adopt gender stereotypes unquestioningly only in order to demonstrate their absurdity. Thus, the protagonist's independence and intelligence must translate into her slightly mannish beauty and sadistic sexuality. She hates the thought of being penetrated and falls madly in love with the effeminate looks, ignorance, and submissiveness of a young, talentless artist. Both lovers symmetrically invert their dress and their use of personal pronouns and become "more and more united in a common thought: the destruction of their own sexes."[29] Raoule refuses to be a Sapho, in her view a banal and vulgar solution to her discontent with gender relations. She is strongly sadistic, but there is nothing phallic about her embraces, which resemble those of the lesbian pair in *Idylle saphique*.

During this period, the novel that most explicitly underscores the correlation between the social and the erotic is *Les Demi-sexes* (1898), by Jane de la Vaudère. The epigraph, a sonnet signed by the author, denounces the social requirement that defines woman as a breeder better off without brains: "And woman, forever ardent and carnal, / should possess only a headless body / With powerful flanks and white teats!" Despite its conventional ending and contradictory discourse, the novel justifies the choice of lesbianism and sterilization as the only possible rebellion and "revenge" in a society that allows men to abandon women with impunity and will not give the heroine an active social role in keeping with her gifts and education.

The four nineteenth-century novels I have been presenting—to

---

27. So do, more seriously, Janine Aeply, in the masturbation scenes of *Une fille à marier* (Paris: Mercure de France, 1969) and Suzanne Allen in the lesbian scenes of *L'Espace d'un livre*, op. cit., 112–13, 180–81, in which the phallic partner rather playfully enacts various sado-masochistic relationships with her passive lovers.

28. Cf., Micheline Besnard-Coursodon, "Monsieur Vénus, Madame Adonis: Sexe et discours," *Littérature* 54 (May 1984): 127.

29. Rachilde, *Monsieur Vénus*, (Paris: Flammarion, 1977), 110.

which should be added *Amants féminins* (1902), by Adrienne Saint-Agen—establish a correlation between woman's will to power, her interest in lesbianism, and her avoidance of penetration, considered as a form of subjection. This refusal undermines the erotic value of the phallus and, by drawing attention to its significance as a *symbol* of power, also tends to put this power into question. Two factors combine to account for this almost total conflation of lesbianism with "feminist" assertion: the severity of the "confinement" of women in the nineteenth century, and the almost general model of male dominance in erotica. These women's response to their exclusion from both society and erotic models was an equally exclusive separatism: a rejection of phallic eroticism, and a reversal *or*, more subtly, a rejection of the power relation.[30] To be sure, these manifestations would have been disowned by the majority of women, but their collective, symbolic significance is unmistakable.

This explanation seems confirmed when one observes that, in the 1920s, when women had more social freedom and Renée Dunan was tirelessly representing female dominance, she did not resort to the mediation of lesbianism. Her erotic novels depict young women whose intellect, strength of character, and social status surpass those of their lovers. *Les Caprices du sexe ou les audaces érotiques de mademoiselle Louise de B.* (1928) include a few comments on the impossibility for a pretty girl to earn even a miserable salary without granting sexual favors to her employer—the aristocratic heroine runs away from home and soon realizes that it will be more profitable to dedicate herself full time to prostitution. She kills two lovers by overexerting them, and sexually dominates all the others. *Une heure de désir* (1929), a more ambitious attempt, gives a minute and quite subtle account of the man's progress and of the two partners' feelings during the hour that it takes for the young woman to surrender her virginity—a tender word from her lover is what finally defeats her. The narration complacently underscores her superiority and lack of prejudice in contrast to her lover's stereotypes and there are hints that her dream of an equal marriage partnership will be disappointed.[31]

Contemporaneous with women's steadily improving status, the penultimate stage in the evolution of erotic writings by women has been their representation of male dominance and female subjection—for the first time from the victim's standpoint. *Histoire d'O* (1954) is the landmark in this respect, but was preceded by the posthumous *Ecrits de*

30. Elaine Marks also makes the point that exclusive separatism is a response to exclusion: see the conclusion of her article in this issue.

31. In *Fort Frédérick* (Paris: Grasset, 1957), narrated in the third person from the woman's point of view, Françoise des Ligneris describes a sadistic woman's relationship with a fugitive criminal.

Laure, written in the 1930s.[32] The irruption of male physical violence into women's fiction coincided with a recrudescence of the Sadean vein in men's erotica and the growing reputation of Georges Bataille in the Paris intelligentsia to which the author of *Histoire d'O* belongs. Women have continued to explore this somber vein, but, especially since 1968, and more than male authors, they have gradually moved away from stereotypes and formulaic models. (The euphoric vein is best represented by the *Emmanuelle* series and its general economy of pleasure, whose orgiastic confusion is paralleled by a hodgepodge of doctrinal discourse and erotic intertext, and in which phallocentrism, social elitism, and the exchange of women coexist with a fervent portrayal of lesbianism.)

For many women, the most unacceptable aspect of pornographic and erotic literature is the representation of their passive acquiescence to, or even pursuit of, abuse and pain. Several feminist critics have already commented on the frequent (though far from general) use of the third person in women's erotic fiction. They convincingly relate it to a division of the self through which the writing subject objectifies a portion of herself (ultimately identified with the maternal body) and disowns it: the more transgressive the experience, the more necessary the use of the third person.[33] Male authors, on the other hand, have favored the eighteenth-century narrative model long after it was discarded in other subgenres: a young woman recounts her erotic, not necessarily masochistic adventures in the first person, usually to her last lover, sometimes to the public at large.[34] In this respect, Sade's *Juliette* is an exception only inasmuch as *she* is almost always the one who inflicts pain. *Illyrine* and *Julie ou j'ai sauvé ma rose,* both written by women, adopt the first-person narration of the time, but there is no masochism involved, Julie is domineering, and Illyrine prefers pleasure to martyrdom. And yet, a number of their followers even in this light-hearted vein wrote in the

32. *Laure, Ecrits, fragments, lettres,* ed. J. Peignot and the "Collectif Change" (Paris: Pauvert, 1977), 112. [First, partial publ.: 1939].

33. A comparable division may operate in the reader. Nancy Huston is the most thorough on these points. See *Mosaïque de la pornographie,* (Paris: Denoël/Gonthier, 1982), 61, 68–69, 26–27, 201, 217.

34. A few examples: *Margot la Ravaudeuse* (1760), *Félicia* (1775), *Thérèse philosophe* (1748), *Le Rideau levé ou l'Education de Laure* (1783), *Caroline de St-Hilaire* (1817), *Les Matinées du Palais-Royal* (1815), *Vingt ans de la vie d'une jolie femme* (circa 1830), *Autour du mariage de Paulette* (1893), *Jacinthe ou les images du péché* (1934), *La Vierge affranchie* (1936), *Chairs ardentes* (1936). Starting with *Caroline* . . . they all belong to vulgar, formulaic pornography and the use of the first person is a fairly reliable sign that the author is male. First-person novels with a male narrator are much fewer: *L'Anti-Justine* (1797), *L'Enfant du bordel* (1800), *Les Dames de Maison* . . . (1830), *Gamiani* (1833).

third person, as do, still, Emmanuelle Arsan and Régine Deforges, whose *Contes pervers* (1980) include only a few episodes of violence against women.

Written in the third person, *Histoire d'O* illustrates, but also complicates the preceding explanation. It provides all the necessary elements to be read as a radicalization and a critique of pornographic stereotypes about what women are but should not be, but it largely transcends its stereotypes. The author's position is highly ambiguous, and therein lies part of her artistry. She does not clearly dissociate herself from her heroine and points at once to the masculine origin of this model and its unquestioning acceptance by the woman in love. O's own sadistic relations with her women lovers parallel and reveal the central male-female power relation. The author develops this double complementarity through a mixture of third-person narration and interior monologue: most of the book is written in Flaubert's *style indirect libre.* The narrative voice blends with O's voice, while performing a dispassionate dissection of her feelings. This leaves open the question of O's subjectivity: the fact that she may be viewed as a male construct[35] does not necessarily mean that her alienated self is only a semblance—this is, of course, where the book is ambiguous—and the emotional, if distanced intensity of the narration projects an effect of interiority.

In the early 1970s, Xavière's move to a first-person narrative, though far from unique by then,[36] is noteworthy for its rewriting of conventional situations. In *La Punition* (1971), her second and strongest book, the prostitute victim and narrator explores and confronts her own masochism and gradually performs a much clearer rejection of it than the third-person narrator of *Histoire d'O.* This difference is reinforced by a reality effect which distinguishes *La Punition* from the oneiric and ritualistic atmosphere of *Histoire d'O* and other erotic fiction. The text functions on two levels. It exploits the erotic power of pain and death and thus belongs to erotic literature. At the same time, the reference to the real is unmistakable. *La Punition* blurs the frontiers between metaphoric death and the real death which ensues from ill treatment.[37] It strips cruelty, transgression, death, and loss of self from their metaphysical or metaphorical dimension. The loss or lack of identity pre-

35. This is argued in detail by Kaja Silverman, in "*Histoire d'O.* The Construction of a Female Subject," *Pleasure and Danger,* ed. Carole S. Vance (Boston: Routledge and Kegan Paul, 1984), 320–49.

36. Among other examples were Suzanne Allen, *L'Ile du dedans* and *Le Lieu commun* (Paris: Gallimard, 1960 and 1966), Janine Aeply, *Une fille à marier,* op cit., 1969. Brécourt-Villars's selection contains a number of first-person erotic scenes before the 1960s. It is not clear how many of these come from purely erotic stories.

37. See Huston, op. cit., 137–38.

cedes the erotic experience instead of following it and explains its suicidal appeal without any romanticizing. Religion and woman's guilt become empty notions, and transgression a dismal farce.

Paradoxically, women's third-person narratives, despite their distancing intent, convey an effect of identification between the narrator and the actions she is describing. We have already seen this phenomenon at work in *Histoire d'O*. Marguerite Duras's two erotic stories, also written in the third person, show some awareness of the ambiguous effect of this practice. In *L'Homme assis dans le couloir* (1962–1980), the male lover is the object of the woman's devouring love and intense masochism, which has a disturbing presence. The narrator sometimes intervenes ("je vois") to introduce a distinction between herself and the woman, but the effect is not sustained. In *La Maladie de la mort* (1982), the narrator clearly distinguishes herself from the male character, whom she addresses as "Vous": this tends to reinforce her identification with the female character. In these two stories as in *Histoire d'O*, the ambiguity of voices suggests an inability on the part of the narrator to establish self-boundaries.

It is finally the first-person narratives which best perform a distancing operation. They seem to force a direct confrontation of the subject of the enunciation with the subject of the *énoncé*, that is, of the narrator with herself, rather than a fleeting displacement onto an *other*, fictitious character. Having inscribed masochism as her own, the writing subject is able to reject it within the fiction. Hence, already in *Ecrits de Laure*, a connection between the use of the first-person to describe a masochistic episode and the subject's gibes at transgression, of which she becomes the less and less willing instrument and victim. Hence, too, in the plot of *La Punition*, the narrator's final, active rebellion.

How do male and female erotic writings differ? How do erotic writings in general, and women's erotic writings in particular, relate to the evolution of the literary canon? The preceding overview suggests some tentative answers.

Women writers' most common move in the nineteenth century, and sometimes in the twentieth, was to invert the model of male dominance by placing the man in the victim's position and objectifying him. This move was often accompanied by a sympathetic representation of lesbianism which, moreover, tended to minimize the power relation. A more subtle kind of inversion took place afterwards: a return of the woman to her traditional role as erotic object and masochistic victim, but with the status of a subject. Where there had been none before, women writers introduced a female subjectivity, whose alienated nature they exposed (*Histoire d'O*) or rejected through their protagonists (Xavière). Marguerite Duras deviates from this trend in one respect: while O and her sisters remain the man's erotic object, the sadistic man in *L'Homme assis dans le couloir* is at once the tormenter and the erotic object. This difference adds another dimension to the male-female sado-masochistic relation, and indeed strengthens it. In contrast with men's, women's erotica always introduce some love or passion, and grant the female body some integrity: as a result, they often call to mind a female narratee, but, at least in the nineteenth century, their actual readership is virtually impossible to ascertain. During the same period, their status was even lower than that of men's erotica and, if they evoked any mention, it was one of opprobrium. A final difference heralds a qualitative change in the model: although women had hardly ever before questioned or subverted the *fundamental dependence of eroticism on power relations*, they have begun to envision at least the possibility of other forms of eroticism, including ones within heterosexual relations. This was apparent in the discursive parts of *Ecrits de Laure*, or in *Emmanuelle II*, and has become an essential aspect in a number of first-person narratives published in the 1970s and 1980s. A similar difference had often characterized female eroticism in mainstream literature, but in less explicit ways.

There has always been a minimum of interaction of erotic writings with mainstream and high literature—the storehouse of canonic works. While writing *Rose et Blanche* in 1831, George Sand complained about being asked by her publisher to insert some spicy passages in her novel: this was in the aftermath of the orgy scene in Balzac's *La Peau de chagrin*. Today, while erotic ingredients seem even more of a requirement in the novel, there are other, more pervasive ways in which the frontiers between erotic and mainstream literature tend to disappear. For instance, the text of Sollers's *Femmes* is somewhat Sadean, not only because of its phallocentric ideology, but also because of its numerous pastiches and parodies and, finally, of its continuous alternation of erotic scenes and disquisitions, whose diversity of topics manifests an encyclopedic ambition. Discursive digressions in the novel have been mostly associated with Balzac, but Sade may well be their initiator in the French novel, and they have always characterized erotic and pornographic fiction. The example of *Femmes*, and many other works like it, are quantitatively important and do participate in the erosion of generic boundaries. But neither in their representation of erotic relations nor in their *écriture* can they be considered innovative.

It is at the intersection of women's erotica and mainstream literature that some signs of renewal can now be found. Given the limited scope of the erotic model, these are easy to identify. Their ideological and formal manifestations are inseparable. Women now explore the male/female power relation even when they reproduce it, in ways that either put it in question, or evade the formulaic model, or both. Their almost general use of first-person narration for more and more daring confessions—whether autobiographical or not—is crucial in this respect. These new erotic stories exploit the traditional motifs but, even when they emphasize the oneiric and fantasy aspect, they do so against the personal, social, and often professional background of women's everyday life, which is hardly a segregated one. This has at least three consequences. First, it endows the succession of erotic scenes with a "reality effect" which brings out the distinct quality of female eroticism and presents it as an integral part of the female subject. Second, it places eroticism in the context of social and gender relations and actualizes the cultural component of eroticism. Third, these stories are distinguished from mainstream literature only by the predominance they give to erotic episodes: they bypass the formulaic and ritualized model and read as less specialized than erotic novels by, for instance, Robbe-Grillet or Mandiargues. This means that they address and may touch a more general public (perhaps comprised of more women than men, but women writers, readers and critics have become a commercial reality which has an impact on maintream literature). Their contribution is double: they develop a new erotic model, and they are introducing this model into mainstream literature.[38]

Until now, the influence of women's erotica had been nonexistent, either as a generic or a cultural model, and their innovations have remained isolated. Modes of loving, perhaps more than any other behavior, have always been mediated by manifestations of discourse, among them fiction. The fact that *Histoire d'O* is, or was, required reading for young recruits in Roissylike societies provides a particularly acute example of this in a specialized area of sexuality. Erotica have inscribed an ideal of male dominance which has been enacted in real life before being inverted or subverted in texts by women. So far, the latter are the only texts which have looked for possible ways out of this circularity. The present survey suggests that erotic literature today participates in the breakdown of generic definitions that is taking place and that erotic works by women, as they reach the general public, are beginning to play a role in the representation of love and sexuality. For the first time, women erotic writers are able to modify generic and cultural models. Changing models effect changes in canon definitions. A provocative by-product of this phenomenon might turn out to be the participation of women's erotica in canon formation.*

38. Several novels of the 1960s and 1970s, already mentioned. belong in this category, as do Mara, *Journal d'une femme soumise* (Paris: Flammarion, 1979); Séda, *Publique* (Paris: Luneau Ascot, 1980); Colette 'Fellous', *Roma* (Paris: Denoël, 1982); France Huser, *La Maison du désir* (Paris: Seuil, 1982); Juliette, *Pourquoi moi?* (Paris: Robert Laffont, 1987). Jeanne de Berg, *Cérémonies de femmes* (op. cit.), despite its conventional paraphernalia, deserves mention here for its use of the first person.

*I wish to thank Phyllis Rackin and Carlos Lynes for their help in editing this article.

MICHAEL DANAHY

Marceline Desbordes-Valmore and the Engendered Canon

Les femmes, je le sais, ne doivent pas ecrire;
J'écris pourtant
—Marceline Desbordes-Valmore (*Une Lettre de femme*)

Freud thought that all men unconsciously wished to beget themselves, to be their own fathers in place of their phallic fathers and so "rescue" their mothers from erotic degradation. It may not be true of all men, but it seems to be definitive of poets as poets. The poet, if he could, would be his own precursor, and so rescue the Muse from her own degradation.
—Harold Bloom, *Yeats*

Among the politicized forces circumscribing women's place in the literary tradition are paradigms of genre which create what I will call the "en-gendered" canon. Not only is the canon brought into being as a body of writings structured by genre, but, in a dual process, it is simultaneously patterned along sexual lines, with each genre explicitly assigned a sexual paradigm. Poetry was made male, while the novel, as the genre of otherness, was made female.[1]

I will argue the paradox that control of the canon rests as much with

1. I have made the argument about the novel elsewhere; to do so in detail would be beyond the scope of this essay and the purpose of this volume. See my "Le Roman est-il chose femelle?" *Poétique* 25 (1976): 85–106. See also Georges May, *Le Dilemme du roman au XVIIIe siècle* (Paris: P. U. F., 1963). Josephine Donovan suggests that the gender formation of the literary canon was instituted as part of the classical tradition in her discussion of Aristotle's *Poetics* (See "Critical Response 2 "Critical Inquiry 3, no. 3 [Spring 1977], 606–07). The classical hierarchy of canonical genres derived from a gender hierarchy, because Aristotle relied primarily on gender-biassed examples to define canons of propriety and appropriateness, which equated women with nonpoets or nondoers, the inferiorized nonpractitioners of *poesis*. Leslie Rabine (in *Reading the Romantic Heroine* [Ann Arbor: University of Michigan Press, 1985]) and Peggy Kamuf (in *Fictions of Feminine Desire* [Lincoln: University of Nebraska Press, 1982]) have shown, on the other hand, that romance (*le roman*), narrative prose fiction, became the genre of patriarchy's political unconscious as early as the twelfth century, because it became the place, structurally and ideologically, where patriarchal culture struggled to repress and represent women in order to resolve its conflicts with nonpatriarchal values.

the canoniz*ed*, as with their canoniz*ers*. Writers themselves build read-ing models and schemata that shape norms prior to and in ignorance of their own canonization; they articulate and transmit formal criteria or lingering images which subsequently regulate not only who will be inscribed in the canon but where, why, and how they will be inscribed. To the extent that one's place in the canon was assigned by genre, it follows that this assignment was controlled by those who held in their hands the power and the instruments to shape the genre in important and influential ways, among which was precisely the formulation of gender-specific images embodying generic paradigms. In other words, gender-specific paradigms of genre are one of the mediating structures that give writers, as well as readers, access to the canon.

The assignment of genders to genres is inherent in a doxological process such as this, because, by its very nature, canonization entails a respect for the paradigms of the past. But to show that discourse about genre simultaneously inscribes a covert discourse about gender is a difficult task, related, in Sandra Gilbert's words, to the effort to "decode and demystify all the disguised questions and answers that have always shadowed the connections between textuality and sexuality, genre and gender, psychological identity and cultural authority."[2] As elusive as this pattern may prove to be, however, it derives from and re-presents Cixous's now famous "tyranny of the binary," which she defined as "the whole conglomeration of symbolic systems—everything, that is, that's spoken, everything that's organized as discourse . . . it is all or-dered around hierarchical oppositions that come back to the man/wom-an opposition. . . ."[3] In other words, the designation of poetry as male and the novel as female implies a literary hierarchy that systematically re-produces the sexual hierarchy. By reading through and beyond an accumulation of nineteenth-century examples, we can see how the hi-erarchy of genres crystallized in esthetic canons which operated dialec-tically, negatively to feminize the novel, but more importantly for our purposes here, positively to masculinize poetry. Thereby, the tyranny of the binary systematically controlled the formation of the French liter-ary tradition itself.

Marceline Desbordes-Valmore consciously experienced this engen-dered canon as part of a system intimidating to women. The Romantics, of course, often contrasted booklearning, which deformed and de-natured the human individual, with the spontaneous, original, creative "natural" self. But Desbordes-Valmore personalized and politicized this conventional theme by satirically depicting the educational and literary systems as a male-dominated environment and attributing their stul-

2. "What do Feminist Critics Want?" *ADE Bulletin* 66 (Winter, 1980): 19.
3. Hélène Cixous, "Castration or Decapitation?" *Signs* 7, no. 1 (1981): 44.

tifying effects precisely to this environment. Also aware that the standing of women was both prescribed and proscribed in the genre "of the masters," as she put it, she wrote of herself in "A M. Alphonse de Lamartine":

> Before the solemn songs you bring,
> Sung alas by both an angel and a man,
> This lyre, mute and without string,
> Incomplete and knowing not how to sing,
> Hardly dares to use the voice it can.[4]

In writing about the sonnet as the canonical form of poetry, she resorted to images of confinement or imprisonment. "This regular genre belongs to men only, who count it a great pleasure for themselves to triumph over their very thoughts by confining them to this brilliant shackle."[5] She knew the works of Louise Labé, dedicated a poem to her, and even lived in Lyon, but in forty years wrote no more than three sonnets among six hundred poems.[6] Nor did she respect the tradition of alternating so-called masculine and feminine rhymes from one stanza to the next.

To see the paradigmatic pattern at work, placing women poets in the tradition, circumscribing—that is, re-placing—Desbordes-Valmore's potential for canonization, we turn first to a member of the Royal Academy of Medicine named Virey (1775–1847). Numerous works on science and hygiene made him a respected authority on women and he captured the dominant ideology of the time in a succinct formula encompassing the interlocking pattern of social and esthetic, sexual and literary categories. "That frivolity of taste," he declared, "those eternal fluctuations in ideas and penchants will forever keep women below the

4. All citations are from *Les Oeuvres poétiques de Marceline Desbordes-Valmore,* ed. Marc Bertrand (Grenoble: Presses Universitaires de Grenoble, 1973), 2 vols. All translations are mine. See, e.g., the series "A mon fils" and "Hippolyte," "Jeune homme irrité sur un banc d'école," "Laissez-moi pleurer," "Les Jours d'été," and *O. p.,* 755 and 757. For what follows, see 225 and "Au revoir," 395, where the poet opts for the novel as a generic self-image: "You no longer take interest in me. / Like the detached leaves of an agreeable novel that have been read, you believed you read me and the page is over."

5. *Lettres de Marceline Desbordes-Valmore à Prosper Valmore* (Paris: Editions de la Sirène, 1924), 2, 151. See also *O. p.,* 2, 798, 690, and the preface to *Bouquets et Prières.* In *Lettres,* 2, 303, she recounts a personal example of the inability of male poets to accept their female counterparts as professional equals.

6. Nancy Vickers has demonstrated that in the Petrarchan tradition of poetry, "his speech requires her silence," that is, the male poet/lover renders the female beloved passive, seen, desired, dis-membered, re-membered. See "Diana Described: Scattered Woman and Scattered Rhyme," *Writing and Sexual Difference,* ed. Abel (Chicago: University of Chicago Press, 1982), 95–109.

level of perfection in the sciences, letters, and the arts."[7] Virey can ascribe his norm for imperfection in letters to one gender, because the norm he had in mind for perfection was indubitably ascribed to the other gender. And we know that this other, unenunciated norm for the superiority or perfection of letters was inevitably already and always poetry, because the novel was held to be intrinsically and generically inferior for the *same* reasons that women were—the superficiality and irregularity of their nature. By thus sexualizing literature, Virey operates a displacement, for he attributes qualities of mind and body to women which, when they appear in literature as esthetic and ethical qualities, were attributed primarily to the novel. The hidden cultural preferences of phallocratic discourse dictate a text in which inferiority in letters was coded to mean the novel, while the full embodiment of perfection meant poetry. Virey's formula elides these connections, but his elision, although hiding the displacement, leaves behind traces of the displacement of these gender-genre connections.

The general privileging of the male inherent in the paradigms leads one to hypothesize a hierarchical preference among genres based on the engendering of the canon. This hypothesis is confirmed by the pervasive use of genre names as value-labels that denigrate or elevate. Just as novelists were not yet admitted to the French Academy, which remained, two centuries after Boileau, the symbol, bastion, and patron of the literary establishment, the very words for novel, *roman* and *romanesque*, remained derogatory while corresponding parts of speech designating poetic qualities—adjectives, adverbs, and the like—remained laudatory. The term *novelistic* was used to designate works of art that were poorly constructed, lacked intellectual, moral, and esthetic substance, and carried no credibility or prestige. Novelistic prose, less polished and less significant than "poetic" prose, was inherently inferior. Throughout the century, the "poetic values" identified in published reviews remained far more crucial to the success of a novel than its "novelistic value." Indeed, "valeur" and "romanesque" remained mutually exclusive terms, and the novel was still widely referred to as "frivole" and "léger," the same coded words Boileau had used to "feminize" the genre.[8] And one anonymous critic writing in *La Revue des*

7. Yvonne Knibiehler, "Le Discours médical sur la femme," *Mythes et représentations de la femme au dix-neuvième siècle*, ed. Duchet (Paris: Champion, 1976), 48. Prominent physicians and medical scientists of the day actually cited novel reading as a cause of hysteria among women; Knibiehler, 51.

8. What conservatives made taboo as a threat to their sense of order, some Romantics construed as a generic advantage. Hugo, for instance, proclaimed that The Revolution "is in the novel speaking softly to women" ("Réponse à un acte d'accusation"). For Hugo, just the same, women were no more apt to become poets than they were soldiers: "I dream of war in my restless soul; I would have been a soldier, had I not become a poet" ("Mon enfance" cf., "He is a genius, because, more than the others, he is a man." in "Le Poème éploré se lamente").

Deux Mondes, typically summarized the hierarchy of genres in the following way. Discussing why any and every tone, thought, style or subject is permissible in the novel, he explained in a burst of vivid imagination that the novel is the epic bedecked in female clothing, promiscuous, indiscriminate, and unselective: "It is an epic in a negligé and struts about at will; it renounces neither the looseness of intimate conversation nor the hard and fast forms of poetry."[9]

The verbal stratagems of major novelists like Balzac who showed due respect for the canons of propriety and accepted engenderized esthetic norms which demeaned the name of his own genre, can serve to indicate the conceptual contortions required to rationalize the engendered canon. Genre labels inscribe a consistent, systematic polarity of opposites that are based on sexual analogy and that codify and regulate literary inspiration on behalf of men.

In contrast to generic paradigms of domesticity and feminine degradation of novels and novelists found in *Illusions perdues,* for instance, the *image* of the poet is associated with male potency. Speaking of Lucien, the narrator notes: "To this poet . . . the present seemed without worry. Success filled the sails of his bark. He had at his command the tools needed for his projects: a well-furnished house, a mistress Parisian society was jealous of, a carriage and team, and, finally, incalculable sums in his inkstand".[10] The horses, the swelling of his sails and his "liquid" treasure all engender poetry as much as a calling to Holy Orders does in the following remark about Lucien. "Neither the miller nor his wife could suspect that, besides the actor, the prince and the bishop, there is a man who is as much prince as actor, a man clothed in a magnificent priesthood, the poet. . . ." Similarly, the narrator of *La Muse du département* belittles Dinah de la Baudraye, the so-called "tenth Muse," for her "novelistic pretentions," while the man for whom she yearns is labelled a "poetic ideal." Typically, Balzac's narrator may treat the image as lost, problematic, ironic, or illusory, but poetry is nonetheless masculinized as the measure of a higher, different

9. See Marguerite Iknayan, *The Idea of the Novel in France: The Critical Reaction 1815–1848* (Geneva: Droz, 1961), 114 and 52–60, and 177–178. For further examples, see Stendhal, *Le Rouge et le noir,* ed. Martineau (Paris: Garnier, 1961), 444, 503, and 506. See also Pierre Barbéris in *Histoire littéraire de la France* (Paris: Editions sociales, 1973), 4, Part 2, 237.

10. *Illusions perdues,* ed. Adam (Paris: Garnier, n.d.), 440, and, for what follows, 543, 250–51, 272–73, and 293. Louise de Bargeton stood in awe of "toutes les existences poétiques et dramatiques" (46). "Romanesques affectations" and "poétique idéal" typify Balzac's use of genre labels that evoke further binary oppositions between negative and/or positive and feminine and/or masculine in, for instance, *Le Père Goriot, La Muse du Département,* and *Mémoires de deux jeunes mariés.* See Richard Bolster, *Stendhal, Balzac et le féminisme romantique* (Paris: Lettres Modernes, 1970), 36–44, 47–49, 54–57, 65, and 77 and Marthe Robert, *Roman des origines et origines du roman* (Paris: Grasset, 1972), 285.

standard at the same time that the quintessential standard for beauty—
the Orient, existence, evil, misfortune, or whatever—is labelled
"poetic."

Consequently, the dilemma of novelists working in a female-identi-
fied genre did not confront the brotherhood of poets who could encour-
age each other to conform to same-sex canons of esthetic propriety.
Vigny proclaimed in "La Maison du berger" that the destiny of poetry
was to "gleam on a male brow." "La Mort du loup," which furnishes an
enduring Romantic figure of the poet, sheds light on Vigny's proposi-
tion. Not incidentally or accidentally, it is one that falsifies the behavior
patterns of wolves under attack and replaces what an experienced hunt-
er like Vigny probably knew with the poet's own projection of *pater-
familias*, sole protector of his offspring and his silent, passive helpmate.
Ignoring the initial slip, Vigny overdetermines the utterly stereotypical
father figure with the impressive and symbolically appropriate physical
characteristics ("ongles crochus," "gueule brûlante," "mâchoires de
fer," and "deux yeux qui flamboyaient") which "poetize" him. His
"great marked paws" yield a kind of writing that contrasts with the vile
utilitarian documents of city dwellers ("le pacte des villes"—pun
intended?). The wolf leaves behind on the earth scratches that humans
may interpret as traces of his presence or passage. "These fresh marks,"
inscribe "the powerful moves and the mighty claws" of Vigny's ideal
embodiment of the poet.

When Lamartine wrote to Desbordes-Valmore that "Providence
. . . marked us in the cradle for one of its most noted gifts,"[11] he may
have had in mind at some unconscious level a visible anatomical mark
as the sign of his own poetic birthright and destiny. At any rate, in "A
Madame Desbordes-Valmore," he allegorized the vocation of the poet as
two kinds of boat. The greater one, transporting only male passengers,
sails on "like a stallion sowing, in its wake, white froth from its bit."
The lady poet, on the other hand, is called to the "frail crew" working
under "humble sail" and lest the sexual patterning escape her notice,
Lamartine reintroduced it on "the floating household." The woman,
"leaning against the swaying mast that she grasps in one hand, held
suspended from her breast a suckling child," while "the man of the
house plowed the furrowed seas." Lamartine's text is strangely reminiscent of Balzac's cited above, for both incorporate "esquif" and "équipage," although the metaphorical vehicles vary in each case.

Turning to Baudelaire's essay singling out Desbordes-Valmore as "a
soul of the elite," we can see how the engendered canon becomes an
overriding force.[12] Ironically, the female poet figures only as an excep-

11. O. p., 1, 357 and for what follows, see 2, 819.
12. Baudelaire, "Réflexions sur quelques-uns de mes contemporains," *Oeuvres complètes*, ed. Le Dantec and Pichois (Paris: Gallimard, 1961), 718.

tion that does not threaten or problematize the pervasive interlocking pattern masculinizing poetry and feminizing the novel. It is true that Baudelaire assigns her to the aristocracy or, rather, to an aristocracy, the one he calls "natural," and which we know from other texts is only a second-class, external one opposed to the greater "unnatural" or spiritual aristocracy of dandies and creators of genius. Two adjectives, *feminine* and *natural*, recur throughout the essay as code words for her poetry; she is a poet of nature and her style is natural, i.e., simple, direct spontaneous, from the heart. To epitomize her work, Baudelaire concludes that unlike a French or Italian garden, she remains "un simple jardin romantique et romanesque."

We must of course read this reading of the female poet in conjunction with all of Baudelaire's other texts on esthetic values, where invariably, the qualities of the vegetal, organic, and irregular symbolize the antithesis of true form in poetry. From such a vantage point, his analysis filled a double function. First he praised her for embodying the "eternal feminine," but to the extent that she incorporates through her femininity the profuse, wild, and uncultivated forces of earthiness that Baudelaire scorned elsewhere, his analysis enabled him to bring into play his esthetic rejection of Romanticism. Thus he articulated the canons for discounting poetry by women. In the same essay, he self-consciously addressed himself to his implied reader and cast this privileged figure in the masculine singular. Desbordes-Valmore does not, in other words, belong to the male elite of fellow poets, whom he takes also as his proper audience in the imagined dialogue.

Consequently, the very terms Baudelaire used to commemorate Desbordes-Valmore as the feminine poet par excellence institute an ironic strategy for reading women poets that covertly preserves intact masculine paradigms for the poetic process and product. But because these terms contain a hidden agenda, rejecting Romanticism in general and rendering the masculinization of poetry immune to criticism, they help us understand the generalized obstacles to creating canonical paradigms for difference. On the other hand, Desbordes-Valmore's conception of her vocation for poetry and images of the poet related to it, because they set her apart from the engendered paradigms, will clarify the politics of tradition that has resulted in a canon that is both gender-based and gender-biassed.

Although women of Desbordes-Valmore's time were consigned to being "muses,"[13] on the off chance that some of them might become poets in their own right, their proper place in a man's world, the brotherhood of poets, was "naturally" prescribed as the "feminine press" of the day. Titles alone on the publications in which Desbordes-Valmore's work appeared make the point. These included *Hommage aux Dames,*

13. Jeanine Moulin, *La Poésie féminine* (Paris: Seghers, 1966), 57–59.

*Hommage aux Demoiselles, Guirlande des Dames, Les Femmes po-
ètes, Almanach des Muses, Almanach des Dames, Almanach des Demoiselles, Chansonnier des Dames, Chansonnier des Grâces, Chansonnier des Belles,* and *Conseiller des femmes.* To contemporaries, they
signalled that women poets, authorized or empowered only to write for
other women, would not gain or be granted access to the canon.

Viewed differently, however, this circumscribed audience shows up
on the other side of the ledger of literary history, no longer as a liability,
but as an asset. The poet's consciousness of being female enables her to
speak of and to her muse as a kindred spirit, free of the sexual tensions
that befall men speaking of and to their Muse. The tones of defen-
siveness, hostility, or embarrassment that frequently characterize lyric
apostrophes based on the usual male/female rhetoric are remarkably
absent. Able to speak woman to woman (as in "A Madame A. Tastu"),
she finds in sororal bonds a source of strength, to which she attributes
her creativity, candor, and courage in speaking.

Speaking about or against the politics of tradition is not Desbordes-
Valmore's principal way of placing women poets in French literature.
Rather, this placement occurs with her insistence on the practice of
poetry as a verbal form of intersubjectivity. It is less a topic she speaks
about than a *topos* she speaks from and which gives her a way of speaking about things. On one level, she engages her readers in it, by not using
falsely generic nouns and pronouns in the masculine singular to speak
paradigmatically or universally. Rather, she impersonates one sex or the
other explicitly. Thus, she grammatically encodes the speakers *of* her
poems, as well as the speakers *in* her poems, while embodying speaking
voices in vegetation, animals, birds, and even inanimate objects, as well
as humans. As a result, the poetic "I," or central, controlling consciousness, speaks concretely and individually as a male at times, as a
female at others, and as nonsexed at still others. The richness of impersonations is a definining characteristic of her voice.

Many of her poems, for instance, consist of dialogues between animals. Among those which are deliberately gendered, sometimes the
dialogue is between two females as in "Le Pélican ou les deux mères" (a
fascinating debate between proponents of opposing ideologies of motherhood, where one mother is "il" and the other, "une autruche," is
"elle") and sometimes between two males as in "Deux chiens" (where
she playfully imagines two dogs speaking to each other). By contrast,
"Les Deux ramiers" are imagined as "the gentle and discrete models for
lovers" and "Les Deux peupliers" as "married," but the implied gender
differences remain unimportant and unmarked, since the couple is not
stereotyped by sex roles. In fact, this, like many of her "love" lyrics, can
be read as a statement not restricted to heterosexual relationships, but
about female friends and the bonds between them.

The same variability prevails among human speakers. In addition to mixed-sex dialogues, some poems stage all male speakers, others all females. And even where a dialogue form is not consciously adopted, the speaker is sometimes gendered male, at other times female. The speaking subject even shifts from "Je" to "on," in "Point d'adieux," or to "nous" in "Nocturne II," while the gender of the speaking subject is kept textually indeterminate. Moreover, in poems which embody only a male or female speaker, the implied audience directly addressed is sometimes gender-marked as male ("Le Prisonnier de guerre") and sometimes as female ("L'Amour"). But the gender of a particular poem's intended audience may also be left indeterminate and finally matter no more than the gender of the speaker.

For engendering the self-image of the poet, Desbordes-Valmore shows the same di-morphism in her embodiments and the same vocal versatility. The child is one of her favorite figures for the poet; in referring to herself as well as her daughter, she frequently makes the word "enfant" and its adjectives masculine. One might suppose, therefore, that its gender does not vary grammatically in her work. Such is not the case, however, for a mixing of the "dominant" and "muted" patterns and voices occurs. The speaker of "L'Impossible" yearns for "Un rêve! où je sois libre, enfant, à peine née,/ . . . Quand tout vivait pour moi, vaine petite fille!" [A dream! where I am free, a child, hardly born./ When everything was alive for me, vain little girl], and in "Ame et jeunesse" the soul of the speaker addresses its body as "be*lle* enfant" (See also "Plus de Chants"). This gender code-switching occurs not only from one poem to another, but even within poems, like "Tristesse," where the poet speaks of herself as "isolée," but echoing the past participle of "L'Impossible" from the same collection, she is also "ce pauvre enfant heureux . . . qui, *né* pour le malheur . . . je le regrette encor, ce pauvre enfant, c'était moi" [this poor happy child . . . who, born for unhappiness, I regret it still, this poor child, it was me.] And in "L'Église d' Aroma," the speaker embodies herself as female but switches to masculine pronouns and adjectives toward the end of the poem and in midline: "Et me voilà parei*lle* à ce volage enfant" [And there I am like this flighty child] (See also "Qu'en avez-vous fait?"). In "La Vallée de la Scarpe," her own portrait of the artist as a young female, she exclaimed, "Oh! qui n'a souhaité redevenir enfant!" echoing a line perhaps borrowed from Byron: "Ah! happy years! once more who would not be a boy!" For the Englishman's (and Baudelaire's) rather blithe, falsely universal paradigms, "La Vallée" provides the appropriate revision. Although she leaves the word "enfant" in the masculine, the context of the poem makes it abundantly clear that her poetic "Je," returning nostalgically to its origins, is gendered differently.

If no one gender prevails among Desbordes-Valmore's *personae*, the reason seems to be that the poet was neither compelled nor afraid to prefer one over the other. Engendering the female poet as male or embodying herself in male speakers and projections did not threaten the identity and unity of her self-concept. On the other hand, she does not accept the male as paradigm for the universal or the poet in particular. Rather, because the projection of the self-image is not consistently or automatically embodied, the reader is put on alert not to take gender for granted; it is problematic and careful attention is required to determine how the pronouns "le" and "la" affect meaning, because the text will engender itself in different ways.

Despite its title, "La Voix Perdue" reverberates with such a tone of self-assurance. The speaker creates two roles, a mother and a daughter, and the mother in turn recounts the metamorphosis of Philomela into a nightingale.

> On a dit qu'autrefois, au sein d'une famille,
> Il vécut sous un front brûlant de jeune fille.
> Cet être harmonieux aimait l'ombre et les fleurs;
> Nul ne pouvait l'entendre et retenir ses pleurs.
> Rossignol, il chantait aux errantes étoiles;
> Jeune fille, il pleurait, dérobé sous ses voiles.

> The legend says, in the family's bosom,
> Beneath the brow of a young girl it lived.
> This creature of harmony loved both flowers and shade
> And no one heard it without shedding a tear.
> Nightingale, it sang to the wandering stars;
> Young maiden, it sobbed invisibly beneath its veils.

Through a series of metamorphoses, the plumed progeny, springing from Philomela's forehead, incorporates the speaking subject, the poetic consciousness or "I" of the poem. First, the mother identifies empathically with her own offspring, seeing in her a reflection of herself, while the daughter in turn is expected to see herself reflected in the young girl, Philomela. But the mother's situation vis-à-vis her offspring is also reflected by and equated with Philomela's, from whose body the bird will spring. Thus, the roles of progenitor and progeny seem interchangeable, as do the three female figures, equated with the same thing and, consequently, with each other. As the dominant speaker in the poem, the older female is identified both directly and indirectly with what the nightingale figures. Escaping from the head of the young girl, it embodies the poet's functions because "it eases the way of the exiled" and speaks "to a mother simple like myself and to a child as shy and charming as you." Also like the poet, "it is destined to be alone, to cast its sobs, free, between the heavens and the earth." The bird is male-gendered grammatically (*le rossignol*) and because he travels with "sa compagne." Despite this fact, however, the older female is reassuring her offspring—and through this figure, her own poetic self-projection—that the changes one may experience, such as "la voix perdue" or switches in gender, need not be feared as the loss of identity or the poet's voice.[14]

Beyond impersonation and gender code-switching, Desbordes-Valmore imagines the poet as having a special ability, that of transforming one self, one speaker, one subject into another. For her, childbearing is a figure of poetic identity and the intimate, organic, and special relationship of the speaker to her own text often leads to such figures of parent and child. In "Un Nouveau-né," she says to and about her son Hippolyte, "Adieu! . . . I am no longer the happy chrysalis,/ Where the soul of my soul throbbed for nine months." This poem reflects the belief then current that the sights, colors, sounds, and rhythms experienced by a pregnant woman were actually communicated to the foetus. Being a creative mother therefore involves selecting appropriate sensory input as textual detail and in the poem she makes these connections explicit. Because the cocoon imagery obviously suggests a womblike existence for the caterpillar, it provides the privileged image of her vocation and work as a period of gestation or slow transformation.

Real caterpillars secrete the strand with which they make their cocoons directly from their mouths. The metamorphosis of the caterpillar orally creating a cocoon around and from itself and emerging as a new form of life suggests that poetry is a verbal cocoon in which the usual relationships between subject and object or self and other are redefined. This is the issue on which we will want to re-mark the differences which set Desbordes-Valmore apart from the engendered canon.

In *Women Writers and Poetic Identity*,[15] Margaret Homans showed how construing relations between the speaking subject and the other, the world of persons and things, in terms of subjects and objects leads to the alienation of the female voice, because it means construing relationships in terms of male subject and female object. She concludes that women had great difficulty identifying their consciousness with the

14. The speaker's poem is itself a strange metamorphosis of the well-known myth dedicated to her daughter Inès who lost both a beautiful singing voice and her life to tuberculosis. Before acquiring a poetic voice of her own, moreover, Desbordes-Valmore had experienced a similar loss of voice physically. Concerning the Philomela myth and its importance when it comes to re-placing women writers in the tradition, see Jane Marcus, "Liberty, Sorority, and Misogyny," in *Representations of Women* (New York: Columbia University Press, 1983), 88–91 and "Still Practice, A/Wrested Alphabet: Toward a Feminist Aesthetic," *Tulsa Studies* (Spring-Fall 1984), 79–96. See also Pat Joplin, "The Voice of the Shuttle," *Stanford Literary Review* 1, no. 1 (Spring 1984): 25–53.

15. Margaret Homans, *Women Writers and Poetic Identity* (Princeton: Princeton University Press, 1980).

speaking subject of most poetry because the Judeo-Christian tradition excluded all women since Eve from control over language and because the romantic view of Mother Nature made woman an object rather than the center of subjectivity. In Desbordes-Valmore's work, however, the presence of difference is not tied to the usual distinctions attendant upon subject/object relationships and the time-honored philosophical issues to which this dichotomy gave rise. The intersubjectivity she achieves with the body of her text means that the speaking subject does not present or structure herself as trapped in the subject/object dichotomy, either as an alienated voice speaking to or about objects, or as an autonomous self dominating them. Nature is thus not the object of contemplation adopted from male poetry as an alien body of fearful, external forces which can swallow up subjectivity in wild vegetation. Rather, the caterpillar embodies the butterfly, the one becomes mysteriously the other, without converting the self or the other into an object of destruction or subjugation. Neither creature is superior, neither inferior.

Thus, in "Elégie," the poet changes one female identity for another, "resembling a chrysalis, / Which prepares its radiant destiny brooding beneath its cold, dark shield." Her images confer value upon a form of life not usually valued positively, life cut off from the outside world, shrouded, veiled, wrapped up or in limbo. Similarly, to evoke the writings of Louise Labé, which she called "feuilles parlantes", she penned the following lines, doubly appropriate for two poets who lived in the silk capital of Europe.

> O Louise! on croit voir l'éphémère éternel
> Filer dans les parfums sa soyeuse industrie;
>
> . . . .
>
> Fiévreux, loin du soleil, l'insecte se consume;
> D'un fil d'or sur lui-même ourdissant la beauté,
> Inaperçu dans l'arbre où le vent l'a jeté,
> Sous un linceul de feu son âme se rallume!
>
> Oui! ce sublime atome est le rêve des arts;
> Oui! les arts dédaignés meurent en chrysalides,
>
> . . . .
>
> Car tu l'as dit: longtemps un silence invincible,
> Etendu sur ta voix qui s'éveillait sensible,
> Fit mourir dans ton sein des accents tout amour,
> Que tu tremblais d'entendre et de livrer au jour.
>
> Louise, we seem to see before us the ever ephemeral
> Weaving its silken industry in and out amidst the scents. . . .
> Feverish, far from the sun, the insect consumes itself,

Warping itself with the beauty of a golden thread,
Overlooked in the tree where the wind cast it,
Beneath a shroud of fire its spirit rekindles;
Yes, this sublime atom is the dream of the arts;
Yes, the arts, disdained, die in their cocoons, . . .
For you yourself have said it, a long invincible silence,
Covering up your voice which was awake with feeling,
Stifled in your breast all love of sound,
You trembled to hear sound or confide it to the day.

But she will not be interred within the conflicts that mark her condition; rather, the invincibly inaudible speaker ("l'éphémère éternel") begins her work among the odors or lingering memories of flowers, Desbordes-Valmore's usual metaphor for her unspoken sexual activity. By an effect akin to synesthesia, the olfactory sensation yields to an impression of blazing glory, so that what has been inhaled, organically ingested by the insect, becomes a visual image as it passes through its body. The shroud of fire made from golden threads is spun from the very substance of the caterpillar's dying flesh. For the process to be complete and subject/object boundaries transformed, the embodiment of poetry requires paradox: the metamorphosis that takes place unseen in obscurity shines forth brightly.

Nowhere is the poet's refusal to subscribe to the engendered canon and her re-formulations of the traditional subject/object dichotomies made more clear than in her treatment of the mother-daughter relationship inscribed in the imagery of Mother Earth which is related to the theme of death. And nowhere is her commitment to difference and to the life of intersubjectivity made more vivid, for she has a dyadic, rather than a polar sense of organic growth, which grounds her consciousness of di-morphic transformations in the soiled matter of permeability. Perhaps because the poet had buried daughters, as well as a mother, images of a future as well as a past self, a progenitor as well as progeny, the earth is never a figure that threatens wholly to absorb her in its bosom or womb.

The organic transformation of flower into fruit supplies an important cluster of images for the kind of intersubjectivity in question. And the pattern which the images establish reiterates the relationships noted in "La Voix perdue" between the mother and the daughter, Philomela and the bird. In "La Tombe lointaine," Desbordes-Valmore postulates a double identification; first, she identifies her mother with flowers ("Les fleurs de ton visage / Languissent sur le mien." "Vers ta grâce ignorée, / Comme on va droit aux fleurs"). Visually, the progenitor's life lingers in the fleshtones of the daughter which are then metaphorically transferred, when the poet identifies herself, through sensory contact, with the analogous metamorphosis of the flower into a fruit. Thus the di-morphic object exteriorizes the organic rapport in which the daughter prolongs the mother, as the fruit does the flower. The poet stresses physical resemblances, as well as the biological and emotional bonds the two share. In reiterating the feeling that she is the prolongation of her deceased mother's life "par tes charmes . . . par tes larmes," she connects her mature identity, embodied at first only as the fruit, ultimately with her power to sing songs. She evokes both her mother's and her own "maternels pouvoirs," specifically in the sound of the former's voice. She asks her mother, "Ce fruit que je respire / L'as-tu vu dans sa fleur? / Ce chant que je soupire / En plains-tu la douleur?" [This fruit I breathe in / Did you see it as a blossom? / This song I sadly sing / Do you pity its suffering?] In this series of parallel displacements, the flower which the mother once saw has become the fruit which the daughter now inhales, while it in turn becomes the song which the poet exhales. The daughter born of the mother is identified with the fruit of the poet.

But the embodiments of the poet in poetry preserve difference. The shared object remains the same organism, but enjoys a common life in two different forms. Difference is also preserved by distinguishing the senses brought into play to appropriate the di-morphic object. While ordinary mortals, a mother or daughter, would be restricted in their separate contacts with an object, each to her own sense organs alone, the poet has enhanced organic connections with both flower and fruit interchangeably. Hence, the poet grounds intersubjectivity in the subtext of organic sharing that mother and daughter enjoy, the one in smelling, the other in seeing.

Elsewhere, reversing direction, the female poet's special power to be di-morphic and speak in a variety of embodiments enables "La Mère qui pleure" to make herself the prolongation of her deceased child, envisioned as a departed bird, whose song the mother's voice prolongs posthumously. If "l'enfance est poète," as we have seen, so too is the "maternal séjour." Identification with Mother Earth, whether through burial, descent or return to the "pays natal," is constructive, rather than destructive, because it furnishes the poet with a self-image. Nature, in being "la Maison de ma mère," is also the "maison du moi." Having a mother, being a mother, having a child, being a child, these separate aspects of her self can unite in earth where these figures are buried. But because it is not a completely closed off, inert refuge, it does not unequivocally threaten her with going to seed, irreversibly vegetating, or being wholly swallowed up. But by the same token, she cannot detach herself completely from it. When she unites in death the child she had with the child she was, the mother is there to denote, to remind her of the poet's call. Conversely, when she merges the mother she is with the mother she had, the child is there to remind her of the same calling.

Since the ties to Mother Nature are not unilateral, she can switch around the bonds in renewing her efforts to figure out the poetic self. The di-morphic figure which Mother Earth yields unifies her consciousness of self as poet, because it offers alternative ways of re-membering, projecting herself into the earth and identifying with it. "Ma mère nous enfante à l'éternel séjour," she exclaims in "Les Sanglots," and often speaks of the cemetery as a garden, a hot house, or a playground.[16] In that metaphorical place and way, the poet successfully metamorphosed language on her own terms, remaking the androcentric Romantic cliché of the "femme-fleur" into a concrete, vivid, bodily experience.

Desbordes-Valmore preserves difference in a third and final sense, more fundamental and general than the ways we have discussed thus far. In her practice, intertextuality is the form of intersubjectivity specific to poets. In evoking the origins of poetic genius, the poetic process, or the poetic product, most Romantics accepted the analogy that, as a tree naturally came only from another of the same species, like was born from like.[17] The poetic subject, on the other hand, fixed for itself a vantage point from which to view this unilinear march from forebear to offspring, life to death, in terms of mutually exclusive polarities, locked in an either/or relationship. Either one was alive or dead, parent or child.

Similarly, the canon valorizes the transmission of poetry from one poet or generation to the next by means of an inheritance or inspiration received from a man's Muse or a Heavenly Father. In Desbordes-Valmore's time and place, legacies still passed primarily from father to son, while the idea of inspiration implied another exclusive attribute of omnipotent divine males, the creation of form *ex nihilo*. As a subject, the poet either possessed creativity or, on the contrary, was possessed as an object by it. To be inspired, moreover, was to be chosen in a special moment from on high, as noted in Lamartine's remark above, anatomically (and therefore automatically) determined at, and by, birth.

To the extent that Romantics used this ideology (the poet is poet, by virtue, not of work, but of nature, of being born a certain way) to reserve poetry to the dominant gender, but also to deny the need for a father, a teacher, or a guide, then women poets had a greater chance to be free of it. They felt no need to affirm it because they had no need to deny the helping "hand" of an oedipal father in their vocation, as do men in the Freudian account. On this point, Desbordes-Valmore echoes Lamartine: "Jamais aucune main sur la corde sonore / Ne guida dans ses jeux

16. In its simplicity and intensity, "Inès" is the poem which makes the earth mother as much a poet as childhood was.

17. See M. H. Abrams, *The Mirror and the Lamp* (New York: Norton, 1958), 172–218.

sa main novice encore. / L'homme n'enseigne pas ce qu'inspire le ciel."
[Never did a hand on the musical string guide in its play his hand still
novice. Man is not instructed in what heaven inspires] ("L'Ame de
Paganini").

Desbordes-Valmore speaks of herself, her vocation, and work neither in terms of being heir to a poetic tradition, nor of being inspired,
neither in terms of possessing nor of being possessed—by feelings, poetic furor, or even men. A tomb is the only inheritance she speaks of, and
even that she cannot rely on: "L'ironie embaumée a remplacé la pierre /
Où j'allais, d'une tombe indigente héritière, / Relire ma croyance au
dernier rendez-vous!" [An embalmed irony has replaced the stone
where, indigent heir of a tomb, I was going to reread my belief in the last
reunion.] The primacy of a male authority figure is factored out, moreover, by the kind of parent and child images she uses. In "La Jeune fille et
sa mère," it is the girl's willingness to ask her mother to authorize her
story that brings the poem into being, just as, in the poem after it, "La
Visite au hameau," the daughter becomes the source or pretext authorizing the mother's monologue.

To the divine ideology of creating form *ex nihilo*, she prefers figures
of transformation within life and designates as a maternal embodiment
the hope that creation is not the ultimate form of destruction, but that
destruction of the worm, the cocoon, or the flower, ultimately means
that creation—of the fruit, of a butterfly—will prevail. For her, the kind
of tension-ridden oedipal anxities evoked above, in the epigraph from
Bloom, simply did not and indeed could not possibly furnish the driving
force behind intertextuality and canon formation. Rather, for the woman poet, for a woman to be a poet, intertextuality occurs once one has
agreed to nurture the other's form *in utero*. In regard to intertextuality,
therefore, before she can read or re-write the text of the other, she must
be its mother. Thus, the feeling of being double takes on a very different
meaning, because a kind of intratextuality must precede intertextuality, just as the intrauterine subjectivity in a poem like "A mon fils
avant le collège" seems to precede intersubjectivity. Likewise, she says
to her son in "Un Nouveau-né," referring to his foetal state, "D'hier
nous sommes deux." But before being two, the di-morphs are one pre-
natally. Not the physical fact alone of maternity, but the consciousness
she developed of it, enabled her to achieve the richness of intertextuality—measured by her numerous citations, paraphrases, translations, imitations, etc.—which in fact she achieved. Projecting herself
into children of both sexes as self-images fostered this ability to embody
both self and other and speak interchangeably, as caterpillar and butterfly, flower and fruit, that makes her a female poet. But the poet speaks
of the birth of poetry and her capacity to give birth without stridently or
defensively restricting fecundity to phallic in-semination and re-pro-

duction. In the surprising life of caterpillars, both males and females of the species live through the kind of maternity figured in the uterine image of the chrysalis.

What all the image patterns suggest, with their various role reversals, impersonations, and gender code-switching, is a kind of maternity, germination, transformation, and intersubjectivity not restricted by biological gender or genital sexuality. Thus, she defines the creative process in terms of "both/and" rather than "either/or" relationships, because one substance or life form is metaphorically incorporated or compounded into another kind. To borrow Nancy Chodorow's words, Desbordes-Valmore had a sense of "permeable boundaries," which permitted her to circulate freely among life forms, not so much *ex*changing one identity for another, as *inter*changing them, making one another, being both one and an other. As we have seen, before being embodied in the fruit, the earlier, the flowering, larval, or mothering self embodied it. A reciprocity between progenitor and progeny, source and issue, spring and stream is set up that collapses boundaries and demarcations or erases the river banks and sharp edges. This reciprocity means that the poet's fruit cannot belong to a progenitor, any more than the progeny does to its mother, the worm to its butterfly or, for that matter, the butterfly to its worm, the fruit to the flower, or vice versa.

In addition to motherhood, Desbordes-Valmore's careers as actress and opera singer doubtless contributed to her experience of intertextuality in terms of a re-sounding, rather than a re-vision of the "inherited" texts of male predecessors. A sort of buzzing serves as the appropriate image. Combining languages and quotes within quotes, in "Imitation libre de Thomas Moore 'When the first summer bee,'" we hear the voice of a speaker who sidesteps the engendered canon, "steals" her way around it, precisely because she is strong in her convictions, sure of her identity. With the honey bee, nature's tireless female worker, she brings together playfully several of the phrases and images that defined intersubjectivity above, including the sexual interplay.

> A tes lèvres, mon âme immobile, épuisée,
> Renaîtra pour mourir sur une seule fleur.
> L'insecte entr'ouvrira mille jeunes calices,
> Ma bouche sur ta bouche en boira les délices,
> L'abeille aux fleurs, moi sur ton sein;
> Pour elle et moi, quel frais larcin.

> On your lips my soul, lifeless and worn,
> Still will spring solely to die on a single bud
> Gently will the insect pry thousands of tender petals apart,
> My mouth on yours will drink in its delights
> The bee on the flowers, me on your bosom,
> For the two of us, how fresh is theft.

What Marceline Desbordes-Valmore says and how she speaks, put her at odds with the usual accounts of and the usual ways of accounting for the poetic canon and for that reason her works did nothing to ensure her standing in that canon. Unfortunately, for instance, they do not appear in the recent French anthology of poems by women, *The Defiant Muse*, which was published by the Feminist Press as part of its series with the express purpose of challenging masculine hegemony over the genre. In the editor's preface, Domna Stanton summarizes some of the obstacles to creativity faced by women poets.

. . . the system that brands all female authors as deviant creates even more formidable obstacles for the woman poet than for the prose writer.

Enshrined as the highest, most esoteric language in Western thought, poetry has been considered the property of a priestly figure whose gifts derive from or refer back to the godhead. . . .

From this perspective, it is understandable why the inferior, vulgar, indeed prosaic language of prose offered women comparatively greater freedom . . .
. . . in contrast to prose, the conventions of poetry, the noblest, the priestly language, may have a repressive impact on women's writing.[18]

Generalizations of this sort have some historical substance and pedagogical validity, but they may also produce unwanted side effects. For they leave intact the engendered paradigms which all along have made it difficult to determine the very existence, let alone the quality of poetry by women of Desbordes-Valmore's caliber.

Denial of access, not to poetry, its language, tradition, experience, training or reward, but denial of access to the canon results in the perception that poetry by women is scarce and/or inferior. When one poses the question in terms of the politics of constructing the canon, the need to explain why women did not write more or better poetry self-

---

18. Domna Stanton, *The Defiant Muse* (New York: The Feminist Press, 1986), xv, xvi, and xxiv. For other contemporary views linking poetry generically to males and the novel to females, see: Simone de Beauvoir, *The Second Sex* (New York: Vintage Books, 1974), 660, 688, and 783–784; Germaine Brée, *French Women Writers* (New Brunswick: Rutgers University Press, 1973), 38, 69, and 80–81; Christiane Rochefort, "Are Women Writers Still Monsters? in *New French Feminisms*, ed. Marks and Courtivron (New York: Shocken Books, 1981), 185; and Ellen Moers, *Literary Women* (Garden City: Doubleday, 1976), 43–47, 81–84, and 119–26. Specific accounts of the dearth of "good" female poets emphasize the ways in which they have been handicapped by lack of education, encouragement, time, discipline, and the like, or, worse yet, silenced for various reasons—historical, linguistic, psychological, and philosophical. But the body of Desbordes-Valmore's writing suggests that when one sets out to show why women did not write *more* poetry than they did or *better* poetry, because female poetry, by definition, does not conform to prescribed standards of the engendered canon, what results is not listening appreciatively to women poets on their own terms, trivializing them instead in terms of the condescending patriarchal preconceptions of females as minor poets, seen in Lamartine's image of the "frêle équipage."

destructs, for the canonizers—readers and publishers—rather than women writers, appear to be the ones handicapped. When one starts out by explaining the scarcity or inferiority of poems by women, one may finish without ears to hear, without further need to discover those who did speak out or ways to appreciate what they were saying. Within the framework of difference, however, Desbordes-Valmore was only too happy to turn a so-called disadvantage dialectically to advantage. She welcomed the long-term benefits of not participating in cultural conditioning that only worked against women who would be poets and rejoiced at feeling free.

> Le front vibrant d'étranges et doux sons,
> Toute ravie et jeune en solitude,
> Trouvant le monde assez beau sans l'étude,
> Je souriais, rebelle à ses leçons,
> Le coeur gonflé d'inédites chansons.
> ["Plus de chants"]

> Temple throbbing with strange and gentle sounds
> Ecstatic, young, on my own,
> I found the beauty of the world without books
> Rejecting its lessons, I smiled
> My heart swelled with songs unscored.

"Women," she wrote in "Une Lettre de femme," "are not supposed to write. Yet I write." Verlaine made this line the first one he quoted from the only woman he ranked among the "poètes maudits," writers in limbo, the canon of the cursed.[19]

19. Verlaine, *Les Poètes maudits*, ed. Décaudin (Paris: SEDES, 1982), 62. See also Eliane Jasenas, *Marceline Desbordes-Valmore devant la critique* (Geneva: Droz, 1962), 125, 155–61. Germaine Brée noted that not a single woman poet is mentioned in any of the surveys and anthologies she consulted in preparing *Women Writers in France*, nor were any included on the "Agrégation" lists studied by Thiesse and Mathieu. Of the fifty-four anthologies I surveyed, seventy percent contained nothing by Desbordes-Valmore.

SUSAN RUBIN SULEIMAN

A Double Margin: Reflections on Women Writers and the Avant-garde in France

I

To say the word "avant-garde" today is to risk falling into a conceptual and terminological quagmire. Is "avant-garde" synonymous with, or to be subtly distinguished from, the experimental, the bohemian, the modern, the modern*ist*, the postmodern? Is it a historical category or a transhistorical one? A purely aesthetic category or a philosophical/political/existential one? Is it still to be taken seriously, or does it "conjure up comical associations of aging youth?"[1] In short, does the word have specific content or has it become so vague and general as to be virtually useless?

With that bow to confusion, I shall proceed as if *I* knew what I meant

---

1. Theodor Adorno, *Aesthetic Theory*, trans. C. Lenhardt (London and New York: Routledge and Kegan Paul, 1984), 36.

Among the works I have found helpful in thinking about these questions are: Peter Burger, *Theory of the Avant-Garde*, trans. Michael Shaw (Minneapolis: University of Minnesota Press, 1984); Matei Calinescu, *Five Faces of Modernity: Modernism, Avant-Garde, Decadence, Kitsch, Postmodernism* (Durham: Duke University Press, 1987); Hal Foster, ed., *The Anti-Aesthetic: Essays on Postmodern Culture* (Port Townsend, Wash.: Bay Press, 1983); Clement Greenberg, *Art and Culture* (Boston: Beacon Press, 1961); Andreas Huyssen, *After the Great Divide: Modernism, Mass Culture, Postmodernism* (Bloomington: Indiana University Press, 1986); Rosalind Krauss, *The Originality of the Avant-Garde and Other Modernist Myths* (Cambridge: MIT Press, 1985); Marjorie Perloff, *The Futurist Moment: Avant-Garde, Avant-Guerre, and the Language of Rupture* (Chicago: University of Chicago Press, 1986); Renato Poggioli, *The Theory of the Avant-Garde*, trans. Gerald Fitzgerald (Cambridge: Harvard University Press, 1968); Harold Rosenberg, *The Tradition of the New* (Salem, N.H.: Ayer, 1959); Charles Russell, *Poets, Prophets, and Revolutionaries: The Literary Avant-Garde from Rimbaud through Postmodernism* (New York: Oxford University Press, 1985). See also my essay, "Naming and Difference: Reflections on 'Modernism versus Postmodernism' in Literature," in *Approaching Postmodernism*, ed. Douwe Fokkema and Hans Bertens (Amsterdam and Philadelphia: John Benjamins, 1986), 255–70.

when I say "avant-garde." And I shall take as a starting point a set of propositions that appear sufficiently obvious to warrant no detailed demonstration. There have existed avant-garde movements in French art and thought. Although they can be traced at least as far back as Romanticism, they came fully into their own in the early years of this century and found what was perhaps their fullest elaboration in the Surrealist movement between 1924 and 1939. The *Tel Quel* group and its allies of the 1960s and early 1970s, as well as various feminist groups after 1968, associated with specific journals and theoretical positions regarding women and "the feminine," also constituted genuine artistic and cultural avant-gardes (*pace* Peter Burger).[2] The hallmark of these movements was a *collective project* (more or less explicitly defined and often shifting over time) that linked artistic experimentation and a critique of outmoded artistic practices with an ideological critique of bourgeois thought and a desire for social change, so that the activity of writing could also be seen as a genuine intervention in the social, cultural, and possibly even the political arena. Finally, although most of the participants in the later movements are still alive and writing in France today, the movements themselves are now dispersed and have not been replaced.

To be sure, qualifications and additions are possible (should the *nouveaux romanciers* be considered an avant-garde movement, and if not, why not? Same question for existentialism). The point I wish to make is that there has existed, at least since Surrealism, a strong and almost continuous current in French literary and artistic practice and thought, based on the double exigency to "be absolutely modern" (Rimbaud) and to change, if not the world (Marx), at least—as a first step— the way we think about the world. Furthermore, this recurrent tendency has expressed itself with remarkable consistency, privileging certain concepts (heterogeneity, play, marginality, transgression, the unconscious, eroticism, excess) and mounting heavy attacks on others (representation, the unitary subject, unitary meaning, linear narrative, the realist novel, paternal authority, Truth with a capital *T*). Alice Jardine has argued that perhaps the most important thread of continuity, subtending all of the above oppositions, has been the "putting into dis-

2. In his influential/controversial *Theory of the Avant-Garde*, Burger argues that the term "avant-garde" must refer only to what he calls the historical avant-gardes, embodied for him chiefly in Dada and Surrealism. According to Burger, the European and American avant-garde movements of the 1960s are merely a "neoavant-garde, which stages for a second time the avant-gardiste break with tradition" and thereby "becomes a manifestation that is void of sense" (61). The notion that the avant-garde project could only happen once, making all other manifestations of it inauthentic "replays," sets Burger against other theorists (notably Huyssen and Russell) who wish to see more of a continuity in the project of modernity.

course of 'woman' ''': "We might say that what is generally referred to as modernity is precisely . . . the perhaps historically unprecedented exploration of the female, differently maternal body."[3] One has but to think of the Surrealists' celebration of *amour fou* (or, in the case of Bataille, *amour obscène*) in poetry and narrative, and their obsessive preoccupation with the female body in painting and photography; of Alain Robbe-Grillet's and other *nouveaux romanciers'* combination of a thematics of erotic violence with a poetics of antirealist transgression; of Phillippe Sollers's attempts to wed Joycean wordplay to erotic exhibitionism (especially in *Paradis*, his last work of the *Tel Quel* period); of Julia Kristeva's theory of the maternal/semiotic and Jacques Derrida's concept of "invagination"; and of contemporary women writers' exploration/inscription of the female body, whether as maternal *jouissance* or as the *jouissance* of female lovers, to assent to Jardine's daring generalization.

One question, of course, is whether the "putting into discourse of 'woman' " by a woman writer is comparable, in its meaning and effects, to its putting into discourse by a male writer. Another important question, which has preoccupied many feminist theorists and which Jardine rightly emphasizes at the outset of her book, concerns the problematic relationship between "woman" as discursive entity, or metaphor, and *women* as biologically and culturally gendered human beings. "It is always a bit of a shock to the feminist critic," writes Jardine, "when she recognizes that the repeated and infinitely expanded 'feminine' . . . often has very little, if anything, to do with women" (35). And putting the dilemma even more sharply: "To refuse 'woman' or the 'feminine' as cultural and libidinal constructions (as in "men's feminity"), is, ironically, to return to metaphysical—anatomical—definitions of sexual identity. To accept a metaphorization, a semiosis of woman, on the other hand, means risking once again the absence of women as subjects in the struggle of modernity" (37). As Jardine points out, the dilemma is especially acute for those American feminist critics who are torn between the heady attractions of (largely French) theory and the no less significant appeal of (largely American) empirical and historical study, where the material situation and the gender of an author are never a matter of indifference. Nancy Miller, who has often and forcefully argued for the materialistic view even while admitting the elegant attractions of French theory, summed up the dilemma in another way a few years ago when she asked, half jokingly: "Can we imagine, or should we, a position that speaks in tropes and walks in sensible shoes?"[4]

---

3. Alice A. Jardine, *Gynesis: Configurations of Woman and Modernity* (Ithaca: Cornell University Press, 1985), 33–34; hereafter cited in parentheses in the text.

4. Nancy K. Miller, "The Text's Heroine: A Feminist Critic and Her Fictions," *Diacritics*, 12:2 (1982), 53.

I would like to take up Miller's challenge by reflecting on a particularly powerful trope associated both with women and with avant-gardes: that of the margin. If, as this trope suggests, culture is "like" a space to be mapped or a printed page, then the place of women, and of avant-garde movements, has traditionally been situated away from the center, "on the fringe," in the margins. One difference is that avant-garde movements have willfully chosen their marginal position—the better to launch attacks at the center—whereas women have more often than not been relegated to that position: far from the altar as from the marketplace, those centers where cultural subjects invent and enact their symbolic and material rites.

It has become increasingly clear that the relegating of *women* to the margins of culture is not unrelated to the place accorded to "Woman" by the cultural imaginary: "Woman, in the political vocabulary, will be the name for whatever undoes the whole."[5] In other vocabularies, "woman" has been the name of the hole that threatens the fullness of the subject, the wild zone that threatens the constructions of reason, the dark continent that threatens the regions of light. What strikes me as new, however, is that the "putting into discourse of 'woman'" in modern French thought has gone hand in hand with a revaluation and revalorization of the marginal spaces with which "she" has been traditionally identified. It is because of that reversal that the complicated relations, at the margins of culture, between women writers and the avant-garde in France must particularly occupy our attention.

In *Les Parleuses*, the series of conversations between Marguerite Duras and Xavière Gauthier published in 1974, the talk turns at one point to why Duras is not really known by the reading public. Gauthier remarks that people know her name, but few seem to have read her texts—perhaps because they are afraid? Duras replies that very probably things will change after her death, but that indeed "I attract misogyny in a particular way." Gauthier (who often speaks more volubly than Duras in these conversations) then observes:

That doesn't surprise me. Precisely because I think that they are totally revolutionary books, totally avant-garde, both from a usual revolutionary point of view and from a woman's point of view, and most people aren't there yet.

To which Duras responds: "Yes, it's something doubly intolerable" [une double insupportabilité].[6]

Doubly intolerable because "totally revolutionary, totally avant-

5. Denis Hollier, "Collages," Introduction, *College de Sociologie*, trans. Betty Wing (Minneapolis: University of Minnesota Press, 1988).

6. Marguerite Duras and Xavière Gauthier, *Les Parleuses* (Paris: Editions de Minuit, 1974), 61; my translation, here and throughout from the French unless otherwise stated. *Les Parleuses* has been published in English as *Woman to Woman*, trans. Katherine A. Jensen (University of Nebraska Press, 1987).

garde," Duras's work (by 1974 she had published among other works the trilogy comprising *Le Ravissement de Lol V. Stein, Le Vice-Consul* and *L'Amour,* and directed *India Song*) is here seen as the quintessence of the marginal. The fact that ten years later, with the publication of *L'Amant,* she would become an international bestselling author does not alter the logic of that characterization (although it did of course alter Duras's own situation[7]): the avant-garde woman writer is doubly intolerable, seen from the center, because her writing escapes not one but two sets of expectations/categorizations; it corresponds neither to the "usual revolutionary point of view" nor to the "woman's point of view." Gauthier does not explain what she means here by the "woman's point of view"—I would guess that she alludes to a certain view of women's writing which does not include experimentation with language. As for the "usual revolutionary" point of view, it seems to refer to an overtly political kind of writing which adopts an oppositional stance to society. Duras tells Gauthier that in her works there is no "refusal" or "putting into question" of society, because "to put society into question is still to acknowledge it. . . . I mean the people who do that, who write about the refusal of society, harbor within them a kind of nostalgia. They are, I am certain, much less separated from it than I am" (62). Her own position is one of total separation, total estrangement. So far out that it escapes the social order altogether? In any case, so far out as to be elsewhere. *L'existence est ailleurs.*

The sudden appearance of the last sentence in the above paragraph, produced as my free association to the word "elsewhere," itself a gloss on Duras's words, suggests to me a curious filiation; for the sentence is the famous concluding sentence of the first Surrealist Manifesto. Breton, declaring the foundation of a radically new movement, states that [his/its] existence is elsewhere; Duras, who accepts to call her works "totally revolutionary, totally avant-garde," declares that she is elsewhere. In one reading of the trope of marginality, "woman," "woman's writing" and "avant-garde" become metaphors for each other. That is one reason why Rosalind Krauss, for example, can write about Surrealist photography that in its practice "woman and photograph become figures for each other's condition: ambivalent, blurred, indistinct, and lacking in, to use Edward Weston's word, 'authority'."[8]

The opposition Krauss establishes between "Straight Photography,"

---

7. Interestingly, Duras continues to see herself as the object of misogyny and even, somehow, as in danger of not being recognized *in France,* despite her worldwide fame. See her interview with Alice Jardine in this volume.

8. Rosalind Krauss, "Corpus Delicti," in R. Krauss and Jane Livingston, *L'Amour Fou: Photography and Surrealism* (New York: Abbeville Press, 1985), 95; hereafter cited in parentheses in the text.

metonymically represented by Edward Weston and implicitly coded as male ("grounded in the sharply focused image, its resolution a figure of the unity of what the spectator sees, a wholeness that in turn founds the spectator himself as a unified subject") and Surrealist photography, which she explicitly codes as female (blurring all boundaries and threatening the spectator of Straight Photography to the point that he finds it "unbearable"—which translates exactly into *insupportable*, as used by Duras) is a move that signals Krauss's allegiance to contemporary French thought. It allows her to valorize Surrealist photography as the (metaphorically) "feminine" Other of "straight photography"; but it is also a move that leads to a significant (symptomatic?) slippage in terminology and conceptualization. Woman, Krauss states, is "the obsessional subject" of Surrealist photography—but in fact, as the illustrations to her essay amply document, woman, or rather the female body, is the obsessional *object* of Surrealist photographic experimentation.[9] Krauss's brilliant discussion of Surrealist "optical assaults on the body" (70) elides the difference between the subject who is agent of the assault (and who is invariably a male photographer) and the object that is the target of the "active, aggressive assault on reality" (65), this object being also invariably the female body.

To call woman the obsessional *subject* of Surrealist photography is, then, misleading in a particularly interesting way, for it suggests, or rather confirms, that the figural substitution of "woman" or "the feminine" for avant-garde practice (the two being united by their common marginality in relation to "straight" or "mainstream" culture) may end up by eliding precisely the question of the female subject; and eliding, as well, the question of history. For if Surrealism, to stick to that example, is studied historically, then the absence of female subjects of Surrealist practice becomes a problem one *cannot* avoid. And I would claim that it is only by working through the problem historically that one can make progress on theoretical ground as well.

Before turning my discourse down the historical path, however, I want to emphasize a more positive and empowering aspect of the "woman"/avant-garde/marginality trope for female subjects. As the remarks by Duras I quoted earlier suggested, there is a way in which the sense of being "doubly marginal" and therefore "totally avant-garde" provides the female subject with a kind of centrality, *in her own eyes*. In a system in which the marginal, the avant-garde, the subversive, all that disturbs and "undoes the whole" is endowed with positive value, a

9. It is true that the English language is partly responsible for this slippage, since "subject" can mean "subject-matter," a synonym for object of representation. But a critic as theoretically sophisticated as Krauss obviously knows the other, more "Gallic" meaning of subject as agent of action.

woman artist who can identify those concepts with her own practice and metaphorically with her own feminity can find in them a source of strength and self-legitimation. Perhaps no one has done this more successfully than Hélène Cixous. Her famous essay, "The Laugh of the Medusa" (1975), is the closest thing to an avant-garde manifesto written from an explicitly feminist perspective. True to the genre of the manifesto, it is written by an "I" who represents a group ("we," in this case women); it alternates in tone between the aggressive (when addressing the hostile "straight" reader) and the hortatory (when addressing the other members of the group), and it suggests a program that implies both a revolutionary practice of writing and the disruption of existing cultural and social institutions and ideologies. What distinguishes Cixous's manifesto from its forerunners (Marinetti's Futurist manifestoes, Tzara's Dada manifestoes, Breton's Surrealist manifestoes) is that Cixous explicitly equates the radically new, subversive text with the "feminine text": "A feminine text cannot fail to be more than subversive. It is volcanic; as it is written it brings about an upheaval of the old property crust, carrier of masculine investments . . . in order to smash everything, to shatter the framework of institutions, to blow up the law, to break up the 'truth' with laughter."[10] Although the "feminine text" that is here projected (not *defined,* but projected into the future as an "écriture à venir"—this too being the hallmark of the manifesto as genre)[11] is not to be restricted to writers who are women, women are nevertheless in a privileged position to practice it: "thanks to their history, women today know (how to do and want) what men will be able to conceive of only much later" (258).

Cixous's metaphorical equation of "the feminine" with the hyperbolically marginal allows her to envisage *women* as the primary subjects of avant-garde practice. In this she differs not only from Krauss (for whom "the feminine" remains a metaphor, applied to work by male artists), but also from Kristeva; for although Kristeva leaves ample space for the maternal/semiotic in her theory of the avant-garde subject, that subject remains of necessity male. Not only are all of her exemplary avant-garde writers male, from Lautréamont and Mallarmé through Joyce, Artaud, Bataille, and Sollers, but she has even discussed, at various times, why in terms of her theory it is virtually impossible for a

10. Hélène Cixous, "The Laugh of the Medusa," trans. Keith Cohen and Paula Cohen, in *New French Feminisms*, ed. Elaine Marks and Isabelle de Courtivron (New York: Schocken Books, 1981), 258; hereafter cited in parentheses in the text.

11. The phrase "écriture à venir," "writing to come," is Maurice Blanchot's; its application to avant-garde writing (specifically, to Surrealist writing) was pointed out in a lecture by Denis Hollier at the 1987 Harvard Summer Institute on the Study of Avant-Gardes, which I codirected with Alice Jardine. I wish to thank Denis Hollier for this insight.

woman to achieve a similar status. In order to be truly innovative, one has to be able to risk giving up "la légitimation paternelle"; but if women take that risk, what awaits them more often than not is madness or suicide.[12] For the male subject, the negativity involved in giving up paternal legitimation is compensated for by a positive maternal support, and the two coexist in a dynamic balance. For the woman writer, there seems to be no viable alternative to either total paternal identification (which involves the absence of negativity, the conformism of the dutiful daughter) or else a regression to the "archaic mother," which involves yet another conformism equally incapable of producing true artistic innovation—the conformism of those who claim that "it's good because it was done by women."[13]

Even as I am writing these remarks, however, I realize that they are in some profound sense not pertinent. It is misleading to use the present tense in discussing either Kristeva's or Cixous's theoretical reflections on "écriture féminine" and its possible or impossible intersections with innovation and avant-garde practice. Those reflections are historically situated in the 1970s, at a time when there existed a strong if already splintered women's movement in France, together with an equally strong current of philosophical and literary theorizing about modernity. Today, as we are nearing the end of the 1980s, my sense is that the collective dynamism is gone and there remain only individual efforts, among women as in the French literary and intellectual arena generally. The music has stopped and the dancing is over, at least for a while. This may be the time, therefore, to put on our sensible shoes and take a walk around some real margins in the imaginary garden of the French avant-garde.

II

From the point of view of one who walks in sensible shoes, it is clear that there is no such thing as *the* avant-garde; there are only specific avant-garde movements, situated in a particular time and place. If we want to talk about the real marginalization of women in relation to "the avant-garde" (by real marginalization, I mean the exclusion of women from the centers of male avant-garde activity and/or their exclusion

12. Julia Kristeva, *Des Chinoises* (Paris: Editions des Femmes, 1974), 47; and "Unes Femmes," *Cahiers du GRIF* 12 (1975), 26. Kristeva's theory of the (male) avant-garde subject is most systematically laid out in *La Révolution du langage poétique* (Paris: Seuil, 1974); see also "Le Sujet en procès" (on Artaud), "L'Expérience et la pratique" (on Bataille), and "Polylogue" (on Sollers) in Kristeva, *Polylogue* (Paris: Seuil, 1977).
13. Kristeva, "Unes Femmes," 24.

from the historical and critical accounts of that activity), we must look at individual cases in their historical and national specificity.

I propose to look at a case that has been much examined by feminist critics of late, in France and in the United States: that of Surrealism. The feminist exploration of Surrealism has proceeded along two tracks, which we might designate, following Elaine Showalter's well-known categorizations, as feminist critique (the rereading of male authors from a feminist perspective) and as gynocriticism (the rediscovery of hitherto "invisible" or undervalued women writers and their work). The pioneering work of feminist critique of Surrealism was Xavière Gauthier's *Surréalisme et sexualité* (1971). Polemical in its effect even though analytical in tone, Gauthier's detailed study of Surrealist poetry and painting sought to show, and to explain in chiefly psychoanalytic terms, "the misogyny of the compact group of male Surrealists."[14] Whether they idealized the female body and their love of it, as they did in their poetry, or whether they attacked it and dismembered it, as they did in their paintings, the male Surrealists, according to Gauthier's analysis, were essentially using the woman to work out their rebellion against the Father.

Gauthier's book appeared a year after Kate Millett's *Sexual Politics;* like Millet's work, it was important because it *posed as a problem* the subject position of male artists in relation to the objects of their representations, women. In recent years, we have seen more nuanced attempts to explore this problem, especially in the field of Surrealist visual art;[15] but there is certainly room for further reflection on the subject position of Surrealism.

As for the gynocritical work, it began with the necessary task of gathering information: who were the women writers and artists associated with Surrealism, and what did they accomplish? The 1977 volume of the review *Obliques*, devoted to *La Femme Surréaliste*, was the first attempt to present a catalogue of "Surrealist women," in alphabetical order, complete with photographs, bibliographies, and brief excerpts or reproductions of their work as well as some interviews and interpretive essays. In 1980, Lea Vergine's *L'Autre Moitié de l'avant-garde*, which sought to document the lives and work of women artists associated with all the major European avant-garde movements between 1910 and

14. Xavière Gauthier, prefatory remarks to "Le Surréalisme et la sexualité" (an excerpt from her book), in *La Femme Surréaliste*, special issue of *Obliques* 14–15 (1977), 42. See Gauthier's *Surréalisme et sexualité* (Paris: Gallimard, collection "Idées," 1971).

15. See, for example, Mary Ann Caws, "Ladies Shot and Painted: Female Embodiment in Surrealist Art," in *The Female Body in Western Culture: Contemporary Perspectives*, ed. Susan Rubin Suleiman (Cambridge, Mass.: Harvard University Press, 1986), 262–87; and Susan Gubar, "Representing Pornography: Feminism, Criticism, and Depictions of Female Violation," *Critical Inquiry* 13, no. 4 (1987), 712–41.

1940, included eighteen women under the heading "Surréalisme;" some of them had also figured among the thirty-six women listed in *La Femme Surréaliste*, while others had not. These two books are precious reference works, but clearly they were only a first step: neither one made any claim to exhaustiveness, nor did they attempt to draw any general conclusions about the participation of women in the Surrealist movement and their contribution to it. In the last few years, important work in that direction has been accomplished by (among others) Whitney Chadwick, Jacqueline Chénieux-Gendron, and Gloria Feman Orenstein.[16] As a result, it is now becoming possible to engage in a more systematic reflection on the place (and placing) of women in Surrealism.

In what follows, I want to develop the two lines of thought suggested above. If indeed the subject position of Surrealism was male, what difficulties did that imply for the artistic practice of "Surrealist women," especially of women writers? And what exactly was the historical position of women artists and writers in the development of the Surrealist movement?

The Surrealist Subject

Since nothing is more instructive than a good example, I shall begin by offering two. The first is a paragraph from an essay by Louis Aragon, one of the founding members of the Surrealist group, published in 1924. He is writing here about the newly established *Centre des recherches surréalistes* (also known as *La Centrale Surréaliste*), which functioned in its first months as a rallying point for all those wishing to participate in the Surrealist project:

We hung a woman on the ceiling of an empty room, and every day receive visits from anxious men bearing heavy secrets. That is how we came to know Georges Bessière, like a blow of the fist. We are working at a task enigmatic to ourselves, in front of a volume of Fantomas, fastened to the wall by forks. The visitors, born under remote stars or next door, are helping to elaborate this formidable machine for killing what is in order to accomplish what is not. At number 15, Rue

16. See Whitney Chadwick, *Women Artists and the Surrealist Movement* (Boston: Little, Brown, 1985), the first comprehensive study of Surrealist women artists, lavishly illustrated; Jacqueline Chénieux, *Le Surréalisme et le roman* (Lausanne: L'Age d'Homme, 1983), which includes serious discussion of work by Surrealist women writers; Gloria Feman Orenstein, "Reclaiming the Great Mother: A Feminist Journey to Madness and Back in Search of a Goddess Heritage," *Symposium* 36, no. 1 (1982), 45–69, which discusses work by both women writers and artists. Chénieux and Orenstein contributed to the *Obliques* issue on *La Femme Surréaliste*. Despite all this valuable work, no one has attempted until now a systematic reflection on the historical relation of women to the Surrealist movement and on its implications for French literary and cultural history, as well as for a possible theory of the avant-garde.

de Grenelle, we have opened a romantic Inn for unclassifiable ideas and continuing revolts. All that still remains of hope in this despairing universe will turn its last, raving glances toward our pathetic stall. *It is a question of formulating a new declaration of the rights of man.*[17]

The second example is from an essay by a historian of Surrealism, Robert Short, published in 1976 in an influential volume:

The criterion that the Surrealists apply to a work of art is its susceptibility to provoke a real change in those who encounter it, to call forth an affective response similar in quality to that evoked by the sight of the woman one loves.[18]

Although these texts are very different, one thing they have in common is that the author does not seem to be aware of all that he is saying. Aragon begins by talking about a woman hung on a ceiling and ends by proclaiming the Surrealist project as a desire for "a new declaration of the rights of man"—apparently unaware that the word "man" in his last sentence asks to be interpreted in its gender-specific sense, especially after all the talk about blows of the fist and machines for killing what is. Robert Short begins by talking about the Surrealists' conception of art and ends by evoking "the woman one loves"—apparently unaware that not all spectators of art are heterosexual males. In a word, both the founding Surrealist and the later historian are writing from an exclusively male subject position, and are unproblematically assigning that position to the Surrealist subject in general. They do this, I would guess, in all innocence, with no malevolent intent: theirs is not the provocation of the self-conscious misogynist, but the ordinary sexism of the man who will reply, when you point it out to him, that he hadn't noticed there were no women in the room.

But in fact, as Aragon tells us, there was a woman in the Surrealist room—her only peculiarity being that she was not made of flesh and blood. The woman in question was a life-size reclining nude figure, armless and headless (was she the inspiration for Max Ernst's first collage novel, *La Femme Cent Têtes*?), suspended from the ceiling of the *Centrale.* Her function was evidently to inspire the "anxious men" who came there to unburden themselves of their secrets. Did any anxious women come to unburden themselves of theirs? How might the floating lady have functioned for them?

Aragon does not mention any living women in the room; but a

17. Quoted in Maurice Nadeau, *The History of Surrealism,* trans. Richard Howard (New York: Macmillan, 1965), 92; my emphasis. I have modified the translation somewhat—notably, I have put verbs in the present tense as they were in the original, published in 1924 and explicitly referring to the "here and now."

18. Robert Short, "Dada and Surrealism," in *Modernism, 1890–1930,* ed. Malcolm Bradbury and James McFarlane (Harmondsworth, Middlesex: Penguin Books, 1976), 303.

famous photograph by Man Ray, "La Centrale Surréaliste en 1924," documents the presence of two living women: Simone Breton and Mick Soupault, wives of the Surrealists André and Philippe. In the standard version of the photograph, the image has been cut off at the top, leaving only the feet of the headless lady visible in the upper left hand corner (fig. 1). There exists another version, however, which shows the entire figure, occupying the upper third of the photograph (fig. 2); below her, standing and seated in two uneven rows, are twelve men and the two women. The men, dressed in dark suits, white shirts, and ties, are writers and artists: Charles Baron, Raymond Queneau, Pierre Naville, André Breton (sporting a monocle), Jacques-André Boiffard, Giorgio de Chirico, Roger Vitrac, Paul Eluard, Philippe Soupault, Robert Desnos, Louis Aragon, and Max Morise. They look for the most part formal, solemn, almost grim, as befits an official group portrait. The two women look different, both from them and from each other: Mick Soupault, demurely dressed, is smiling slightly, like a good and tolerant wife; Simone Breton (whom Breton was to divorce a few years later, when he met his next "amour fou") is resting her head sideways on her arm—one eye is covered by her dark hair, while the other looks at the camera with a burning stare. She is the only one who looks openly provocative, almost shocking: in one version, her legs are crossed, exposing a bit of bare flesh above her knee-high stocking (fig. 1).

    Why do I dwell on this image? Because I think that it points up, as clearly and more graphically than Aragon's text, the degree to which the subject position of Surrealism, as it was elaborated at the very inception of the movement, was male. The photograph also makes explicit what is only implied in Aragon's text: the problematic position of actual women who might wish to integrate themselves, as subjects, into the male script. I read Simone Breton and Mick Soupault in the photograph as female subjects—but as alienated subjects who have adapted themselves to the male vision of "woman," in what Luce Irigaray calls the masquerade.[19] Together, they figure the two poles of femininity between which male desire hovers: the chaste asexual wife/mother and the burning-eyed whore. Needless to say, I know nothing about the real personalities of Simone Breton and Mick Soupault—my remarks refer to their image in the photograph, which can itself be considered as the construction of a male subject. The photograph fascinates me because it lends itself so beautifully to be read as an emblem: above, the imaginary faceless woman on whom the Surrealist male artist can project his fantasies—fantasies which then become externalized, transformed, elaborated into works, poems, stories, paintings, photographs; below,

19. See Luce Irigaray, *This Sex Which Is Not One*, trans. Catherine Porter with Carolyn Burke (Ithaca: Cornell University Press, 1985).

Figure 1. Man Ray. *The Surrealist "Centrale,"* 1924

Figure 2. Man Ray. *The Surrealist "Centrale,"* 1924.

two flesh and blood women who produced no works, but who *embody* aspects of the imaginary woman hanging from the ceiling.

How much meaning can one extract from a single image or a single text? More examples are needed—for instance, another "official" group portrait, a photomontage published in 1929 in *La Révolution Surréaliste* and often reproduced since then (fig. 3). The montage consists of the photograph of a painting by Magritte, framed by the portraits of sixteen Surrealists with their eyes closed; the painting represents a female nude, standing in a pose reminiscent of Botticelli's *Venus*, frontally exposed; above and below her, as part of the painting, is the inscription: "Je ne vois pas la   cachée dans la forêt," [I do not see the   hidden in the forest], the image of the woman filling in the hole left between the words.[20] The Surrealists, all male, who frame her, adopt the position of the "Je," not seeing; at the same time, she is given *to be seen* by the spectator, who sees both the woman and the Surrealists (including Magritte who painted her) with their eyes kept resolutely shut. This too seems to me to be an emblem of the Surrealist subject, who does not need to see the woman in order to imagine her, placing her at the center but only as an image, while any actual woman is now out of the picture altogether.

Now here is the crucial question: given the overwhelmingly male subject position of Surrealism, how did a number of women artists, who *did* produce works, manage to elaborate an imagery and a script that involved neither a masquerade of femininity nor male impersonation— which in aesthetic terms would result in purely formal imitation, the adopting of formal solutions without discovering them as a personal necessity. Luce Irigaray has touched on this problem in an essay dedicated to one of the Surrealist women whose writing has recently become known, Unica Zürn. "If woman is to put into form the *ulē* [Greek: *matter*] that she is, she must not cut herself off from it nor leave it to maternity, but succeed in creating with that primary material that she is by discovering and exposing her own morphology. Otherwise, she risks using or reusing what man has already put into forms, especially about her; risks remaking what has already been made, and losing her-

---

20. This painting should be compared with Magritte's famous 1926 painting, "Ceci n'est pas une pipe," which shows a pipe accompanied by the inscription ("This is not a pipe") that gives the work its title. Although both paintings are playing with representation, they do so in diametrically opposed ways: the "reality" of the painted pipe is negated by the inscription, which highlights the difference between image and word, image and thing; the painted woman, on the contrary, is so "real" that she can *replace* the word that would be used to designate her. In the first instance, the differences between visual representation, language, and reality are emphasized; in the second, these differences are blurred—as if, where woman was concerned, the real, the imaginary, and the symbolic were interchangeable (for a male subject?).

Figure 3. Photomontage of Surrealists around a painting by Magritte, 1929.

self in that labyrinth."[21] A woman Surrealist, in other words, cannot simply assume a subject position and take over a stock of images elaborated by the male imaginary; in order to innovate, she has to invent her own position as subject and elaborate her own set of images—different from, yet as empowering as the image of the exposed female body, with its endless potential for manipulation, disarticulation and rearticulation, fantasizing and projection, is for her male colleagues.

As we are coming to realize, a significant number of women artists and writers did succeed in creating their own version and vision of Surrealist practice, without merely imitating male models. Over the past ten years, there have emerged significant bodies of work produced by women who previously were either never mentioned or mentioned only in the most cursory manner in general histories of Surrealist art or of the Surrealist movement: Leonora Carrington, Dorothea Tanning, Kay Sage, Eileen Agar, Ithell Colquhoun, Toyen, Unica Zürn, Leonor Fini, Valentine Hugo—the list can be prolonged. These women were (are) primarily visual artists, but some have also produced wonderful written work—notably Leonora Carrington, who is a painter but whose short stories from the 1930s and 1940s, as well as her novel, *The Hearing Trumpet* (written in 1950) are finally finding an audience; and Unica Zürn, a graphic artist whose autobiographical texts, *Sombre Printemps* and *L'Homme Jasmin*, written (originally in German) not long before her suicide in 1970, have acquired almost a cult status in Paris.[22] Among the women who are primarily writers, two whose names have found their way into some general studies without receiving sustained attention are Joyce Mansour (1928–1986) and Gisèle Prassinos (born in 1920).[23] One of my own favorites, better known as a filmmaker (*La*

---

21. Luce Irigaray, "Une lacune natale (pour Unica Zürn)," *Le Nouveau Commerce* 62/63 (1985): 42. Irigaray's cryptic remark about "not leaving her *ulē* to maternity" would need to be commented and qualified, given that for so many contemporary women writers—including Irigaray herself—the maternal body has provided a fertile source of imagery and inspiration; one of the major texts by a woman Surrealist, Leonora Carrington's *The Hearing Trumpet,* is based on a complicated playing with and valorization of the mother's body and the mother's *voice*).

22. Carrington was the only woman included in the original version of Breton's *Anthologie de l'humour noir* (1939). Her works currently in print include *En bas* (Paris: Losfeld, 1973—in English as *Down Below* [Chicago: Black Swan Press, 1983]); *The Hearing Trumpet* (San Francisco: City Lights Books, 1985); *Pigeon volé: contes retrouvés* (Paris: Le Temps Qu'il Fait, 1986). For a detailed bibliography of her works, see J. Chénieux, *Le Surréalisme et le roman,* op. cit. Carrington is particularly interesting in that she wrote both in French and English; two volumes of her stories in English are scheduled for publication by E. P. Dutton in fall 1988. By Unica Zürn, see *L'Homme-Jasmin* (Paris: Gallimard, 1971), and *Sombre Printemps* (Paris: Belfond, 1985), with a biographical postface by Ruth Henry.

23. Neither Mansour nor Prassinos is included in Michael Benedikt's supposedly comprehensive anthology in English, *The Poetry of Surrealism: An Anthology* (Boston:

Fiancée du pirate, Néa, Papa les p'tits bateaux) but also the author of several books of stories and a novel, whose name appeared in *La Femme Surréaliste* but is rarely mentioned today even by critics interested in Surrealist writing by women is Nelly Kaplan (born 1936), writing under the pen name Belen.[24]

Only a careful study of individual works and artists will allow us to answer the question of the female subject in Surrealism. In the meantime, however, one can speculate about the strategies employed by women artists and writers, both in the way they managed their lives (when and under what circumstances did a given artist become associated with the Surrealist movement? Was her work included in major exhibitions or anthologies organized by male Surrealists? Did she break with the movement, and if so under what circumstances? What was the subsequent evolution of her artistic career?) and in the ways they situated their work within Surrealism. Since the women were generally younger and started producing later than the men who were associated with the movement, it is not unlikely that their version of Surrealist practice included a component of response to, as well as adaptation of, male Surrealist iconographies and mythologies—this being especially the case in the realm of sexuality. Here, Irigaray's notion of "mimicry," the playful or ironic counterpart of the masquerade, might provide a useful analytical category in approaching individual works. In mimicry, a woman "repeats" the male—in this case, the male Surrealist—version of "woman," but she does so in a self-conscious way that points up the citational, often ironic status of the repetition.[25]

Another, specifically stylistic concept that would be useful in looking at the work of women artists is Mikhail Bakhtin's concept of "internal dialogism." The "internally dialogized" word (but this is also true of

---

Little, Brown and Co., 1974); nor do they appear in Paul Auster's more recent bilingual anthology, *The Random House Book of Twentieth-Century French Poetry* (New York: Vintage Books, 1984). Benedikt's anthology, covering two generations of Surrealists, includes no work by women; Auster's, covering the whole century, includes one woman: Anne-Marie Albiach. In France, Gisèle Prassinos' *Les Mots endormis,* containing selections from her poetry of the 1930s as well as later work, is in print (Flammarion, 1967); all of Mansour's books are out of print. They include: *Cris* (Paris: Seghers, 1953); *Rapaces* (Paris: Seghers, 1960), and *Carré Blanc* (Paris: Le Soleil Noir, 1965). *Rapaces* is available in a shortened bilingual edition in the U.S.: *Birds of Prey,* trans. Albert Herzing (Perivale Press, 1979).

24. Belen's comic, erotic novel, *Mémoires d'une liseuse de draps* (Paris: Pauvert, 1974) is currently available; her books of stories are *Et délivrez-nous du mâle* (Paris: Losfeld, 1960), and *Le Réservoir des sens* (Paris: La Jeune Parque, 1966).

25. See Irigaray, *This Sex Which Is Not One,* 76. As Irigaray suggests, mimicry may be only an "initial phase," a first strategy adopted traditionally by the oppressed. This raises the question of how one might go beyond mimicry, to other possible strategies not based on an ironic relation to a preexisting situation.

the image), Bakhtin shows, is often polemically related to another, previous word that is absent but that can be inferred from the present response to it.[26] Gloria Orenstein has suggested, replying not on Bakhtin's concept but on the anthropological concept of "muted" versus "dominant" groups, that the work of women who were personally linked—through love or marriage—to well-known male Surrealists like Max Ernst (Leonora Carrington and Dorothea Tanning), Yves Tanguy (Kay Sage), or Hans Bellmer (Unica Zürn) can be read as "a double-voiced discourse, containing both a 'dominant' and a 'muted' story."[27] In Bakhtinian terms, we can speak of the women's work as dialogically related to the men's, often with an element of internal polemic. I would suggest that such internal dialogue is to be found not only in the work of women directly involved with male Surrealists to whose work they were specifically responding, but was a general strategy adopted, in individual ways, by women wishing to insert themselves as subjects into Surrealism.

Women in the History of Surrealism

Henceforth, it will be difficult for any responsible teacher or student of Surrealism not to devote some serious attention to the work of women. And if it is true that the work of women Surrealists is in internal dialogue with that of the "mainstream" male Surrealists, then our understanding of the former will necessarily influence, or even alter, our understanding of the latter. Read in the light of women artists' and writers' responses to it, the aesthetic (and political, in the broad sense) achievement of Surrealism will not necessarily be diminished, but it will look somewhat different.

At the same time, the question arises: will the discovery of a significant body of work by women oblige us to rewrite the history of the Surrealist movement? In one obvious sense, it will: the hitherto invisible women will have to be recognized.[28] In another sense, however, it

26. See M. M. Bakhtin, *The Dialogic Imagination*, ed. Michael Holquist, trans. Caryl Emerson and Michael Holquist (Austin: University of Texas Press, 1981), 282ff.

27. Gloria Feman Orenstein, "Towards a Bifocal Vision in Surrealist Aesthetics," *Trivia* 3 (Fall 1983), 72. The quoted phrase is actually from Elaine Showalter's essay, "Feminist Criticism in the Wilderness," in *Writing and Sexual Difference*, ed. Elizabeth Abel (Chicago: University of Chicago Press, 1980).

28. Just how invisible the Surrealist women were is demonstrated by William Rubin's otherwise excellent 1968 book (the catalogue of a major exhibition at the Museum of Modern Art), *Dada, Surrealism and their Heritage* (New York: Museum of Modern Art). Among the dozens of artists mentioned by Rubin, the only woman is Méret Oppenheim, whose fur-covered teacup (1936) is perhaps the best-known Surrealist object. It has also been, almost invariably, the *only* work by Oppenheim mentioned or displayed in books or exhibits on Surrealism.

won't—and to understand why, we can look at a contrasting case, that of Anglo-American modernism. The recent work of feminist scholars has shown that both the nature and the history of Anglo-American modernism begin to look completely different if one takes into serious account and gives its full historical weight to the work of early women modernists like H. D., Gertrude Stein, Dorothy Richardson, and Djuna Barnes, among others. The presence of major women writers at the beginning of the modernist movement, in a literary culture which could already boast a long tradition of major writing by women, has allowed contemporary feminist critics to argue that the elimination and/or belittling of the work of women modernists (including even Virginia Woolf, who fared better than most but whose late novels were often undervalued) was very like a conspiracy perpetrated by both the male modernists and the traditional (male) historians of modernism. In the Anglo-American case, in other words, one can speak of a concerted exclusion of women's work from the modernist canon, an exclusion which Sandra Gilbert and Susan Gubar interpret as "a misogynistic reaction-formation against the rise of literary women" on the part of the male modernists whose work came to define that canon.[29]

In the case of Surrealism, one cannot make quite the same argument, especially as far as writing is concerned, because the women's work was not present in the early years of the movement, when its most significant work was produced and its "project" was elaborated. Here is an instance where the importance of historical and national specificity becomes obvious.

Let us consider some dates. The founding of the Surrealist movement in 1924 was signaled by two publications: Breton's *Manifeste du Surréalisme,* and the first issue of *La Révolution Surréaliste,* the "official" organ of the movement which continued publication through 1929; in 1930, as a result of several years of discussion and internal debate regarding the Surrealists' position vis à vis the Communist Party, *La Révolution Surréaliste* was replaced by *Le Surréalisme au Service de la Révolution,* which continued publication (although less frequently) through 1933. In the meantime, a number of defections, exclusions and new arrivals occurred—these can be traced through the signataries of the numerous collective declarations published in the two journals. In 1932, the movement was shaken by the departure of one of its most visible and outspoken founding members, Louis Aragon, who joined the Communist Party and began attacking his old comrades.

29. See Sandra Gilbert and Susan Gubar, "Tradition and the Female Talent," in *The Poetics of Gender,* op. cit., 183–207. For an informative historical study, devoted chiefly to English and American women modernists in exile, see Shari Benstock, *Women of the Left Bank: Paris, 1900–1940* (Austin, Texas: University of Texas Press, 1986).

After 1933, when *Le Surréalisme au Service de la Révolution* folded (together with any further hope for active collaboration between the Surrealists as a group and the Communists), the movement no longer had an official journal. (The journal *Minotaure*, published from 1933 to 1938, was largely open to Surrealist work, but it did not have the status of official organ, as the two earlier journals did). The movement was further weakened in 1935 by the suicide of another of its founding members, René Crevel, and by continuing attacks from the Communists. Although the Surrealists continued to publish collective statements and to proclaim an antifascist revolutionary politics, their heroic period as an avant-garde movement was coming to an end. According to Maurice Nadeau, the historian of the movement, Surrealism as a genuine avant-garde movement died around 1935. This was, of course, not a view shared by Breton and his friends. Surrealism continued to maintain itself as a movement and to organize collective manifestations in the late 1930s and throughout the war, when many of its members were in New York. After the war, it gained new adherents and staged a major international exhibition (1947), started several new journals with Breton as *Directeur*, and was not officially dispersed until 1969, three years after Breton's death. But for a long time by then, it had been no more than a surviving remnant.[30]

Historically, this is the significant fact: between 1924 and 1933, during the most dynamic and "ascendant" period of the movement, not a single woman was included as an official member. In the twelve issues of *La Révolution Surréaliste*, whose index reads like an honor roll of Surrealism (ranging from Aragon, Arp and Artaud through Desnos, Eluard and Ernst, to Tzara, Vaché and Vitrac), there is *one* untitled poem by a woman, Fanny Beznos—whose biggest claim to Surrealist status is that she is mentioned in Breton's *Nadja*. A certain Madame Savitsky has a reply to the *Enquête* on suicide ("Le suicide est-il une solution?") in the first issue; a woman artist, Valentine Penrose, has a brief reply to the *Enquête sur l'amour* published in the last issue. And that's all. In the six issues of *Le Surréalisme au Service de la Révolution*, there are one-time appearances by three women writers (one of them being Nadejda Kroupskaia, writing about her husband Lenin—the other two are unknown) and visual work by three women artists, Gala Eluard, Marie-Berthe Ernst, and Valentine Hugo. Of the twenty or so major group declarations published during this period and reproduced in Nadeau's

---

30. It is almost touching to note that there exists, in 1987, a Surrealist Group in Chicago that publishes collective declarations. A leader of the group, Franklin Rosemont, has edited a selection of Breton's writings in English, with a book-length introduction which, although adulatory toward Breton and truculent toward almost everyone else, provides a good indication of a certain American strain of Surrealism. See André Breton, *What Is Surrealism? Selected Writings*, edited and introduced by Franklin Rosemont (Chicago: Monad Press, 1978).

Histoire du Surréalisme, not a single one carries the signature of a woman. The first major document containing the signatures of women (Dora Maar, Marie-Louise Mayoux, and Méret Oppenheim) dates from 1935 ("Du Temps que les Surréalistes avaient raison").[31] After 1935, women are fairly regularly included in exhibits and group publications: in the 1930s, in addition to Hugo, Maar and Oppenheim, we find the names of Fini, Carrington, Agar, Toyen; in the 1940s and 1950s, those of Mansour, Remedios Varo, Tanning, Kaplan, Zurn; in the 1960s, Annie Le Brun.

What conclusions can we draw from all this? First, that it is not only because of sexist bias that historians of Surrealism have tended to exclude women's work from their accounts (although sexism has played a role, since many historians mention the work of younger male Surrealists but not that of the younger women); the fact is that no women were present as active participants in the early years of the movement. Their absence can, of course, be explained as the result of an active exclusion on the part of the male Surrealists, who wanted to maintain their "men's club." But this already suggests a difference from the Anglo-American case, where women were present as active agents at the founding moment of various avant-garde projects, either as writers (H. D. and Imagism, Stein and *transition*) or as publishers and editors who promoted the work of women as well as of men.[32] It was only later that the contribution of these women was either erased from the record or else diminished. In the case of Surrealism, by contrast, women were excluded before they even got started—and this was *especially* true of writers, who even in later years remained a very small minority among women Surrealists.

The relative absence of women writers can be explained in specifically French terms, both sociological and literary. Whereas the nineteenth century in England established a significant tradition of writing

31. Reproduced in Maurice Nadeau, *Histoire du Surréalisme* (Paris: Editions du Seuil, 1964), 422–32. A 1934 declaration, opposing the Fascist demonstrations of 6 February and calling for a united front of workers and intellectuals against Fascism, contained three women's signatures (Nadeau, 381–86). However, this was not a specifically Surrealist declaration, like "Du Temps que les Surréalistes avaient raison." Prior to 1934, I did not find women's signatures on any document reproduced in Nadeau's book. The English translation of *Histoire du Surréalisme* includes many fewer documents than the original French edition.

32. On the role of women editors, see Benstock, *Women of the Left Bank*, chapter 10. Interestingly, there *were* women artists and performers participating in the early days of various Dada movements (even though they were generally ignored by later historians): Sophie Tauber and Emmy Hennings in Zurich, Hanna Höch in Berlin, among others. Could we then see French Surrealism as already a defensive reaction to the rise of "avant-garde women"? Or is it that, given the heavily literary orientation of the French movement in its early years, the relevant category here is that of *writing* and "literary women" in France, which I discuss below.

by women and integrated several women writers into the major canon (Austen, the Brontes, Eliot), while the same century in the United States produced the phenomenon of bestsellerdom by women writers (who, even if they were belittled by their male colleagues, could still not be ignored), the nineteenth century in France had a quite different literary effect: there were *fewer* major women, and fewer best-sellers by women, than in the seventeenth and eighteenth centuries. Germaine de Staël and George Sand, recognized as major by their contemporaries, were eclipsed and belittled by the end of the century, remembered more for their scandalous lives than for their literary achievement. As for the blockbuster best-sellers, no woman even came close to Eugène Sue (whose popularity resembled Harriet Beecher Stowe's in the United States). If one adds to these literary considerations the social fact that France, unlike England and America, did not have a vigorous suffragette movement (French women did not get the vote until 1946), one begins to understand why early twentieth-century French women writers had less to build on, and fewer reasons for self-confidence, than their English and American counterparts. The sad fact is that with the single major exception of Colette (and perhaps Anna de Noailles, who never achieved the same degree of recognition), there were no outstanding women writers in France in the first half of this century, and certainly none who had the tenacity to construct an *oeuvre* (much less the kind of innovative, rule-breaking *oeuvre* that can be qualified as "avant-garde" and that requires the self-confidence of, say, a Gertrude Stein) until Simone de Beauvoir. Beauvoir's own achievement looms all the larger when one considers this fact; but one can also understand why, in *The Second Sex*, she lamented the absence of true audacity in women's writing (including her own).

The second conclusion one can draw from the history of Surrealism's relation to women artists and writers is that as the movement grew weaker and more embattled, it became more welcoming to women, especially young women from other countries. It is striking to note how many of the "Surrealist women" are *not* French: Carrington, Colquhoun, and Agar are English, Oppenheim Swiss, Mansour Egyptian, Fini Argentine and Italian, Kaplan Argentine, Varo Spanish, Toyen Czech, Zurn German. There were also a great many non-French male Surrealists (Ernst, Dali, Bellmer, Man Ray among them), but the *writers* of Surrealism remained overwhelmingly French. In the case of the women, the only native French writer in the 1930s was Gisèle Prassinos— and she was less a member of the group than a "child prodigy" they discovered and promoted.[33]

33. Prassinos's first volume of poetry and prose texts, *La Sauterelle arthritique,* was published in 1935, when she was fifteen years old, with a preface by Paul Eluard. J. H.

One might speculate that competition from foreign women was less threatening to the Surrealists' male egos than competition from their own. Eileen Agar suggests as much in a recent interview: "André Breton's wife [Jacqueline Lamba, Breton's second wife] was a very talented painter, he wouldn't even look at her work. But they were very nice to me, I think they were so pleased, there were so few surrealists at the time who were giving their heart and soul to it that I think they were pleased to welcome me."[34] Although no dates are mentioned, Agar seems to be referring to the mid-1930s. By then, Surrealism as a movement was on the wane (as her remarks suggest) and needed new blood. Furthermore, most of the women whom it welcomed in the 1930s were ten to fifteen years younger than the founders of the movement.[35] They therefore brought youth as well as renewal—not a small consideration for a movement that prided itself on its youthfulness. This was even more obviously the case after the war, by which time Breton and his friends were elderly gentlemen, more than eager to welcome young women like Joyce Mansour, Nelly Kaplan or Annie Le Brun—especially since the young men who might have been their heirs were not about to join a moribund "avant-garde" movement. They were busy founding the new avant-gardes of the period: the rise of the *nouveau roman* and of *Tel Quel* overlaps with the last years of Surrealism.

If it is clear, historically and sociologically, what women brought to Surrealism, it remains to be asked what Surrealism brought to women. In a negative perspective, one could argue that it brought them nothing, since by the time they came to it the movement's truly dynamic moment was over. Christine Brooke-Rose, writing about avant-garde literary movements in general, has ruefully noted that "women are rarely considered seriously as part of a movement when it is 'in vogue'; and they are damned with the label when it no longer is, when they can safely be considered as minor elements in it."[36] Although the history of

---

Matthews, in his long and interesting study on *The Imagery of Surrealism* (Syracuse: Syracuse University Press, 1977), quotes Eluard's preface but has nothing to say about Prassinos. (He does devote half a page to Mansour, however; and he subsequently published a short monograph on her work: *Joyce Mansour* [Amsterdam: Rudopi, 1985]).

34. Mary Blume, "Portrait of a Surrealist," *The International Herald Tribune*, August 17 1987, 14.

35. Most of the first generation male Surrealists were born around the turn of the century: Breton in 1896, Aragon in 1897, Eluard in 1895, Desnos in 1900, Ernst in 1891, Man Ray in 1890, Bellmer in 1902. Of the women, only Valentine Hugo was older (born in 1887); Toyen (1902) and Agar (1904) were around the same age. The other women who came to Surrealism before 1945 were at least a decade younger: Maar was born in 1909, Tanning in 1912, Oppenheim in 1913, Carrington in 1917, Fini in 1918, Prassinos in 1920.

36. Christine Brooke-Rose, "Illiterations," unpublished MS., 19. Quoted by permission of the author.

Surrealism seems to bear out this assertion, some qualifications are necessary. It seems obvious that for the women who came to it during the late 1930s and 1940s, and even after the war, Surrealism was able to provide both a nourishing environment in the form of group exhibitions and publications, and a genuine source of inspiration. That may explain why some of these women, like Dorothea Tanning or Annie Le Brun, are strongly hostile to any feminist critique of Surrealism, and why Tanning has refused so far to be included in shows or publications devoted exclusively to women's work.[37] It is also true, however, that since they were not present during the founding years of the movement, it is easier to relegate them to the status of "minor elements."

The final conclusion we can draw is that if women are to be part of an avant-garde movement, they will do well to found it themselves.

37. Annie Le Brun expresses outrage and anger at the feminist critique in her collection of essays, *A Distance* (Paris: Pauvert/Carrère, 1984). Dorothea Tanning is represented only by a letter of refusal in Vergine's *L'Autre Moitié de l'avant-garde,* and is absent altogether from the issue of *Obliques* on "La Femme Surréaliste."

III. Questioning the Canon in the Twentieth Century: A Future for Tradition?

ELAINE MARKS

"Sapho 1900": Imaginary Renée Viviens and the Rear of the *belle époque*

PREFACE

The questions of this essay are the questions raised by those words of the title of this volume situated on the far side of the colon. What is involved in the act of "placing women in French literature"? Who constitutes the group labeled women? Monique Wittig, for example, insists that lesbians are not women. And what, in 1987, is "French literature"? A rapid perusal of histories and manuals of contemporary French literature reveals that French literature is no longer the chronological, national monolith it was before 1968. Renée Vivien, an avowed lesbian, British and American by birth, and writing in French, has been "placed" by North American and French critics in the tradition of lesbian writers, a tradition that is not limited to or by national boundaries, although it has tended to be Eurocentric.

I would argue that the notion of "French literature" is so embedded in theological and nationalist discourses that changes according to gender in the canon cannot significantly address fundamental questions of culture and reading. Indeed, who is in and who is out, although of considerable importance for understanding how the canon came to be constituted in its present form, is less important than how texts are read and for what purpose. It may be more politically effective to read excluded or marginal texts not as forgotten or neglected pieces that will now take their rightful place, but rather as case histories of the ways in which prescription and proscription operate in discourses that inform literature and culture.

In the essay that follows I try to show what the proponents of a French national literature, the proponents of a French women's literature, and the proponents of an international (Western) lesbian literature have in common; how their grounds for inclusion or exclusion in a representative body of work depend either on the critics' adhesion to

*certain principles of representation and narration, or on their views of
the writer's sexual identity and origins.*

Renée Vivien, pseudonym of Pauline Tarn, 1877–1909, was born in
London, England of an English father and an American mother and
spent much of her childhood in Paris. Her father died in 1886, and she
began to write verses in French in 1887 at the age of ten. The published
stories of her life, those that have been written by others than herself,
focus on women whom she desired successively and, in some cases,
simultaneously: Violette Shillito, Natalie Clifford Barney, Eveline Pal-
mer, Hélène de Zuylen de Nyevelt, Kérimé Turkhan-Pacha, Jeanne de
Bellune, Emilienne d'Alençon, Madeleine Rouveirollis; and older men
who were her mentors and friends: Amédée Moullé, Charles-Brun, Eugène Vallée. Her female relationships usually involved geographical
displacements: as a child between London and Paris and, later, trips to
the United States (Bar Harbor and Bryn Mawr), to Mytilene on the island
of Lesbos, and to the Middle East. They also involved Renée Vivien's
identification with and worship of the Greek Lesbian poet Sappho
whose fragments she translated into French.

At her death in 1909—she was thirty-two years old—Renée Vivien
had written approximately twenty separate volumes composed mainly
of poems, but also of short stories, a novel, and a biography of Anne
Boleyn. She had written a multitude of letters and an unpublished diary,
part of a collection belonging to Salomon Reinach and deposited at the
Bibliothèque Nationale, to be made available to scholars and other readers in the year 2000. Until the Second World War, her life and her work
received regular if discreet attention by critics interested in "littérature
féminine," in the Sapphic tradition in verse and in mores, and in deathbed conversions to catholicism. In 1951, André Billy, in his *L'Époque
1900*, coined the phrases "Sapho 1900, Sapho cent pour cent . . ."[1] im-
plying that Renée Vivien was *the* exclusively lesbian poet of the *belle
époque*, and rekindled a mild interest in her biography and in her poetry.
The feminist and gay liberation movements of the late 1960s and the
1970s primarily in the United States, but also in France, focusing on
sociocultural contexts and subversive discourses capable of disrupting
patriarchal and/or heterosexual constructions, represented Renée Vivien either as a decadent writer, an imitator of Baudelaire, politically
unaware and therefore dangerous as a model; or as a conscious lesbian-
feminist living within a lesbian community in Paris at the turn of the
century, one of the first women writers to rewrite Western myths from
an enlightened lesbian-feminist perspective. Since her early death, vari-

1. André Billy, *L'Epoque 1900: 1885–1905* (Paris: J. Tallandier, 1951), 227.

ously attributed to some excessive combination of alcohol, drugs, anorexia nervosa, and the desire to die, Renée Vivien has become a cult figure for a group of French male admirers, biographers, and critics such as Charles-Brun (1911), Salomon Reinach (1918), Le Dantec (1930), Paul Lorenz (1977), and Jean-Paul Goujon (1986). Complete editions of her poetry were published in Paris by Lemerre in 1923–1924 and in 1934. In 1986, Régine Desforges published a new biography of Renée Vivien by Jean-Paul Goujon, *Tes blessures sont plus douces que leurs caresses* and, in a single volume, the *Oeuvre poétique complète de Renée Vivien,* an edition with an introduction and notes by Jean-Paul Goujon.

Her writings in prose are not as easily available in French. Her one novel, *Une femme m'apparut,* originally published in 1904 and revised in 1905, has had no other French edition. The 1904 version is available in English in a translation by Jeannette H. Foster, published in 1976 by the Naiad Press with an introduction by Gayle Rubin. *La Dame à la louve,* a collection of short stories also published originally in French in 1904, was translated into English as *The Woman of the Wolf and Other Stories* by Karla Jay and Yvonne M. Klein and published by Gay Presses of New York in 1983. Renée Vivien's biography of Anne Boleyn was published for the first time in French in 1982 by A L'Ecart.

Renée Vivien has been placed within a variety of traditions, French and comparative, including a Baudelairean tradition, a Lesbian tradition, a tradition of significant women writers "haunted" by "the person and the poetics of Sappho,"[2] and a tradition of turn of the century minor French women poets. Her critics and biographers have, almost without exception, relied on a certain concept of the *belle époque* as the context within which her texts were written and her life, before it was written, was lived. These stereotypical, standardized discourses *on* the *belle époque* describe a period in which nature, love, and women were glorified, including the figure of the lesbian, a period of artisitic innovation and feminist activity with Paris as the cultural center of the Western world. But there are other discourses *of* the *belle époque,* discourses that tell of and react to the "Death of God," discourses that explicitly or implicitly often use the clichés of social darwinism to construct anti-semitic, nationalist, racist, and sexist theories thereby strengthening and solidifying the binary categories superior/inferior, white/black, aryan/jew, male/female, order/anarchy. These other discourses, from the underside of the *belle époque,* are still prevalent today. Therefore, the appropriate intertexts for Renée Vivien, writer and woman, include not only Sappho, Colette, Natalie Clifford Barney, and *l'art nouveau,* but also Nietzsche, Freud, and Charles Maurras.

2. Susan Gubar, "Sapphistries," *Signs* 10 (Autumn 1984): 43–62.

In 1905, the year of the rehabilitation of (Captain) Alfred Dreyfus, Charles Maurras, one of the leaders of the movement *Action Française* and the principal pedagogue of right-wing ideology in France between the 1890s and 1944, published in the same volume as his *L'Avenir de l'intelligence* an essay called "Renée Vivien" as part of his *Le Romantisme féminin.*[3] In 1976, the Naiad Press published Jeannette H. Foster's translation of Renée Vivien's *A Woman Appeared to Me* with a preface by Gayle Rubin that in many ways, but not in all, is diametrically opposed to the text by Charles Maurras.[4] I would like to confront the discourse of the nationalist, monarchist, and antisemite with the discourse of the lesbian-feminist, cultural and social analyst, and to raise through this confrontation a series of questions that relate to the placing of women writers in French literature. I will attempt to show how both Maurras and Rubin, in brilliant and provocative essays, use the available biographical and textual data to create an imaginary Renée Vivien, to pursue a genealogical illusion, a utopian vision of unity that reinforces a coherent ideological discourse from which metaphysical anguish and the enigma of sexual identity, the thematic core of Renée Vivien's poetry and prose, have been banished. I will also argue that because of the anomalous status of women writers in relation to the traditions of French literature and because of the assumptions about women that inform discourses on women writers at different historical moments, many critics seem unable to resist the power of their own ideological whims in the interpretation of women's texts.

By placing *Le Romantisme féminin* in the same volume as his *L'Avenir de l'intelligence*, Charles Maurras informs his readers that the question of women writers and the question of gender cannot be viewed in isolation. His essay on Renée Vivien is embedded in his desire to return to another France, the France of the ancien régime, the France of grace, of charm, and of lightness. Renée Vivien and the three other women writers he discusses—Madame de Régnier, Madame Lucie Delarue-Mardrus, and the Comtesse de Noailles—are presented individually as important, original poets and collectively as a dangerous phenomenon. The very title of the collection of four essays condemns these women writers within Maurras's system: they are either not French by birth or not French in spirit, that is to say that they are "romantic," foreign, through their adherence to a Germanic or Anglo-Saxon literary tradition; they are not working within the French clas-

3. The edition of Charles Maurras that I have used is: *L'Avenir de l'intelligence*, suivi de *Auguste Comte, Le Romantisme féminin, Mademoiselle Monk, L'Invocation à Minerve* (Paris: Flammarion, 1927). All translations from the French are mine, unless otherwise indicated. References will henceforth be given in the text.

4. Renée Vivien, *A Woman Appeared to Me*, trans. Jeannette H. Foster, with a Preface by Gayle Rubin (Tallahassee, Florida: Naiad Press, 1976).

sical tradition, therefore they are marginal; they are not men and therefore they are or should be feminine: resigned, sweet, and patient. What
is important in this scheme is that the male/female difference cannot be
separated from the French/foreign binary opposition or from the clas-
sical/romantic opposition. These four women writers are, in essence,
sexually different and racially impure. Moreover, if they manifest any
sign of the "risque lesbien," they are a danger to the nation. Let us look
more closely at *L'Avenir de l'intelligence* and *Auguste Comte*. These
texts will assist us in placing Charles Maurras, as he places "Renée
Vivien," in French letters.

But, for those Catholics who have left the faith, this form of nostalgia can
become so absorbing that the apologists of their religion have developed an
extremely cogent argument. Human life, they say, has only one axis without
which it breaks apart and drifts. Without divine unity and its consequences—
which are discipline and dogma—mental unity, moral unity, and political unity
disappear at the same time; they only come together again if the first unity is
reestablished. Without God, there is no longer either true or false, there are no
more rules, there is no more law. Without God, a rigorous logic equates the
worst folly with the most perfect reason. Without God, killing, stealing are
perfectly innocent acts; there is no crime that does not become unimportant, no
revolution that is not legitimate; because, without God, only the principle of
free examination exists, a principle that can exclude everything but that can
establish nothing. The Catholic clergy gives us the choice between its dogma,
with the extreme degree of organization that accompanies it, and this absolute
absence of measure and regulation which annuls or which wastes activity. God
or nothing is the alternative proposal to those tempted by doubt. [Charles Maurras, *Auguste Comte*, 105.]

Charles Maurras, in 1905, was nostalgically in search of an order that
would resurrect what he imagined to have been the golden age, the
garden of Eden of the ancien régime, the period before the French Revolution, a period in which the adjectives French, catholic, and classical
were synonymous. *L'Avenir de l'intelligence* calls for a counterrevolu-
tion, an alliance of intelligence with the old religious and philosophical
traditions against those who, like Emile Zola and the "new intellectuals," were threatening civilization. Writing towards the end of the
Dreyfus Affair, Maurras brings together, in the camp of his enemies,
Rousseau, romanticism, and foreign influences, the protestant critical
spirit and the inability of jewish intellectuals and critics to understand
"nos humanités." Charles Maurras was not a believer. He was, like
Auguste Comte, one of the "Catholics who have left the faith," one of
the catholics "without God." His attempt to hold on to certain moral
and aesthetic values in spite of the "Death of God" explains his interest
in Auguste Comte's positivism and his initial attraction to the poetry of
women writers who seem to annnounce a return to simplicity and

sincerity of feeling in their poems. Maurras's quest for unity and order refuses contradictions, banishes anarchy and hermeticism, and posits a harmony between "lettres françaises," "l'intelligence," and "le sens national." Maurras is blatantly nationalistic. France, in his texts, has already replaced the kingdom of God, and if he supports the catholic church as the only institution capable of encouraging adherence to the old values, it is because he views the catholic church as a French institution. Moreover, Frenchness, for Maurras, cannot be acquired:

People say that culture is moving from right to left and that a new world is being formed. That may be. But those who have been newly promoted are also newcomers, unless they are their clients or their valets, and these foreigners, recently enriched, are terribly lacking either in seriousness and reflexion in spite of their weighty appearance, or in lightness and grace in spite of their false Parisian polish. I find their brutish minds superficial! They are so practical, so pliant that they lose the heart and soul of everything. How could these people have a genuine taste for our humanities? What can they understand about them? Understanding of that kind cannot be learned at the university. All the diplomas in the world will not make this Jewish critic who is erudite and profound appreciate that in *Bérénice* "charming places where my heart adored you" is a manner of speaking that is not banal, but simple, moving, and very beautiful. [Charles Maurras, *L'Avenir de l'intelligence*, 12]

It would appear then that Renée Vivien, Anglo-American and protestant, is *ipso facto* excluded from participating in this Frenchness. But because she is a woman, other standards apply. Maurras does not expect Renée Vivien to have "des idées philosophiques vraies," but he does expect her to have "des émotions justes . . ." ("Renée Vivien," 165). Because her texts cannot be judged by the same criteria as those by which the texts of Baudelaire, for example, are judged, Maurras does not immediately dismiss her work. His double standard implies that women writers may be placed both in relation to "lettres françaises" and in relation to other women writers. Although Maurras seems convinced in his essentialism, convinced that Frenchness cannot be learned if one is not born into it, he is nevertheless surprised by the quality of Renée Vivien's French and by her knowledge of Latin and Greek, as well as of English literature: "Her use of the French language, whether in prose or in verse, is remarkably fluid. There is neither impropriety in the choice of words nor a false note in the harmony of sounds. She knows that the mute *e* is responsible for the charm of our language. She plays with the eleven-syllable line of verse that Verlaine considered the most accomplished of all" "Douceur de mes chants, allons vers Mitylène . . ." (148) [Sweetness of my songs, let us sail towards Mitylene. . . . ("Renée Vivien,"] Not only is Renée Vivien the faithful disciple of Baudelaire and of Verlaine, but she is often, according to Maurras, their rival.

Indeed, what is most striking about Maurras's essay on Renée Vivien is the serious attention he gives to her poetry and, at the same time, the ironic and indulgent manner in which he treats women, and particularly young women, as thinkers. His text abounds in contradictions. He focuses on two texts by Renée Vivien, "La Genèse profane" in *Brumes de Fjord* (1902) and "Prophéties" in *Cendres et Poussières* (1903). In both cases he compares Renée Vivien's words to those of Charles Baudelaire, and in both cases he insists on Renée Vivien's superiority and her difference. Her superiority because she is a young woman and therefore more natural and more sensual, particularly in relation to the sense of touch; and her difference because she is a woman. It is this tautological concept of absolute difference accepted by Maurras as clear and evident, as an unquestioned assumption, that his essay does not and cannot justify.

"La Genèse profane," which Maurras compares favorably to Baudelaire's "Blasphèmes," is a prose poem in twenty-one stanzas that narrates a "profane" version of *Genesis*. Jehovah, who incarnates strength, creates the sky, man, the heterosexual embrace, and the poet Homer; Stan, who incarnates cunning, creates night, woman, the caress, and the poet Sappho, the Lesbian. And while Homer told of the life and death of warriors, Psappha sang of:

. . . Les formes fugitives de l'amour, les pâleurs et les extases, le déroulement magnifique des chevelures, le troublant parfum des roses, l'arc-en-ciel de l'Aphrodità, l'amertume et la douceur de l'Erôs, les danses sacrées des femmes de la Crète autour de l'autel illuminé d'étoiles, le sommeil solitaire tandis que sombrent dans la nuit la lune et les Pléiades, l'immortel orgueil qui méprise la douleur et sourit dans la mort, et le charme des baisers féminins rythmés par le flux assourdi de la mer expirant sous des murs voluptueux de Mitylène.

. . . The fugitive forms of love, the pallor, and the ecstasy, the magnificent unfolding of hair, the troubling perfume of roses, the rainbow of Aphrodite, the bitterness and the sweetness of Eros, the sacred dances of the women of Crete around the altar illuminated by stars, the solitary sleep while the moon and the seven sisters disappear into the night, the immortal pride that scorns pain and smiles at death, and the charm of feminine kisses rhythmically marked by the muffled beat of the sea expiring under the voluptuous walls of Mytilene.

Maurras uses this poem as an example of the "esprit général" that pervades Renée Vivien's poetry and that informs the reader about Renée Vivien's views on religion, ethics, history, and literature. He finds this poem more Baudelairean than Baudelaire's own poetry, more forceful and more blasphemous. But he also finds the poem "un peu chargé." Maurras recognizes that Renée Vivien has created her own imaginary Psappha, a Psappha Baudelaireanized, christianized, and romanticized. What is interesting is not that praise and criticism alternate, but that there is so little precision in Maurras's comments when he is not engaged in classifying. If one recalls his emphasis in *Auguste Comte* on what is implied in a concept of a world without God, it is curious to note that when a similar theme occurs in the texts of a woman writer, it is not recognized. Seventy-one years later, Gayle Rubin treats this same theme in an apparently very different manner: "Renée Vivien read widely in myth, legend and ancient literature. She rewrote many of western culture's most cherished myths, replacing their male and heterosexual biases with female and lesbian ones. In these excerpts from 'The Profane Genesis' Vivien changes the biblical story into the creation myth of lesbian poetry" (x–xi). Maurras's essay is moving towards a particular definition of feminine difference, and Rubin's is primarily concerned with discovering ancestors for contemporary lesbian-feminism. Neither Maurras nor Rubin is prepared to read in Vivien's prose poem a Nietzschean rewriting of religious and metaphysical texts. Maurras will allow a woman poet to imitate Baudelaire but not to propose other directions. Rubin will read a lesbian poet only in terms of post-1968 lesbian-feminist consciousness.

Towards the end of his essay Maurras reveals the theory of feminine difference on which the *belle époque* relied for many of its representations of women:

Nature has arranged things so that women are bound to conceive of almost everything that touches them strictly in connection with vague ideas of happiness, luck, fatality, and destiny. The future is for them an innate obsession. In vain does the wise Horace warn them that things of the future are not precisely fixed. Women think of themselves as the protectors of being. All women listen to the magnificent resonance in their very entrails of the slightest conjecture about the relationship between what is or was with what will be. A maternal instinct constructs their universe in the form of a cradle, everything must work together to receive their fruit. A superstition, without a doubt. The superstition is complete. A woman without superstition is a monster. One notes, not without pleasure, that in spite of all her devilishness, Renée Vivien did not think of making herself into a thinker. A holy man murmurs: "That is what will save her." . . . That is, at any rate, the most natural element of her profoundly feminine art. ["Renée Vivien," 166]

Maurras judges Renée Vivien's "art" on the basis of its conformity to a particular theory of the feminine. This theory depends on the absolute program laid down by nature and on a particular relationship to the future determined by a "maternal instinct." Maurras's presentation emphasizes the notion that what is natural is both inevitable and inferior. But there is no escape. Either a woman is natural and inferior, that is to say feminine and superstitious, or she is a monster, a thinker, someone who breaks the natural order. The feminine, according to Maurras, is both a constraint and an obligation. The feminine defines limits that must not be transgressed. Within these limits women poets are judged on the degree to which male critics "frissonnent" and "frémissent" in contact with their poems, the degree to which poems by women produce effects which are sensuous and powerful. As an example of this power, Maurras extracts from the poem "Prophéties" the line: "Tu te flétriras un jour, ah! mon lys!" [One day, you will wilt, ah! my lily!] which he reads as superior to lines on the fear of aging in the poetry of Charles Baudelaire. The difference, for Maurras, is that Baudelaire's "frémissement apparaît un simple exercice de rhétorique," whereas Renée Vivien achieves her effects "par la magie du chant" (167). Renée Vivien, the accomplished versifier of the opening pages of the essay, has been transformed at the end into a feminine magician, qualified by the adjective "diabolique" and replaced by the noun "perversité." The monster is emerging.

Maurras's praise of the feminine disappears from the last chapter of *Le Romantisme féminin*, "leur principe commun," in which he discusses what Renée Vivien and "Mmes de Noailles, de Régnier et Mardrus" have in common. As in the essay on Renée Vivien, there is in "Leur principe commun" a significant difference between the beginning and the end of the chapter. Maurras begins by placing the four women poets in the tradition associated with the names of Rousseau, Chateaubriand, and Hugo. "We can no longer study Romanticism without referring to Mlle Renée Vivien, Madame de Noailles, Madame de Régnier and Madame de Mardrus: by resuscitating and enlarging the scope of Romanticism, they illuminate it" (207). The rest of the chapter is subdivided into eight parts: "L'Origine étrangère," "D'étrangetés en perversions," "L'Indépendance du mot," "L'Anarchie," "Le Génie féminin," "Le Prestige d'être bien soi," "La Profanation," and "Le Dessèchement." As the titles suggest, Maurras raises questions that are not considered in the essay on Renée Vivien, questions about the dangers of romanticism, the dangers of women forming a community of women writers, a secret little world (here, too, the resemblance with anti-semitic rhetoric of the period is striking), and, finally, the greatest danger of all, perhaps the very definition of monster, the "risque lesbien."

Maurras's text represents romanticism in terms of the feminine and, through a series of metaphors, concludes that these four women writers are dangerous to the human race. The first and most negative aspect of romanticism is that the authors who practice it and the ideas that have influenced them are foreign. The term "métèques indisciplinées," which Maurras borrows from a young nationalist writer, M. Duchot, is used to identify the four women writers who benefit from the advantages of a French culture but who cannot accept "la discipline nationale." It is also used by Maurras to remind his readers that Rousseau, Germaine de Staël, and George Sand were not French: "The lack of discipline of our young *métèques* only continues a tradition that, although it was introduced in France, has nonetheless remained separate from the true tradition of French literature. One must understand the heterogeneity of Sand, of Staël, and of Rousseau or desist from censuring their heirs; for the latter are but a wave, the last wave, of that gothic invasion for which Geneva and Coppet opened the way" (208). The opposition now in place is that between France, inheritor of the classical, Greek spirit and Germany, guilty of having infected, over the past one hundred and fifty years, Greece, Spain, and Italy with its mediocrity. Maurras is not at all troubled by the facts: for example, not one of the four women writers he discusses is of German descent. It is sufficient for him "que leur sang ne fût point de veine française très pure" (210). From this moment on the text takes off, as do polemical texts based on irrational premises, in a series of fanciful accusations that recall such outrageous and popular antisemitic texts of the *belle époque* as Edouard Drumont's *La France juive* (1886). The pure and the impure designate French and non-French; the Romantic tradition, for Maurras, is, by definition, impure. Maurras reads the same "perversité sensuelle" in Baudelaire's *Fleurs du Mal* and in Renée Vivien's poems. He accuses the "mallarmistes" of being feminine in their worship of the word, and, except for their refusal of obscurity, he finds the same glorification of the word in the writing of the four women.

But even more dangerous for Maurras than this verbal materialism is the importance given to the ego, an importance he interprets as a sign of revolt. Renée Vivien is accused of wallowing in eccentricity, in evil, in images of death, decrepitude, and illness. The same sensibility that was praised earlier in *Le Romantisme féminin* as direct and natural is now condemned; the expression of feeling has become unhealthy. But, in an unexpected shift, Maurras insists that romanticism has always been feminine and that the male poets associated with the romantic movement were subjected to a change of gender; they were feminized. Suddenly, it is as if Hugo, Chateaubriand, Lamartine, Michelet, Baudelaire, Verlaine had been contaminated by the feminine, a feminine that had installed itself perniciously in the very core of romanticism.

The remainder of the essay is a diatribe against women. In support of his passion, Maurras quotes an anonymous woman philosopher who, writing for several Parisian newspapers under the pseudonym Foemina, contends that women are more subject than men to bodily discomforts, that women are governed by the maxim: I suffer, therefore I am. The insistence on egoism as the feminine trait par excellence seems to be a satisfactory explanation for Maurras as to why women were the original discoverers of the aesthetic of harmony. From "métèques" to "criminelles" to "bacchantes" and "ménades," women writers constitute, according to Maurras, not only a danger for French letters but for the entire human race. Again, the parallel with antisemitic rhetoric is obvious:

> Today, more than one woman of distinction repeats an old paradox reformulated as a syllogism and propagated as if it were a religious or moral doctrine. Woman, they say, is uniquely capable of understanding and of receiving, of giving and returning the essence of love that her heart desires: "men are hard," "lovers are brutal. . . ." These women are being listened to. We must not exaggerate the malignancy of the symptom furnished by our cafes or our women's clubs and certain other characteristics of American or British customs. As far as this topic is concerned, the philosopher has to trust nature, which tells him not to lack confidence in life. It is nonetheless true that a society of women is in the act of being organized, a secret little world in which man only appears as an intruder and a monster, a lecherous and comic toy, in which it is a disaster, a scandal for a young girl to become engaged, in which a marriage is announced as if it were a burial, a tie between a woman and a man as the most degrading misalliance. Under the pale grey female Apollo who illumines this world, girls and women suffice unto themselves and arrange between themselves all affairs of the heart. [229–30]

The question on which Maurras ends his *Le Romantisme féminin* is whether or not the "cité de femmes," the "secret petit monde" and the "risque lesbien" it implies, is a danger to or a preserver of the naturally feminine. He presents the arguments of those to whom he refers as "superficial observers" as if they were direct quotations. He avoids giving the source of the quotations, and it is likely that these arguments are Maurras's own version of what a positive reading of these women as preservers of femininity might be. Maurras proposes two major points as counterargument. The first is that one should not exaggerate the "risque lesbien" because women are naturally fortified against lesbianism. The second is that these young women should be applauded rather than censured. Because their goal is to become ever more feminine, they do not participate in the movement of other women who are attempting to become like men and to take the place of men. These young women are, therefore, protectors of femininity, they are benefactors. Maurras's response to his confected objections is categorical. He sees the "risque lesbien" as a powerful, disruptive force, and although he persistently opposes what is natural to what is acquired, he senses that a construction of reality which is projected, repeated, and studied can take on a life of its own or become a second nature. He is aware that words produce their own reality. The bacchantes who repeat "I, I, I" must inevitably be disloyal to civilization. They do not become more feminine, but rather they join with the others in the goal of imitating men, of pretending to be like men. Even more than the female doctor or lawyer, they become like an "être insexué," they become dry. And to be dry implies to be without "charme."

What emerges from Maurras's conclusion is that women who think about their sexuality are most apt to do so in groups and that these groups are likely to be inclined towards lesbianism. The formula, then, is: it is not feminine to think *or* a woman who thinks is *ipso facto* a lesbian. Reading the poetry of Renée Vivien, Maurras does not recognize the marks of a thinking woman but rather the marks of a feeling woman. Examining the women writers one by one, examining the text of their lives, Maurras is struck by a lesbian presence which he can only attribute to a narcissistic concentration on the self. The real danger, then, of "romantisme féminin," is not only that it feminizes men, that it impedes clear communication, and that it relies on foreign, non-French, impure values, but that it changes the natural sexual orientation of women. The effects produced by the texts of "romantisme féminin" are powerful enough to create a second nature. Maurras, in *Le Romantisme féminin*, implicitly equates the menace of lesbianism with the menace of foreigners, protestants, and jews.

The key word in *Le Romantisme féminin* is the word "charme," the same word that directs Barbey d'Aurevilly's discourse on women in his prefatory dedication of *Les Bas-bleus* (1878).[5] This undefinable "charme" can only be identified by men of exquisite feeling, thereby eliminating jews and foreigners. It is the ability of women to seduce men. It is unrelated to literature, art, or science, and it is essential to the maintenance of a social and an aesthetic harmony. Without this "charme" that emanates from women, men's pleasure, and consequently the meaning of men's lives, evaporates. The "risque lesbien," viewed as threatening to this "charme," must be diagnosed and the monster eradicated. According to Maurras, the two domains capable of eroding this "charme" are metaphysical anguish and the investigation of sexuality. "Sapho 1900," to the dismay of her critics,[6] was concerned with both.

5. Barbey d'Aurevilly, *Les Bas-bleus*, ed. V. Palmé (Paris: Sociéte générale de libraire catholique, 1878). It is also the key word in Philippe Sollers's novel, *Femmes* (Paris: Gallimard, 1981).

6. Colette, in her 1928 portrait of Renée Vivien, incorporated in 1932 as a chapter of *Ces plaisirs . . .*, renamed in 1941 *Le Pur et l'impur*, insists on the childish, puerile behavior of Renée Vivien and represents both her anguish and her sexuality as eccentric and unhealthy. Indeed, although her style bears little resemblance to that of Charles Maurras, Colette reproduces, through elaborate anecdotes, Maurras's ideological positions. Toward the beginning of her text, Colette refers to "the hidden tragic melancholy that throbs in the poetry of Renée Vivien" [*The Pure and the Impure*, trans. Herma Briffault (New York: Farrar, Straus & Giroux, 1978), 80]. But because Colette and Renée Vivien never talked together about their writing and because Colette only occasionally saw Renée Vivien in the act of writing, Renée Vivien, the writer, is absent. Colette focuses

What is for Charles Maurras in 1905 a dangerous "secret petit monde" is for Gayle Rubin in 1976 a "lesbian renaissance." Renée Vivien is no longer a contradictory, menacing figure but the producer of "one of the most remarkable lesbian oeuvres extant" (iv). Charles Maurras was defending his version of Frenchness and maleness against contamination by impure texts and persons. Gayle Rubin celebrates her version of lesbian-feminism by extolling texts and persons who represent "forerunners of the contemporary gay women's movement" (vii). For Maurras as for Rubin, Renée Vivien's texts and life are subversive. In one case the subversion is villainous; in the other it is heroic.

"Sapho 1900" is an ideal textual figure for those critics who maintain a Manichean, theological view of the world and for whom good and evil, as well as absolute presence, can be located in specific texts. Gayle Rubin welcomes narratives that attack and challenge heterosexual privilege and male bias and that can be read both as fictions and as historical documents. She writes with equal passion about Renée Vivien's texts and Renée Vivien's life. She is primarily interested in the fact that Renée Vivien was a lesbian and that lesbian history, difficult to research, is even more difficult to transmit.

Rubin reads the 1904 version of *A Woman Appeared to Me* as a "novel [that] is also a historical document, part of the archival remains of one of the most critical periods in lesbian history" (iv). In presenting historical and biographical contexts for the novel, Rubin insists on the changes in the concept of homosexuality that occurred towards the end of the nineteenth century, particularly the change from an understanding of homosexuality as a form of behavior to an understanding of homosexuality as an identity or a fixed character. She does not connect this change to the development of racial theories. During this same period, for example, to be jewish became a question of racial as well as religious difference, a question of character. And this character, for both homosexuals and jews, depended on theories of strict biological determinism. Rubin does not make the connections that are implicit in Maurras's text between the representation of lesbians and jews. Her text, with its emphasis on the "specialized homosexual communities" in "nineteenth-century cities" (v), seems to glorify any evidence of lesbian society without concern for the ideological premises on which it was constructed. When Rubin writes: "The variety of lesbian society in Paris before 1910 has been charmingly described by Colette" (v), the adverb

---

on Renée Vivien's face, her lisp, her claustrophic apartments, her eating and her drinking habits, and her manner of speaking about her lesbian love affairs. Colette's Renée Vivien is only incidentally a writer. She is, rather, an exemplary dark figure of the *belle époque* and, as Colette's definitive title suggests, corroborating Charles Maurras's conclusions, one of the impure.

"charmingly" warns us that in spite of apparent differences there may be a significant resemblance between Maurras's fear of lesbianism and Rubin's welcoming of it.

But contemporary investigations, such as Bram Dijkstra's[7] into the connections between discourses and representations of women, lesbians, blacks, and jews during the *belle époque* must make us suspicious of any discourse that conflates difference and identity and any community that depends on this conflation for its existence. And so it is incumbent upon readers of Gayle Rubin's text to question the unqualified praise she lavishes on Renée Vivien and Natalie Clifford Barney in such phrases and sentences as: "their shared vision of a society in which women would be free and homosexuality honored" . . . or "searching for their own roots, they discovered Sappho and Hellenism. They endeavored to recreate a Sapphic tradition" . . . or "the two women declared themselves pagans, spiritual descendants of the Greeks" (ix). The search for roots and origins betrays the theoretical and ideological presence of social darwinism and its intersections with religious discourse. We have noted Maurras's insistence on the Greek connection as the basis of the French, male, classical tradition. How curious, then, to find a Greek connection, albeit a "Sapphic tradition," honored by Rubin because it was honored by Renée Vivien and Natalie Clifford Barney. History does not necessarily imply roots, but roots always imply an origin, a source from which one traces an identity that excludes all forms of difference. There is a tendency in the first part of Rubin's essay to uphold the notion of a lesbian community based on a fundamental, "racial" difference that would be as exclusive as Maurras's French, male, catholic community.

In the second part of her introduction, Gayle Rubin looks more closely at the text of *A Woman Appeared to Me* and the changes made by Renée Vivien in her retelling of myths and legends. Rubin is at her best in pointing out the play in the text between heterosexual and lesbian and male and female biases and the ambiguities this play creates for the reader confronted with familiar figures and symbols—such as Saint John, or snakes, or a prostitute—that no longer adhere to their usual sexual interpretation. Like Maurras in the first part of his essay on Renée Vivien's poetry, Rubin supplies the reader with intertexts and temporarily forgets or abandons ideological rhetoric in favor of precise examples from the texts and relevant anecdotes from Renée Vivien's life.[8] She shows convincingly Renée Vivien's interest in stories that deal with independent women, rebels who refuse men and male desire.

7. Bram Dijkstra, *Idols of Perversity* (Oxford University Press, 1986).

8. Gayle Rubin fails to mention that the title of the novel is a quotation from the thirtieth canto of "Purgatory" in Dante's *The Divine Comedy*. The essential reversal in the text is that a woman, a Beatrice, appears not to the male narrator, Dante, but to the female narrator of *A Woman Appeared to Me.*

Until the last sentence of the introductory essay, there is no sustained attempt, as there is in the beginning of the essay, to make of Renée Vivien's texts or her life and loves a paradigm for a lesbian tradition. The examples from *A Woman Appeared to Me* and from stories such as "The Veil of Vashti" or "The Eternal Slave" are quoted in their uniqueness or related, when appropriate, to other texts in nineteenth-century French literature. The same is true of Rubin's account of the amorous relations between Barney and Vivien. They are not presented as exemplary. The last sentence is, therefore, disappointing: "At the time of Barney's death, she, Renée Vivien, and the other women linked to them were already being rediscovered by a new generation of lesbian feminists searching for their ancestry" (xxix).

It would be as serious an error to consider Renée Vivien's lesbianism a danger to the human race, as Maurras ultimately does, as it would be to treat Renée Vivien as an "ancestor" for a new generation of lesbian-feminists. If she is an "ancestor," then lesbianism is a family affair, and a family, unlike a freely chosen community of associates, is a closed, imposed biological group. Lillian Faderman, in *Surpassing the Love of Men*[9] censures Renée Vivien for imitating "French decadent literature," for imitating nineteenth-century male writers who wrote about and who represented lesbians in their poetry and their fiction. Faderman's condemnation depends on the notion that there is an authentic lesbian experience, one that has been understood and transmitted by United States lesbian-feminists since the 1970s. Neither Rubin's lesbian family nor Faderman's authentic and inauthentic lesbian "experience" is a satisfactory reading or placing of Renée Vivien. If it is unpardonable to proscribe her because she and her texts are dangerous to humanity, it is equally unpardonable to prescribe or proscribe her because she either is or is not part of an imaginary lesbian-feminist family.

It is not Renée Vivien's place in French or in lesbian literature that it is important to determine but the multiple discursive contexts of the *belle époque* that traverse her texts. This cannot be accomplished by critics eager to establish their own arbitrary categories of classification. For it is, in the long run, the desire to classify that links Maurras and Rubin and that makes it difficult for them to approach Renée Vivien's texts. There is not one of Renée Vivien's critics who has acknowledged her preoccupation with metaphysical anguish and with sexual identity. Blinded by their own rhetoric and discourse, her critics have tended to classify "Sapho 1900" in terms of a real lesbian identity rather than as a symbolic epithet. The result has been the creation of a succession of imaginary "Renée Viviens."

---

9. Lillian Faderman, *Surpassing the Love of Men* (New York: William Morrow and Co., Inc., 1981).

CHRISTIANE MAKWARD, WITH
ODILE CAZENAVE

The Others' Others: "Francophone" Women and Writing

To put it dramatically, if "canonical" means inclusion in basic college courses, discussed in literary history, bibliography and criticism, and published as paperback "classics,"[1] literary francophone women do not exist in the canon. Of course, thanks to literary awards, the works of Antonine Maillet and Simone Schwarz-Bart seem to enjoy the status of "modern classics," but most of our colleagues can't spell their names yet, let alone consider seriously teaching them in survey courses. (As it is, the thematic approach is the francophone woman writer's best chance for topical inclusion in syllabi.)

Unlike women writers of France, whose status has fluctuated with trends and the idiosyncracies of literary critics and historians, the francophone woman writer—at least outside of Europe—is a relatively modern phenomenon. While French-Swiss women's writing can be identified as early as 1536—when Marie Dentière published her chronicle of Genevan religious strife—the history of French-Swiss women's fiction begins with Dutch-born Belle van Zuylen de Charrière in the latter part of the eighteenth century. In the New World, Quebecois literature prides itself on French-Canadian novelist Laura Conan who published *Angéline de Montbrun* in 1884. At the other end of the chronology, only the last decade has seen the birth of Black African women's fiction.

If we are to challenge traditional assumptions about French literature and begin to "place" the works of non-French women who have written in French, the first concept in need of scrutiny—if indeed it should be used at all—is that of "francophone" ("French-speaking"). Like "feminist," "francophone" has the treacherous value of a handy label. Certainly the Quebecois quarterly *Présence Francophone* is not in

1. I owe this functional definition to Paul Lauter, "Race and Gender in the Shaping of the American Literary Canon," *Feminist Studies* 9, no. 3 (Fall 1983): 434.

question here, having provided a valuable forum to critics and writers from around the French-speaking world since 1970. One senses however that there is an old ideology at work in occasional statements and pieces such as "Brève Histoire du Mouvement Francophone" (1973) where the author worries that the French language might be "slighted" or treated with disrepect: "Ici et là, le français demeure un instrument de colonisation ou de domination; ailleurs, cette langue est bafouée." [Here and there, French remains an instrument of colonization and domination; elsewhere it is slighted.] What ghosts of Empire still lurk in this century-old word, and an ideology which surfaced as a "sauve *que peut*" [save what can be saved] French political tool of the sixties. Ironically, it is probably in countries like Quebec and Belgium, whose political-cultural identifies have been chronically threatened by Parisian or Anglo-Saxon engulfment, that we find the most receptive territories for the "new [francophone] humanism" described by the author, based on "respect for people, their language and their culture."[2]

In the academy the term "francophone" is to be decoded skeptically: just as "French literature" still largely means French literature by men, the term "francophone," while suggesting an effort to balance geographical regions, often covers only what is of interest to the user in devising a syllabus, a project or a program. The label may first serve as a neutralizing reference to a delusive/elusive entity. A balance of gender along with the various geographical subareas may be achieved only exceptionally and remains utopian for most areas. Beyond a willingness to pay homage to the culture and the language of the nation responsible for the term, there seems to be little sub-stance to the concept. The label "francophone" itself tends to disappear with fame: whoever gives serious thought to the fact that Marguerite Yourcenar was Belgian and lived in Maine . . . ? Not metropolitan French critics to be sure.

Women writers in French outside France? Nowhere is circumspection more necessary and more difficult to achieve than in attempting to group women's literary production arising from such diverse geographical entities as Belgium and Switzerland in the Old World, Quebec-Acadia in the New, and in the Third World North Africa and the Middle-East, West and Central Black Africa, and the West Indies, to name the major sources of francophone writing. There is probably more intellectual common ground between Aimé Césaire and Jacques Chessex (from Martinique and Switzerland respectively) than between Simone Schwarz-Bart and Anne Cunéo (also from the West Indies and

2. Anne Voisin. *Présence Francophone* nos. 7–8 (Fall 1973–Spring 1974): 125–27. On the concept of "francophonie" see also Maryse Condé's interview in *Journal Français d'Amérique* (11–24 April 1986, 10–11) where she questions the creation of the Ministry of Francophony with Lucette Michaux Chevry, a West Indian woman, as chief executive.

Switzerland respectively): while both men might be described as erudite and "territory proud," the women are divided by their opposite stance on feminism despite the fact that Schwarz-Bart lived in Switzerland for many years.

Francophone women writers living outside of Europe have one important trait in common, however. They are subject to specific tensions and conflicting allegiances which arise not only from their identities as women but also as citizens of threatened or unstable political entities. In Quebec, North Africa and Lebanon, the political questions werc/arc still pressing even when not life-threatening. This spawns a type of creative writing that will necessarily be scrutinized for political relevance. In the Arab world particularly, the women's movements have gained and lost precious ground and "a room of one's own" is simply not imminent for Franco-Arab women with an interest in creative writing. They often must resort to exile in order to maintain creative integrity. In the West Indies and Black Africa, civil rights cannot be taken for granted and serious political disruptions can occur. In most countries, women's rights or the equivalent of an Equal Rights Amendment are either absent or on the books purely as a matter of form.[3] The woman writer in these areas can hardly afford politically to produce "new languages," even in the unlikely event that she has had access to the "Grandes Ecoles" of the "métropole," or passed the prestigious "concours" open to French citizens only.

The relation of the writer to the French language varies tremendously from one country to the next, and here again we can see that history and geography define particular linguistic attitudes, competencies, and politics. In the New as well as the Old World francophone communities, French is the mother tongue—as much a part of the local identity as the regional attributes that residents have cultivated and preserved. This, of course, is not the case for Arab or Black women writers. Nor is it true for the West Indians, with the exception of their educated upper-middle class. European and North American writers have had an ambivalent relationship with the French language: loyalty and devotion to it as the basis of their cultural identity against threatening alien communities (German, Anglo-Saxon or Flemish), insecurity and rejection under the gaze of Parisian cultural imperialism. Those contradictions are still alive in Quebec today where a Madeleine Gagnon and an Hélène Ouvrard, for example, stand at odds on the usefulness of dialect or *joual* in writing. In Switzerland, the French-Swiss region of "Romandie" is not that much more remote from Paris than

3. A helpful source of information on these issues is Robin Morgan's *Sisterhood is Global* (Garden City, N.Y.: Anchor Press/Double Day, 1984). We can only regret that no more than four francophone countries are treated: Algeria, Haiti, France, and Senegal along with two marginally francophone nations: Lebanon and Morocco.

Belgium, but a clearer distance from French customs seems to be main-tained deliberately; perhaps the Swiss are innately less impressed by French intellectual ways. A few, however, assimilate them totally. In-deed, they can ultimately become Parisians like Robert Pinget or Cla-risse Francillion, or they can be perfectly dual commuters like the poet Pierrette Micheloud.

Yet it is only in Quebec and Belgium, and only among the most highly educated writers, that the French language is treated/mistreated experimentally/jocularly with as much freedom as in France by new generations of women. There lies a quintessential difference for the Third World francophone women whose mother tongue is not French and whose ethnicity guards them from assimilation. Even though the whole colonial apparatus was geared towards that very goal, and "as-similation" was official cultural policy, women's access to education was severely restricted. This accounts for the emergence of African women writers several decades later than their male counterparts. For these writers, the French language is neither an object of reverence nor a source of existential anxiety. It has not yet reached the luxurious status of a personal enemy in need of masterful deconstruction, but rather functions as an unfamiliar road to new forms of power. Here, the pri-mary value of language in literary usage is that of an instrument to promote change or reveal its possibility.

Having questioned the label "francophone" and sketched out dif-ferences between Old, New and Third world women writers in French, we shall review briefly the circumstances of their creativity and the specific differences between the various constituencies in the field. Just as access to public schools or the end of the male's privileged access to education in the late nineteenth century ushered in the possibility of gender-balanced creativity in France, differences in educational and cul-tural politics and in history play an important role in the formation of francophone creativities.

Francophone literatures, and women writers within them, have clearly flourished in the recent past—nearly three decades after "les indépendances," two decades after "la révolution tranquille" in Que-bec, and over a decade since Woman's Year of 1975. Indeed, the last ten years have seen the consolidation of these area studies, with the pub-lication of new journals, reference works, and several significant over-views.[4]

4. The most recent and useful of these are two on African women writers: Brenda F. Berrian's *Bibliography of African Women Writers and Journalists* (Washington, D.C.: Three Continents Press, 1985) and *Ngambika, Studies of Women in African Literature* (Trenton, N.J.: Africa World Press, Inc., 1986) edited by Carol Boyce Davies and Anne Adams Graves. This section on African criticism may be credited more specifically to Odile Cazenave.

While the area of African literary criticism is not new, the recent focus of attention on African literature by women has revitalized critical interest. In a roundtable devoted to "Male vs. Female Narrative Theory" at the 1987 African Literature Association conference at Cornell University, panelists attempted to identify the specific traits of African feminine writing as it stands in relation to the general body of literature. Critics argued that it is neither best defined by theme (e.g., polygamy, ritual sexual mutilations, infertility), nor by narrative structures such as autobiography or the epistolary form. Also rejected were such aspects as the immediacy of communication—which may or may not be related to the epistolary or the autobiographical mode—and elements of the oral tradition, although these emerged as somewhat less circumscribed and thus more promising for analytical speculation. Only the question of the "sexualization of space"—or the different "spaces" inhabited by women and determined by culture—received serious consideration as a trait specific to African women's literature. Yet, until more research is accomplished, it will be unclear whether this special relation of women to space is distinct from African thematics. A healthy skepticism resulted from this discussion, with participants pointing out the limitations of theoretical approaches, and even questioning the necessity of defining a specificity of feminine African writing.

Critical readings of African literature have traditionally been dominated by male Western-oriented and -trained critics. Thus when Davies and Graves undertook their anthology of women writers in Africa, they did so fully aware that these writers now have to wage the same war as their African male counterparts had to, about twenty years ago, when European critics controlled the emerging field. This valuable new scholarship seeks to extend interpretations of African literature in a gender-balanced way, as well as to reconsider—or challenge in a fresh manner—the traditional assumptions underlying prefeminist African criticism. The book's treatment of "images of women," self-representation by women, and women's issues in criticism shows, however, a disproportionate emphasis on anglophone realms of African literature; although dedicated to the memory of Mariama Ba, and including analyses of her only two books, it barely touches on any other female author in French.[5]

---

5. Clearly, more work is needed in this area with approaches that would move beyond Arlette Chemain Degrange's very useful overview of male novels: she brings out the narrative female prototypes of the "Black Venus with a generous heart," "the suffering woman," and "the diligent woman" with both a political awareness and a constructive-active voice. Arlette Chemain-Degrange. *Emancipation féminine et Roman africain,* (Dakar: Les Nouvelles Editions Africaines, 1980).

Davies's introduction, "Feminist Consciousness and African Literary Criticism," specifically addresses African feminism and its implications for writers. She constructs a prospective frame for this new area of feminist criticism, showing that the developing body of African women's writing is only now in a position to receive serious and fair evaluation; critics are no longer doomed to function within male and Western paradigms. In order to achieve valid analyses, she cautions critics to remain aware of the dual foundations of race and gender while "taking what is of value from both mainstream feminist criticism and literary criticism." Davies proposes the following objectives in the shaping of a feminist criticism of African literature: 1. developing the African canon (working to give women's texts the status of standard reference comparable to the one enjoyed by a core body of African male writings); 2. examining stereotypical images of women; 3. analyzing the writing and development of an African female aesthetics; 4. examining women in oral traditions. Other tasks will include that of evaluating the omission of women writers from the canon, and of challenging their creativity while encouraging it. Somewhat didactically, Davies also suggests that women writers must keep in mind "appropriate" portrayals of women, warning them against the traps of stereotypical female roles. She calls for feminine/feminist writing on themes of motherhood, the vagaries of polygamous marriages, the consequences of the colonial heritage and/or of an urban environment, the balance between male and female relationships and the development of a separate self. Davies also maintains that while these themes are neither specifically African nor feminine, they are a fruitful approach for critics in delineating the African literary profile.

As far as French-writing African women are concerned, Berrian's bibliography—albeit not as exhaustive or reliable as it could be—enables the reader to estimate the corpus of French African fiction by women as comprised of some twenty-five volumes of narrative and autobiographical works by about a dozen authors from Senegal, Cameroon and the Ivory Coast. The poets, more numerous but less productive, are geographically more scattered. In the area of dramatic texts, a scarcity of works for the stage seems to parallel what can be observed of French women writers prior to the contemporary period. Sociological considerations and unequal access to education need hardly be evoked to explain the "stage fright" of women writers who have had little exposure to this ancient occidental ritual.[6]

6. Géo-H. Blanc has pondered the question in the French-Swiss protestant context (*Alliance Culturelle Romande* [Geneva] Cahier 26, November 1980), and English Showalter analyzes this phenomenon for eighteenth century French women writers in his article in this issue, pp. 95–111.

What was true of France until the turn of the century can and will be observed in the Third World for some time to come. Robin Morgan's *Sisterhood is Global* shows consistent patterns: with each progressive age group (primary education, junior-high and senior-high) the ratio of boys to girls becomes greater. Currently, the gross overall figure is about one girl to two or three boys in school, puberty being the most dramatic factor in girls' attrition rate. In Zaïre the female student population drops from 22% to 9% during the first three years of secondary school.[7] In Senegal a teacher training school for girls was opened a full thirty years after the one for boys. By the midseventies, some fifteen years after independence (1960), the number of school children had quadrupled, but girls still made up only a quarter of the school enrollment. For the African continent as a whole the corresponding statistics show an even clearer disadvantage for women, and it must be further noted that the education of girls is normally oriented towards domestic/secretarial skills at the junior level, and towards nursing and education at the college level.

Much bleaker still is the corresponding figure on the Haitian scene where Marie Chauvet (1919–1972) stands in relative isolation as the accomplished author of several volumes of fiction, including the powerful *Amour, Colère et Folie* (1968). The French language is used by a scant 15% of the Haitian population[8] and illiteracy remains high, having been brought down only from 81% to 75% between 1968 and 1980. In contrast, younger generations on the islands of Martinque and Guadeloupe (DOMs or Départements d'Outremer since 1946), are given a better foundation in spelling and writing skills, since social and educational policies are identical to those in France.

Among the themes surfacing in Caribbean francophone literature is the "syndrome" identified by writers such as Edouard Glissant as "linguistic schizophrenia" or "Caribbean madness." These labels describe the anguish arising from the repression of Creole, the mother-tongue of a majority of French West Indians, which combines African syntax and seventeenth century popular French lexical sources. Another specific West Indian trait emerges quickly for the reader of Carribean women writers: "epidermic neurosis" or awareness of skin tone.[9] This question and the more familiar "feminine neuroses"—sometimes designated as

7. I am here using miscellaneous sources and references quoted in a working paper: "Différences-Afrique: Continent deux fois noir."

8. See Marie-Thérèse Colimon's interview on her own career in Condé's essay on French-Carribean women writers: *La Parole des femmes. Essai sur les romancières des Antilles de langue française* (Paris: L'Harmattan, 1979).

9. "The darkness ladder" is indicted most forcefully by Simone Schwarz-Bart in *A Dish of Pork with Green Bananas*, with André Schwarz-Bart (Paris: Editions du Seuil, 1967).

"bovarysm," the inability or reluctance displayed by literary heroines to dissociate sex from love—provide the basic framework of psychological narratives written by a handful of women over the past forty years: Mayotte Capécia, Michèle Lacrosil, Jacqueline Manicom, Marie-Magdeleine Carbet, etc.

With the fiction of Simone Schwarz-Bart and Maryse Condé we enter the new age of French-Caribbean women's writing where female characters cease to be victims; at the very least they are shown as rebels in spirit and sometimes in actual fact, or as "modern," philosophically conscious characters. But more generally, this writing should be seen in the context of intended readership and the interaction between critics, writers, and readers examined by Maryse Condé in her essay on French-Caribbean women writers.[10] Both a writer and a critic herself, Condé finds in a recurring theme of Caribbean fiction—the questioning and/or rejection of motherhood—an essential difference between African and Caribbean women writers. Condé wonders if this theme is a denial of prevalent tradition or an ultimatum to men justifying their own behavior by their partner's abnegation; refusing motherhood would have a sexual-political function here. Condé takes issue with the pressures on women writers not to discomfit the reader, and to offer positive characters instead of expressing their existential darkness: "But to demand positive heroes from writers strikes us as highly risky. This leads to a form of literary authoritarianism which could entail the writer's sclerosis, her silence, or could engender a type of literature where slogans would replace thought . . . isn't to sow discomfort the most beautiful part for a writer to play?" (76–77).

About the same time that Condé was formulating these thoughts in her energetic, spontaneously "oral" style, with an occasional reference to "strident" feminism (her own choice of words), Simone Schwarz-Bart was moving back to the West Indies from Switzerland. Understandably, her views were grounded differently from Condé on the question of providing positive images to Caribbean readers.[11] Although Schwarz-Bart never paid "feminist" attention to women's issues, her readers will instantly sense a genuine love of women in her novels. . . . Whether the gynocentrism of her masterpiece, The Bridge of Beyond [Pluie et Vent sur Télumée Miracle, 1972], combined with sociopolitical factors, accounts for the relative lack of critical attention is open to speculation.

10. Maryse Condé, La Parole des femmes. Essai sur des romancières des Antilles de langue française. (Paris: L'Harmattan, 1979).

11. At the time she published Ti Jean L'Horizon (Paris: Editions du Seuil, 1979), and unless she was maligned or misquoted by her interviewer, Simone Schwarz-Bart was so ill-informed about Caribbean and Black women writers in general that she thought she "must be the only one." Interview with Simone Schwarz-Bart in Flash-Afrique-Antilles, Oct.–Nov., 1979.

"Positive images" of women (and somber male figures) are conveyed through myth and archetypal situations in all three of Schwarz-Bart's novels. A fascinating comparison could be made between Condé and Schwarz-Barts's treatments of "roots," or the return journey to Africa. Condé's achievements include substantial works for the theatre, thus further suggesting that Caribbean women's writing in French has entered maturity.

The women of Quebec, with a fully diversified body of works, could have claimed maturity too as early as two or three decades ago. In 1975, Nicole Brossard, herself a conspicuous figure among the new generation of Quebec women writers, wondered about the unusually important part played by Canadian francophone women on the literary scene.[12] Indeed the figures are identical (13% of citations) for women in French and in Quebecois literary history, founded on traditionally conceived tools such as the Gallimard/Pléiade *Histoire des littératures françaises, connexes et marginales* and the 1976 *Dictionnaire pratique des auteurs québécois* by Hamel, Hare, and Wyczynski. Another classic source, *La Littérature canadienne-française* by Bessette (1968) opens with a female figure, Marie de l'Incarnation, a nun who penned some 13,000 letters and founded a new order in Quebec, and credits yet another woman, Laure Conan, with founding the novel in French on Canadian soil in 1884.

It is important to understand the effects of geographically determined attitudes on the emergence and treatment of literary women. The powerful figure of the mother in Franco-Canadian traditional society, for example, is reflected in its literature. For political and religious reasons, women in the New World were under obligation to procreate abundantly. As recently as the midseventies one could still hear of women being refused the sacraments because they had not lately borne a child. Two and a half centuries earlier, shiploads of "Royal daughters" were sent to New France to speed up settlement of the territories, and it is still a demographer's wonder how the population grew from 60,000 to one million between 1763 and 1867. The very harsh conditions under which this miracle took place, and the later stresses of the industrial age, demanded from these pioneer women survival skills which seemed only to strengthen their status in the culture.

Such is the thrust of Gabrielle Roy's *Bonheur d'occasion* (1945) which chronicles the life of a poor family in Montreal during World War II, and was quickly hailed as an authentic painting of the Quebecois people. The good fertile mother archetype, as well as the all-consuming, domineering mother figure, have inspired countless narratives and dra-

---

12. See the special issue, "La Femme et l'écriture," in the Québecois literary journal *Liberté* 106–07 (1976).

matic texts, especially after 1970 when Quebec women "took over" the stage with the resounding success of *La Nef des sorcières*, a collective work created in 1976, and the scandalous *When Faeries Thirst* by Denise Boucher (1974). This author was legally challenged for her audacity; putting on stage the archetypal figures of Virgin and Prostitute, she made them sound extremely familiar, very real and . . . terribly disgruntled. Indeed the success of Quebec women's theatrical enterprises is one of the most distinctive features of the francophone literary scene. Prior to the new feminist era, Anne Hébert and Suzanne Loranger's plays had been well received. But it was the women's movement of the late sixties, which created new links between anglo- and francophone women in North America (e.g., Nicole Brossard's film on the new American feminists), that energized and inspired a younger generation of writers who functioned in groups and recognized the value of mutual support. Sexuality and the female body were placed at the center—as in current "performance art"—of these new women's creations, for all to look at in order to un-learn old voyeuristic or male-identified patterns.

In the past fifteen years Quebecois women writers have emerged as a forceful presence in the French-speaking world. They have garnered several prestigious awards on the Parisian scene, they have organized noteworthy literary events and cultural happenings; they travel to France without being overshadowed by their French counterparts. Their names (Bersianik, Blais, Boucher, Brossard, Gagnon, Hébert, Lamy, Lasnier, Loranger, Ouvrard, Maillet, Théorêt, etc.), have become familiar to an ever widening group of French and American critics, feminists and American students, thanks in part to their geographical accessibility and to the supportive cultural policies of Quebec province. Even more clearly, however, this flourishing is due to an unusually gifted group of women and their fruitful interaction with critics who have, in turn, produced outstanding works: the collected essays of writers and editors like Suzanne Lamy and Irène Pagès, Paula Gilbert Lewis, Louise Forsyth and Karen Gould.

This positive picture does not imply that Quebecois writers have conquered the French reading public, whose judgment swings in harmony with "Apostrophes" and the book industry's publishing plans, one of the more elusive realities with which writers and scholars must contend. Since "études féminines" in France seem to be in hiatus for the present (perhaps to infuse discreetly new life), we can only hope that the talented productions of Quebecois women will be given fair space and attention in the French academic and literary world. Still, there are serious gains to report: Quebecois studies, with its healthy representation of women writers, is currently offered in some French universities (Rennes, Haute-Bretagne for instance). As a new "planetary" vision begins to compete with traditional "European" and "francophone" visions of the French, as more and more young people hop about and insist on finding out for themselves what happens across the Atlantic, and as more and more women work in the decisive areas of education, research, and publishing, Quebecois writers should fare best of all among "francophone women," since the worst they have to contend with is Parisian "provincialism" and the simple arithmetic of French literary production and marketing.

Conversely, Belgian as well as French-Swiss women writers have suffered from a lack of separate identity in the eyes of the French. The French-Swiss body of works by women includes a few plays, none of which has achieved "export" status, although Anne Cunéo, a bilingual writer who functions in a sociofeminist militant mode in Zürich, may come close. Dramatic texts for the radio (e.g., plays by S. Corinna Bille), and a respectable body of film scripts for television are by now sufficiently numerous to warrant investigation. Women's poetry has not yet received serious assessment, but the works of Pierrette Micheloud, Anne Perrier, Vic Martin and the younger generation's Monique Laederach and Mousse Boulanger, are often read on Swiss radio stations. Of all creative modes for Swiss francophone writers the narrative genre fares best. As I observed earlier, the line started, ironically, with immigrant Belle van Zuylen de Charrière's satire of her native Dutch society in *Lettres Neuchâteloises* (1784), followed by *Lettres écrites de Lausanne* (1785). Prior to Charrière's works, several Swiss women had written religious essays, pamphlets, chronicles and poetry: Marie Dentière and Jeanne de Jussie in the early sixteenth century, and in the eighteenth, Marie Huber—"la belle théologienne"—was considered by some a precursor for Rousseau's "natural religion." Indeed, Huber was noted in her day, and essays such as "Le Monde Fol Préféré au Monde Sage" might well yield exciting feminist readings today. Charrière believed that works must be read "beyond" the regional context; she advocated resistance to French literary authoritarianism, which pervaded the ranks of Swiss critics in their assessment of their homeland's artistic production. Among the more famous victims of such constraints was Isabelle de Montolieu (1751–1832). Her *oeuvre* includes over a hundred volumes, among which the popular *Caroline de Lichtfield* (1786) and *Châteaux suisses* contributed in a vital way to the emergence of a French-Swiss consciousness. At the same time, her work was criticized as being unsophisticated, sentimental, marred by regional turns and enamored with natural scenery.

One Swiss woman never fails to find space in French literature manuals, not so much as a Swiss writer but as the woman Napoleon banned from French soil. Germaine de Staël exemplifies most adequately the Swiss model of the European visionary, not only because of her well-known essays which paved the way for comparative literary theory but also for her cosmopolitan novels, *Corinne* and *Delphine*, set not in Geneva, but in London, Paris, and Rome. She is the only Swiss woman writer of genuine "canonical" stature in the French tradition though not for her novels. Certainly the new feminist scholarship on Staël—most recently Charlotte Hogsett's *Literary Experience of Germaine de Staël* (1987)—has helped remedy this distortion in the critical perspective.[13]

Some forty authors and 180 titles constitute the field of modern French-Swiss fiction by women. The first generation of professional or semiprofessional writers emerged in the 1930s, and their most distinctive figure is the charismatic pastor. Unlike the Catholic priest, he is not a forbidden love-object. The women around this spiritual power figure—his dear one or wife, sister, daughter, student or servant—suffer neurotic distortion through love, from incestuous and rebellious to delirious and sacrificial. The most accomplished of these "pastorals" can be credited to Monique Saint-Hélier, Clarisse Francillon, Dorette Berthoud, and Elisabeth Burnod. The pastor as a focal problem fades from women's fiction in the 1960s, replaced by concerns about women's autonomy and professional vocation—writing, art, teaching, or office-work—along with themes of social consciousness (e.g., Rivaz's short stories in *Sans alcool*) and xenophobia (e.g., several of Cunéo's stories). Experimental writing has remained limited, in both poetic and narrative discourse, and passion, adultery, and marriage are not treated extensively. If one excepts the best known, most versatile and productive of Swiss storytellers, S[téphanie] Corinne Bille (1912–1979) sensuality, sexuality, and the entire "discourse of the body" are either missing or inscribed in the negative mode: hysterical traits, neuroses, abortion and repression of lesbian affection as seen in Anne Cunéo, Anne-Lise Grobéty or Mireille Küttel, the three most "daring" among the living authors.

In Swiss, African, and Arab women's fiction, exile is still the price to be paid by a writer who decides to speak out. In the land of Calvinism, where women were Europe's last to gain the vote, where social space is as restricted as physical space, it is particularly delicate and difficult for a woman not to be identified with her characters and ostracized by

---

13. After Staël, transcending borders and regional traits was to be a dominant feature of Swiss fiction for the next century and a half. This is illustrated by the lesser-known Valérie de Gasparin, whose work was recognized and praised by Sainte-Beuve. A diplomat's wife and accomplished traveler, she willingly shared her perceptions of social and religious issues such as marriage, conventual life and orders, the degradation of faith and moral values. Noëlle Roger (Hélène Pittard-Dufour, 1874–1953) is another little-known, yet accomplished, Swiss writer whose novels–some twenty-five titles–reveal a special talent for fabulation and reflect the author's lifetime of travels as the wife of an anthropologist.

countryfolk "above reproach." Such is the fate of most North-African women writers today, but Bille, who traded comfort, security and social respectability for freedom and creativity, did not escape it entirely in postwar Europe. Long considered, even at home, as a traditional region-alist, her best writing is indeed always related to Valais. One might compare her style to Colette's though it is shyer, more honest, and more passionate, perhaps. Like Colette, she was the well-loved daughter of a charming father and a strong mother, whom she painted as a young woman in *"Virginia,"* (*Deux passions*, 1979). This text is the pendant novella to her masterpiece, *"Emerentia."* Bille received the 1975 Goncourt award for her short story, *La Demoiselle sauvage*. Her output, considering her life-style, was monumental. Including posthumous col-lections of stories and unpublished notebooks, correspondance, and au-tobiographical texts, the complete works will include about thirty titles.

Similarly, vast amounts of energy and scholarly passion are still needed to analyze the fiction of Switzerland's Catherine Colomb, par-ticularly the circumstances and maturation of her original, novelistic style. The continuity of tone from one novel to the next; the extraordi-nary mixture of irony, sensitivity and nostalgia; the strangely realistic harmony with the milieu evoked (north shore of Lake Geneva); the disintegrated point of view, and the baroque musical aspects of her composition have not yet received adequate critical attention in spite of her prestige at home. Her ground-breaking style, developed in her first novel during World War II, must eventually be recognized as a forerun-ner of the New Novel—as of her compatriot, Pinget, whose polyphonic "romans de la parlerie" [novels in obsessional spoken style] are very much akin to hers.

We need to ask whether it makes a difference for Belgian women writers to be "francophones" in perfect control of the French lan-guage—indistinguishable from that spoken across the border in Lille—and to live, in the case of Brussels, within three hours of Paris by train.[14] Among the more positive utterances made about "belgitude," one can

14. The forthcoming dictionary and repertory of women writers in French Madeleine Hage and I have compiled over the years—with collaborators—includes articles on sever-al Belgian women, but the question of "belgitude" is not addressed. (Previously refered to as "Ecrits de femmes," the proposed format and title is *Pour un dictionaire des écri-vaines de langue françaises*). My remarks on this area are based on secondary sources only, including Françoise Lalande's article in the *Dictionnaire des Littératures de Langue Fran-çaise*, J.-P. de Beaumarchais et al., eds. (Paris: Bordas, 1984); Maurice Gauchez's *Histoire des Lettres Françaises de Belgique des origines à nos jours* (Bruxelles: Edition de la Renaissance d'Occident, 1922); Adrien Jans, ed., *Lettres Vivantes; Deux générations d'écrivains français en Belgique—1945–1975* (Paris: Renaissance du Livre, 1975). No feminist or gynocentered study of Belgian literature has come to my attention todate but I do not claim familiarity with this body of critical works.

name a healthy blend of traditionalism and avant-garde sensitivity, a dark sense of humor, a bourgeois sense of comfort and a daring imagination, all layered over the fundamental substratum of skepticism . . . about self, other, and even genius. Among the negative traits drawn, one finds a slowness of pace, a label shared with the Swiss, and just about anyone living more than ten miles from the capital. . . . Only a tiny segment of the French population is aware that some of "their" most celebrated artists and writers are Belgian-born, including Magritte and Marguerite Yourcenar.

Literary feminists have not speculated diacritically on the apparently weaker "individuation" of Belgian writers. Authors such as Suzanne Lilar and her daughter Françoise Mallet-Joris, Dominique Rolin or Gabrielle Rolin, Françoise Collin, Liliane Wouters, or Claire Lejeune are known, and often read, but many more are not, because, like the Swiss, they are discreet and stay "home." New readings and gynocentric evaluations are needed for those Belgian writers who have received only cursory treatment by well-meaning, hurried historians. There is every reason to believe that it *does* make a difference to be situated in a culture which straddles the linguistic borders between the French and Germanic languages, especially when that culture is only a century and a half old. The scenery, weather, food, homelife, folklore and mythology—not to mention the skin and underlying bodies—are Northern, that is non-Latin, Alpine, or Ile-de-France. Flanders is defined by a specific set of geographical features, together with equally specific socioeconomic conditions resulting from the industrial revolution. Perhaps the ultimate irony for the French Belgians is that, like women, they suffer (benefit?) from more fluid ego-boundaries. There is something truly puzzling about the amount of displaced anger directed at "belgitude" by some writers, from Baudelaire to Michaux, and in the fact that the Belgians are the last "minority" considered fair game for ethnic jokes in neighboring France.

Among the earlier writers claimed as Belgian, Mme Caroline [Boissart] Popp (1808–1891) collected and wrote—with sprightly humor—legends, tales, short stories and "landscapes," and was noted for founding the Bruges gazette. Marguerite Van de Wiele (b. 1859) appears to have been a prolific novelist who depicted the bourgeoisie in the manner of the popular novelist Daniel Lesueur (pseudonym of Jeanne Lapauze). One source compares Van de Wiele to Daudet and Dickens. A Belgian playwright, Marguerite Duterme, saw her work performed at the Théâtre de l'Oeuvre (*Vae Victis*, 1905) and received several awards for *Le Musée d'amour* (1922) whose title seems to echo Rachilde's *Tour d'amour*. Her distinctive achievement in the theatrical milieu of her day was unusual. In the same genre, Suzanne Lilar's dramatic texts are hardly known today but were noted in their time. An intriguing figure needs to be recovered from obscurity: Felixa Wart-Blondian was recently identified as a feminist journalist, suffragette and socialist who created consciousness-raising shows with a group of thirty-eight young women!

Turn of the century poets such as Hélène Canivet and Jean Dominique (pseudonym of Marie Closset) sound rather traditional but then, so did Marceline Desbordes-Valmore in the hands of "traditional" literary historians, as has been demonstrated elsewhere in this issue by Michael Danahy. Vera Feyder, who started publishing in the early sixties, and Renée Brock (1912–1980), Maud Frère (1923–1979), Madeleine Bourdouxhe (b. 1906), Marie Gevers (1883–1975), and Louis [sic] Dubrau (b. 1904) are all substantial novelists. They obviously need to be "placed" with fresh criteria and compared to peers in the context of other francophone writers of fiction. The same can be noted about the many distinguished poets who are responsible for the extraordinary "explosion" of contemporary feminine poetry. Janine Moulin, Andrée Sodenkamp, Annie Kegels, Lucienne Desnoues, Claire Lejeune, Hélène Prigogine, Liliane Wouters, Sophie Podolski, Françoise Delcarte have all become known since the Second World War.

North African and Middle Eastern women who write in French are a post-World War II phenomenon. More of these writers originate from Lebanon and Algeria than from other nations of the Maghreb and Machrek. In both countries, the population is larger and the French influence deeper, although in the case of Lebanon, a French education was primarily a matter of class and culture, French being the creative medium chosen by writers who wished to reach Western audiences. Many of the first generation of writers settled in France after going there as students, often failing, for political reasons, to readjust to their home countries. Such is the case of Andrée Chedid, who can no more be labeled an African or Arab writer than Tunisian-born lawyer/feminist Gisèle Halimi or Egyptian-born Joyce Mansour. Marguerite (Taos) Amrouche, an Algerian Berber fiction writer was also of that generation, but her work is considered Maghreb rather than Parisian.

A new type of Arab writer has now emerged: one who identifies both as a French writer and as a North African, and yet does not neutralize or "transcend" her situation. Indeed she makes that situation her prime focus as a writer. Leila Sebbar is the most accomplished woman in this category. Certain cultural or political influences may be invoked to explain why the more talented Lebanese women often emerge as poets (Nadia Tueni, Venus Khoury-Ghata), while the Maghreb women are novelists primarily. Djamila Debêche, Aïcha Lemsine, Salah Garmadi, Mina Boumedine, among others, have published narrative texts often inspired from direct experience, as seems to be a rule with emerging literatures and repressive environments. Essayists have also been part of the female literary scene since the Algerian war. Fadela M'Rabet, Denise Brahimi and Zoulika Boukortt are known for their critical writings. Indeed, women and the wars of Algeria and the Middle East suggest a topic to be pursued through Franco-Arab women writers' works for which Chedid's texts would offer a prime source.

The most accomplished of the new Arab francophone women writers is probably Assia Djebar (b. 1936), author of half a dozen volumes of fiction, and of film scripts and essays on Arab women. Through this remarkable sequence one can follow her struggle to achieve freedom of speech as an Algerian woman, to maintain allegiance to her country while developing her own literary discourse. The dilemma of serving one's kin while preserving one's own integrity as an individual whose needs have outgrown the confines of the political scene at home is one that Djebar explores at length in *L'Amour, la Fantasia* (1985).[15] Over the years her writing has evolved from a modish, naive narrative into a refined and sophisticated discourse. After her earlier novels about Algeria during the war of independence, she turned to the history of colonization, focusing on Algerian women's history and the current situation, at home as well as in France. Her texts, accessible to a wide audience, display an imagery and a sensuality, a political dimension, and an unmistakable modern woman's voice which assure her prominence among Franco-Arab literary women.

What, then, constitutes an important writer in these "francophone" areas? The case of Djebar is exemplary, but also the exception: many of these writers are still marginal *because* of sex, color and creed. The problem for francophone women is that they must gain recognition on so many fronts to achieve—or even come close to—canonical stature. Their audience is irreducibly heterogenous. They must win appreciation in Paris and at home, with the male establishment which determines publication and promotion, with the male readership which has greater buying power, and, not least, with the female readership if their work is at all gender-conscious and gynocentric as is true of most of the younger writers. But what if their "natural" readership is kept from learning to read, as in Algeria where the 1977 literacy rate was 14% for females and 42% for males? And what if their "message" is threatening to the current order, where every other male still believes that he does not have enough power, that women have already caused enough hardship, and that he can't see himself reading women's work any more than he can see himself cooking? What if the commentators use this vast

15. Forthcoming translation by Marguerite Le Clézio as *Arabian Quartet 1* (London: Quartet Books).

array of inflexible social and political criteria rather than "purely literary" ones? Or if they do use literary ones, but still fail to read for a message, for feeling, for testimony, for information, for female lore?

The closer francophone women writers are to the literary standards that dominate the Parisian scene, the better they will fare—and to date no outspoken francophone feminist writer has been a "bookstore success." The less culturally confined their work, and the more standard their French, the more easily they will achieve success. Of course, there have been certain exceptions: Maillet's success in France—beyond her unquestionable talent and humor—must have been that she struck the chord of "terroir" in her judges and the lettered French public. You cannot read Maillet's texts with pleasure if you have only a high school education; her language is hard to enjoy even though it is based (*because* it is based) on (Acadian) dialect. Old French, yes; "broken" French, no: Condé, Schwarz-Bart, Mariama Ba, had she lived, or Djebar—or even Gagnon and Boucher—would not have dared use distorted or dialectical French ("joual," "petit nègre," "sabir," or new brands thereof) because it would have guaranteed them failure to gain recognition on the French front. What is possible in the United States for a Toni Morrison will remain impossible as long as the French offspring of Third World people do not buy more books. Only when they do will the media and the publishers work to promote the literary works of "foreign" or "minority" women writers.

A gap exists between those highly educated writers who live in capital cities, who interact with groups of women, who are often seen in Paris, and who set trends or react to them in their works, and the "stayed" women writers who produce for their home audience. Most African writers, many older non-Parisian writers, and those without a college education are working in that manner. This implies that being successful as a francophone writer involves being recognized in Paris and sold to the French. No woman writer lives off her (creative) pen in the francophone world who does not have a marketable name in France. Fortunately, national pride and purse occasionally function in harmony to enable "other" writers, female or male, to publish, but we should have few illusions about "francophony" as a support network. Differences in age, sex, education and culture are more insidious and therefore probably more difficult to overcome than obvious racial differences.

Our concern should be how and why we read as professionals, as opposed to how and why the public reads, beyond commercial manipulation, which only has short-term consequences. There is no doubt that the less educated the writer, the more she is going to measure her effort and model her goals upon the traditional canon imposed in grade school. Some would-be poets will start with endeavors in the style of

Baudelaire—or even venture seriously an "ode to the rose" *à la* Ronsard. At the other end of the (reader-writer competence) scale, the sophisticated among us will appreciate the tale of a rose—quite unrelated to the recent *Name of the Rose*—which came from Poland via Brazil to find place in Hélène Cixous's *Illa*. . . . all just words of rose and love. Much of the poetry by francophone women has the quality of naive art. Only when a woman has a thorough grasp of the canon will she be able to play with it, demythify it, question it, and ultimately change it. As feminist teachers we can speed up the process and lead students and readers to shed some of the invisible blinders we may still be wearing. It is to be hoped that feminist critics can and will play a role in analyzing literary productions in their psychosociological context and give them full significance as gendered artefacts *in situ* rather than measure them against unspecified universals.

ANNE-MARIE THIESSE AND
HÉLÈNE MATHIEU

The Decline of the Classical Age and the Birth of the Classics

THE EVOLUTION OF LITERARY PROGRAMS OF STUDY FOR THE AGREGATION EXAM SINCE 1890

"How should literature be studied in secondary education? What point of view should dominate? What relationship should there be between its study and the more general ends of education?" Such was the broad essay question in French literature proposed to the candidates for the Agregation exam for young women in 1901. Apparently all the problems raised by the teaching of literature are evoked in this supremely pedagogical topic. Yet the essential question is not stated: *What is literature as educational material?* How is this domain of academic study called Literature defined, and how is it constituted? By the *Classics*, respond numerous contemporary studies on current practices in education, which go on to denounce the restriction of Literature to a limited corpus of writers canonized by textbooks and rehashed in the classroom. But these *Classics* which function as so many landmarks in the manuals of literary history[1] used in secondary education are themselves the product of the history of the teaching of Literature. Criticism today needs a study of the social history of the concept of the *Classic* and its application. To this end, we have researched crucial, little exploited archival material: the programs of study in French Literature for the competitive Agregation exam.[2] These sources reveal, more precisely

1. *Manuel scolaire* will be translated as "manual" throughout. Lagarde and Michard is typical of the modern manuals; each volume anthologizes a century of literature which is then divided by period, by genre, or by historical movement, and presents texts by major authors, with introductions to each division citing historical background. From the eighteenth century on, manuals have been the primary tool for the teaching of literature in French secondary schools.

2. Created in the eighteenth century, the men's Agregation took the form of a national competition in 1830. The women's Agregation was created in 1884. It is a competi-

than official rulings, the manner in which literature is conceived as an object of academic knowledge to be acquired and transmitted.

FROM MIMETIC DISCOURSE TO THE EXPERIMENTAL METHOD

The Aggiornamento *of the Third Republic*

Up until the end of the last century, candidates to the Agregation exam in Letters had only to know and study the works of the seventeenth century,[3] the only works judged worthy to figure in the programs of study next to Greek and Latin texts. For the teaching of the Humanities was based on rhetoric, i.e., an apprenticeship in the rules of discourse and writing by the imitation of models, preferably models from Antiquity. A legacy from the lower schools of the ancien régime, this coursework in rhetoric permitted the children of the bourgeoisie to acquire a linguistic competence indispensable in a parliamentary regime.

Our Humanities courses, to be worthy of this name, must initiate our young men [*jeunes gens*] into the precepts of taste, the art of writing, its rules, and up to a certain point, literary history. On the other hand, in our form of government, and for the development of our bar, oratory studies are appropriate for a rather numerous class of citizens, and ancient rhetoric contains a wealth of precepts which are not outdated.[4]

The notion of *classic literature*[5] thus designates a group of works fulfilling a *normative* function for written and spoken discourse, the supreme

---

tion for the recruitment of professors in secondary education, and is organized by discipline (Letters, Math, Philosophy, Physics, etc.). Preparation for the exam takes place in the Universities and the "Ecoles Normales Supérieures." Those who succeed (the "agrégés") constitute only a minority of teachers (200 positions per year before World War II, 800 in the early '60s, 2000 today); they are considered the elite of the teaching profession. The competition is very selective and the number of candidates is much higher than the number who actually succeed in the competition: in fact, a good number of professors in secondary education have, at some time or other, studied to take the competitive exam. (For lack of a term that might correspond to "Agrégation" in English, the French term will be retained.) [Translator.]

3. With the exception, however, of the historical works of Voltaire and a few texts by Montesquieu.

4. Victor Cousin, Minister of Public Instruction, Ruling of 14 July 1840. Cited by J. B. Piobetta, *Le Baccalauréat* (Paris, J. B. Baillière, 1937).

5. In this essay, *classic* refers to literature of any period that plays a role in the French pedagogical programs. *Classical* literature denotes either the literature of the seventeenth century (often referred to as the "great" century) or that of ancient Greece and Rome.

referent being Greek and Latin literature.[6] Need it be noted that this definition of classic literature canonizes works characterized by their linguistic and stylistic distance from "vulgar" language (contemporary French) and from literature created at that moment? At the same time, it sets literature apart as an ancient patrimony whose transmission to the dominant class, and to that class only, is assured by academic institutions. This double effect of teaching Letters (the mastery of a *classical* language, namely of a class dialect, and the acquisition of a cultural capital redoubling in the symbolic order the power given by economic capital) was the real stake in the struggle for academic reform that occupied the first years of the Third Republic.

The defeat of 1870, the events of the Commune, and the threat of a monarchical reaction weighed heavily on the approach of the Third Republic to education; the educational system, which had hardly evolved since the ancien régime, found itself suddenly thrown into question. The republican bourgeoisie, which had just come to political power, found itself obliged, to strengthen its position and its legitimacy, to create a national ideological consensus, and to close the considerable technical, economic, and military gap between France and Prussia. Attacks raged against a system of education condemned for its old-fashioned character and, above all, its inability to prevent the disasters of 1870 and 1871. If the creation of free elementary schooling, which proved to be the true "ideological cement"[7] of republican France, easily resolved the debates on the education of the masses, the dominant class remained divided as to the education dispensed in secondary schools, which it reserved for its own children.[8] It was around the question of Latin (and of Greek), the cornerstone of the old system, that crystallized the controversy whose object, more or less implicit in the arguments advanced, was to know whether secondary education should have a practical, short-term end, or whether it should dispense a "liberal" culture functioning as a class marker for the social élite. These divergent views actually covered over oppositions within the dominant

6. In a way, this acceptance of the term *classic* persists in France in the opposition Classical Letters/Modern Letters. Secondary, or "Modern," education does not require the study of ancient languages (Latin or Greek), while so-called classical education implies the study of at least Latin. Currently, the Agregation in Classical Letters includes exams in French language and literature, Latin and Greek; the agregation in Modern Letters includes tests in French language and literature, comparative literature, the translation of a living language and the translation of Latin.

7. The expression is from J.-P. Azema and M. Winock in *La IIIe République* (Paris: Calmann-Lévy, 1971).

8. Before 1933, public secondary education was not free. There were few scholarship students: between 1892 and 1895, for example, one secondary student in eight had a scholarship, but only 0.5% of the children in this age group had a scholarship to study in a *lycée*. Secondary students belonged essentially to a financially comfortable social class.

class: the lower middle class expected secondary education to give its children knowledge useful in the exercise of a profession; the upper middle class, rich in economic and/or social capital, and thus assured of positions for its sons, remained attached to the principle of the Humanities that designated them as the legitimate heirs of the aristocracy. The debate was resolved by the creation of two orders of secondary education: classical studies and so-called "specialized" education,[9] without Latin, oriented towards modern languages, sciences, and economics: the creation of an Agregation in specialized education authorized the radical difference between the two orders, of which one was, quite obviously, considered inferior.[10]

This division of secondary schooling into two orders, one of which was open to modernity while the other preserved the old system, made it possible to proceed with a certain updating of the programs of study in French literature, stopping short of global reform: the programs of study for special secondary education and the corresponding Agregation exam allotted a certain place to nineteenth-century writers, while "normal" education remained devoted to *classical* writers.

The situation was absurd in many respects: at the beginning of the Third Republic, only a minority of high school students, who followed a devalued course of study, had access to postrevolutionary literature, the others studying only works written under the ancien régime! Above all, there existed an aberrant distinction between their respective methods of teaching French literature: the study of literary history and the study of texts. Introduced sparingly in programs of study in 1840 in the form of questions on different periods of Greco-Latin and French literature, literary history, by definition, was not limited to the seventeenth century for the French domain. But insofar as the study of nonclassic works was not written into the program, the course was limited to a dry encyclopedic nomenclature, a catalogue of dates, titles, and schools, as is indicated in this program of study for the baccalaureat degree in 1840: "[the candidates must be able to] cite those poets who stood out in each of the periods of French poetry, following the hierarchy of genre, indicating the dates of their birth and death, and the titles of their principal works." Manuals then appeared on the academic market, which gave excerpts from those texts destined to illustrate the course of literary history. But the program continued to require knowledge only of the "great works" of the "great century" from future teachers. It was not that the University, which increasingly controlled the education of

9. *Enseignement spécial* is related to what we now call "tracking" in American education.

10. The specialized education experiment was of short duration. The 1902 reform of the Baccalaureat eliminated it, and replaced it with a section linking science and modern languages, without Latin, where, for the most part, "weaker students" were oriented.

Table 1. The Distribution of Points for the Competitive Agregation Exam

A) *Agregation in Letters (1890–1914)*		
	1890 distribution	*1908 modification*
Written		
Essay question in French	12	15
Essay question in Latin	12	0
Grammar and prosody	10	0
Latin translation	10	10
Translation into Greek	10	10
Translation into Latin	—	10
Greek translation	—	10
Oral		
Explication[11] of a Greek text	10	10
Explication of a Latin text	10	10
Explication of a French text	10	10
Explication and commentary of a Greek or Latin text	10	0
A lesson on a topic in Classical literature	10	0
A lesson on a topic taken from the program in French Comp.	—	10
Analysis of an Old French text	—	2.5

B) *The Agregation in secondary teaching for young women* in Letters, Letters section (bill of 7/31/1894 which introduces the distinction between sections of Letters and of History)

	distribution
Written	
Composition on a topic of morals or education	4
Composition on a literary topic	4
Translation of a modern language	3
Oral	
Explicated reading of a French text	4
Lesson in morals	4
Exposé on a question of language or grammar	4
Explicated reading of a text in a modern language	3

11. *Explication de texte,* or *explication française* is a formula for the written and oral presentation of a passage of literature by students, whose first efforts are guided by a questionnaire (prepared by the professor) to "help the child to better understand and feel more subtly the beauty of a page of French." A given page would represent the essence of the work from which it was taken, the oeuvre of the author, the period and genre, and ultimately, the French language itself. Its goal is to "reconstitute from *the words* of the

professors, was powerless to provide a more complete approach to French literature: an intense activity of research and the edition of texts was organized, in the last quarter of the century, around prestigious academics like Paris, Bédier, Huguet, or Lanson. But the weight of tradition and the conservatism inherent in a masculine and time-honored secondary education precluded the first step indispensable to any renewal in education—the updating of the knowledge required of teachers. Thus the task of renewal was left to an academic order devoid of any tradition: the secondary education of young women.

The Feminine Precedent

Founded by the Camille Sée Law of 19 January 1880, public secondary education for young women met very explicit ideological needs: to tear the young women and future wives of the bourgeoisie away from the influence of the Church and reactionary ideas in order to win them to the Republic.

Raised in the school of superstition, [the young woman] will marry a man raised in the school of reason; she will be of the seventeenth or the middle of the eighteenth century, the man will be of the end of the eighteenth or the nineteenth.

exclaimed Camille Sée to the Chamber of Deputies, entreating the State not to leave the education of women to the Church.

To the founders' minds, this women's pedagogy was not intended for any specific professional ends: it accorded a minimal place for scientific subjects (which distinguished it from the degree in the other track) and did not mention the study of ancient languages;[12] French language and literature constituted the principal subject. Thus, a pedagogy of "Modern Letters" was put into place as a parallel to the "normal" course of study for men, which was still dominated by classical humanities, and it was likewise sustained by a system of recruitment of its own professors (the creation of the Ecole de Sévres[13] in 1881, of the Agregation in Secondary Education of Young Women in 1884). This women's Agregation was distinguished from the men's not only by the lack of an exam in Latin or Greek; historical grammar, for women, took the place of the exercises in prosody and rhetoric imposed on male candidates. Above all, the preoccupation with training women (and women teachers) in the nineteenth century involved a very rapid widening of the

---

text the ideas, the sentiments, the intentions that moved the author . . . by taking on his point of view" and "to follow its development and continuity." [From *Extrait des Instructions du 30 septembre 1938.*]

12. The young women did, in fact, immediately demand Latin courses, which were offered on an optional basis.

13. The Ecole Normale Supérieure de Jeunes Filles. See note 1. [Translator's note]

programs to include contemporary works. Just nine years after the national funeral organized by the Republic for Victor Hugo, the author
figured on the program for the womens' Agregation. The graph on page
215 shows how the programs for the womens' Agregation, from 1890 on,
stopped imitating the model for the men's Agregation and substituted
works of the nineteenth century for those of the seventeenth century.
Somewhat later, and with more regularity, the men's programs followed
the line of the women's programs.

At first, of course, it was above all the works of the nineteenth
century that competed with those of the seventeenth, by virtue of the
ideological stakes we have evoked: but insofar as the exclusivity of the
"Grand Siècle" found itself under attack, works of other periods could
be introduced gradually into the programs, to such an extent that in
1914 the principle which still prevails in the Agregation (equal distribution of centuries) had been sketched out. It should be noted that in the
same period the men's Agregation accorded a place of growing importance to exams in French literature, at the expense of tests in ancient
languages and literatures (see the table on page 212).

The works included in the program were thus destined to provide
testing topics for oral *explications de texte;* but, as was indicated in a
note of the period, when the test in written composition in French
called for knowledge of literary history, it had to be related to those
works included in the program. Out of the separation that prevailed
until that time between the study of texts designed for an apprenticeship in the rules of writing and an autonomous discourse of literary
history, came a method of study conjugating these two elements. Thus
appeared in the training of teachers what was for decades the official
basis of literary pedagogy: *the teaching of literary history through
texts.*[14]

Positivism and the Science of the Literary

Knowing texts, and using them as a support for literary history—the
approach fulfilled quite well the requirements of positivist thought and
was one of the numerous academic attempts at transposing experimental methods in the sciences into the humanities. At the same time that
scientific pedagogy was the poor relation of academic programs, the
scientific approach fascinated professors of literature who tried to bor-

14. Literary history through texts was for a long time the basis of literary education in
secondary schools, as is demonstrated by the enormous success of the series of manuals
edited by Lagarde and Michard. Violently contested in the '70s by proponents of pedagogical reform, in practice it has remained the basic reference for literary studies, even if
the official programs no longer refer to it explicitly.

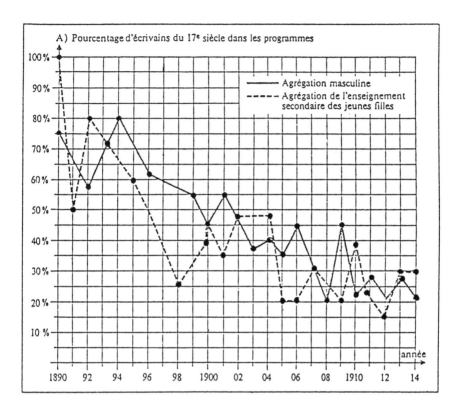

A) Pourcentage d'écrivains du 17ᵉ siècle dans les programmes

——— Agrégation masculine
----- Agrégation de l'enseignement secondaire des jeunes filles

année

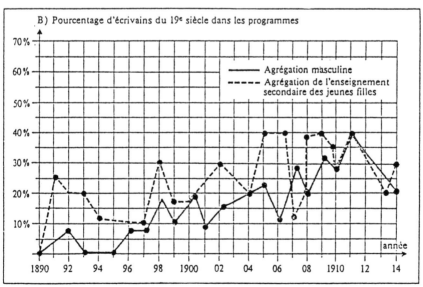

B) Pourcentage d'écrivains du 19ᵉ siècle dans les programmes

——— Agrégation masculine
----- Agrégation de l'enseignement secondaire des jeunes filles

année

row techniques used to study the living organism in order to investigate literary texts. Witness an astonishing essay question in French literature given at the competitive entry exam for the *Ecole Normale Supérieure de Jeunes Filles* in 1908: "Can the method that Claude Bernard described in his *Introduction à la médecine expérimentale* apply to literary studies, and if so, in what way?"

Does this mean that, under the auspices of positivist thought, a science of literature, however embryonic, appeared at the beginning of this century? Describing the method ("go to the text," analyse it) was not enough: more important was to define the corpus of texts set aside for this kind of study. Thus, if the "Grand Siècle" reigned no longer as absolute master over secondary and university programs, the term "classic author" continued to define "the author to be studied," at the cost of a slight reworking of the concept. A note to the program for secondary studies for the year 1890 reads:

> The committee wondered if it was desirable to limit the choice of authors to the classics. It has decided that by the word *classic* must not be meant only authors of the seventeenth century, but also writers of the eighteenth and nineteenth centuries.[15]

A concession to postrevolutionary modernity (note the omission of the sixteenth century and the Middle Ages), this extension of the notion of the *classic* remained problematic, since it did not mention the criteria according to which the label of *classic* was to be discerned. Because the principle of selection of the *classic* works and authors has never been made explicit since that time, except tautologically (the *Classics* are the Great Writers, that is to say, the Authors on the program), only a study of the de facto corpus can make possible the analysis of the principle of selection. To do this, the programs of exams and of competitions are more useful than the manuals, which reflect only imperfectly the real practices of teaching (many authors mentioned in the manuals were never actually studied). Examined over the period of a generation, the programs of literary study for the Agregation give a list of the Classics of a period, those writers who were the object first of university study, then secondary study. Knowledge of those authors was judged indispensable to future professors (clearly, teachers of literature were all the more likely to lecture on authors represented on their Agregation, as they would have devoted a year to their study). We have thus systematically analyzed these programs of study for two periods of twenty-five years: from 1890 to 1914 (the first period of extensive updating) and

15. Cited by Philippe Lejeune, "L'enseignement de la 'littérature' au lycée au siècle dernier," *Le Français aujourd'hui*, 9 February 1970.

1956 to 1980,[16] which, by comparison, allowed us to establish the invariable and the changing characteristics in the definition of "classic" works.[17]

THE PANTHEON OF FRENCH LETTERS

The Immortals[18] in the University

Restricted to perhaps ten authors until 1890, the group of the "Classics" widened considerably between 1890 and 1914: between these two dates, 58 different authors were cited at least once on the program of study for the women's Agregation, and 56 on that for men. At the time, the number of authors included in the program each year varied from five to twelve, and the current rule (one author per century) was not yet in use; it is thus all the more surprising to discover that the programs of study for the Agregation in Letters,[19] between 1956 and 1980,[20] selected exactly the same number of authors: 62. Moreover, these three programs show the same number of authors cited at least twice in 25 years: 33, 33, and 32 respectively. . . . That this number should not change is somehow strange, all the more so because twentieth-century authors were taken into account by the programs of the last 25 years![21] Like the

16. This study was done in 1979, which explains the choice of dates. The programs of succeeding years did not bring about modifications likely to change the conclusions of the study. The programs indicate, as authors for the sixteenth, seventeenth, eighteenth, nineteenth, and twentieth centuries: Ronsard, Bossuet, Beaumarchais, Flaubert, Supervielle (1981), Rabelais, Corneille, Choderlos de Laclos, Verlaine, Gracq (1982), Régnier, Madame de Sévigné, Voltaire, Stendahl, Sartre (1983), Turnèbe, Pascal, Marivaux, Rimbaud, Proust (1984), Ronsard, Molière, Rousseau, Hugo, Desnos (1985).

17. This information was obtained by consulting the *Bulletin administratif de l'Instruction Publique* and the *Revue Universitaire* for the period 1890–1914. In addition, the *Bulletin trimestriel de l'Association des Elèves de Sèvres* regularly gives the essay questions in literature for the women's Agregation. For the recent period, we referred to the programs that appeared in the *B.O. de l'Education* as well as to the annual jury reports. The programs for men's and women's Agregation exams were identical between 1956 and 1980. The system has been totally coed since 1976.

18. *Les Immortels* are the forty members of the French Academy who, once honored by election, cannot resign.

19. We are referring to the program in French Literature common to the Agregation exams in Classical Letters, Modern Letters, and Grammar.

20. We have not taken into account medieval authors whose place in older programs was marginal and extremely variable. Even now, they have a relatively secondary role since tradition has it that they are never the object of the essay question in literature, which is the principal part of the written exam. This persistent discrimination should be studied further.

21. This study was written in 1980.

Forty Immortals of the French Academy, the authors of the Agregation may renew themselves to some extent, but their number remains immutable. Even as in the case of the current program, which retains but one author per century, per year, 125 different choices (five authors per year, over a period of 25 years) would have been possible, and this, among the thousand or so writers who have known some notoriety since the Middle Ages. It was thus not material imperatives that restrained the choice, but a principle of overselection of literary stars, which was carried out at the expense of more recent writers. One out of two is the approximate ratio of authors selected several times for the programs of study to the total number of writers appearing in these programs; but this figure is much less balanced for the more recent period: one third of the nineteenth-century writers included in the men's Agregation from 1890 to 1914, and only one sixth of twentieth-century writers included in the programs from 1956–1980 were selected at least twice. This is no doubt an indication of the difficulty in distinguishing a sure and durable set of values for the selection of *modern classics*, especially in the absence of any clear criteria for selection. (N.B.: living writers are barred from the programs, today as at the beginning of the century).[22] One finds this same phenomenon in the manuals, where the presentation of contemporary authors is limited to a long nomenclature, a nondescript enumeration which avoids any particular attention to highlights. Only the women's Agregation at the beginning of the century rose to counter this principle because of its modern orientation. Inversely, almost all the seventeenth-century writers cited were cited many times over—time-honored tradition had canonized the classical authors of the classical century.

The Major Criteria for Selection

The classics selected early in the century remain, for the most part, the same works chosen today, as the table on page 219 indicates. Of the 29 writers from the sixteenth to the nineteenth centuries included more than twice in the Agregation between 1956 and 1980, 22 were paid the same honor between 1890 and 1914. . . . Two among them (Beaumarchais and Garnier) appeared once in the programs of the *Belle Epoque*. Five others (Marguerite de Navarre, Scarron, Flaubert, Nerval, and Baudelaire) enjoyed a slightly scandalous reputation that justified their exclusion from the programs of secondary study in the Third Republic. The criterion of morality was in fact of great importance in the selection

22. On the other hand, the death of a famous writer may assure his or her inscription in the programs of study for the Agregation. Thus Sartre figured on the program of 1983. One exception should be noted: Julien Gracq was listed in his lifetime on the program of 1982.

Table 2. General classification of the authors in descending order of frequency on the Agregation programs

1890–1914				1956–1980	
Men's Agreg.		Women's Agreg.		Agreg. in Letters	
Racine	20	Molière	13	Rabelais	4
Corneille	19	Corneille	12	Ronsard	4
Bossuet	16	Hugo	11	La Fontaine	4
Molière	16	Bossuet	10	Molière	4
La Fontaine	15	La Fontaine	10	Marivaux	4
La Bruyère	15	Racine	10	Diderot	4
Voltaire	10	Voltaire	9	Rousseau	4
Pascal	10	Rousseau	8	Montaigne	3
Rousseau	10	Montaigne	8	D'Aubigné	3
Hugo	8	Pascal	7	Racine	3
Fénelon	7	Lamartine	6	Pascal	3
Montaigne	6	Fénelon	5	Corneille	3
Vigny	5	La Bruyère	5	Voltaire	3
Chateaubriand	5	Montesquieu	5	Musset	3
Montesquieu	5	Vigny	5	Hugo	3
Marot	5	Michelet	4	Valéry	3
Du Bellay	5	Boileau	4	Garnier	2
Boileau	4	Ronsard	4	Marot	2
Sévigné (Mme De)	4	Chateaubriand	4	M. De Navarre	2
Rabelais	4	Sainte-Beuve	3	Du Bellay	2
Lamartine	4	Diderot	3	La Bruyère	2
Michelet	4	Sévigné (Mme De)	3	La Fayette (Mme De)	2
Bourdaloue	3	Leconte De Lisle	2	Scarron	2
P.L. Courier	3	Staël (Mme De)	2	Montesquieu	2
La Rochefoucauld	3	Fromentin	2	Beaumarchais	2
Saint-Simon	3	Balzac	2	Vigny	2
Ronsard	3	Renan	2	Balzac	2
Régnier	3	Chénier	2	Flaubert	2
D'Aubigné	3	Marot	2	Nerval	2
Malherbe	3	D'Aubigné	2	Baudelaire	2
La Fayette (Mme De)	2	Amyot	2	Claudel	2
Marivaux	2	Du Bellay	2	Proust	2
Estienne	2	Musset	2		

of classic authors, and particularly when their study was being proposed to women: included four times on the men's Agregation before 1914, Rabelais did not figure on the women's Agregation.

In a phenomenon related to the question of morality, women writers were rarely considered worthy of study: among the literary stars on the programs under consideration, only two women appear on each (again, a strange preservation of the number!). Mme de Lafayette, cited twice between 1890 and 1914 on the men's Agregation and twice between

Table 3. Authors mentioned just once in a program of study

| | 1890–1914 | 1956–1980 | |
	Men's Agreg.	Women's Agreg.	Agreg. in Letters
XVI	La Boétie Noël Du Fail	Montluc Vauquelin La Boétie Garnier Tristan Noël Du Fail Lemaire Des Belges M. D'Angouléme Des Perrier	Montluc Régnier
XVII	Vaugelas	Mᵐᵉ De La Fayette Saint-Simon Descartes	Boileau Bossuet
XVIII	Diderot D'Alembert Beaumarchais Fontenelle Saint-Évremond Lesage Vauvenargues	Vauvenargues Marivaux Rollin Mᵐᵉ Rolland Buffon Beaumarchais Saint-Simon	Saint-Simon Prévost (Abbé) Chénier Lesage
XIX	Sully Prudhomme Taine Musset Sainte-Beuve Dumas fils Staël (Mᵐᵉ De) Fromentin Balzac Renan Leconte De Lisle Stendhal Sand/Flaubert Sand	Fustel De Coulanges Taine Musset Hérédia Gautier Sand	Chateaubriand Michelet Mallarmeé Standhal Verlaine Lamartine Sainte-Beuve
XX			Alain Fournier Péguy Barrés Malraux Giono Saint-John Perse Giraudoux Montherlant Éluard Camus Breton Bernanos Colette Apollinaire Gide

1956 and 1980, doubtless owes this durable favor to the exemplary character of her heroine, incarnation as she is of the values of the Eternal Feminine (depth of feeling, sacrifice of passion to duty).

The writers mentioned just once in 25 years on the Agregation are indicated in the following table. Medieval authors, who were not always explicitly mentioned on older programs, were not taken into account.

This table indicates the ratio of writers mentioned at least twice in the programs for the Agregation, to the total number of writers figuring in these same programs. The last two lines indicate an analogous ratio: the number of writers to whom a full chapter is devoted compared to the total number of writers cited, in two current manuals in use in secondary classes (*Lagarde et Michard, Chassang*).

Table 4.

	XVI^c	XVII^c	XVIII^c	XIX^c	XX^c	Total
Agreg. in Letters (1890–1914)	7/19	15/16	5/12	6/19*	—	33/56
Women's Agreg. (1890–1914)	6/15	10/13	5/12	12/18	—	33/58
Agreg. in Letters (1956–1980)	8/10	8/10	6/10	7/14	3/18*	32/62
Lagarde et Michard	6/9	12/28	9/27	16/46	5/139	48/239
Chassang	4/32	11/53	5/47	15/80	2/179	37/391

The decline of Mme de Sévigné is linked to the almost total disappearance of the epistolary genre from the program. In the same way, Mme de Staël, who had been represented only by her essays, is eliminated when that genre falls from favor. As for the introduction of Marguerite de Navarre, it is doubtless related to the rise of the novel as genre. Like the French Academy or the Pantheon of Great Men of the Nation, the group of Classics remains a masculine universe which tolerates women only in the smallest numbers. It is still remarkable that the women's Agregation early in this century, in spite of its innovative and modern character, did nothing to promote women's literary production, just as the current Agregation (where female candidates are far more numerous than male) has contributed to a situation in which women teachers are persuaded that great literature is written by men.

Ideological and political criteria were, finally, a determining factor in the canonization of the *Classics*, and they seem to have changed little since the beginning of the century: excluded from the programs of the Third Republic, the materialists of the eighteenth century, the revolutionary orators, and the socialists of the nineteenth century are still absent from recent programs. This ostracism is exercised even against naturalist writers like Maupassant and Zola, who were included only once in the Agregation programs of the last 25 years (in the same period, Valéry appeared three times!).

But an enumeration of the criteria for selection of writers cannot be relevant without an examination of the principle of selection that takes into account the use for which these texts were destined.

Table 5. A Breakdown by Genre of Works on the Program

A) Agregation in Letters (1890–1914)					
	XVI	*XVII*	*XVIII*	*XIX*	*XX*	*Total*
Novel	4	3	7	5	—	19 = 7.5%
Memoirs	—	3	2	2	—	7 = 2.8%
Theater	—	53	5	6	—	64 = 25.4%
Poetry	18	22	5	17	—	62 = 25%
Epistolary	—	6	8	2	—	16 = 6.3%
Essays (history, rhetoric, criticism, philosophy)	10	50	13	10	—	83 = 33%

B) Agregation in the secondary education of women (1890–1914)					
	XVI	*XVII*	*XVIII*	*XIX*	*XX*	*Total*
Novel	—	4	2	7	—	13 = 6%
Memoirs	—	—	2	4	—	6 = 3%
Theater	1	33	4	4	—	41 = 19.5%
Poetry	18	19	3	25	—	66 = 31.5%
Epistolary	—	10	9	—	—	19 = 9%
Essays	9	28	14	13	—	64 = 31%

C) Agregation in letters (1956–1980)					
	XVI	*XVII*	*XVIII*	*XIX*	*XX*	*Total*
Novel	6	4	8	5	14	37 = 32.7%
Memoirs	1	—	4	1	—	6 = 5.4%
Theater	3	10	6	2	2	23 = 19.8%
Poetry	12	5	1	15	8	41 = 33.3%
Epistolary	—	—	—	—	—	0 = 0%
Essays	3	6	5	1	1	16 = 14.9%

The Typology of the Classic and its Evolution

The above comparative table gives a classification by genre and by century of all of the works chosen for the Agregation in the periods under consideration. It can be observed that although the overwhelming part played by the theater, as well as that played by poetry, hardly vary at all, the same is not the case for the novel (and the short story), which were particularly underrepresented at the beginning of the century and which now occupy first place in the programs of study. Considered "paraliterary" by scholars in 1900, even though it was clearly the major form of literary creation at the time, the novel has today acquired legitimacy, represented on the Agregation by the novelists of the twentieth century, but also by those of preceding centuries (this would surely explain the rediscovery of Marguerite de Navarre). The gap between scholarly literature and living literature is thus not only chronological and purely a question of dates: a classic is a work *formally* dead (the pedagogical exploitation of the novel is simultaneous with the theoretical crisis of the genre; one can only point to the absence of forms of contemporary writing like film, which would be no less accurately placed in literary studies than theater).

According to a tendency which has hardly changed since the turn of the century, each literary form is particularly associated with one century with which it thus establishes a relationship of elective affinity: the theater belongs primarily to the seventeenth century (even if eighteenth-century theatrical works have benefitted recently from a certain rehabilitation), poetry to the sixteenth and nineteenth centuries (the poetry of the seventeenth century is overrepresented on older Agregation exams by the *Fables* of La Fontaine) and works of prose fiction (novel, tale, and short story) to the post-Classical age. This has resulted in a representation of the *canonical form* of the three great genres and of their *classical type:* tragedy and comedy governed by the rule of the three unities, poetry by alexandrines or octosyllabic meter, and prose fiction by the psychological novel. This has simultaneously produced a perception of those works that fall outside the norms of classical form as peripheral (archaic or degenerate, according to the case). This perspective cannot be corrected with a literary history which is only the linking-together of works retained as classics and thus is inclined to study, in Hegelian terms, periods of the birth, flowering, and decline of genres.

This principle of the restriction of genres to their canonical form is analogous to that which, in recent times, identifies an author with one or two privileged genres: at the turn of the century, Racine figured on the programs of the Agregation as a tragedian, but also as poet, as the historiographer of Port-Royal and as correspondent; similarly, Voltaire was studied for his tragedies, his correspondence, and his historical work as much as for his philosophical writings. The current Agregation does not tolerate polygraphs, and recognizes Racine only for the classical model of his tragedies and Voltaire for his articles in the *Encyclopédie* or his philosophical tales. One may wonder whether this process is not a way of eliminating, simply by not mentioning them, all the problematic aspects of a work and of a biography inscribed in social history, reducing writers to the unique function of producers of classic texts. Literature thus finds itself defined as a set of three redundant corpuses (by century, by writer, by genre), which are equivalent and mutually illustrative: the seventeenth century is represented by Racine and classical tragedy; the eighteenth century by Voltaire and philosophical prose. . . . By carrying this idea to its limit, it would be possible to inscribe all of classical literature on a *table* with three columns, from which any "aberrant" form would be logically eliminated. But perhaps the management of the literary patrimony for pedagogical use is working towards precisely this goal: the presentation of literature as a closed and autonomous universe, as a veritable museum of fictional works inherited from the past (and thus outmoded)?

But the corpus of classic texts and writers constituted at the turn of the century has not been preserved intact today: political and social imperatives have markedly restricted the corpus and have worked against academic conservatism (a principal target of current attacks, which see it as solely responsible for all present ills).

The Management of the Patrimony

The epistolary genre, whose place on the programs of 1890–1914 was far from negligible, has completely disappeared today. At the turn of the century, it was represented not only by Mme de Sévigné, but also by Racine, Bossuet, Voltaire, Mme Roland, etc. It is also remarkable that Flaubert figured in the programs only for his correspondence with George Sand. Furthermore, examiners frequently drew material from two collections of *Lettres du XVIIe et du XVIIIe siècle*, published by Gustave Lanson, which contained letters by famous people who did not belong *stricto sensu* to the literary world (the painter Nicolas Poussin, for example). The study of epistolary texts was thus seen as an apprenticeship in the art of writing and more precisely, in "knowing how to turn out a good letter." This was a skill required particularly of women, who, more than men, had to study correspondences (9% of the texts for the women's Agregation, as opposed to 6% of the men's).[23] As for the

23. Even the written assignments in French literature given to young women were often to be composed in an epistolary form, as in this topic given on the competitive exam at the Ecole de Sèvres in 1902: "In his comedy *La Frivolité*, Louis de Boissy mocks the taste of French men and women for foreign literature. . . . A society woman writes to Boissy, requesting that he make a fair distinction. . . . Develop. . . ."

elimination of this genre, and the teaching practices associated with it, it should be attributed less to an awareness of progress in telecommunication than to a widening in the social recruitment of secondary school students and their teachers.

The case of oratory discourse is analogous, and will enable us to explore this point in greater depth. At the turn of the century, Bossuet and Bourdaloue figured regularly in the Agregation programs, even though the criterion of ideological selection should have eliminated them in the years of dispute between Church and State (if Bourdaloue did not figure in the women's Agregation, was it for ideological reasons, or because the art of rhetoric was designated more particularly for men just as the epistolary art was reserved for women?) The interest of the Agregation juries of the period, composed of academics who could not be suspected of clericalism, in Catholic orators can be explained as an attachment to these masters of the art of rhetoric, whose study allowed students to be able to "speak well, write well, and consequently, to read well." If the religious orators have today fallen into disuse, it is not that education has been definitively secularized—Claudel is one of the three star writers of the twentieth century on the Agregation. The part of the literary patrimony that the Third Republic had inherited from the pedagogy of religious and royal middle schools has been abandoned today for reasons that have doubtless to do with the social evolution of the school public.[24] Of course, religious eloquence may well seem boring and obsolete in a country where attendance at religious services continues to decline. But the art of speaking has lost none of its importance in a world where mass media plays a role of ever greater importance. And it is astonishing, even troubling, that texts in which a contemporary rhetoric is deployed are not proposed for study (political speeches, for example, or articles from the press.)

The essay is another category that has been reduced in the programs. Under this general term, we have assembled a diverse group of works whose common denominator is that they are not works of fiction (memoirs, relatives of fictionalized biography, were counted separately). In spite of the extensive character of the definition, this rubric has known a marked decline since the turn of the century (33% and 31% of total works in the program between 1890 and 1914, 14.9% between 1956 and 1980). Today, the essay means little more than Montaigne's

---

24. "It is doubtless not by accident that rhetoric was suppressed, as secondary education was democratized, however feebly—the study of the art of writing and speaking, however rigorously normative it may be, is 'dangerous' if it is not strictly reserved for the use of the dominant class. . . . A dangerous kind of knowledge, which if too widespread, would challenge the method of Lagarde and Michard and allow people to read Chateaubriand and Senancourt, and even newspapers, in a new way. It would also make it possible for official speeches to be understood in a manner undesirable to the dominant class." France Vernier, *L'écriture et les textes* (Paris: Editions Sociales, 1974), 31.

Essais, Pascal's *Pensées*, or the philosophical works of Voltaire, Montesquieu and Rousseau; however, at the turn of the century, texts as different as Vaugelas's treatise on grammar, Fromentin's writings on esthetics, Fustel de Coulanges's historical writings, an *Histoire naturelle* by Buffon or by Michelet, critical works by Sainte-Beuve or Taine, etc., could figure on the programs.

The question of literarity is never explicitly posed: but on the Agregation exam, the domain reserved for literature is identified more and more with the totality of *classic works of fiction;* thus it is precisely those works that promote a better understanding of literary texts that are rejected from the program: texts of esthetic criticism (painting, plastic arts, or cinema), historical, philosophical, or indeed, scientific works, and even works of literary criticism or linguistics![25] But the process of elimination goes still further, leading to a random division of literature.

Atomized Literature

Academics who, at the beginning of the twentieth century, established programs of study for the Agregation did not hesitate to present literary works in the form of fragments. When they did not simply refer to a collection of selected passages [*morceaux choisis*] already in existence, they were given to making such arbitrary excerpts themselves: the candidates were thus called upon to study the *Mémoires d'Outre Tombe* from page 326 to page 353, the third and fourth parts of *La Princesse de Clèves*, or the fifth act of *Rodogune!* This principle of selecting classic pages from classic works was for the most part due to an attitude of prudence. The literature of the nineteenth and sixteenth centuries thus appeared for the first time in the programs of the women's Agregation in the form of excerpts from *Morceaux choisis des auteurs français pour l'enseignement secondaire des jeunes filles* by Albert Cahen and *Morceaux choisis des auteurs français, poètes et prosateurs, des origines à nos jours* by Petit de Julleville. Current programs are indeed more respectful of the integrity of literary works (or the selections seem to be less absurd in the first place), but the effect

---

25. For several years, a double practice has dominated in French classes in secondary schools. On one hand the study of classic literary texts that teachers are supposed to know and have studied; on the other hand, exercises on how to do a resumé and analysis of a text, which do not belong to the domain of fictional literature, but are chosen instead from sociology, esthetics, history, etc. Thus contemporary texts which have not undergone the process of selection as classics are starting to be introduced into secondary schools. The pedagogical treatment conferred on them is clearly different from that used on literary texts—it is a question of extracting the thought independently of any considerations of style. As if the content could be dissociated from the form. . . .

remains the same: one novel or one play given to be studied is supposed to sum up the whole of an author's oeuvre. It is above all in secondary education that reigns the formula of selected fragments, those great purveyors of general ideas and aphoristic summaries.

Beyond this often-denounced process of reducing texts to their "essence," there is a need to question another mode of excerpting literature—division into century and genre—which is less apparent because it has been "naturalized" by practice. We have seen how the principle which prevails today in the Agregation of studying one writer (represented by just some of his writings) for each century was laid out in the years 1890–1914. This truncation of literature is all the more arbitrary in that it fails to account for literary or even historical periods. The teaching of literature was, however, more or less officially founded on this principle, as much in secondary education (where each grade corresponds to the study of a century) as in the University (where professors must define themselves as specialists of one and only one century—as sixteenth-, seventeenth- or nineteenth-century scholars). Similarly, and this was not the case at the turn of the century, current programs carry out in the choice of texts a precise balance between the three canonical genres of poetry, theater and novel. What results is thus a recipe for the composition of classic literature: a mixture of equal parts of ingredients coming from two great categories (century and genre), the result being *normally* invariable. This principle of excerpting, inspired by an outmoded model of historical studies, owes its justification entirely to its constant and almost exclusive use in the practices of teaching and research. We have ourselves taken them up in this study; is that to say, to use the language of anthropology, that we have been victims of "indigenous categories"? Yet, on the one hand, without reinventing an original nomenclature, it would have been impossible to set forth the results of our work; on the other hand, the use of this classification has itself permitted us to clarify its implications (the affinity between century and genre, for example). It appeared to us as well that if the distribution of works according to this double principle of excerpting posed no difficulties for the programs of 1956–1980, such was not the case for those of 1890–1914. If "every taxonomy involves a theory,"[26] the critical usage of taxonomy reveals the theory and its historical evolution (in the progressive reduction of the concept of literarity).

The introduction of comparative literature among the tests making up the Agregation exam in Modern Letters (as opposed to the Agregation in *Classical* Letters) has somewhat subverted the mode of classification of classic works by bringing together works of different periods and

26. P. Bourdieu, J.-C. Chamboredon, J.-C. Passeron, *Le Métier de sociologue* (Paris: Mouton/Bordas, 1968), 74.

genres. Furthermore, insofar as comparative literature calls on foreign works,[27] or those not belonging to the domain of the classic, it denounces the arbitrary and restrictive character of literary studies founded only on French Classics. But the alternative adopted, which associates works different in *form,* but analogous in *content,* is still problematic: the risk is to substitute for the old nomenclature an endless list of *themes* recurrent in literary works (a varied list including the fantastic as well as the political, Christian symbolism as well as the imaginary voyage, etc.). Is this not the consequence of a conception of literary education defined solely as *the study of texts* selected for their *representative* character (of a genre, a century, or a theme)?

The virulent attacks that were made against French literary education and university research in literature in the '60s and '70s often targeted "literary history," long identified with the chronological linking of classic works and the commentaries, just as classic, that were associated with them. The principal result of calling the discipline into question has been the abundance of new methods of textual analysis applied most often to classic works. However radical this challenge has seemed, it is no less invested in the French tradition of the discipline which greatly privileges the text over its context. Studies on the social history of literature (the history of publishing, of readership, of the status of the writer, of the discipline itself, and of its teaching) have remained outside the programs and outside the field of literary research. Currently, research in these areas is being done, but it is in general directed by historians and sociologists. What the programs of study for the Agregation illustrate is the century-long tendency of the literary discipline in France to construct a landscape composed of *isolated monuments* that loom out of an ahistoric past and a social vacuum in order that they might be given over to commentary. All in all, the exhaustiveness of this catalogue of masterpieces matters little: is the essential point that the works thus removed from their context and their use in society are grouped to compose a vast still life?

Translated by Lauren Doyle-McCombs

27. The study of foreign works has also made an appearance in secondary schooling, but predominantly in the penultimate year of that level. In the last year, which is given over to studying for the baccalaureat exam, French literature holds an all but exclusive place in literary studies. Students are supposed to have knowledge of foreign literatures through modern language classes; in practice, lack of time precludes the teaching of literature courses. Among the foreign authors recommended for presentation in the penultimate year (the decision of 14 November 1984) are: Defoe, Jimenez, Kipling, Stevenson, Swift, de Vasconcelos, Bradbury, Buzzati, Calvino, Carroll, Cervantes, de Queiros, Hemingway, Poe, Pushkin, Steinbeck, Hussein, Tolstoy.

ALICE A. JARDINE / ANNE M. MENKE

Exploding the Issue: "French" "Women" "Writers" and "The Canon"?

FOURTEEN INTERVIEWS

"How can one possibly write an article on the canon at the end of the twentieth century?" was our initial response to the invitation to participate in this issue. The question of literary history for a postmodern sensibility attuned to the need to reconceptualize History did not seem to be the most compelling one to us. While sympathetic to the efforts of those committed to revising the canon, we nevertheless could not ignore our sense that the epistemological assumptions upon which such an endeavor is based may no longer be tenable. Neither did it seem to us that inclusion in the by-definition Western, white, Christian, male canon is what those writers who have been excluded from it are struggling for today.

At the same time, however, it has become increasingly clear that the very work that has most convincingly elaborated postmodern, post-structuralist theory—and helped create new contexts for the writers mentioned above—could itself rapidly disappear if the power of institutions (and their ideologies) to (de)legitimize certain kinds of knowledge is not taken seriously. It therefore seemed important to us, particularly at this moment in time, to find a way to map some of the fields of force operating between the new topologies of knowledge and their continued dependence upon archaic structures of power. To do this, we decided to turn away from History with its third-person pronouns, past-tenses, and "fixing" of narratives—and to turn toward Discourse itself with its implications of the "I" and "you," its emphasis on the "now," and its insistence on process. Despite the complicated status of interviewing (looking to the author as an authority on texts), we decided to assume the contradictions and ask questions of some of those intimately involved with these issues. In the context of this *Yale French Studies* issue: women writers and the literary tradition in France today.

It soon became clear, as we were deciding who to interview for this project, that we would be forced to reproduce for ourselves the process of canon formation itself. We knew that we were beginning with and would be limited by our own knowledge, subjective preference, ideology, complicated personal and professional relationships, and a resistance to pluralism as well as to party lines. We decided that rather than attempt to cover the field of all women writing in French today, we would focus most particularly on those women writing in Paris whose work has been perceived in the United States as "French Feminism," and we would examine the political and intellectual effects of such a representation. This group of women is comprised of both fiction and theory writers who have already had a marked impact on feminist literary theory in the United States either directly or indirectly, and whose work is located within the fields of force mentioned above.

We then proceeded to formulate six questions (five identical and one specially designed) for each writer. This is where the process became more complicated. For we wanted to make apparent in the formulation of the questions themselves our own problems with the entire problematic. We wanted to remain "in between"; to show that we were "representing"—albeit in no simple way—a desire not entirely ours. This required complex rhetorical moves on our part—moves that very often led to long pre- and post-interview explanations of our double-talk. What was finally most interesting about this process were its chiasmatic effects.

We felt that these were American questions, translations of an American academic desire, projections having to do with a canon that is ultimately perhaps not as French as it is American (French literature in the United States). Our combined desire was to problematize this American desire. The responses of the women in France forced us, however, to acknowledge our strong (if reluctant) complicity with this American desire. We were surprised. Most of these writers, after all, are far from being widely taught in French universities. It was hard for us to understand how so many could profess indifference to inclusion of their own work in the canon. And inclusion was not the only problem: for many of these women the word "canon" does not refer to the literary tradition, and few of them see it as an area of feminist concern.

However, the above-mentioned complicity was most certainly not one-sided. If there was a combined desire on the part of these women in France, it was to expose the "American," when not "irrelevant," nature of our questions. Yet it seems to us that the strong, when not passionate, tones of these women's responses betray a reluctant acknowledgement of their oppression as women by the literary establishment and an often covert recognition that they are not, after all, indifferent to the effects of these highly theoretical matters on the destiny of their own work, especially in the United States.

The following short texts were excerpted in most cases from much longer interviews, yet the wide range of concerns still comes through. Many of those concerns were the direct result of reactions to our questions. First of all, several writers we invited to respond to our questions simply refused (including Nathalie Sarraute and Marguerite Yourcenar). Those who did respond were often interested not in answering the questions but in questioning them and then relating them to other issues that seemed more urgent to them. Is the question of the "canon" not hopelessly passé in our high-tech, media culture? What can be the meaning of a national ("French") canon in an increasingly transnational world? Why bring up "writing" (as fiction, as *écriture*) in the context of its enemies (criticism, the institution)? And, for many, there was the question of why we wanted to concentrate on the metaphysical category of "women" when the crucial field of force is occupied by the construction of sexual difference through notions of the feminine and the masculine.

If there was one theme shared by the interviewees, it was a resistance when not violence vis-à-vis university discourse and its tendency to ring the death knell for creative thinking and writing. Many of the writers maintain that women in the university today run the real danger of becoming more male than men—and all agree that the French University system is hopeless on both scores. Beyond that there is little "sameness" in these interviews.

By USA feminist standards, the attitudes expressed toward women range wildly: from (rather foreign) implications that there have been so few women in both the fictional and theoretical canon up until now because "only good work survives" or because "women just don't make good theoreticians," to (more familiar) pessimism with regard to how much things have really changed, amid warnings that women must remain vigilant.

The most remarkable aspect of these collected responses (and the aspect we ultimately felt most drawn to) is their strong resistance to the notion of the "canon" itself. For even when the writers did admit that such a thing exists, they wondered why anyone would want to be *in* it. One of the most often repeated points was that there is no *one* canon—especially in the twentieth century.

Perhaps the canon is, in fact, a myth (in the strong Barthesian sense of that word). To construct an image of one canon is to deny process—canons change continually. To construct an image of *one canon* is inevitably to become involved with the law—and the sacred. Do we want to do away with the canon or bring women into it? Either way, to fight the battle in these terms is to accept the sacred and its relationship to the law. The implication of this insight is that the primarily Anglo-American war with the canon is an (undeclared) holy war, an ecclesiastical battle. It does seem to us that these unavoidable associations for the

French of the "canon" with the Church, the sacred, and the law have become naturalized in English. In speaking with these women in France, it was finally that naturalization itself which became strange, rendering our questions foreign, even to us.

We are extremely grateful to the women writers who agreed to allow us to "canon"-ize—in the musical sense of compose—their voices here.

The interviews, conducted between 8 May 1986 and 6 November 1987, eventually took on every conceivable permutation of oral/written forms. The majority of the interviews took place in person in French. However, Claudine Herrmann, Luce Irigaray, and Michèle Montrelay wrote their texts. Jeanne Hyvrard read from a prepared text and also answered extemporaneously. Hélène Cixous, Françoise Collin, and Sarah Kofman used the oral excerpts as the basis for a written text, while Monique Wittig's interview took place in English over the telephone. Excerpts from the interviews were chosen for maximum montage effect. Every writer was given the opportunity to review both the excerpts selected and the translations. In the end, few of the writers were satisfied with the process of limiting their comments to excerpts, which they felt decontextualized their remarks. They agreed, nonetheless, to let us publish these excerpts in this issue of Yale French Studies, *given that a collection of the interviews in their entirety will be co-edited by us for Columbia University Press.*

QUESTION #1: What does it mean to you to write at the end of the twentieth century?

QUESTION #2: Is it valid/of value to write as a woman, and is it part of your writing practice today?

QUESTION #3: Many women writing today find themselves, for the first time in history, at the center of such institutions as the university and psychoanalysis. In your opinion, will this new placement of women help them to enter the twentieth-century canon, and if so, will they be in the very heart of this corpus or (still) in the footnotes?

QUESTION #4: Today we are seeing women produce literary, philosophical, and psychoanalytical theory of recognized importance, and, parallel to this, we are also seeing a new fluidity in the borderlines among disciplines and genres of writing. Will this parallelism lead only to women being welcomed alongside men, or to a definitive blurring of these categories?

QUESTION #5: Given the problematic and the politics of the categories of the canon, and given the questions we've been dealing with, do
you think your oeuvre will be included in the twentieth-century canon,
and if so, how will it be presented? In your opinion, what will the
content of the canon be?

CHANTAL CHAWAF[1]

Question #1—It brings up the possibility and the necessity of seeking
out new directions . . . of trying to verbalize areas . . . not yet inscribed
in literature . . . which increase our consciousness and conscience as
well as our knowledge of women, the feminine, life, and men. This
would facilitate the communication and rapport between men and
women. . . . One type of strategy . . . is indispensable if one wants to
survive and continue to be free to create and explore: there is power and
resistance in stepping aside enough to preserve an area . . . a terrain, a
realm for writing the body. . . .

Question #2—Obviously it is, it's like breathing. . . . It's a privilege to
be a woman today . . . but a woman's identity is also a problem for her
because of the experience she has of her body, of her female identity
with respect to her mother, and because of her experience, actual or not,
of motherhood—she doesn't have to be a mother or have children herself to experience motherhood. . . . A woman stays closer to the feminine because she identifies with her mother and therefore with the
body, pregnancy, the whole world of the flesh, of affects . . . gestation,
generation, of the prenatal, the preverbal, and the pregenital. . . . Eth-
ically and metaphysically in women a whole current of thought opens
up to life and a symbolization of the living. . . . Woman has the mar-
velous ability to open up a passage between language and this body
which has been deprived of words . . . and limited to its organs . . . but
which is in fact an immense and infinite thing.

Question #3— . . . Just being a woman or of the female sex doesn't
mean a woman's work will change things for women with respect to
this particular cultural problem. Women who work in such institutions
must have another perspective as well, one that is different from that of
the institution. Unfortunately this is not the case for all the women in
these systems. . . . Women do, however, need [to be in the institution],
but being there requires awareness, a good deal of courage, and perhaps a
combative, strategic spirit as well as diplomacy and subtlety. . . .

1. Translated by Anne M. Menke.

Question #4—It seems to me that if everything went well it could change things. If it doesn't, if it puts women on one side and men on the other, then men and women haven't been communicating, then all the work on the feminine hasn't been assimilated. . . . When, however, men are interested in what a woman is working on, then something happens, and the men are transformed. . . . But there is a social barrier connected to barriers of power, self-interest, economics and politics that needs to be shaken up; it's much harder to shake up those barriers than one individual man. . . .

Question #5—For us—I'm speaking in the plural— . . . to be happy about appearing in the canons in the twentieth century . . . they would at the very least have to reflect what I have tried to do and change, and what has changed through what I have done. If it is the kind of canon that completely coopts your work and classifies you as a continuation of the nineteenth century or as pastiche, then I'm not interested in being a part of it. . . . The only chance I have of being included is if the canon-makers acknowledge both that my work surpasses me as an individual, and that more than symbolic work needs to be done. . . . It also depends on society and its evolution. . . . We women in addition need solidarity among ourselves; in France at least this is far from always being the case. . . .

Question #6: Do you think that it's possible to talk about the specificity of women's writing today?

—It's still too early. . . . There are not yet enough women who have shown that they have something specific to accomplish artistically and culturally through literature. . . . Instead of talking about specificity, I'd rather say that there are still domains into which literature hasn't been introduced or which haven't yet been introduced into literature. It is precisely these domains that have been turned over to hospitals, psychoanalysis, and psychiatry. They have been called regressive, but are essentially the domains of the body, the feminine, and desire. They haven't been expressed yet and can't be, for without . . . a language or a tongue, there is no way to symbolize them. That remains for us to do, that is our job. . . . In the end, though, this task goes beyond women's specificity because it can be done by any artist or creative person, but of course as women we have quite an experience of and closeness to the body and the mother since regression is the return to the maternal. . . .

HELENE CIXOUS[2]

Question #1—When I think in terms of the twentieth century, I think in terms of the age of mass media, the age of the greatest possible threat to its opposites, by which I mean, in particular, writing as a practice distanced from the media-imposed star system. Writing at this point means more than what it did when I first started to write. When I began I was pushed by a subjective total need, stemming from my earliest childhood, to enter the land of writing. There I came to the realization that writing was being threatened from all sides by the events of the time, the violence of the age, a violence which in fact goes by the name of mass media. I understood that writing was not only a matter of writing as meditation on the human passions, that it was also a necessary, immediate gesture of defense of writing itself and of what it represents, which is to say a certain kind of thinking which refuses simplifications, which wants absolutely to take into account all the contradictions that make up living itself.

Question #2—When I began to write I didn't ask myself any questions. So then the questions came to find me. I couldn't not respond, because I would have felt that I was betraying a people to which I belong. I belong to the people of women. And I belong as well to other peoples: the Jewish people, the Algerian people. I cannot not respond if one of my peoples is put in question. In short, there is a part of me that answers to the name "woman."

Question #3—This question seemed "American" to me. But all in all, I don't think that I really know the French university system. I have the feeling that women in French universities have little interest in women's problems. The majority of French university women are aligned with men. I don't think it is the women in universities who will contribute to making sure there is more room for women.

Question #4—I don't believe that the borders between literary, philosophical, and psychoanalytical categories are going to suddenly disappear. On the other hand, it is obvious that neither is there any pure literature, pure philosophy, pure psychoanalysis. What interests me is the passage into literature of a portion of philosophy, the passage into philosophy of a portion of psychoanalysis, etc. The fact remains though that one will always be dominant.

2. Translated by Deborah W. Carpenter.

Question #5—I have nothing to say to this question. Here again is this story of the "canon" which is really an American notion. But perhaps it is your use of the singular that troubles me. In my opinion what there is in France is not "the" canon, but categorizations which are ideological and vary from one theory to another. One always attempts to code. But there is an infinite variety of codes.

Question #6: From Hélène Cixous, theoretician and practitioner of *l'écriture féminine*, to Hélène Cixous, historical dramatist à la Shakespeare: this trajectory has provoked strongly opposed reactions. Some see this displacing of the feminine in favor of giving man back his place at the center of the story/history as a splendid success; others are worried that in the process of this return to History the "repressed feminine," barely glimpsed these last few years, already seems to be disappearing. How have you experienced this trajectory?

—I've followed a certain path, and along the way my orientation hasn't changed. There was a period in my work, one which to my mind is inevitable for anyone who writes, of work on the ego. One must go through the ego to get to the other and to others. For one to personally become the world stage, one must be capable of ego effacement.

What matters to me is what is fragile. This is what seems to me to be the vocation of writing: to safeguard what is simultaneously necessary, rare, alive, and precarious. For me women are this precarious people, at once totally present and totally absent, one that can be forgotten at any moment, or remembered at any moment. With that I took a step further, that is, toward others, not only toward women, but not to the exclusion of women, toward others who are similarly threatened, and in this case, it was Cambodia that had all these characteristics: a people at once cultured, sensitive, and threatened with disappearance. I didn't sacrifice women, I tried to concern myself with an absolutely adorable people in danger of death at this moment, a people of great tenderness, the bearers of a strong femininity. I couldn't have worked on a virile people.

FRANÇOISE COLLIN[3]

Question #1—First of all, it is writing in my own time, the only one given to me. . . . And it is true that today writing doubtless no longer commands center stage as it once did, that it can even seem archaic in a culture dominated by images and telematics. But the relationship to the archaic interests me: it seems to me to protect something essential. The archaic in that sense does not belong to the past. . . . Writing, in the twentieth century, makes it impossible for language (for words) to die.

3. Translated by Patrician Baudoin.

Question #2—Everything depends on what sort of writing you are talking about. If I am writing within a feminist framework, then yes, I situate myself as a woman among other women—which does not mean that I write in a style that is necessarily "feminine."

When I write fictional writing, I have no other place to stand in but the one imposed by what I am writing. Writing, then, consists of distancing everything that could stand as a screen, everything that could be normative in any way. The law I obey is an inexpressible, internal law. That my woman-being reappears is possible and even likely, but it is a being over which I have no say, that I do not predefine.

It seems to me that my fiction-writing always sort of controls my theoretical and feminist texts, makes it impossible for them to become fixed as ideology or even as theory, and behaves with a sort of irony which makes "lying" impossible as well.

Question #3—Creativity for me has nothing to do with the institution; creativity liberates one from the institution. However, the reception of texts, their critical understanding, their distribution, and therefore, as a boomerang effect, their confirmation, does happen thanks to editorial, newspaper, university and media-related institutions. The presence of women in these institutions does mean that texts by women will have a greater chance of finding their legitimation. But, then again, the institutionalization of the feminine or of feminism very quickly creates a new norm.

Question #4—The beginnings of feminism did in fact foster transdisciplinary thought where borders between categories were subverted. But it does not seem to me that what is happening today in feminist studies is faithful to that first movement. By inscribing itself in a university (and publishing) environment, feminist research has rediscovered those divisions—even if the borders are still somewhat porous. Current feminist work seems to be located within existing categories: feminist (literary) criticism, the renewal of history, sociological development, the revision of philosophy, etc. . . . Theory, moreover, has completely cut itself off from action, and more generally from the political even though the coupling of theory and practice had been one of the fundamental ambitions of its beginnings.

Question #5—Is there a "canon" of the twentieth century? The notion of a canon is always retrospective: it enables literary historians to construct frameworks for reading after the fact. But these frameworks are modified from one era to another: the shape of the past changes with time.

I think that works that matter do not conform to any canon—or that they set up their own canon.

I never ask myself anything about the canon. I don't know if I belong to my time or not. By writing, I accomplish a task which is mine, a task whose origins are obscure, and I endeavor to remain faithful to them. As I write, of course I hope to be read, but I don't write what might be read, I don't write from the perspective of a probable reading. I would rather elicit the birth of new, male and female, readers. Of that, there is no guarantee.

Question #6: You are a philosopher in a university, but also director of the independent, interdisciplinary journal *Cahiers du GRIF*. Could this double activity be the strategy that feminists have searched so hard for—to avoid the double pitfalls of recuperation and marginality?

—This question really made me laugh. Because my thought has some rigor, people immediately suppose that I belong to a university institution, as if the university were the guarantor of thought. In fact, I was excluded from teaching in the university, and while I owe a great deal to my philosophical training, the best work I have done I owe to my relative marginality—which, moreover, has cost me a lot. Having said this, belonging to an institution affords an enviable security, a social legitimacy, and the support of an environment that I do not underestimate. But does it not also sterilize the imaginary? It is difficult to be both on the inside and on the outside. That is the whole problem confronting young feminists who simultaneously denounce the institution and do everything they possibly can to belong to it. It is understandable that for previously excluded individuals—and this is the case of all minorities—entrance into the institution amounts to winning a certain sort of victory. But true victory is beyond that.

MARGUERITE DURAS[4]

Question #1—Writing. I've never asked myself what era I was living in. I've asked myself this question in relation to my child and his activity later on, or when wondering what would become of the working class, that is, in relation to political issues or political circumstances. But not in relation to writing. I think that writing is beyond everything.

Question #2— . . . I'm still writing now. . . . I don't have any major problems anymore in terms of the reception of my books. The way men in society respond to me hasn't changed . . . misogyny still comes

4. Translated by Heidi Gilpin.

first. . . . But I know about safety valves, about how things are supposed to work. That is, from time to time I write theoretical articles, on criticism, and that frightens contemporary critics . . . and women too. It has to do with feminine writing [*écriture féminine*]. There are many women who side with men. . . .

Question #3—I think that those women who can get beyond this feeling . . . of having to correct history . . . would save a lot of time. . . . All the women who are correcting history, who are trying to correct the injustice of which they have been victims, of which they still are victims—because nothing has changed, we have to remember that in men's heads it's all still the same—. . . these women who are attempting to correct man's nature, and that which has become his nature, call it whatever you like, are wasting their time. . . . I think that if a woman is free, alone, she can go ahead like that without barriers, that is how she will create fruitful work. . . . I don't care about men. I've given up on them. It's not a question of age, it's a question of intellectuality, of one's mental attitude. I've totally given up on trying to put men on a logical track, totally. . . . For women, the worst is behind them: they've already taken the biggest step. They've crossed over to the other side. All the successful books today are by women, the important films are women's films. The difference is fabulous. . . . One book, like *The Lover*, for example—which was a slap in the face for everyone, for men—is a giant leap forward for women, which is much more important. For a woman to command international attention is enough to make men sick. It just makes them sick. . . .

Question #4—I don't know, it's dangerous. Because their criteria have been tested for a long time and they manipulate them with great skill and diplomacy. Men are not politicians, they're diplomats. That's even lower.

Question #5—I don't know what it will be, and I don't know how it will be, or who will decide. The only thing that reassures me is the fact that I've become a bit of an international phenomenon now, and even a pretty big one. And what France won't do, other countries will. So I'm safe. But I have to speak in those terms. I am not safe in France. There my position is still shaky. . . . I got involved in men's business. First, I was involved in politics. I was in the Communist Party. I did things which are considered to be in bad taste for a woman. . . . The thing about my literary work is that I've never mixed political theory with literature. It never turns into rhetoric. Never. Even things like *The Sea Wall* remain a story. That is what saved me. . . .

Question #6: We are asking you these questions about the future destiny of the work of contemporary women, when in fact your work seems to have been canonized already. Actually, you are one of the few people who not only have seen their work come out of an unfair obscurity into the limelight, but who have also seen it attain worldwide recognition. How has becoming a celebrity influenced a vision that was intentionally critical and other?

—You know, *The Lover* came late in my life. . . . I was accustomed to events like that which operate completely independently from you. It comes on you like lighting and takes place in inaccessible regions. You can't know why a book works when it works that well. . . . A tiny little book that's a worldwide hit—that's strange. So I was not at all a young girl in the face of those events. As for the end of your question—"a vision that was intentionally critical and other"—that has nothing to do with it. I understand the implication of your question that being famous somehow inhibits, intimidates. No, no, on the contrary. . . . That reminds me of something Robbe-Grillet told me one day: "When you and I are in the 500,000 copies range, that will mean we have nothing else to say." So I have nothing else to say, and he still has another book.

CLAUDINE HERRMANN[5]

Question #1—Writing seems to me to be dangerous in a world where the very future of humanity is in jeopardy. I wonder sometimes if our descendants will know how to read and if books won't be a passing stage of the general evolution of things.

Writing should, in good logic, be what our editors think it is: addressing the present, at least, or, perhaps, the coming year. Still, things don't exactly happen that way for me. When I write, it seems to me (although I am willing to admit readily that this point of view is irrational), that I meet up with what escapes from time, with what is external to the entropy that surrounds me and possesses me. It is surely not that I imagine myself addressing posterity or that I am basking in excessive illusions about the perennity of what I write, but the very act of writing displaces me inside and gives me the impression of communicating with what is invisible and what cannot be destroyed. In that respect I am probably much like other writers who came before me, the only difference being perhaps that I am not trying to place that feeling back into a system. Naturally, time is recaptured when the book appears and you have to deal face to face with what is now called "promotion." But that, too, is the twentieth century. . . .

5. Translated by Patricia Baudoin.

Question #2—Although the books that have shaped my thought were mostly books written by men, I know that today if there is anything in me that is personal and that is worth expressing, it is necessarily related to my experience and my woman's language [*langage de femme*], simply because I have no other. Even what is imaginary is transmitted through my own circuits and becomes feminized along the way. I became conscious of that with speech well before writing: in my young lawyer's speeches, I tried so hard to imitate the forms of discourse that were then in fashion. As I tried, however, to express in my own language what I really thought, the result would surprise me. That is what happens when I attempt to borrow a male concept: it becomes other. Sometimes I do an exercise that consists in narrating an essentially virile scene, a naval battle, for example. . . . You would be surprised to see how it turns out. . . .

Question #3—I am wondering about the word *institution*. Just yesterday we still spoke of learning institutions, of legal institutions—so that I wonder to what institutions women belong today. . . . Are we talking about "society," as in an academic institution, or the official forces of labor, or have these two meanings become synonymous? Nearly all women who have written in the past held a position of importance in the society of their times. Today this position often takes the shape of a paid position, but I think that what is essential for a writer (but, when speaking about "works," is that about literary or scholarly works?) is to be in touch with the world, and for some women writers, who are not any less writers, that contact can be rather tenuous. I am thinking of Emily Dickinson.

Question #4—I think personally that the production of *women*, to the extent that women will not be satisfied following in tow (or being in waiting), will be inscribed alongside men's productions, except in the exact sciences, if there are any left. . . .

Question #5—I have absolutely no idea where my work, which I hope only to be able to complete, will stand. I wonder unsuccessfully about whether it will ever appear in a canon. That word for me has nasty connotations and I don't particularly care to be catapulted into the world of the official. I do nonetheless like having women and men readers and I do recognize that the usefulness of the canon lies in how it multiplies reading possibilities. I hope I am insulting no one by saying that this canon is a necessary evil. . . . Besides that, the future raises this question for me: there will certainly be more and more books and less and less time to teach them, because of the growth of other areas of knowledge, so, where do we cut back? I have no idea. Nevertheless, I hope that in this mythical canon, there will be proportionately more women than there are today.

Question #6: In the United States, if there is a lively literary criticism, it is feminist criticism. Here in France, on the other hand, your book *Les Voleuses de langue* figures among the rare, serious contributions in this domain. Why has the meeting of literature and feminist theory inspired so few French women?

—Entrance into the French university system takes such a toll on everyone that it becomes difficult to attack it once one has entered its fortress: it has shaped your mind, submitted (or seduced) your intelligence and if you were not ready to be smitten, you would not have spent the best years of your life taking exhausting and competitive entrance exams. Today you can be critical of the impressive corpus of French literature only in accepted forms. Now, feminist criticism, as I see it, is radical and functions without courtesy like a lever. . . . What is more, to show yourself as culturally feminist offers the—justified—fear of displeasing those who will have to vote on your advancement. The French university is tied to its tradition and I can guarantee that it has no feminist tradition. . . . As for imagining that someone on the outside could launch into such a critical adventure, don't even think about it, for in France there is a solidly entrenched idea according to which, outside the university, there is no true knowledge. This reminds me, strangely, of "Out of the Church, far from salvation" [*Hors de l'église, point de salut*]. It is, by the way, the Sorbonne that, a very long time ago, used to point out the doubtful points of the faith. Today, it has got its hands on knowledge, for the better perhaps, but also for the worst. . . .

JEANNE HYVRARD[6]

Question #1—I write in order to stay in touch with the sacred and culture. To overcome the antagonism of memory and of forgetfulness, of eternity and of time, of fusion and of separation. To attest to my belonging to a Western civilization that in this century, nevertheless, crushes me. To transmit the forms and the values of the European heritage I received. To accompany the revolution in cybernetics, in procreatics, and in geonomics (the overall management of the earth's resources). To forge the new tools that enable me to think the revolution and join it. In short, to survive. . . .

Question #2— . . . As far as I'm concerned, for ten years I didn't write "as a woman" although my texts helped me to break with the imposed

6. Translated by Patricia Baudoin.

models. The pressures and discriminations that I have been subjected to as a woman writer have caused me to think about the imprisonment of French women in the literary arena, a cultivated version of knitting. . . . Having recognized this, I had to choose between being satisfied with the conceded territory ("write and keep quiet") and accepting the challenge of building on feminine networks to break through the dam. I tried to do that with *Canal de la Toussaint* by setting up philosophical tools to think through logarchy (a power system resting on the predominance of the logos) whose vehicles are Western males. It is indeed as a woman that I wrote *Canal de la Toussaint*, but the logarchy that is crossed is not uniquely masculine, just as the forged tools are not reserved for women. . . .

Question #3— . . . Everyone knows that it isn't enough for a woman to be Prime Minister for politics to diverge from that of her masculine homolog. . . . What seems to be more worrisome is the integration of women into the masculine hierarchies based on the fiction that "women are men like all others." The cybernetics revolution can purely and simply make the notion of literary body and canon disappear. As for the bionomics (the management of "human capital": perception and economy of human beings leading to considering humans as stock parts that can be changed or thrown out according to profitability forecasts) in the process of taking shape, it could well render feminism itself obsolete. . . .

Question #4— . . . One might think that the dam erected against women will erode in proportion to the accumulation of a body of writings that are not only feminine and feminist, but that grow out of woman-thought (sets of mental tools enabling thought about issues specific to women)—the sheer quantity would then make censorship impossible. This could lead at once to the establishment of women alongside men and to the disappearance of these categories. Woman-thought is not only destined for use by women but can also be used by men. . . .

Question #5— . . . How can I know what will be said of me? That many of my contemporaries have already managed to present me as a typically West-Indian writer offers humorists all sorts of hope. But what kind of criticism will dare utter: "She was a housewife who dreamt of cooking up a chocolate Bavarian cream for her big family, but who was cornered, given the events that historically intervened in her life, into taking recourse in writing to emancipate herself and to rethink the world that was condemning her to death?"

Question #6: "Although I was born and raised within the boundaries of France, and am white like all my ancestors, in everything from linguistics dissertations to the *Bordas Encyclopedia,* I am presented as a writer "typically representative of West-Indian literature," (*Le Français, contrelangue*). Instead of refusing this false impression, you retorted: "There is in my texts no exploded identity, but the anticipation of a new planetary identity." Does that transnational identity render the idea of a canon obsolete since one of the canon's major functions is to preserve a national culture through its language?

— . . . I am not really convinced that there exists a nation other than fantasmagorically. . . . History is constantly being rewritten by the victors and has a lot in common (this is not meant negatively) with mythology. We can wonder, then, whether the national culture's canon isn't itself a fantasy. . . . National cultures will not necessarily be rendered obsolete by the third culture (a transnational culture overarching Western and other cultures) that is being born. But their places, their meanings, their roles and their value will be determined by the outcome of the struggle. . . . But we can also imagine that in an integrated world economy, the national fantasy will no longer be necessary and will relinquish its place to other ideologies born of communications and bionomics. We could begin to witness the emergence, for example, of the canon of a fusionary culture (dominating and dominated in the logarchy), that legitimates new values. . . .

LUCE IRIGARAY[7]

Question #2—I am a woman. I write with who I am. Why would that not be valid/of value, unless there were contempt for the value of women, or refusal of a culture in which the sexual/gendered[8] represented a dimension of subjectivity? But how could I be a woman on the one hand and write on the other? This scission or split between the one who is a woman and the one who writes can only exist for those who confine themselves to verbal reflexes, taking on the protective coloring of already constituted meaning. My whole body is sexed/gendered. My sexuality is not limited to my sexual organs and to a few sexual acts. I think that the effects of repression and above all of the lack of a sexual culture—civil and religious—are still so powerful that it is possible to make statements as strange as these: "I am a woman" and "I don't write as a woman." These declarations also conceal an allegiance to the cultures of men-amongst-themselves. Indeed, alphabetical writing is historically linked to the civil and religious codification of patriarchal

7. We have agreed with Luce Irigary to publish the full answers to two of the questions instead of excerpts from each one. They were translated by Margaret Whitford.
    8. Sexed/gendered translates *sexué.* [Translator's note]

powers. Not to contribute towards giving a sex/gender to language and to its written forms is to perpetuate the pseudoneutrality of the laws of traditions which privilege masculine genealogies and their codes of logic.

Question #4—The fluidity between disciplines and between different types of writing is not very great at the present time. The fact that branches of knowledge and new technologies are increasing in number means that the compartmentalization of knowledge is more watertight than it used to be in the past. In previous centuries, philosophers and scientists used to engage in dialogue. Nowadays, they are more often strangers to each other, because their languages have become mutually incommunicable.

Between certain disciplines such as philosophy, psychoanalysis, and literature, are there new possibilities for exchange to take place? This is a complex question. There are attempts to move from one field to another, but these attempts are not always sufficiently well-informed to be pertinent. What we are witnessing is a modification in the use of language by certain philosophers who are turning back towards the origins of their culture. Thus Nietzsche and Heidegger, but also Hegel before them, interrogated their foundations in Ancient Greece and in religion; Levinas and Derrida are interrogating their relation to the texts of the Old Testament. Their gesture goes together with the use of a style which comes close to that of tragedy, poetry, the Platonic dialogues, the way in which myth, parables and liturgies are expressed. This return looks back to the moment at which male identity constituted itself as patriarchal and phallocratic. Is it the fact that women have emerged from the privacy of the home, from silence, which has forced men to question themselves? All the philosophers I've mentioned—except Heidegger—are interested in feminine identity, and sometimes in their identity as feminine [féminins] or women. Does this lead to a confusion of categories? Which ones? In the name of what? Or whom? Why? I think that what you are calling categories refers to branches of knowledge, not the logical categories of discourse and truth. The installation of new logical forms and rules goes with the definition of a new subjective identity, new rules for determining meaning. That is a necessity too, in order for women to be able to situate themselves in cultural production, alongside and with men. Turning back towards the moment at which they seized sociocultural power(s), are men seeking a way to divest themselves of these powers? I hope so. Such a desire would imply that they are inviting women to share in the definition of truth and the exercising of it with them. Up to now, writing differently has not done much to affect the sex of political leaders or their civil and religious discourses.

Is it a question of patience? Is it our duty to be patient in the face of decisions which are made in our place and in our name? Certainly, I don't think that we have to resort to violence, but we do need to ask ourselves how to give an identity to scientific, religious, and political discourses, and to situate ourselves in these discourses as subjects in our own right. Literature is all well and good. But how can we persuade the world of men to rule their peoples poetically, when they are interested above all in money, in competing for power, etc.? And how can we as women run the world if we have not defined our identity, the rules of our genealogical relationships, our social, cultural and linguistic order? For this task, psychoanalysis may be of great assistance to us, if we know how to use it in a way that is appropriate to our bodily and spiritual needs and desires. It can help us to free ourselves from our confinement in patriarchal culture, provided that we do not allow ourselves to be defined or seduced by the theories and problems of the world of masculine genealogy.

SARAH KOFMAN[9]

Question #1—In your question what is most important for me is not the fact that I am in the twentieth century, but that I write. I write when I am not just translating a certain oral content, when I am not just aiming to defend certain ideas. In my writing activity, my referents—and in this respect I can belong only to the twentieth century—are the great thinkers on writing: Blanchot and Derrida. My own psychoanalysis also played a big part, although I wrote my first book, *L'Enfance de l'art*, before entering analysis. But it enabled me to introduce into myself and into my work a certain play, a certain irony that is but one with writing. . . .

Question #2—Obviously one starts with the fact that I am a woman, and that I write as a woman. In fact, I write as a philosopher first. But I have shown—and I am not immune to this law—in my book on Auguste Comte that even in a philosophical text that is presumably rational and systematic, independent of all empirical and pathological subjectivity, and therefore of sexuality, one cannot separate the text from the sexual position of the author . . . but the author's position is not to be identified with his or her anatomical sex. In other words, for me, one isn't a man or a woman: those categories are anatomical and social, and can be traced back to the metaphysical tradition that starts with Aristotle. . . . When you say to me "do you write as a woman?," I cannot accept this metaphysical formulation. . . .

9. Translated by Patricia Baudoin.

Question #3— . . . What is important is to know whether there are women in the twentieth century who are doing theoretical work that is significant enough for them to be integrated as authors in a curriculum. . . . I don't think, on this point, that women are excluded as women. I am not speaking about literature here, but about philosophy. Now, the fact is that, in this area, few women have accomplished sufficiently important and original work to merit a place in any curriculum. That does not mean that I think that the difference here stems from anatomy, it comes instead from the received education that results, in general, in women being far more submissive to what they read, more repetitive than innovative, and also more mimetic of a master whom they need to stimulate their research. . . .

Question #4—From a philosophical point of view, I think [this parallelism] is extremely important; originally, however, there was not necessarily any parallel between the two problems. We owe to Nietzsche this idea that philosophy and literature are not separable. . . . This blurring of the boundaries between philosophy and literature is part of the system of crossing out, of putting under erasure all the metaphysical opposites, including, among others, this opposition between the feminine and the masculine. . . . I don't think that "women's" productions can lead in themselves to the blurring of these categories. It is nevertheless important that both women and men be able to produce in areas that have thus far been reserved for either one sex or the other, and in this way to blur the boundaries. . . .

Question #5—It is rather difficult for a writer, and a bit pretentious, to say "my work will be included." And what is a "work?" I'm in *Who's Who.* So there are traces, and my books are traces. In addition the feminist movement was such that any woman's work cannot be effaced. And those who compile *Who's Who,* far from excluding women, because there are few famous women, tend to include all of them. They are presented as women but perhaps not with all of the nuances that I give that expression. . . .

Question #6: As a philosopher and a Derridian, how would you go about discussing the notion of the canon?

—It is rather amusing to see first of all that, while you seem to be aiming at questioning categories and metaphysical opposites, with this last question you are reintroducing a simple category: philosophy. Secondly, too, while your questionnaire seemed to me to want to stress the originality of women's work, you classified me from the outset as a Derridian and therefore as subordinate to a male philosopher. . . . I still want to keep the title of philosopher, but in quotation marks, for I believe that the specificity of philosophy is conceptual, rigorous reflection and I do want to claim that. On the other hand, I am troubled by your qualifier, "Derridian," not that I want to cover up my very strong ties to Derrida—a true encounter—but when I'm asked to think about the notion of a canon, that excludes classifying it in a genre. "If I think, I can only think on my own. If I think "as a Derridian," then I am precisely no longer thinking. . . .

JULIA KRISTEVA[10]

Question #1—It means trying to keep things as personal as possible by avoiding every kind of pressure, whether it's from groups, the media, public opinion, or ideology. . . . It means preserving a margin of surprise and not-yet-known . . . because, contrary to appearances, I think we're beginning to see a uniformization of mentalities, information, and education. . . .

Question #2—For me it's a requirement. But I feel that requirement is dependent upon . . . the need to write in my own name. It seems to me that helps protect the writer from the risk involved in writing "as a woman," for that can end up being a uniform of sorts: writing like all women. . . .

Question #3— . . . Obviously the fact that women are now in institutions is a tremendous gain . . . but their position still has to be consolidated and improved. . . . And that does not mean the battle has been won once that's been attained. I think it's important to stay constantly vigilant. That's my practice in any case. . . . It is important to insist upon the fact that nothing can be taken for granted and that no one's situation is comfortable. Women must understand that the battle will never be over. . .

Question #4— . . . What struck me in your question . . . is the issue of blurring sexual difference. In the future sexual difference could fade away. . . . That's a fairly troubling problem to which there are two solutions. First, let's say that this really is going to happen: the difference between the sexes will no longer exist in the twenty-first century. Instead there'll be a kind of perpetual androgyny . . . and we'll see the end of desire and sexual pleasure. For after all if you even out difference, given that it's what's different that's desirable and provokes

10. Translated by Anne M. Menke.

sexual pleasure, then you could see a sexual anesthesia of sorts. . . . When we get to the point of sexual homeostasis, won't we see some sort of symbolic anesthesia and therefore little creativity? Or instead—since the type of societies and psychic life we've known up until now have not tolerated this homeostasis—won't new differences be created? . . .

Question #5— . . . It seems to me the question you're asking is really about education and the transmission of information. I see this transmission as a TV with fifty to a hundred stations, each of which is very different and transmits different information—although they cancel each other out—but which give one the feeling they're all part of the same ideology or, in any case, of something not easily discernable but which is precisely a form of possible resistance to anything surprising or anything that could undermine the norm, and so on. In any event, it's my impression that [in the future] there won't be any canon in the current sense of the word given the plurality of information which the media has already started to carry and which the schools and universities are working against. . . .

Question #6: In the diversity of your work, one always finds epistemological problems that have been posed across time examined from today's perspective. This perspective is a knowingly critical one and, since it is also that of a psychoanalyst, it has no choice but to take sexual difference into account. How is it possible to work in that way without at least appearing to repeat on a theoretical level the historical gesture of organizing knowledge by relegating women subjects and their texts to the background?

—I don't happen to agree with the position that, to the extent that the gesture that organizes knowledge is based on effacing sexual difference in the name of an absolute or neutral subject, women must refuse that gesture. . . . Women must take their place inside the cultural field by trying to discover objects of knowledge men haven't. In doing this, do women respond as women? No doubt they do, especially when one considers that we are always constituted bisexually and that a woman who makes her own that historical gesture of organizing knowledge is exhibiting her phallic component. Now I don't see why women shouldn't exhibit that component. However, once women do exhibit that component . . . they are also uncovering their specificity which is not a phallic specificity. . . .

LEMOINE-LUCCIONI[11]

Question #1— . . . It means strictly nothing at all. Because I don't see myself writing in any other century. . . . I started in the middle of the century, in the '40s; it is so much a permanent function for me to write, I even started earlier. I started[12] my life as writer by writing short stories, with the distinct feeling of writing women's stories, as a woman, even if the "reciter's" first name often was "Michel." . . . If certain changes intervened, it's not an effect of the turn of the century. It's the result of my encounters. . . . I met Jacques Lacan. After several years of training (for I was an absolute novice), I started writing works of so-called psychoanalytic theory. I never went back to the short stories, even if regrets themselves often find their way back. . . .

Question #2— . . . My first work, *Partage des femmes*, was a woman's book. . . . In my latest book, which was first entitled *Le Lien social*, but now is called *Psychoanalysis of Quotidian Life*, I lay out how I place myself, as a writer and analyst, and as a woman, at one of the transmission links of psychoanalysis. . . .[13] [Is it valid to write as a woman?]. . . . The stakes are extremely important, and that has to do with the role of women in Lacanian theory. For Lacan, woman would be a symptom of man, insofar as she marks the place where there is nothing more to say. It is of course the man who has nothing else to say about what he encounters there as empty, an emptiness figured, as you know organically. . . . So of course this, this is a phallic perspective, a man's perspective. So should woman shut up about herself, as unconscious? Of course not, because as far as that goes there's no such thing as men *and* women. There is a phallic function for women too, and to that extent she speaks, she's not just a hole. . . . What is true is that it puts women in a divided position (that I went over, in detail, in *Partage des femmes*), a division which doubles the already divided subject. . . .

Question #3— . . . It's difficult to predict, isn't it, what will become of women, because I think they are so transformed, and men, too, that these are problematics which will be left behind. . . . But really, women have occupied, without any difficulty whatsoever, whatever space they wanted on the psychoanalytic terrain. . . .

Question #4— . . . The borders are shifting, as they are between the

---

11. Translated by Patricia Baudoin.
12. The following passage, up to "Michel", is an excerpt from a letter to Alice Jardine and Anne Menke dated 18 May 1986.
13. Excerpt from letter dated 18 May 1986.

sexes; that does not mean that a difference shouldn't be maintained, but maintained in motion, not fixed. I prefer speaking about differentiation rather than difference—there is a differentiating function, it might be a moveable one, it might choose its own terrain, *I* don't know. That does not mean that soon we're just going to move into another whole new monstrous social configuration compared to ours, but it is true that we can imagine many, many profound transformations. It could all go as far as the suppression of engendering. . . .

Question #5— . . . A canon, that's not predictable, it emerges after the fact, it's a state of things, otherwise what would it be? Besides, would I, personally, conform to a canon? Look, I don't confer . . . a sure value on what I do at the level of theoretical invention. . . . I don't think women are gifted for theoretical invention. For instance I don't think it's accidental that Freud is a man, that Lacan is a man, that Einstein is a man, and I don't think, as many women do, that at the end of several centuries of feminist revolution, women will be capable of it. This is not modesty because I think they are capable of other things, and that what we write, men don't write. . . .

Question #6: As a psychoanalyst and disciple of Lacan, how do you interpret our project on the canon?

— . . . I'm not interpreting at all, it's not a question of interpretation. You are trying, I think, to define something. I told you earlier how wary I am of definitions personally, but I don't interpret your desire to classify and define, nor even to predict. . . . This concern for having a place reveals [a] worry. It's probably a totally legitimate one. I would worry even more if I were a man about the place I would have in the twenty-first century. But about man as human being, you know . . . should humanity commit suicide, I wouldn't find it strange, provided I had the time to think.

MARCELLE MARINI[14]

Question #1— . . . My writing is that of a critic. . . . It is not always or not often academic . . . and it does not respect university canons. This type of writing belongs to a genre called the essay. . . . Since it cannot be defined formally, it is, in my opinion, an important form for women to explore and inhabit . . . for it is one . . . that maintains its marginality in the face of any system that attempts to totalize. . . .

14. Translated by Anne M. Menke.

Question #2— . . . I think that this aspect varies considerably at the time one is writing, when one is really inside writing. Fortunately one cannot always be mindful of what sex one belongs to. I believe it is very very important for women to come to the point where their specificity fades into the background and where they use their experience and what they have to say to communicate to everyone and not to play the role of a woman. . . .

Question #3— . . . Women will only make their way into the twentieth-century canons if . . . they participate in the elaboration of these canons. Two things could hinder this. Either women will be marginalized . . . or else . . . their work will become part of some man's discourse. His text will be remembered instead of hers, and in it her ideas will be presented as his. . . . Men have taken everything they have to say about their feminine side from women. There's no reason to criticize them for this, for it's only natural that they should receive things from women. The problem is men use what they've taken as their own . . . and are nourished by it, but they never acknowledge their indebtedness to women. . . . In times of crisis of the imaginary, or of theories or certitudes—because there is a crisis of certitudes and models now— women always have a chance. It's clear we're in one of those periods, but there have been many cases in History, especially in the field of literature . . . of phenomenally successful women who were unknown thirty years later. There is no guarantee . . . —women today could get caught in History's trap and be left behind when the tradition is established. . . . The only guarantee I know of is to be sure there are successive generations of women. . . .

Question #4— . . . Predictions are difficult to make, it seems. One hopes, I believe one should hope—at least that's my personal position— for a blurring of these boundaries, I would even say a blurring of enunciations, so that identity and the way sexual identity is represented are transformed as well. . . .

Question #5— I'm pessimistic about that. . . . I can only speak for my own narrow field of literary criticism. As far as I'm concerned, it does not even exist. It's not really a scientific field, it's a field of research, reflection, and writing, a crossroads of many other kinds of discourses. . . . My field is not a discipline in the scientific sense of the word, or in the way Foucault understood this term as having procedures that could be repeated. . . . I think that literary criticism has been tossing around a whole slew of discourses for the last twenty years and that it now must use them in a more conscious way. It has to . . . refuse to be a separate discipline and instead be a site of tension, meeting and confrontation. . . .

Question #6: You are already trying to change things from inside the University by teaching women's writing from a feminist perspective. You're in a good position then to tell us about how the institution is reacting to this kind of action.

— . . . When I decided to write a book about Marguerite Duras, I wanted to write it without any kind of institutional constraint. So I had to make a choice, that is, I didn't write a dissertation, I wrote a book and had it published by a publishing firm. In other words, I went on my own to another institution instead of the one I was in. That wasn't a very smart thing to do strategically or tactically, since it meant I didn't get my Ph.D., but it was essential for me to do it. That brings up a very important point—the price one pays. The only way to make progress is to be willing to pay the necessary price. . . . As for the University's reaction, it has varied because the University has changed. The fact that a lot of students from other universities and abroad come to my seminar has supported my efforts; the University stands to gain from their contributions. . . . That does not mean there isn't constant irony and more or less discrete questioning of "that feminist seminar" or things like it. . . . What I do is tolerated by the University, but is there any acknowledgement that my work is valuable and pertinent intellectually or culturally? It's considered work, but perhaps work done for nothing. . . .

MICHELE MONTRELAY[15]

Question #1—That means: 1) searching, and making a contribution through my work, so that the part of the human being known since the nineteenth century as the "unconscious" can be understood more and more rigorously, with its "laws," its structure, its dynamic, etc. . . 2) witnessing. A physicist does not have to prove the existence of matter (except perhaps to himself!). A biologist does not have to convince anyone that a cell is a reality, nor an historian that Louis XIV or Julius Caesar were in fact real human beings. Everything happens, instead, as if the reality of the object of my discipline, although acknowledged theoretically, needs to be proven again and again. The unconscious is the object of censorship and repression—that is its essence. That can be verified not only on an individual basis, but also on cultural and social levels. We acknowledge that the unconscious exists, but no one really believes in it. . . . Now, that object does indeed exist. The unconscious possesses laws and structures. . . . A science, ours among others, exists only on the condition that it enlarge, specify, and refine its models and its experimentation, as time goes by. I am trying to contribute to this. That work is also a political battle. . . . I am profoundly convinced that

---

15. Translated by Patricia Baudoin.

in our civilization, psychoanalysis, as theory and as treatment, is one of the most precious, highest, most symbolic forms of freedom. This practice, indeed, simultaneously recognizes the existence of violence, of homicidal desire, in every human being, and wagers that he won't be the same, that he will transform himself as soon as a place opens up where another can hear about it. These are fantastically high stakes for freedom, something totalitarian states understand well, judging from the extent to which psychoanalysis has been the object of persecution there. . . .

Question #2—Never do I say to myself: "I write as a woman, I will be able to transmit this message better than a man, or less well." What is important, I repeat, is the unconscious, the female unconscious, or the male unconscious which I'm busy with these days. . . . Nonetheless, I have to note, after the fact, that I certainly would not have written the texts I can now reread, if I'd been a man. That's for sure! "Writing as a woman," that can also mean: writing to express, to defend points of view, truths, rights that belong to women. It can mean: to be a feminist writer. I never was one. . . .

Question #3—That new space enables them [women] to acquire credibility, notoriety, a workplace, all more easily. As for the canon, history makes that decision. What will be the values which in the next centuries will decide to place this woman, and not that one in the canon? I do not know, but I'm inclined to think that women will find a place there thanks to values that are foreign to institutions. Because these women will be recognized either as brilliant, or as pioneers and precursors.

Question #4—Paradoxically, at this time, I feel that my work is better understood in interdisciplinary meetings than in psychoanalytic milieus, especially French milieus. I don't attribute that to my being female, but to the fact that in these meetings, each person is less threatened, more at ease. Questions of propriety and jealousy lose their immediacy, and do so regardless of gender.

Question #5— . . . I would like for it to be said of my thought, that while being a woman's—I mean while being gendered feminine—it is rigorous and bold. . . . True rigor and logic must move through avenues where a writer's subjectivity, imagination, values, and anguish are put into play. . . .

Question #6: In your work, *L'Ombre et le nom*, you explore the relationships between primary imagination and the feminine. You speak of this feminine in terms that one could qualify as traditional, such as the "shadow," [*ombre*], the "nonrepresentable," the "outside," [*dehors*], etc. Far from criticizing such a metaphoric description of femininity, you confer value on it by designating it as an essential supporting element of the culture, a support that shouldn't be endangered. What do we risk if women, in spite of everything, move out of the shadow to touch the male corpus of the canon?

—All women will not move out of the shadow. Only some will. Perhaps, during the course of this new generation, more will. But allow me to come back nevertheless to some of your formulations. It is not because more men than women have a place in the "canon" that it remains male for all that. What enters the canon is what lasts, therefore what matters, artistically and scientifically, what is a *work* in the strong sense of that word. And all human work worthy of the name is what, each time, in its own way, reconciles and unites the masculine and the feminine. . . .

CHRISTIANE ROCHEFORT[16]

Question #1— . . . It means I'm in that century. How do you expect me to think about what it would mean to be in any other one? . . . I've lived through several historical periods, some in my childhood which I remember, some good ones like the sixties, and now we're in a very frightening, terrifying period—the eighties. . . . I'm pretty up on history and contemporary history, I mean I'm like a sponge that soaks up what's going on. Well, that means I've got to deal with the century I live in. . . .

Question #2—A lot of stupid things, especially in reference to biology, have been written about "writing as a woman." . . . Of course, people do have different experiences but writing as a woman is like writing as a Black, a coal miner, a samurai, an Indian Buddhist, or the CEO of some huge corporation. What it means is that each person has a certain material that differs from that of the person next door. That's what it means to me—I have a certain material. It does not mean there's a specificity of writing. . . .

Question #3— . . . There are a lot of people, men and women, who aren't in the canon but who are worthwhile. Having said that, there are a lot more worthwhile women who ditn't make it into the canon because no one paid any attention to them. . . . I think that's been taken care of today now that we have an old-boy republic and an old-girl republic to boot. . . . Things are evening out but within that old-boy, old-girl net-

16. Translated by Anne M. Menke.

work. . . . There probably won't be as many women who disappear . . . completely. . . . So I think this equalizing business is a good thing. Well, that's more or less going to be the case in publishing for the simple reason that they can make more money if they publish women's books too. . . . It has nothing to do with being more liberal. . . .

Question #4— . . . We're seeing far too much literary theory being written today considering literary theory isn't at all important. . . . First there was the terrible period when literature was theoretically analyzed by using autobiography and biography. . . . Now we're in the terrible period when literature is being analyzed by using—what? . . . Literature has nonetheless remained outside of all that. . . . It's a separate entity, except when every now and then a philosopher comes along who knows how to write. That happens sometimes, as with Nietzsche for instance. That changes everything but it's pretty rare, and by the way, only then is he a good philosopher. . . . It's a good idea to be interdisciplinary, whether the subject being studied is women or elephants. . . . [But] why talk about blurring category distinctions? I'm not so sure it blurs them. On the contrary, I think it should clarify them. . . . It's about time people were interdisciplinary. Classifying things is a result of the nineteenth century, so I don't see what women have to do with it. . . . Everybody needs to do it. . . .

Question #5— . . . I couldn't really say. I'm already in the grade school . . . and high school books. I don't know if I'll go any higher than that though. . . . I am subject to a particular kind of ostracism. . . . It's not easy to classify me because I go by my own rules. . . . I'm not part of any consensus, so to the extent that the words canon and consensus can be confused . . . my work doesn't stand much chance of being included. . . . To tell you the truth, I couldn't care less. I did have something happen to me once, though. A friend of mine told me about this friend of hers that was half-crazy—this guy had been sent to fight in the Algerian War even though he was of Berber descent. He deserted from the army . . . and lost his mind. . . . At some point someone lent him one of my books, *les Petits enfants du siècle*. It gave him back his courage and calmed him down. He was cured by it and felt better afterwards. . . . Things don't happen in literary history or in literary anthologies, they happen in life. . . . Now *that's* immortality. . . .

Question #6: People don't usually smile while they're reading a book that's supposed to be feminist, but they do when reading *Les Stances à Sophie* for example. Will this funny kind of marriage between criticism of masculine society and feminine-style humor help a body of work such as your own be included in the canon or will it act as an obstacle to inclusion?

—It's an obstacle because not everyone has a sense of humor. . . . I remember that in the beginning of the women's movement there were about fifteen of us . . . and a couple of us said, "We're not going to have any demonstration unless it's funny!" Without humor there can be no revolution or change. You can be sure you've got it wrong if it isn't funny. . . . We didn't win of course, humor never does. The truth is, humor is a minority too. . . .

MONIQUE WITTIG

Question #1—If I were to answer this question from the point of view of literary history, I would remind us that our century has taught us more than once what the revolution of the novel is about. I am thinking of Stein, Proust, Joyce, Dos Passos, Faulkner, Woolf, Sarraute, etc. These are the giants of our century. I always keep them in mind, for they taught us that form is meaning. They taught us to tear off limb by limb a new literary reality from the literary landscape of the time. The accent on form is what is new to this century. And a writer's work today is on form. But to invent a form that is new and raw is difficult. We aren't here to make pretty things. We might ask who is writing the new American experimental novel today? Is it not our work as writers to experiment so as to fight the canon, to break it down? A writer never works in (or to be in) the canon. All of the above writers were fighting the canon.

Question #2. . . . . .

Question #3—To say that writers have been excluded from the canon because they are women seems to me not only inexact, but the very idea proceeds from a trend toward theories of victimization. There are few great writers in any century. Each time there was one, not only was she welcome within the canon, but she was acclaimed, applauded, and praised in her time—sometimes *especially* because she was a woman. I'm thinking of Sand and Colette. I do not think that real innovators have been passed by. In the university, we ruin the purpose of what we do if we make a special category for women—especially when teaching. When we do that as feminists, we ourselves turn the canon into a male edifice.

Question #4—First of all, I do not think this process is specifically linked to women. Secondly, I think the disciplines have on the contrary strengthened their boundaries.

Question #5—That's a provocative question to which no writer with any modesty can respond.

Question #6: Deciding the content of the canon is a classification process that is doubly complicated in your case.

First, given the positive way *L'Opoponax*, with its stylistic innovations, was received in France, one can imagine that a category will be proposed in order to include it in the canon. But when one adds to this formal experimentation an even more radically other exploration of sexuality, as in *Les Guerillères* and *The Lesbian Body*, one can expect to see a complete refusal of your work on the part of the guardians of the dominant culture.

Secondly, to make this process even more problematic, especially in relation to the questions we have asked you, you refuse the category of woman and declare that you are instead a lesbian. What do you think about the fact that you have been so successful at disconcerting these efforts at categorization?

—First, the question of the canon is a question for literary criticism, not for fiction writers.

Secondly, there is confusion created when a purely sociological matter is transported into literary criticism. For example, women are a sociological group whose very existence vis-à-vis the sociological group of men is barely accepted. The fact that these two groups exist in a conflictual political situation is not yet taken seriously so it is important not to jump ahead, past this essential fact. Lesbians, by their very existence, are fugitive women—people trying to escape their class. It is true that the notion of woman is the ideological aspect, the alienated representation of oneself which seems to emanate from the group but is in fact imported from outside. That is to say: women exist as a class while woman is an imaginary formation (to use an expression by Guillaumin). These are sociological issues. Now to return to the literary problem: I can no more say I am a lesbian writer than I can say I am a woman writer. I am simply a writer. Writing is what is important, not sociological categories. I do think some changes of form are more open to history than others; but working, writing—for the writer—is an individual process, never a collective one.

Contributors

PATRICIA BAUDOIN teaches in the Department of Foreign Languages and Literatures at MIT. She has just completed a translation, *The Constraints of a Rivalry: The Super Powers and Africa (1960–1985)*, forthcoming from the University of Chicago Press, and is currently writing a book on the impact of translation on Western Culture since the Renaissance.

DEBORAH CARPENTER is a graduate student in the Department of Romance Languages and Literatures at Harvard. Her English translation of Hélène Cixous's *Le Venue à l'écriture* is forthcoming from Editions des Femmes.

ODILE CAZENAVE holds Master's degrees from the University of Strasbourg in Linguistics and English, and from the Pennsylvania State University in French literature. She has special interests in women's studies, stylistics, and African literature. She has recently taught as a guest lecturer at the University of Yaounde. Her doctoral dissertation examines the European-African interracial relationships in francophone literature from West Africa including connections between music and narrative patterns.

MICHAEL DANAHY holds the Ramberg Chair in French Literature at Hollins College, where questions of women writers, their standing in the literary canon, and the politics of tradition are very much alive. Besides teaching and research devoted to problems of pedagogy as well as literary criticism, he occasionally publishes poetry.

JOAN DEJEAN teaches French at The University of Pennsylvania. She is the author of several books on seventeenth- and eighteenth-century French prose fiction, most recently, *Literary Fortifications: Rousseau, Laclos, Sade.*

LAUREN DOYLE-McCOMBS is a doctoral candidate at Yale University and is writing her dissertation on "Plotting Novelistic Space: Women in the Novels of Proust and Blanchot."

LUCIENNE FRAPPIER-MAZUR is professor of French and a member of the Group in Comparative Literature at the University of Pennsylvania. A specialist of Romanticism and the nineteenth-century novel, she has written on Balzac, Stendhal, Nodier, Sand, Gautier, and Mallarmé.

HEIDI GILPIN is a graduate student in the Department of Comparative Literature at Harvard. She is an editor of *Copyright*, a new journal of cultural criticism.

ALICE A. JARDINE is Associate Professor of Romance Languages and Literatures at Harvard University. She is the author of *Gynesis: Configurations of Woman and Modernity* and coeditor of *The Future of Difference* (with Hester Eisenstein) and *Men in Feminism* (with Paul Smith). She is an editor of the new journal of cultural criticism, *Copyright*.

ANN ROSALIND JONES is Associate Professor of Comparative Literature at Smith College. Her research interests include Renaissance fiction and poetry, women's writing in the sixteenth and twentieth centuries, and contemporary literary theory.

CHRISTIANE P. MAKWARD, Associate Professor of French at the Pennsylvania State University, holds degrees from the University of Dakar and the Sorbonne. She has taught in West Africa, Quebec, and the United States. Her research interests include the new novel, feminist theory, stylistics, psychoanalytic criticism and contemporary women writers in French. Founding editor of a quarterly *Bulletin de Recherches et d'Etudes Féministes Francophones* (1976–1983), she has published numerous articles in books and journals (*Poétique, Ecriture, Revue des Sciences Humaines, French-Swiss Studies*, etc.) Forthcoming books include *Pour un dictionnaire des femmes de langue française*, with Madeleine Hage (University of Maryland) et al.; *Women's Drama from the French*, an anthology with Judith Miller (University of Wisconsin), and essays on Corinna Bille.

ELAINE MARKS, Professor of French and Women's Studies at the University of Wisconsin-Madison. Author of books on Colette (1960) and Simone de Beauvoir (1973); coeditor of *Homosexualities and French Literature* (1979) and *New French Feminisms* (1980). Editor of *Critical Essays on Simone de Beauvoir* (1987). Currently working on "La Question juive in French writing 'after Auschwitz.'"

HELENE MATHIEU, agrégée de Lettres Modernes, teaches at the Ecole Normale d'Instituteurs and is a consultant at the Ministry of Culture.

ANNE M. MENKE is a Ph.D. candidate in Romance Languages and Literatures at Harvard University, writing a dissertation on French Women's Erotic Fiction. Her translation of Julia Kristeva's *Le Langage, cet inconnu* is forthcoming from Columbia University Press.

NANCY K. MILLER is a Distinguished Professor of English at Lehman College and the The Graduate Center, CUNY. She is the author of *The Heroine's Text: Readings in The French and English Novel, 1722–1782*, *Subject to Change: Reading Feminist Writing*, and editor of *The Poetics of Gender*.

STEPHEN G. NICHOLS is Edmund J. Kahn Professor of Humanities and Chair of Romance Languages at the University of Pennsylvania. He is the author of *Romanesque Signs: Early Medieval Narrative and Iconography* and editor of *Images of Power: Literature/Discourse/ History* (*Yale French Studies* 70). He currently has a Guggenheim Fellowship to complete a book on problems of text and image in medieval manuscripts.

MARIE-NOELLE POLINO was a student at the Ecole Normale Supérieure, Paris, and a visiting lecturer at Yale University in 1986–87.

NAOMI SCHOR is Nancy Duke Lewis Professor and Professor of French Studies at Brown. Her most recent books are *Breaking the Chain: Women, Theory, and French Realist Fiction* and *Reading in Detail: Aesthetics and the Feminine*. She is currently completing a study on George Sand.

ENGLISH SHOWALTER, JR. was executive director of the Modern Language Association from 1983–85 and is currently Distinguished Professor of French at Rutgers University, Camden. He is the author of books and articles on the eighteenth-century novel and on Albert Camus. He is currently working on a nine-volume edition of the letters of Mme de Graffigny.

SUSAN RUBIN SULEIMAN is Professor of Romance and Comparative Literatures at Harvard University. She is the author of *Authoritarian Fictions: The Ideological Novel as a Literary Genre*, coeditor of *The Reader in the Text: Essays on Audience and Interpretation*, and editor of *The Female Body in Western Culture: Contemporary Perspectives*. She has published numerous articles on modern French literature and on literary theory, and is currently working on problems of avant-garde writing.

ANNE-MARIE THIESSE, agrégée de Lettres Modernes, has been at the Centre National de la Recherche Scientifique since 1982. She writes on the sociology of contemporary French literature.

NANCY J. VICKERS is Professor of French and Italian at the University of Southern California. She has written on Dante, Petrarch, and Shakespeare as well as on politics and patronage in the reign of François I.

MARGARET WHITFORD lectures in French at Queen Mary College, University of London and is currently writing a book on Luce Irigaray.

Impressionism
Art, Leisure, and Parisian Society

Robert L. Herbert

"This full scale revision of Impressionism immediately supersedes all other studies in the field."—Robert Rosenblum

Exploring the themes of leisure and entertainment that dominated Impressionist painting, Robert L. Herbert shows how completely Impressionism was integrated into the social and cultural life of its times.   70 b/w + 240 color illus. $50.00; $60.00 after 1/1/89

The Studios of Paris
The Capital of Art in the Late Nineteenth Century

John Milner

In this engaging book, John Milner vividly recreates through words and pictures a painter's life in *fin-de siècle* Paris. Enhanced by a wealth of illustrations not only of the art of the period but also of the studios and characters involved, this is a book sure to enchant any lover of art or Paris.   252 b/w + 51 color illus. $39.95

The Other Woman
Feminism and Femininity in the Work of Marguerite Duras

Trista Selous

Marguerite Duras, the internationally famous French novelist, film writer, and director, has never called herself a feminist. Critics who use Lacanian psychoanalysis, however, have argued that Duras's writing subverts masculine conventions of language, making way for—and indeed introducing—a new, "feminine" language. Trista Selous here offers a fresh interpretation of Duras. $30.00

Pleasures of the Belle Epoque
Entertainment and Festivity in Turn-of-the-Century France

Charles Rearick

"*Pleasures of the Belle Epoque* gives us the best of both worlds. It is both visually excellent and offers the first serious examination in English of commercial musical and variety entertainment in Paris in the early Third Republic . . . . An entertaining and important book."—Richard Holt, *History*

"Required reading for any serious student of turn-of-the-century French gaiety."—S. Hollis Clayson, *Art in America*   70 b/w + 8 color illus. $17.95

Monet
Nature into Art

John House

In this beautifully illustrated book John House discusses the career and painting techniques of one of the greatest Impressionist painters, providing the fullest account ever written of Monet's working practices and the ways in which they evolved.

"This is the best book on Monet we have."—Marina Vaizey, *Sunday Times* (London)   150 b/w + 110 color illus. $24.95

Yale University Press
Dept. 795
92A Yale Station
New Haven, CT 06520
(203) 432-0940

The following issues are available through **Yale University Press,** Customer Service Department, 92A Yale Station, New Haven, CT 06520.

63 The Pedagogical Imperative:
Teaching as a Literary Genre
(1982) $13.95
64 Montaigne: Essays in Reading
(1983) $13.95
65 The Language of Difference:
Writing in QUEBEC(ois)
(1983) $13.95
66 The Anxiety of Anticipation
(1984) $13.95
67 Concepts of Closure
(1984) $13.95

68 Sartre after Sartre
(1985) $13.95
69 The Lesson of Paul de Man
(1985) $13.95
70 Images of Power:
Medieval History/Discourse/
Literature
(1986) $13.95
71 Men/Women of Letters:
Correspondence
(1986) $13.95

72 Simone de Beauvoir:
Witness to a Century
(1987) $13.95
73 Everyday Life
(1987) $13.95
74 Phantom Proxies
(1988) $13.95
75 The Politics of Tradition:
Placing Women in French
Literature
(1988) $13.95
Special Issue: After the
Age of Suspicion: The
French Novel Today
$13.95

Special subscription rates are available on a calendar year basis (2 issues per year):

Individual subscriptions $22.00

Institutional subscriptions $25.90

- -

ORDER FORM Yale University Press, 92A Yale Station, New Haven, CT 06520

Please enter my subscription for the calendar year
☐ **1988** (Nos. 74 and 75)   ☐ **Special Issue**   ☐ **1989** (Nos. 76 and 77)

I would like to purchase the following individual issues:

_____

_____

For individual issues, please add postage and handling:
Single issue, United States $1.50
Each additional issue $.50
Connecticut residents please add sales tax of 7½%.

Single issue, foreign countries $2.00
Each additional issue $1.00

Payment of $ _____ is enclosed (including sales tax if applicable).

Mastercard no. _____

4-digit bank no. _____ Expiration date _____

VISA no. _____ Expiration date _____

Signature _____

SHIP TO: _____

_____

_____

- -

See the next page for ordering issues 1–59 and 61–62. **Yale French Studies** is also available through Xerox University Microfilms, 300 North Zeeb Road, Ann Arbor, MI 48106.

The following issues are still available through the **Yale French Studies** Office, 2504A Yale Station, New Haven, CT 06520.

Add for postage & handling

Single issue, United States $1.00
Each additional issue $.50

Single issue, foreign countries $1.50
Each additional issue $.75

- -

YALE FRENCH STUDIES, 2504A Yale Station, New Haven, Connecticut 06520

A check made payable to YFS is enclosed. Please send me the following issue(s):

Issue no.   Title   Price

_____   _____   _____

_____   _____   _____

_____   _____   _____

Postage & handling   _____

Total   _____

Name _____

Number/Street _____

City _____ State _____ Zip _____

The following issues are now available through Kraus Reprint Company, Route 100, Millwood, N.Y. 10546.

36/37 Stucturalism has been reprinted by Doubleday as an Anchor Book.
55/56 Literature and Psychoanalysis has been reprinted by Johns Hopkins University Press, and can be ordered through Customer Service, Johns Hopkins University Press, Baltimore, MD 21218.

The Yale Journal of Criticism

Published twice yearly in April and October

Among *YJC's* recent contributors:
Herbert Marks • Peter Brooks
Harry Berger, Jr. • Anita Sokolsky
Michael Cooke
Roberto González-Echevarría
Christine Poggi • Margaret Homans
Norman Podhoretz • A. Bartlett Giamatti
Jonathan Culler • Cornel West
Jonathan Freedman

edited by Lars Engle, Jonathan Freedman, Christopher Miller, Sheila Murnaghan, and Sara Suleri

Editorial Board: Peter Brooks, *Chairman;* Marie Borroff, Paul Fry, Roberto González-Echevarría, Michael Holquist, Margaret Homans, Louis Martz, Jonathan Spence, Bryan Wolf

The Yale Journal of Criticism provides a new forum for acts of confrontation and discovery in all fields of the humanities. Produced in association with the Whitney Humanities Center at Yale University, *YJC* will publish essays of an interpretive and theoretical nature that heighten and extend the growing dialogue between divergent disciplines.

"Scholars and intellectuals from every quarter will want to read it." —Philip Lewis, Editor, *Diacritics*

"How welcome is *The Yale Journal of Criticism,* drawing on both the editorial talents and choices of young critics, and the experience and traditions of one of the finest centers for humanities scholarship in America." —Natalie Zemon Davis

_____ Please enter my one-year subscription to *The Yale Journal of Criticism* (2 issues, $15.00)

_____ Please send me the inaugural issue (1:1) of *The Yale Journal of Criticism* for $9.95

Yale University Press
Dept. YJCX, 92A Yale Station
New Haven, Connecticut 06520

My check for _____ is enclosed. Add $1.50 for postage/handling *(plus 7.5% tax in CT).*

Or charge _____ MasterCard_____ Visa

Account # _____ Exp. _____

Signature _____

Name _____

Street _____ City _____

State _____ Zip _____

Editor: Harold F. Mosher, Jr.
Publisher: Northern Illinois University

A quarterly journal publishing articles, reviews, and bibliographies on stylistics and on the theory and practice of new approaches to literature, especially those dealing closely with texts.

Style Celebrates Proust

Volume 22, Number 3 (Fall 1988). Guest Editor: John Halperin

John Halperin, "Proust Disparu"; Eloise Knapp Hay, "Proust, James, Conrad, and Impressionism"; Marcel Muller, "Tropes and Dialectics in Proust"; Nancy Lane, "Self, Desire, and Writing in *Remembrance of Things Past*"; Linda A. Gordon, "The Martinville Steeplechase"; Diane R. Leonard, "Proust and Ruskin"; David R. Ellison, "Proust's 'Venice'"; Michael Riffaterre, "On Narrative Subtexts"; James H. Reid, "Lying, Irony, and Deconstruction"; Richard E. Goodkin, "The Proustian Octave"; Mary Ann Caws, "Proust Recalled with a Kierkegaardian Twist"; Maureen E. St. Laurent, "Possession of Consciousness in Remembrance of Things Past"; Pascal A. Ifri, "Proust's Male Narratee."

Already Published in Volume 22

Number 1: *Narrative Theory and Criticism*
Gerald Prince, "The Disnarrated"; Seymour Chatman, "On Deconstructing Narratology"; Jiwei Ci, "An Alternative to Genette's Theory of Order"; Gérard Genette, "A Reply to Jiwei Ci's 'Alternative'"; Nilli Diengott, "Narratology and Feminism"; Susan Lanser, "Feminism and Narratology"; Nils Ekfelt, "Style and Reality in E. T. A. Hoffmann"; Tamar Yacobi, "New Worlds and Themes in Dan Pagis's Poetry"; Monika Fludernik, "Unity of Vision in *Winesburg, Ohio.*" Reviews of Wallace Martin's *Recent Theories of Narrative,* Thomas Pavel's *Fictional Worlds,* Katharine Young's *Taleworlds and Storyrealms,* Kathryn Hume's *Fantasy and Mimesis, On Referring in Literature,* and others.

Number 2: *Visual Poetics.* Guest Editor: Mieke Bal. Mieke Bal, "Introduction: Visual Poetics"; Norman Bryson, "Intertextuality and Visual Poetics"; A. Kibédi Varga, "Stories Told by Pictures"; Michael Ann Holly, "Cultural History as a Work of Art"; Ernst van Alphen, "Reading Visually"; Arie-Jan Gelderblom, "Allegories in the Garden"; Harriet Guest and John Barrell, "Some Plates from the *Songs of Innocence*"; John Neubauer, "Morphological Poetics?"; Timothy Mathews, "Apollinaire and Cubism?"; Linda Hutcheon, "Postmodern Border Tensions"; L. A. Cummings, "A Semiotic Account of Gothic Serialization"; Alice Benston, "Theatricality and Voyeurism in Balthus."

Ordering Information

To purchase a single issue or to subscribe, address orders, accompanied by a check payable to *Style,* to:

The Associate Editor for Business Affairs—*Style*
Department of English, Northern Illinois University, DeKalb, Illinois 60115-2863

Annual Subscription Rates
(4 numbers per volume)

Institutions $25/Individuals $17/Students $10/
For postage outside the U.S., add $4.

Single Numbers $6/
For postage outside the U.S., add $1 per copy.

Please send me _____ copies of the special issue of *Style* on Proust, Volume 22, Number 3, at $6 each (*plus $1 for foreign postage*).

☐ Please enter my subscription to *Style* beginning with volume 22.

My check in the amount of $ _____ is enclosed.

Name _____

Address _____

City _____ State _____ Zip _____